THE new ROCK'N'ROLL

STUART COUPE AND GLENN A. BAKER

Omnibus Press
London/New York/Sydney/Cologne

This book attempts to provide a reference to the hundreds of new bands that have appeared since the 1977 punk explosion. It seemed only right to me, as overall editor, that both the selection and the content of the essays by the authors would have an Australian bias, since the two authors both live in Sydney. I don't think that any important US or UK artist has been left out as a result of this (indeed the authors may have been overcautious because of it) and I feel that the book has been enhanced and given more of a world view by the inclusion of many lesser known Australian and Japanese bands. I also feel that, by living in Australia, they have an overview which would be impossible when writing from the chauvinist music capitals of London and New York, where the excitement of social contact and the sheer density of hype, fashion and gossip make evaluation difficult.

There are disadvantages of course, as becomes apparent in their introductory essays. They have seen very few of the new US and UK bands live and have to approach them purely on the basis of their recorded output, which, in the case of the very recent bands, may consist of just a few singles. A UK band doesn't normally tour the Far East unless they have an album to plug. This gives the Australian bands the advantage and so it is not surprising that they are seen as the future of rock'n'roll.

I don't personally think that rock'n'roll is in a stale backwater, in fact I think it is healthier and more interesting now than it has been for several years. The specialist subject of this book means that the authors have not been able to include recent fine records by David Bowie and others in their assessment. Even so, in my opinion, Culture Club, Bow Wow Wow, The Thompson Twins, Eurythmics, Michael Jackson and other recent chart bands represent a stage of consolidation and evaluation in rock.

The synthesizer and other new instruments are no longer being used as gimmicks but are being seriously explored. A new interest in African and Latin music has influenced the rhythmic base of rock'n'roll as well as racking up album sales for King Sunny Ade and Kid Creole and the Coconuts, and particularly reggae continues to influence UK rock, in the use of dub and echo, through the work of groups such as Black Uhuru. The performance art fringe in New York of such artists as Philip Glass, Robert Ashley and The Love Of Life Orchestra which originally influenced rock via the work of David Byrne and Brian Eno continues to make itself known through Laurie Anderson and provides another area of experiment and discussion, all these artistic divertisements being framed by a constant flow of hard hitting straight-forward rock bands such as Gun Club. Experiments may not give such obvious satisfaction as fully fledged work but ultimately yield results which are a step into the future. To me, this is a period of experiment.

Miles, London, 1983.

CONTENTS

© Copyright 1983 Omnibus Press
(a division of Music Sales Pty. Ltd.)

Coupe, Stuart, 1956 —
The new rock'n'roll.
Includes index.
ISBN 0 949789 02 X.
1. Rock music — Dictionaries. I. Baker,
Glenn A., 1952 —. II. Title.
780'.42

Exclusive Distributors:

Omnibus Press
139 King Street, Sydney.
NSW 2000, Australia

Book Sales Limited
78 Newman Street, London,
WIP 3LA, UK

To The Music Trade Only:

Music Sales Australia Pty. Ltd.
27 Clarendon Street, Artarmon.
NSW 2064, Australia

Music Sales Limited
78 Newman Street, London
WIP 3LA, UK

Music Sales Corporation
799 Broadway, New York City,
NY 10003, USA

Art directed and designed by
Gary Fletcher and Jack Jagtenberg
Photoset by Anna Pappas at Get Set
Typesetting Pty. Ltd., Sydney
Photograph selection by Glenn A. Baker
Jacket design and art by Gary Fletcher,
from a photo by Mark Green
Printed in Japan by Dai Nippon Printing
Co. Ltd., Tokyo

Index compiled by Phillippa Weaver
Photographs supplied by London
Features International, Festival Records,
WEA Records, EMI Records,
Polygram/Astor Records, RCA Records,
Mushroom Records, CBS Records, Gap
Records, Powderworks Records, Deluxe
Records, Liberation Records, Big Time
Records, Why Fi Records, Rivet Records,
Green Records, Regular Records, RAM
Magazine, Bob King, Marjorie McIntosh,
Annie Sidlow, Joseph Stevens, Peter
Simons, Nick Clark.
Manuscript typing by Rhonda Barton.

Special thanks for kind assistance to: Greg
Taylor at RAM, Helen Finn, Viv Hudson,
Annie Waterhouse, the staff of The
Record Plant in Sydney, Bob King, Norm
Lurie, Miles, David Jarrett, Gail
Madigan, Paul McNally, Lorelle Baker,
Jules & Steve at Phantom Record Store,
Yanni Stumbles, Paul Worstead, Annette
Yore, Tony Barrell, Toshi Kamei, Peter
McLain, Jane and Billie, Studio 318, Steve
Bunk, Warren Costello, Neil Hamilton,
Roger Grierson, Julie at Music Sales, Meg
Broughton, Rick Tanaka, Daymon
Wynters, Tom Czarnota, Brendon
Akhurst, Clive Miller and everyone who
helped him, our parents, multitudes of
faceless bio writers, and everyone who
bought the first book.
An A1-Super-Duper-Whiz-Bang-Golly-
Gee-We-Owe-You-One-How-Can-We-
Ever-Thank-You-What-A-Sport thank
you to Kent Goddard.

To the Sex Pistols,
who unwittingly
turned boredom and
malice into a
marketable
commodity.
And Lester Bangs,
who loved the best
people in this book,
hated the rest,
and always knew
why.

To be perfectly honest, the title of this book is a misnomer. What we are dealing with here is the realm beyond Andrew Loog Oldham's Industry of Human Happiness — the Land of Lost Visions. With very few exceptions there is no new rock, only mutton cleverly dressed as lamb slipping by the taste buds of the unaware. The talent of discernment has never been more essential for artistic survival.

In 1980's *The New Music*, the forerunner to this tome, we observed: "In almost identical manner to the first British wave of 1963-'65, the first years of the New Music produced loud, frantic, hard-edged powerhouses, more interested in intensity than structure. But, just as that first beat wave became moulded into an intelligent, exhilarating musical mainstream, so punk rock underwent a similar metamorphosis. A truly phenomenal expansion diverted an army of buzz-saw guitarists toward the myriad sub-trends

THEY SHOOT PUNKS DON'T THEY?

BY GLENN A. BAKER

of ska, mod, rockabilly, synthesizer, powerpop, etc. Just as the Stones and Beatles drew upon the best of rock's past, so too do the New Music participants.

"Now on the threshold of the eighties, contemporary music has rarely looked so healthy. Hundreds of small labels have given us thousands of fascinating singles, and even the giant record corporations have accepted new wave music as the obvious, if not necessarily desirable, future of rock."

Three years on, it may be noted that our predictions were accurate, though our joy is far from unbounded. New Wave most certainly did become the future of rock, the mainstream force. Pale, pimply synthesizer duos, proficient on their electronic warhorses a scant few weeks, have made the charts (well, at least those in England and Australia) their own. The disposable age has taken us beyond fast foods and domestic utensils into the music we fondly refer to as rock'n'roll. Haircut 100 leader Nick Heyward was remarkably accurate when he recently observed, "A pop band at the moment is really about small things,

like socks and vests and nice hair and the way the singer's eyebrows are shaped."

Never has rock music enjoyed such massive total acceptance in western society and never has it wielded less real power. Passive in its incumbency, it appears to have forsaken the greatest strength it ever possessed — unity. When screaming hordes hurled themselves against barriers in Liverpool, London, New York, Sydney and Stockholm, frantic in their desire to communicate a oneness of devoted purpose to the four frail lads beyond their thrusting grasp, rock possessed a voice and an energy field that could, and eventually did, spin this globe a wee bit off its axis.

Ah but then we were ignorant, easily led. Now, given the perspective of distance, disillusionment and daring discovery, we have all chosen our own diversions and scattered off in a dozen directions. The once great battering ram of rock has become frail swords in a hundred hands. The music strains that now fall under the convenient utility term of rock'n'roll run a gamut longer than the Trans Siberian Railway. We're all just too lazy to invent another term.

So the New Romantics disdain the Punks, who antagonise the Oi Boys, who beat up both them and the Rastas. . . and so the mad merry-go-round trundles. When each sub-culture manages to duck out of its dressing rooms for a few moments to whip up an odd bit of music, they all reunite for a common act of piracy. The cyclical nature of rock has never been more pronounced than in the early Eighties. Most of the primary colours of music have been around and back a good three times now; so it's just a matter of getting ready to jump on as it goes past, like a packed bus in the rush hour. "History has shown us," we cautioned in our introduction to *The New Music,* "that, inevitably, this fertile resurgence will collapse into self-indulgence and complacency." We just didn't expect it to happen quite so fast!

"I don't see that there are *any* particular changes in popular music," observed critic Lester Bangs just prior to his death. "Just because it's The Pretenders instead of Foreigner, is this such a vast change? None of the groups now are *about* anything. So the songs are short, so they don't have 90 minute guitar solos. So what?! All I see is a whole lot of groups that are recycling a lot of stuff that has been recycled once too often anyway. I can't buy that this is an organic movement. Most of the groups that are being marketed and packaged, and moulded and shaped and all that stuff that new wave was supposed to be against, don't have anything challenging or even individual to say. The original groups that came out of CBGB's in '75-'76, Television, Talking Heads, Richard Hell & The Voidoids, or out of London like The Sex Pistols and The Clash, all had something unique to say and a unique way of saying it. I can guarantee you there will be no Throbbing Gristle repackages from Japan in the year 2000."

The means by which the snarling wild beast of 1979 was tamed into the confused lap dog of 1983 was documented with uncommon perception in 1970 by author George Melly in the essential 'Revolt Into Style'. Heed his words well: "Each successive pop music explosion comes roaring out of the clubs in which it was born like an angry young bull. Watching from the other side of the gate, the current Establishment has proclaimed it dangerous, subversive, a menace to youth, and demanded something be done about it. Something is. Commercial exploitation advances toward it holding out a bucketful of recording contracts, television appearances and worldwide fame. Then, once the muzzle is safely buried in the golden mash, the cunning butcher nips deftly along the flank and castrates the animal.

"After this painless operation, the Establishment realizes it is safe to advance into the field and gingerly pats the now-docile creature which can then be safely relied upon to grow fatter and stupider until the moment when fashion decides it is ready for the slaughterhouse. . . I don't mean to suggest that there has ever been a conscious agreement drawn up between the Establishment and the entrepreneurs

THE CLASH on stage in Sydney, Australia — holding on to a thread of their original idealism.

of rock. It is simply that their interests happen to coincide."

If my words up to this point reek of rampant negativism, then they may be as accurate a barometer of the times as the music I seek to lampoon, lament and occasionally laud. What we are all witnessing, as it emerges from the New Romantic clubs of England and the pathetically contrived 'punk' haunts of Los Angeles, is the traditional response to a depression — a 'let's party while the ship goes down' ethic. Remember 'They Shoot Horses Don't They?'

We might have been able to dismiss our misgivings as mere petulance if it were not for the plummeting in position of almost every artist so bold as to express some human soul and passion (Graham Parker, Elvis Costello, Mink DeVille, Southside Johnny, for starters); and the dizzying elevation of a score of five minute style'n'synthesizer wonders with the character and charm of a bent subway token. (The Clash standing as the obvious contradiction to this generalisation.)

Style has always been the spouse of rock but never have the external trappings taken on such vital importance — at the expense of the music it is intended to embellish. "What we want to do is create a soundtrack for what goes on in our clubs by making records," explains Spandau Ballet's Gary Kemp. "In fact, the music is irrelevant. The people in the clubs are more important." Such candour is rampant, in fact it's almost an exorcism of guilt. "The trouble with experimentation is that it becomes a hip thing to do and it's just played out too much," offers Les Pattison of Echo & The Bunnymen. "A lot of these kids just don't have any talent. Any farmyard horse can kick a synth."

Synthesizers may be viewed alternatively as the culprits or heroes of early Eighties rock. Without a governing body to issue the equivalent of driving licenses for their operation, we are forced to suffer the consequences of their falling into irresponsible hands. Of all the retributions which the Germans and Japanese have covertly inflicted upon us for kicking their collective arse in the last big bang, this is surely the most unforgivable. As the dB's Will Rigby has sagely observed, "Giving synthesizers to the Europeans was like giving whisky to the Indians."

That folks, as they say in bad movies, is progress. We have the sea of synths and albums of flimsy fabrication predicated upon an almost kindergarten dress-up day fashion climate. But we *also* have, obscured and squeezed for breath, a sizeable number of artists who have carried on the core traditions of rock'n'roll — power, exhilaration, sensitivity, imagination and individuality. Those entities save this book from being a mere catalogue of this month's trends.

We make no apologies for the inclusion of personal favourites. While every attempt has been made to appraise and expose every distant corner of the New Music (which has a geography like the Norwegian coastline), there will be those who are displeased by the omission of acts that they consider vital to the survival of the race.

What we have tried to do is de-emphasise the importance of Britain and America as major product sources and direction pointers, because this has plainly ceased to be the case. Perhaps, as Australians, we are able to distance ourselves from the lemmings' rush and view our subject from a clearer perspective. From this far-flung southern observatory we are watching the giant music centres move further to opposite outfields. Britain is clutching wildly at straws trying anything and everything, a different trend every three months. Like a jaded voyeur who can't get it up any more, even with triple X pornography, British rock is flogging off over any freshly-painted old whore; getting its jollies more from the memory of what it once looked and sounded like than the reality of its current state of being.

America can't seem to bury its overpowering conservatism and traditionalism. Mid-western ballpark dinosaur boogie bands still sell most of the rock records; radio continues its love affair with Air Supply, Kenny Rogers, Lionel Ritchie, Neil Diamond et al, or discovers, as in the case of the Stray Cats and Toni Basil, two year old British trends; record companies dash out with fat chequebooks and sign the 'new Knack', or 'new Joan Jett' or whatever, bereft of any degree of vision; and the charts generally ignore those American acts that *are* moving in an imginative direction (B-52's, Missing Persons, dB's, Marshall Crenshaw, Talking Heads/Tom Tom Club, and many others). So while the British fall over the edge and the Americans are too scared to go near it, some of the secondary markets are emerging to fill the gap. Australian rock is being treated more seriously on an international level — its freshness, vitality, unique flavour and lack of extremities (well, except for The Birthday Party!) marking it as some of the most properly accessible music being made.

JOSIE COTTON — and why not?

To a lesser degree, Japanese rock is beginning to assert itself proudly and, although still basically contained within its own borders, has the potential to strongly penetrate international mass markets. Both these countries have been examined in this book and their most important acts highlighted.

For better or for worse, this *is* new rock'n'roll; the good, the bad and the ugly.

The main reason the punk/kids rock scene is so healthy is because the kids who are playing it and the kids who are getting off on it are all hungry, and that breeds good, rock, rock, ROCK!... They are hungry for music that they can identify with, THEIR music, not product. Hungry to make it, to be stars. Hungry for good times and ecstasy. Hungry to burn it all down and start again. Listen, when you see Elizabeth Taylor or Princess Margaret at a Who or Stones concert drinking champagne backstage with your heroes, and you've queued for six hours for your overpriced ticket and the officials at the stadium treat you like dirt and your girl gets her head opened up by a bottle and there's the rock aristocracy up there in the clouds sipping your wages, there's only one thing you can do, no matter what age you are, there's only one thing you can do — vomit."

(Tony Parsons — New Musical Express, 1976.)

As I write this I'm 26 years old and, regardless of what happens to rock'n'roll in the future, I'll always have a

grabbing those early singles and experiencing it all from the start... and I never could get excited, or motivated, to be the first person on the block with Yes' *Tales From A Topographic Ocean,* or Jethro Tull's *Thick As A Brick.*

I'll never know what it was like to queue up outside the local record store waiting for it to open on the day *I Want To Hold Your Hand* was released.

But I sure know what it felt like doing that the morning *Anarchy In The UK, God Save The Queen, White Riot,* and *New Rose* arrived.

There's something essentially exciting and affecting about being there, not just reading about it in the rock'n'roll history books.

That was especially true when it came to the live scene. Rock critic/guitarist Lenny Kaye put it nicely in Rolling Stone in June 1972 when he described his response to the Young Rascals in terms of Long Island, where he lived:

"I know this may sound a little overboard, but there once was a time when the Young Rascals were the greatest rock'n'roll band in the world. I say this without flinching and in full realisation that such combinations as The Rolling Stones and The Beatles were in the process of turning out their finest work. And I say it knowing far too well that if you never had a bit of Long Island psyche to guide you on your way, the chances are quite good that the group never made much of an impact on you one way or another."

In line with that, living in Adelaide in 1978, it was impossible not to consider Young Modern the greatest band in the history of the universe. A few months later nothing bar Radio Birdman existed, and today I can't conceive that any band anywhere plays better rock'n'roll than The Hoodoo Gurus.

Ya just gotta be there.

In many ways, for kids my age, and younger, The Sex Pistols, The Clash, The Ramones, will always be

A MORE PERSONAL APPROACH TO THE NEW ROCK'N'ROLL

BY STUART COUPE

special fondness for the rock'n'roll that sprang from the 1975/'76 outburst of bands, the 'do it yourself' response to a decade of superstardom and rock'n'roll tedium.

I used the quote from Tony Parsons to preface one of the first pieces I wrote about the punk explosion, The Challenge To The Superstar Syndrome, for Australian rock'n'roll mag, RAM.

Along with most of my friends in those days I believed passionately in what was happening in rock'n'roll. There was a comraderie, a set of symbols that you were with us or against us. You either had the new Saints single or you didn't. Simple. Either you wore a Radio Birdman badge or you didn't. Equally simple.

Hey, this was the first time in our lives that rock'n'roll had really mattered to US.

I come from a generation that wasn't around for any of the other important movements in rock'n'roll's cyclical history.

Like tens of thousands of other kids, when my love affair with rock'n'roll began, the heyday of Elvis, Jerry Lee, The Beatles, Stones, Who, Dylan, ad infinitum, was over.

When *Sgt Peppers* is the first Beatles album you hear all the way through it's kinda not the same as

more significant than The Beatles, The Rolling Stones, etc. because we identify more immediately with that period.

We experienced the social, cultural, and political environment that spawned those bands. We wore the badges, wrote the fanzines, watched the bands, played in them, bought their singles, charted their line-up changes.

The late Sixties and early Seventies were arguably the most boring period in rock'n'roll's short history. Big business had moved in. Everything was 'product' aimed at 'moving units in the marketplace'. Nothing was being created that made anyone really proud to be a rock'n'roll fan.

The early Seventies were the years of Hip Easy Listening, Disco, Heavy Metal, and the Laid Back West Coast Sound. Not forgetting Art Rock. I mean, how exciting is it choosing between The Eagles, Poco, and Crosby Stills Nash and Young?

Rock'n'roll became caught up in technicalities. John McLaughlin sure could move his fingers quickly up and down a fret board but could he play rock'n'roll? I'd hope we agree on the answer to that.

Concepts were the go, triple albums were common, 20 minute guitar solos were the norm, a 30 minute drum solo

PRINCE

THE CRAMPS

hardly raised an eyebrow. Radio was clogged with dull, spiritless, bland rock'n'roll, and the people we'd made stars in the Sixties by supporting them when they had something to say, became richer and richer, had less and less to say, and cared less and less about the people who'd made them what they were.

Greed and commercial interests were killing rock'n'roll as everyone searched for the formula that would make them a million dollars and overnight superstars — and most were prepared to sublimate themselves to the quest.

Instead of separating generations, rock'n'roll was drawing them closer together.

Cliched as it sounds, the arrival of punk/new wave was like a breath of fresh air, a re-awakening.

At last, here was rock'n'roll made for anyone by US. It was immediate, accessible, exciting, and spirited.

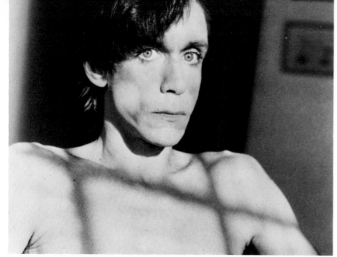

IGGY POP

JOHNNY THUNDERS

always being shoved down our throats by major record companies as 'this week's next week's big thing'.

I kinda got to thinking that although the major record companies continue to pump out the good, bad and mediocre of accessible new rock'n'roll there's dozens of great bands still carrying on the 'do it yourself' philosophy, and dozens of independent labels still turning out records from hungry rock'n'roll bands who want to be stars but know that the only way to do it is not to change with each week's fashion but to follow your heart and do what feels right. For the great ones there's no choice anyway.

Two days ago I bought English band The Milkshakes' album, *Fourteen Rhythm and Blues Greats* on Wall City Records. It hasn't been off the turntable since and is complete proof that there's young bands out there producing GREAT rock'n'roll.

And contrary to some people's opinions I refuse to see bands like The Milkshakes and, say, New York's Fleshtones as nostalgic revivalists.

Essential to making great rock'n'roll is listening to, and absorbing influences and inspiration from the great heroes of rock'n'roll's past.

As Andy Schwartz points out on his sleeve notes to *Blast Off,* The Fleshtones' cassette-only album, that band's sound, "had been around since early 1976, carefully crafted in outer-borough basement rehearsals, perfected in the course of countless house parties and local club gigs. It was a unique, timeless blend of mid-'60s proto-punk (? and The Mysterians, Count 5, et al) and the manic '50s R&B personified by Little Richard, with added touches of surf music and James Brown soul."

It's all about absorbing influences and translating them into something unique and distinctive.

It's something Lester Bangs discussed in one of his last articles — Bad Taste Is Timeless (Music and Sound, Output, May/June 1982).

In true fashion Bangs was getting stuck into most of the well known new music bands, writing at one point: "But preferring Hank Williams or Charlie Parker or the Sun Sessions or the Velvet Underground to Squeeze and Rickie Lee Jones and the Go-Gos and the Psychedelic Furs is not nostalgia, it's good taste."

Much as I'm in agreement with most things Bangs wrote

Some of the bands were great, others diabolical — but that's the way it's always been. People who romanticise the Fifties and Sixties frequently tend to have a blinkered approach that everything from those periods was fantastic — which is obviously garbage.

Like so many people I've gone back to those years and discovered the likes of James Brown, The Searchers, The Remains, early Kinks, Ben E King, Otis Redding, Sam and Dave, Carl Perkins, The Ronettes, Shangri-las, Johnny Cash, The Supremes, Stevie Wonder, The Byrds, etc, etc — the great, and not so greats, of rock'n'roll's erratic, varied output.

And, as any sensible person must realise, added to the list of rock'n'roll greats must be The Sex Pistols, The Clash, The Ramones, Television, New York Dolls, The Jam, and numerous others, depending on your predilection.

"But nothing's happening, it's all dead and there's nothing new that's worth listening to," argued a friend just the other day.

For a few minutes I was tempted to agree, thinking that maybe I wasn't buying as many records as I usually do.

Then I had a quick run through the records that've impressed me most recently and realised that, amidst all the dross, rock'n'roll is alive and well but not

RICHARD HELL

over the years I feel he should have added something to that story. The best new rock'n'roll bands *are* the ones who've been listening to Hank Williams, the Velvets, or say John Fogerty, James Brown, the early Stones, etc etc and have assimilated those people's ideas into their own vision.

Anyone of any worth draws from what's come before but the great divider is the line between the imitators and those who take their influences and create something totally new, or at least totally theirs.

It's pretty obvious all the influences running through the music of a band like The Cramps but do they sound like any other band in the history of rock'n'roll? Everybody and nobody.

When Keith Streng from The Fleshtones quips, "Is 24 tracks 16 too many?" all he's saying is that The Fleshtones make their rock'n'roll firmly aware of what's going on in the Eighties but with their heart in the Fifties and Sixties.

The Milkshakes, The Fleshtones, U2, The Blasters, Tom Verlaine, Richard Hell, Sylvain Sylvain, Johnny Thunders, The Undertones, Talking Heads, Prince, Rick James, Orange Juice, Simple Minds, Go-Betweens, Laughing

RADIO BIRDMAN

TACTICS

Clowns, Paul Kelly and The Dots, Panther Burns, Scientists, The Cramps, The Saints, Radio Birdman, Elvis Costello, The Ramones, Tactics, ABC, Zantees, Au Pairs, The Clash, Do Re Mi, Riptides, Bush Tetras, Jim Carroll, Marshall Crenshaw, Dexys Midnight Runners. . . an off-the-top-of-my-head and very personal selection of just some of the performers whose records and live performances convince me that things ain't as bad as some people say.

Sure, in my opinion, there's loads and loads of garbage around — always has been, always will be. In *The New Rock'n'Roll* we've attempted to have a pretty thorough look at who's around but there's no suggestion that these are all favourites of ours.

Take all the cold, austere, alienated, atmospheric music played by so many of the new synthesizer bands. Hate the stuff personally. Maybe it does reflect the lives of many of those drawn to it but I'd prefer not to wallow in the mire.

But the encouraging aspect is the number of kids having a go on their cheap synths. In some ways it's the Eighties equivalent of the mid-Sixties garage punk scene where everyone was picking up a guitar and thrashing away.

A lot of it was mindless junk but every so often there was the truly inspired group, or single.

So it was in the Sixties, and so it is today. Me, I'm still as in love with rock'n'roll as I ever was, be it listening to old rhythm and blues, soul, Merseybeat, or The Scientists' new independent single that came out last week.

Most of all I'm glad that rock'n'roll in the Eighties can inspire people like Shredder (whoever he is) to write this paragraph about the (truly amazing) Gun Club for a small Sydney fanzine called Form 38:

"So if you're fed up with overbearing politics — a flock of sappy bands, and the radio's newwavepopdull bands, and if you're so fed up that you could just give two wet farts about life, grab a large bottle of vodka, and your car keys, a wicked female, and head on to the closest Gun Club performance. And put your godforsaken life back into the right perspective."

That's written with the spirit I felt listening to The Easybeats' single *Friday On My Mind*, the first record I ever bought. . . and there's a lot of that spirit in every record and band that's sent chills down my spine since then.

I guess it could be the same for you.

PION

Joan Jett

Captain Beefheart

David Bowie

Velvet Underground

Robert Wyatt

Jim Morrison

Kraftwerk

The Dictators

EERS

Richard Hell

New York Dolls

Split Enz

Nick Lowe

Roxy Music (with Brian Eno

A

A Certain Ratio

Like the late Joy Division, A Certain Ratio hail from Manchester and record for the Factory label. But there the similarities end, for A Certain Ratio are one of the pioneers of the modern English funk movement, which Joy Division certainly weren't.

The nucleus of the group is Jeremy Kerr (bass), Peter Terel (guitar), Martin Moscrop (guitar and trumpet), and Simon Topping (vocals and trumpet). Donald Johnstone joined as drummer when the group decided to replace their drum machine. Vocalist Martha Tilson was in an earlier lineup but has since departed.

A Certain Ratio's first release was a cassette, *The Graveyard And The Ballroom,* in 1979. One side was recorded at the Graveyard Studios with Martin Hannett producing, while the other is a live recording of their Talking Heads support gig at London's Electric Ballroom. In 1980 the group released a 12" EP, entitled *Blown Away.* In July 1980 their first single, *Shack Up,* came out and the track also appeared on an EP only released in America in January 1981. Soon after *The Double 12"* EP was issued which included both the *Blown Away* EP and the US EP.

Later in 1981 A Certain Ratio produced their first LP, *To Each. . .,* followed by the single, *Waterline.* In January 1982 their second LP, *Sextet,* was released.

A Flock Of Seagulls

Formed in Liverpool in the winter of 1979 by Mike Score, A Flock Of Seagulls had a week or two in 1982 as 'this week's next big thing'.

After a series of mini tours the band struck up a creative communion with Bill Nelson (formerly of Be Bop Deluxe), the guitarist turned record producer/ independent label owner. This union led to the recording of a single, the A-side of which, *Talking*, was produced by Nelson and came out on his own Cocteau Record label. The single initiated enough interest for the band to sign a long term deal with Jive Records.

Nelson also produced Flock Of Seagulls' second single, *Telecommunication,* which made the lower reaches of the British singles charts. The song went on to become number one in the US National Dance Rock Charts, becoming a club favourite throughout the rock dance clubs in the United States and Canada. In the wake of this success

KING SUNNY ADE

> **"Any idiot with two fingers crossed can make a record. Get a beat, throw in some lyrics and someone somewhere is going to like it."**
> *— Mike Score, A Flock Of Seagulls*

the band toured England with Altered Images and Psychedelic Furs.

A third single, *I Ran,* again produced by Nelson took Flock Of Seagulls to the top of charts around the world.

The band's first LP was produced by Mike Howlett, who's worked with the likes of Orchestral Manoeuvres In The Dark, and Sniff'N' The Tears. Album two, *Listen,* was issued in 1983.

The current line-up is: Mike Score (guitar, vocals, keyboards), Frank Maudsley (bass guitar, vocals), Paul Reynolds (lead guitar) and Ali Score (drums).

ABC

ABC are one of the new breed of English bands who have virtually disavowed live work, preferring to concentrate all their energies in the studio. The group was formed in early 1981 by vocalist Martin Fry, who had previously been in Vice Versa. He assembled Steve Singleton (sax), Mark White (guitar), Mark Lickley (bass) and David Palmer (drums).

The group immediately attracted

> *"We wanted to re-invent disco music. If we could make pop music more ridiculous and less pompous, that'd be one of our earliest aims realised."*
> — *Martin Fry, ABC*

ABC

attention in the UK with their first single, *Tears Are Not Enough,* released late in 1981. The single charted very highly, and they enlisted ex-Buggle Trevor Horn (who had been producing Dollar) to hone their followup *Poison Arrow* into shape. The single was a smash hit in England and also broke the band in Australia where it went Top 5 early in 1982.

ABC's third single, the engaging *The Look Of Love,* was quickly followed by their debut album in mid 1982, *Lexicon Of Love,* which again soared up the UK charts. They recorded at Abbey Road studios with

the assistance of the London Symphony Orchestra. Following their chart success, the group finally began performing live and embarked on a tour of England.

ABC's heavily contrived 'dapper' image seems to be already wearing a bit thin on the rock media. The Face has taken to calling them A Blatant Con, and accusing them of becoming lazy under the production of Trevor Horn.

The release of *All Of My Heart* marks the fourth single taken from *Lexicon Of Love,* which has been transformed from a debut to 'best of' album.

Adam Ant

Adam (real name Stuart Leslie Goddard) was born on November 3, 1954 and comes from the Marylebone area of London. His first involvement with the music industry was when he was at Art School in North London playing with a band called Bazooka Joe. After this came a band called the B-sides.

The earliest incarnation of the Ants included Lester Square and Andy Warren, two former members of the B-sides. During the early days of punk, Adam used to hang around Malcolm McLaren's Sex shop wearing black leather bondage gear. McLaren claims he suggested to Adam that he adopt the pirate image.

Adam and The Ants' first hit was *Kings Of The Wild Frontier* in April 1980, followed a few months later by *Dog Eat Dog.* Next came *Ant Music, Stand and Deliver,* and *Prince Charming.* Adam's albums include *Dirk Wears White Sox, Kings Of The Wild Frontier,* and *Prince Charming.*

The longest lasting Ants line-up was Adam (vocals), Terry Lee Miall (drums), Merrick (drums), Marco Perrone (guitar), and former Roxy Music member Gary Tibbs (guitar).

Deciding to disband the Ants, Adam continued with a solo career, entering the charts with *Goody Two-Shoes.* The b-side, *Red Scab,* a live-in-the-studio affair, was consistent with Adam's policy of issuing non-album b-sides. Adam's first solo album was *Friend or Foe,* the title track being released as a single.

With songs like *Ant Rap* and *Goody Two-Shoes,* Adam has finally achieved a significant penetration into the vast American market. He is presently concentrating most of his energies toward that direction. This may be at the expense of his once huge British popularity. . . but then he has been written off before!

ADAM ANT

ALTERED IMAGES

THE ALLNITERS

A FLOCK OF SEAGULLS

Bryan Adams

Angling furiously to be the next lean, pouting, leather-clad, James Dean type rocker, Canada's Bryan Adams gives every indication that he will succeed. Certainly his songwriting ability has preceded him into the spotlight, via hit compositions for Ian Lloyd, Prism, Loverboy and Bonnie Tyler.

Based in Vancouver, Adams has recorded three albums for A&M, all

BRYAN ADAMS

received with mounting praise. Throughout 1982 he slogged hard across North America, opening for The Kinks, Loverboy and Foreigner. His second and third albums, *You Want It-You Got It* and *Cuts Like A Knife,* were co-produced by Bob 'I Never Sleep' Clearmountain and shimmer with a crisp vitality. Musically they straddle the void between traditional hard rock and new wave.

Wrote Salt Lake City's Deseret News: "He knows about people and their relationships. He writes about people we know and because he captures the gist of certain relationships the songs are humorous while the ballads evoke all the intended emotions."

After all, any man who seriously considered titling an album, *Bryan Adams Hasn't Heard Of You Either* can't be all bad.

King Sunny Ade And His African Beats

What Bob Marley is to Jamaican reggae music, so King Sunny Ade is to Nigerian JuJu music. With some 40 albums to his credit, Ade is a superstar of cosmic proportions in

his homeland, usually selling around 200,000 copies of every album, as part of a total Nigerean record market of 12 million albums annually.

JuJu music is the proud property of the Yoruba people. A tough modern dance music, it is deeply rooted in a complex call-and-response interaction between drums and singers. Popular since the '20s, it took definite shape with the introduction of electric Western instruments in the '50s, particularly the electric guitar and, recently, the synthesizer.

Ade, now in his mid-30s, is quite literally a king, being a member of the royal family of Ondo. Apart from leading his 20-member band, the African Beats, he runs a record label and the Ariya Nightclub in Lagos (where he and the band play torturous four-hour sets).

JuJu Music, Ade's first album for Island Records, was recorded in Lome, capital of the West African state of Togo, and mixed in London. It comprises standards from his huge repertoire and is a perfect introduction to 'The Chairman' and his music.

The Allniters

Sydney-based Allniters formed in 1981 around a collection of rude boys and reggae/ska enthusiasts who frequented the small and legendary Sussex Hotel in the city. Their first performances were at the Sussex and the fashionable Arthur's in Kings Cross.

Within three months they were signed to the independent Green

Records and their first single, *She Made A Monkey Out Of Me,* was released in June 1981.

The band made a number of interstate tours and established a strong following with the vibrancy of their live shows.

The Allniters number ten members — Peter Travis (vocals), Brett Pattinson (percussion, vocals), Martin Fabok (guitar), Phil 'Ted' Ayres (sax), Stuart Crysel (guitar), Mark Taylor (organ), Steve Luke (trombone), 'Fred' Perry (bass), Dave Lennon (drums), and the latest acquisition, Julie Conway (vocals).

A second single, *You Shouldn't Stay Out Late?/What Gives You The Right,* was released in February 1982, again on Green.

Early in 1983 The Allniters signed with Powderworks Records and recorded another single — *Hold On/ Mister Yunioshi,* a version of a Henry Mancini song which featured guest vocals from well known personality Jonathan Coleman.

Altered Images

Altered Images were formed in 1979 but it wasn't until 1981 that they began to have any noticeable impact on the charts. However, when they did, it was impressive — three English hit singles in eight months and numerous awards for Best New Band of 1981.

Altered Images' name was inspired by a design company credited on a Buzzcocks single sleeve. The band was formed by three school friends: Johnny McElhone (guitar), Tony McDaid (bass), and Michael 'Tich' Anderson (drums). Jim McIven (guitar, and keyboards) joined after a brief period with Berlin Blondes, and soon after beautiful lead singer Clare Grogan completed the line-up.

The band established a small but loyal following around Glasgow. Their manager, Gerry McElhone (Johnny's brother), sent Siouxsie and the Banshees a demo tape of *Dead Pop Stars* (later their first single), and *Beckoning Strings* (included on their debut album), which gained them a support spot when the Banshees played Glasgow, and later a position on the tour.

Around that time Altered Images met John Peel, the influential Radio One DJ, who frequently played *Dead Pop Stars.* Eventually, the band came to the attention of major record companies and signed with Epic in Britain and Portrait in America.

Altered Images began recording their debut album with Banshees' bass player Steve Severin producing, but his version of *Happy Birthday* wasn't as commercial as the band wanted, so they started looking for another producer.

Martin Rushent, hot on the heels of his success with Human League, expressed interest and his version of *Happy Birthday* sent Altered Images to number 2 on the British charts by selling almost half a million copies.

Rushent also produced *Pinky Blues,* the band's next album, which contained two further hits — *I Could Be Happy,* and *See Those Eyes.*

After *Pinky Blues* was released, McInven and Anderson left the band, being replaced by guitarist Stephen Lironi, and a variety of session drummers.

Linking with producer Mike Chapman, the group cut the hit *Don't Talk To Me About Love,* followed by *Bring Me Closer.*

Laurie Anderson

Thirty-five-year-old performance artist Laurie Anderson became popular in rock'n'roll circles with the success of her single, *O Superman* and the subsequent *Big Science* album.

The eight minute *O Superman* has been described as "a minimalist, Vocoderized, mesmerizing composition exploring life in a technocracy".

A big hit in Europe, and an underground favourite in America, it was originally recorded for New York independent label One Ten Records, with an initial pressing of 5,000.

Although *O Superman* is dotted with American catch-phrases, Anderson has said that the song's success had a lot to do with the universal nature of its message.

"I don't think it's particularly unique to the United States," she said. "Especially since there was

more response to it out of the US. I think it's a very American song in a lot of ways. It has a lot of cliches; it's about any high-tech society. German audiences in Berlin probably understand it even better than American audiences."

Anderson's album, recorded for Warner Bros, is a collection of spoken pieces, instrumental passages and stripped-down songs with a rock sensibility, if not language. The material is from a work in progress titled *United States 1-1V.*

On *Big Science,* Anderson sings and plays keyboards, Vocoder and violin (something she studied for 15 years). Other performers on the album are co-producer Roma Baran, drummer David Van Tieghem, and reed men Bill Obrecht, Perry Hoberman and Peter Gordon.

Anderson has also appeared on a double album, *You're The Guy I Wanted To Share My Money With,* performing sections of *United States.* Others on the record are William Burroughs and John Giorno.

Angelic Upstarts

The Angelic Upstarts were formed back in the summer of 1977 after being inspired by The Clash on the White Riot Tour. The four young musicians — Mensi (vocals), Mond (guitar), Decca (drums) and Steve (bass) were all brought up on the Brockley Whims Estate in South Shields, Yorkshire. Steve was thrown out of the band early on for drug problems and replaced by Ronnie Wooden from Lancaster. Decca also left the band in their initial stages but later returned.

In August 1978 the group financed and released their debut single, *The Murder of Liddle Towers.*

LAURIE ANDERSON

Angelic Upstarts then signed to J.P. Productions, a subsidiary of Polygram, but were sacked with out releasing a record after Mensi became involved in a punch-up with a Polygram security officer.

The group then signed to WEA and released three singles — *Never 'ad Nothing, Teenage Warning* and *We Gotta Get Out Of This Place* — and two albums — *Out Of Control* and *We Gotta Get Out Of This Place* — during 1979 and 1980. Though all these records charted, the group were dissatisfied with WEA and in

ANGELIC UPSTARTS

mid 1980 left to sign with EMI.

In July 1980 they released their debut single for EMI, *Last Night Another Soldier,* and in January 1981 followed it with another two singles, *England* and *Kids On The Street.* Their third album, *2,000,000 Voices* came out later that year, as well as two further singles, *I Understand* and *Different Strokes,* and the *Live* album.

The Angelic Upstarts released their fifth album, *Still From The Heart,* in April 1982.

The Anti-Nowhere League

The Anti-Nowhere League are one British band that refuse to concede that punk is dead. The group formed late in 1980 and consists of Animal (vocals), Winston (bass), Magoo (guitar) and P.J. (drums).

Throughout 1981 The Anti-Nowhere League gigged consistently around the London circuit and built up a strong street following. Their first single, *Streets Of London,* a cover of the old Ralph McTell hit, rose quickly to the top of the alternative charts on release in December 1981. The group achieved further notoriety in February 1982 when 10,000 copies of the single were seized by the police who claimed that the altered lyrics were obscene. This marked the first time in the UK that an obscenity charge had been considered because of the lyrics of a song.

In early 1982 the group released their second single, also on the WXYZ label, called *I Hate People*, which was followed up later in the year by their first album, *We Are The League.*

The general stance of The Anti-Nowhere League is rather well expressed by a random sampling of their song titles — *So What? Let's Break The Law, I Hate People* and *Ballad Of J.J. Decay.*

The Associates

The origins of The Associates lie in Scotland's 1976 cabaret combo, The Ascorbic Ones, comprising Billy Mackenzie and Alan Rankine. The following three years saw Mackenzie and Rankine form and disband a succession of groups until finally The Associates emerged on ex-Polygram A&R man, Chris Parry's Fiction label. Their first release was in fact on their own Double Hip label, a version of Bowie's *Boys Keep Swinging.*

But the Parry connection prevailed and in 1980 their debut album, *The Affectionate Punch,* emerged with the addition to the duo of Australian drummer John Murphy. This immediately established The Associates' reputation and was one of the most critically acclaimed LPs of 1980 in the UK.

> "It's all gone. . . so what if I have to pay it all back. Who cares? I'm drunk, I'm happy, I'm having a good time and my record is on the charts."
> *Captain Sensible*

Their option was surprisingly not picked up by Fiction and they immediately became the hottest unsigned property in the UK. Whilst playing the field with their various suitors, the band entered into a liaison with Beggars Banquet subsidiary Situation 2, which eventually resulted in one-by-one contracts for a series of five singles which in 1981 were amalgamated into an album, *Fourth Drawer Down.* The singles, all designed to show off differing aspects of their music, picked up ecstatic reviews in the English press and went high in the independent charts.

In early 1982 The Associates released a new single, *Party Fears*

Two, which charted high in the UK and soon after their third album, *Sulk,* was released. Also in early 1982, Billy Mackenzie appeared as one of the featured vocalists on the BEF album, *Songs Of Quality And Distinction.*

Au Pairs

The lineup of the Au Pairs is Lesley Woods (vocals and guitar) and Jane Munro (bass) with Paul Foad (guitar) and Pete Hammond (drums). Though the group formed in Birmingham in 1979, it was not until 1981 they made their recording debut and then it all tumbled out in a rush.

That year they released three

singles, beginning with *You* and followed by *It's Obvious* and then *Inconvenience* (which was also released with an added cut as a 12" EP). Their debut LP was released in mid 1981, titled *Playing With A Different Sex,* and it rose to the UK top 10 and topped the independent charts in that country.

The Au Pairs also appeared on three different compilation LPs in 1981: *Urgh! A Music War, Life In The European Theatre* and a German live set, *Venus Weltklang.* As well, Smart Distribution in England released a C60 live cassette of the group. The Au Pairs have toured extensively through the UK and Europe and their exciting live work has boosted their growing reputation.

THE ASSOCIATES

B

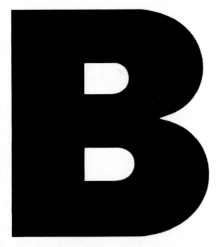

THE B-52's

The B-52's

The B-52's — Fred Schneider (vocals), Kate Pierson (keyboards and vocals), Cindy Wilson (vocals), Ricky Wilson (guitar) and Keith Strickland (drums) — got together in Athens Georgia in October 1976, after a jam session at a friend's house. They called themselves The B-52's after the Southern slang term for the smooth, high bouffant hairdos worn by the female members of the band.

The B-52's first gig was at a Valentine party in 1977, and in those days they played with guitar and drum backing tracks, live vocals, guitar and percussion. Disaster struck the night someone pulled the plug on the tape recorder in the middle of a show. From then on the group concentrated on playing all their instruments live.

The B-52's released an independent single, the quirky *Rock Lobster* (later to be their first and only top 10 single — in Australia), and very quickly became the favourite band of the hip New York music scene. They were snapped up by Warner Brothers and their debut self-titled album, produced by Chris Blackwell of Island Records, was released in June 1979. They arrived for a UK tour to promote it but found themselves 'too fashionable' for much of the rock press. The public liked them though and they returned the next month for more gigs.

The B-52's toured Australia in June, 1980 selling out concerts in every capital city. Like the Motels, The B-52's enjoy an antipodean success quite disproportionate to their meagre homeground standing. In August 1980, they released their second album *Wild Places* which contained the single *Private Idaho,* a minor hit in Australia.

After a long period of recording inactivity, The B-52's released a six track mini LP, *Mesopotamia,* in February, 1982, produced by David Byrne of Talking Heads. *Party Mix* also hit the market — another six track mini LP, it featured 'club mixes' of old and familiar material.

A sell-out Australian tour in June 1980 instigated a short-lived fashion craze of vinyl mini-skirts, white vinyl boots, knitting needles poked through heaped hairdos, and leopard-skin tights. A December UK tour garnered good reviews and a retrospective feature in NME. After that came a long period of silence, broken by the release of the *Whammy!* LP in 1983.

Bad Manners

Bad Manners are: Louis Alphonso (rhythm guitar), Brian Chew-it (drums), Chris Kane (keyboards), David Farren (bass), Gus Herman (trumpet), Fatty 'Buster' Bloodvessel (lead vocals), Andrew 'Marcus Absent' Marson (saxophone), Martin Stewart (organ), Winston Bazoomies (harmonica).

This bizarre outfit whose music fits somewhere between ska and R&B rely heavily on their oddball onstage antics for their appeal, although they have managed a couple of top 20 hits in England.

Bad Manners come from North London, and formed when a band called Back Stage Boogies heard some of them singing in a van and invited them onstage to do some backing vocals.

Deciding that performing wasn't such a bad idea the band started seriously rehearsing early in 1980. In 1981 they had an English hit with *Can Can,* and have recorded four albums — *Ska and B, Looney Tunes, Gosh It's Bad Manners,* and *Forging Ahead* — all for Magnet Records.

Bananarama

The Bananarama trio had their origins in Bristol school chums Sarah Dallin and Keren Woodward. After graduation they moved together to London where Sarah worked in the pensions department of the BBC and Keren attended the London College of Fashion on a journalism course. There Keren met Siobhan Fahey and soon the three of

BAD MANNERS

them were sharing a flat in Soho.

On the floor below, ex-Sex Pistols hit in 1983 with *Na Na Hey Hey Kiss Him Goodbye*.
began to nurture hopes of forming a group and this aim was aided by Cook and Jones who used them as backing vocalists and percussionists. In mid 1981 Paul Cook produced Bananarama's debut single, *Aie A Mwana,* which received lavish praise from the UK music press.

The trio's big break came though when The Fun Boy Three saw their picture in a magazine and took a liking to their name. They invited Bananarama to sing backup vocals on their debut album and when the album garnered a hit single in *It Ain't What You Do, It's The Way You Do It,* the girls were on their way. Fun Boy Three repaid the debt by singing on Bananarama's second single, *Really Saying Something,* which gave the girls their first UK hit in their own right in early 1982. The trio's third single, *Shy Boy,* provided them with another UK hit and also went top five in Australia. It was followed by the album *Deep Sea Skiving* and a further UK hit in 1983 *Na Na Hey Hey Kiss Him Goodbye.*

BANANARAMA (TOP). THE BARRACUDAS (ABOVE)

The Barracudas

The Barracudas were formed in 1978, originally calling themselves RAF, and changed to their present name in the spring of 1980. Devoted to the folk-rock sounds of the Leaves, Turtles and Byrds, and the Southern California surf consciousness, they attracted attention with a stream of excellent, surf influenced pop singles — *I Want My Woody Back, Inside Mind, Radios In Revolt, Summer Fun, We're Living In Violent Times,* and *Watching The World Go By.*

The line-up that recorded these singles and the band's debut album *Drop Out With...* was: Robin Wills (guitar and vocals), Jeremy Gluck (vocals), David Buckley (bass and vocals), and Nicky Turner (drums and vocals). Wills had played with French band Lou Chrysler Et Les Noustiquaires, Gluck with Canadian outfit Yohawks, and Buckley with Sky-Scrapers.

After the album release The Barracudas went through an extensive period of inactivity, resurfacing in 1982 with an excellent album, *Mean Time,* released in France on the Closer Label, distributed by New Rose Records.

At this stage The Barracudas contained only Gluck and Wills from the previous line-up. New members were former Flamin' Groovies guitarist and vocalist Chris

> **"Our music is designed for listening to intently or as quality muzak — none of the sounds are particularly obtrusive."**
> **— David Sylvian, Japan**

Wilson, Jim Dickson, former member of Australian band The Survivors, on bass and vocals, and drummer Terry Smith. The group's sound had altered significantly as well, forsaking '60s surf/folk-rock for late '60s psychedelia and late '70s New Wave.

Toni Basil

In 1982 the multi-faceted Toni Basil added hit records to her extraordinary tally of achievements. Primarily a dancer/choreographer, she has been a familiar figure in the realms of cinema, theatre and rock music for almost twenty years.

She can be traced back to the 1965 film *Village Of The Giants,* in which she appeared in a minor (mostly dancing) role. The following year

Toni cut a solitary single for A&M Records — the Graham Gouldman composed *I'm 28* (also recorded by P.J. Proby). She danced with Davy Jones in the 1968 Monkees' movie *Head,* portrayed a whore in 1969's *Easy Rider,* was seen as a hitch-hiker in 1970's *Five Easy Pieces,* choreographed and appeared in 1973's *American Graffiti,* choreographed David Bowie's *Diamond Dogs* tour, and staged Harlettes sequences for Bette Midler's sleazy stage productions.

Toni's return to vinyl was somewhat of an accident. A prime mover in video production, she created the *Word Of Mouth* video cassette using music tracks as a virtual backdrop. The soundtrack featured songs from such diverse sources as Devo, Bacharach & David and her producer, Greg Mathieson. For one rather spectacular sequence, featuring a troupe of real cheer leaders, the irresistible Mike Chapman/Nicky Chinn pop gem *Mickey* was utilised. Such was the appealing combination of visual and audio that the song soared to number one in England and Australia in 1982, followed in characteristic fashion by America a year later.

Bauhaus

Bauhaus's origins date back to 1977 and a Northampton punk band called The Submerged Tenth which included David Jay (bass) and Kevin Haskins (drums). The group folded after only three dates and the two then formed The Craze with Daniel Ash (guitar). That was also short-lived but led to a meeting with singer Peter Murphy and the formation of Bauhaus.

The group's first release came out on Small Wonder Records in mid 1979, the 12" EP *Bela Lugosi's Dead.* On the strength of that record the group signed to 4.A.D. Records and

BAUHAUS

in January 1980 their debut single, *Dark Entries* came out. In June they released another single, *Terror Couple Kill Colonel,* and in October their first album, *In The Flat Field.*

In 1981 Bauhaus switched to the Beggars Banquet label and in early 1981 released two singles, *Kick In The Eye* and *The Passion Of Lovers,* followed in October by their second LP, *Mask.* That same month 4.A.D. issued the notable *Telegram Sam* single, a cover of Marc Bolan's T-Rex classic. In February 1982, Beggars Banquet re-released *Kick In The Eye* in both 7" and 12" EP versions and it was a major hit on the UK alternative charts.

In November 1981 David Jay collaborated for a single with poet/painter Rene Halkett (a student of the original Bauhaus art movement in '20s Germany), called *Nothing.* The group's third album, *The Sky's Gone Out,* was released in late 1982.

British Electric Foundation

When The Human League split in two in late 1980, synthesiser players Ian Craig Marsh and Martyn Ware set themselves up as a production company, The British Electric Foundation. The stated purpose was to be involved in a variety of different production and recording ventures. By intending only to license their own product through Virgin, the duo ensured that they would retain total control over their records.

Their first project was Heaven 17,

BEF/HEAVEN 17

a collaboration between Marsh, Ware and vocalist Glenn Gregory. The debut single, (*We Don't Need This*) *Fascist Groove Thang,* was released in March 1981 and proved to be a minor UK hit. On the same day under the British Electric Foundation banner, the duo released a cassette-only album, *Music For Stowaways.*

In late 1981 Heaven 17's debut album, *Penthouse And Pavement,* came out and became a top 30 success in England, followed by *Luxury Gap* in 1983. In early 1982 BEF established themselves as a production company par-excellence with the album, *Music Of Quality And Distinction,* which showcased a variety of vocalists, including Tina Turner, Gary Glitter, Sandie Shaw, Bernie Nolan and Glenn Gregory, all produced and backed by Marsh and Ware. *Luxury Gap* was released in mid 1983.

Neither BEF or Heaven 17 are intended as a performing group, though they did do a few club dates in England and New York.

The Beat

The Beat first came together as a quartet late in 1978, in their hometown Birmingham and played their first gig in March 1979 with a lineup of David Wakeling (guitar and vocals), Andy Cox (guitar), David Steele (bass) and Everett Moreton (drums). Their set comprised a mixture of originals and reggae covers and it was at that gig they first encountered Ranking Roger, who was 'toasting' the headlining punk band.

The bookings started rolling in and Roger started toasting them with regularity, so much it came as no surprise when all decided he

"Music is what you make of it. An artist reflects the environment he's in. If he's committed enough he may even want to change it."
— Hugh Cornwall, The Stranglers

should join the band full time. A support tour with The Selecter followed and through this they met The Specials. The Specials had just formed the 2 Tone label and, impressed with what they heard, offered The Beat the chance to make a single. A saxophone player was needed for the session and 50 year old Jamaican Saxa, who had been

THE BEAT

spotted playing pubs in Handsworth, got the job.

In early 1979 The Beat released their first single on the 2 Tone label, the Smokey Robinson classic *Tears Of A Clown,* which gave them a UK hit first up. In early 1980 the group formed their own label, Go Feet, and released a double A side single, *Hands Off. . . She's Mine/Twist And Crawl.* This was soon followed by another single, *Mirror In The Bathroom,* which reached No 3 on the UK charts in June 1980, coinciding with the release of their debut album, *I Just Can't Stop It,* which reached No 1 in Britain. Shortly afterwards they starred in the film *Dance Craze.*

Following extensive tours of the UK, Europe and America, in early 1981 The Beat released another double A side single, *Too Nice To*

Talk To/Drowning, which gave them a further British hit. Their second album, *Wha'ppen?,* came out in mid 1981 and they consolidated its success with extensive touring for the remainder of the year. In early 1982 The Beat released *Hit It* as a single, though it didn't emulate the success of their earlier hits. In late 1982 a third album *Special Beat Service* and accompanying single *I Confess* appeared. The *What Is Beat?* album followed in 1983.

The Belle Stars

An all-girl seven piece band, The Belle Stars have been together for less than eighteen months.

Prior to the formation of the group, four members of the present line-up (Sarah Jane, Stella, Miranda, and Judy) were in the all-girl 2 Tone

band, The Bodysnatchers, who had a hit with *Do Rock Steady.*

The Belle Stars signed to Stiff Records in April 1981 and released a series of singles — *Hiawatha, Slick Trick, Iko Iko,* and a four-track EP featuring *Another Latin Love Song, Having A Good Time, Miss World,* and *Stop Now.*

Surrounding these releases The Belle Stars spent a large amount of their time touring, having supported Madness, The Clash, The Police, The Beat, Pretenders, Joe Jackson, and Elvis Costello. They also headlined numerous shows and toured throughout Europe.

The present Belle Stars line-up is: Jennie (vocals), Sarah Jane (guitar), Miranda (saxophone), Clare (saxophone, keyboards), Lesley (bass), Stella (rhythm guitar), Judy (drums).

THE BELLE STARS

Late in 1982 The Belle Stars scored a hit record in the UK and Australia with their single, *The Clapping Song,* followed by *Sign Of The Times* and *Mocking Bird.*

The Birthday Party

The nucleus of the group which became The Birthday Party came together around 1973, when they were at Caulfield Grammar School in Melbourne, playing at school dances and the like. They first began performing seriously in 1977, after leaving school, as The Boys Next Door and were heavily influenced by the punk revolution — taking the themes of alienation, anger and musical rebellion and amplifying them into what amounted to a new music form.

The lineup at this stage had stabilised as Mick Harvey (guitar), Nick Cave (vocals), Tracy Pew (bass) and Phil Calvert (drums). They soon aroused the interest of major labels, and were signed to Melbourne based Mushroom Records, where they recorded their debut LP, *Door Door,* released in early 1979.

By late 1978 Rowland Howard (guitar) had joined the band, completing the lineup. Mushroom Records soon took a dislike to the

'uncommercial' trend that their music began taking, and in 1979 the band began working with Melbourne independent label, Missing Link. In August of that year they released a five track 12" 45rpm entitled *Hee Haw,* changing their name to The Birthday Party.

In early 1980 the debut self-titled album was released and in March they journeyed to England. They struggled in London for recognition and their first UK single, *Mr.*

Clarinet, was issued independently. Only Ivo at 4.A.D. and John Peel gave them any encouragement.

In September 1980 they recorded their first Peel session and released *The Friend Catcher* as a single on 4.A.D. Records. This won them a small amount of critical acclaim and in November they returned to tour Australia. While there they recorded their second LP, *Prayers On Fire.* In March 1981 they returned to England and released the album on 4.A.D. to mass critical acclaim and a quick trip to the top of the Independent chart. *Nick The Stripper* was taken from the album and released as a 12" single in Australia.

In late 1981 a new single, *Release The Bats,* intensified the band's cult status in the UK. Following a disastrous tour of the US, the Birthday party returned to England in December 1981 to tour with guest support artist Lydia Lunch. In mid 1982 a live LP, featuring Lunch on one side and The Party on the other, was released, entitled *Drunk On The Pope's Blood/The Agony Is The Ecstasy.*

In January 1982 The Birthday Party headed back to Australia for a triumphant tour. When they returned to the UK however it was without bassist Tracy Pew, who had to serve a couple of months in Melbourne's Pentridge Jail on drunk driving charges before he could rejoin the band.

A third studio album, *Junkyard,* was released in mid 1982. It was essentially a refinement of previous ideas. In an air of uncertainty, the group moved to the stimulating atmosphere of Berlin during November in search of a new direction claiming that they were sick of London. During the move drummer Phil Calvert was sacked on

THE BIRTHDAY PARTY

the logical grounds that he was no longer needed, and he joined The Psychedelic Furs. His place was taken by Jeff Wegener from the now-defunct Laughing Clowns.

Wegener lasted five gigs before returning to the Clowns, whereupon guitrist Mick Harvey began playing drums.

The four piece Birthday Party toured Australia in May 1983. Their most recent recording is *Bad Seed,* a four-track EP released on 4AD.

Black Uhuru

The embryonic Black Uhuru ('uhuru' means freedom in Swahili) was formed in the mid '70s by Ducky Simpson, together with Garth Dennis (who is now with the Wailing Souls) and a friend called Don Carlos. The group played hotel and small club gigs throughout Jamaica, without making any great impression in the burgeoning reggae market. They did however cut a single called *Folk Song* for Dynamic Sounds' Top Cat label.

Garth Dennis and Don Carlos quit the group soon after the release of that single. Ducky's next move was to team up with Michael Rose, a

> **"I have no (music) ambitions. I would rather have my face on the front of a corn flake packet."**
> — *Emma Townshend, The Laundrettes*

long-time friend, and a singer called Errol from The Jays. The new lineup recorded an album called *Love Crisis* for Prince Jammy. The album was released on Count Shelley's label in Britain.

The album brought little financial reward however. Errol decided to leave the group, while Ducky and Michael concentrated on songwriting. They still had plans for a new Black Uhuru lineup, this time with a woman singer complementing the male harmonies. By coincidence Ducky was walking past an apartment window one day and heard a girl singing Bob Marley's *Natural Mystic.* It was the right voice for Black Uhuru.

Puma Jones, an American from South Carolina, joined the group in late 1978. Her previous musical experience had included some backup vocals for Ras Michael & The Sons Of Negus. Michael, Ducky and Puma checked out Sly Dunbar to see whether he would produce the group. Sly liked what he heard and in partnership with Robbie

BLACK UHURU

Shakespeare produced the group's *Sun Is Shining* single.

The Sly & Robbie/Black Uhuru relationship was further cemented with such singles as *General Penitentiary, Abortion, Plastic Smile, Guess Who's Coming To Dinner?, Shine Eye Gal, Rent Man* and *Wood For My Fire,* released by Cash & Carry Records. They also released the *Showcase* album.

In 1979 the group was signed to Island Records and their debut album for that label, *Sinsemilla,* was released to extraordinary mainstream acclaim in the summer of 1980. It was, of course, produced by Dunbar and Shakespeare.

In the summer of 1981 Black Uhuru toured Britain for the first time, playing a series of sell-out concerts to support the release of their second Island album, *Red,* which went Top 30 in the UK. They toured again later in the year (again with Sly & Robbie in the backing band) and a live album, *Tear It Up,* was recorded and released in February 1982.

In support of the *Chill Out* studio album Black Uhuru returned for a European tour in April 1982 and finished with two shows at the Wembley Stadium in London as support for The Rolling Stones.

Blam Blam Blam

New Zealand's Blam Blam Blam evolved directly from The Plague, a band-cum-theatre troupe formed in 1977.

The Plague was led by Richard von Sturmer whose name also appears on several Blam Blam Blam songwriting credits. The band evolved into The Whizz Kids who were: Andrew (Snoid) MacLennan (later of Pop Mx and The Swingers), Ian Gilroy (later The Crocodiles and

The Swingers), Tim Mahon, Mark Bell, and (later) Don McGlashan. They did several demos and one single, *Occupational Hazard,* before Andrew and Ian left.

In late 1980 The Whizz Kids became Blam Blam Blam. They appeared on the influential compilation *Class Of '81* released by Propeller Records in March 1980, and soon after signed to that label. The band toured New Zealand with Split Enz as part of the highly successful Screaming Blamatic

BLAM BLAM BLAM

Roadshow (with The Newmatics and The Screaming Mee Mees).

The first Blam Blam Blam release in New Zealand was the four-track self-titled EP, released in April 1980, which went to number 19 on the charts. Next came a single, *There Is No Depression In New Zealand,* a tongue-in-cheek song which was especially apt as it came out in August just as the country erupted into a mass of anti-Springbok riots. It became the theme song of the anti-tour movement and reached number 11. The band's third single was *Don't Fight It Marsha, It's Bigger Than*

Both Of Us. Then the band's original EP was coupled with *No Depression* and that single's flip side, *Got To Be Guilty,* and released as a mini-album in Australia and New Zealand.

Blam Blam Blam's debut album was called *Luxury Length* which was produced by Paul Streekstra and the band.

The band's present line-up is: Don McGlashan (drums, brass, percussion, vocals), Tim Mahon (bass, guitar, vocals), and Mark Bell (guitar, bass, vocals).

Blancmange

Blancmange started life early in 1979 in London as the culmination of various musical liaisons between Neil Arthur and Stephen Luscombe.

After being involved with improvised and experimental music for around six years, and the demise of his workshop group, Miru, Stephen joined Neil's band L360 as a keyboard player, although the association lasted but a few weeks. The eventual decline of L360, and also of Neil's garage band, The Viewfinders, led to the foundation of The Blancmange one wet January afternoon in Stephen's flat, where, with no more than a handful of kitchen utensils, a few battered instruments, and a couple of cassette recorders, the duo worked on the first series of oddities and aural distractions that were to form the basis of a series of semi-improvised performances through 1979. The release in April 1980 of the EP *Irene and Mavis — The Blancmange,* universally ignored by press and public alike and finding its way into

the bargain bins with a speed hitherto unknown, marked a change of direction for the duo. Although maintaining the style and uniqueness of the earlier pieces, the emphasis became on songs rather than sound experiments. The first performance of the new music was in July 1980 at a self-organised concert with three other bands at the Centro Iberico, West London.

A performance in September at the Bridge House, Canning Town led to the beginning of the association with the infamous Stevo, and ultimately inclusion of the track *Sad Day* on the Some Bizarre album, released in January 1981. Further concerts in and around London increased audience exposure and contacts and in February 1981 Blancmange embarked on their own mini-tour of the North, and their inclusion on the 2002 review in March.

The February dates included a meeting with Martyn Ware of BEF, and led to his production of demo tapes in May following the signing of a publishing deal with Cherry Red Music in the same month.

Little activity occurred until September, with the surprise news that Blancmange were to be the support on the Grace Jones European tour that autumn. Being unable to go to Europe, they made do with the three London dates in October, and this proved to be a turning point as far as presentation of the music was concerned.

Following tour stints with Depeche Mode and Japan, Blancmange came to the attention of London Records and were inked in early 1982. Their first single *I've Seen The Word* generated a deal of interest which became manifest in the UK and Australian hit status of *Living On The Ceiling* and *Waves.*

The Blasters

Breathing life and passion into what may loosely be described as the Rockabilly Revival (did it ever go away?) is Los Angeles quintet The Blasters, undoubtedly one of the most exciting live acts in North America.

Their music is a frenzied amalgam of rockabilly, rock'n'roll, rhythm &

THE BLASTERS

blues, soul, country & western, urban blues and western swing. They approach these revered forms with affection and reverence but not to the point that it gets in the way of having a good time. Purists may puke but The Blasters are turning a new generation onto the joys of quality roots music.

After one little-known album on the Rollin' Rock label in 1980, Dave Alvin (guitar), Phil Alvin (lead vocals), Bill Bateman (drums), John Bazz (bass) and Gene Taylor (piano) were signed by Slash Records and a 1981 self-titled album appeared highlighted by a number of Dave Alvin originals, including *American Music, Marie Marie* and *Border Radio.*

BLANCMANGE

In May 1982 the group toured England and a steaming performance at The Venue in London was captured for a six track mini-LP, *Over There*. This disc featured fiery workouts of Jerry Lee Lewis, Roy Orbison, Ed Bruce, Little Richard and Big Joe Turner songs. On Richard's *Keep A Knocking*, saxman Lee Allen played the same lick he did on the 1956 original. A bonus seventh track, Frankie Ford's *What Will Lucy Do?*, was only included on the cassette edition.

Blondie

Blondie are the archetypal band of the late '70s and early '80s, overriding the categories of new wave, punk rock, powerpop and anything else the critics care to invent. Their music, born in the '60s with influences of The Beatles, Byrds, Hollies, Who, Ronettes, Janis Joplin, Procol Harum, Jimi Hendrix and hundreds of others, cuts through all styles.

Guitarist Chris Stein and singer Debbie Harry formed the band back in 1973, prior to which Debbie had been a Playboy Club Bunny, sung with a Mamas & Papas style band called Wind In The Willows (whose one Capitol album was re-released after Blondie's success), been the fourth member of girl group act The B Girls (who actually toured Canada) and third member of The Stilettos.

They started playing CBGB's and the New York Club circuit in 1976 and first came to prominence with the compelling Private Stock label single, *X-Offender*. This led to a recording of a debut self-titled album with producer Richard Gottehrer also for Private Stock. The lineup at that stage was Harry, Stein, Gary Valentine (bass), Clem Burke (drums) and Jimmy Destri (keyboards). Chrysalis Records bought the group and album from Private Stock and re-released it.

The group began playing outside New York and in March 1977 toured America for the first time, with Iggy Pop. (David Bowie was playing keyboards for Iggy.) In late 1977 they toured England with Television and in September the same year had their first hit in Australia (for that matter, anywhere) with *In The Flesh*, a number one. The group immediately toured Australia and made the famous quote that the best thing about Australia was the heroin.

Plastic Letters, the band's second album, released in 1978 was produced by Gottehrer and featured new bass player, Frank Infante, who joined after Valentine left to follow a solo career. *Plastic Letters* was a

BLONDIE

much tougher rock album than its predecessor and contained another hit single in *Denis* (originally a 1963 Number 1 US hit for Randy and The Rainbows). At this point English bassist Nigel Harrison joined and Infante moved to rhythm guitar.

The *Parallel Lines* album finally broke them worldwide and established Blondie as creators of perfect pop singles. They enlisted legendary Australian expatriate hit producer Mike Chapman and the resulting album, recorded at the Record Plant in New York, contained five tracks that have all topped charts somewhere in the world: *One Way Or Another, Picture This, Sunday Girl, Hanging On The Telephone* and of course *Heart Of Glass*. King Crimson leader Robert Fripp made a guest appearance playing guitar on *Fade Away And Radiate* (he also plays on the live version of *Heroes* on the 12" *Atomic* single).

Heart Of Glass, with its infectious disco-based rhythm, was a worldwide number one and the first studio disco/new wave crossover. In some countries the line "pain in the ass" was edited out to save offending sensitive ears.

Late in 1979 Blondie's fourth album, *Eat To The Beat,* appeared,

> **"I could never understand what a record producer was meant to do until I met Mike Chapman. He drove us to insanity at times."**
> — Nigel Harrison, Blondie

again produced by Mike Chapman. It was another collection of excellent pop songs; highlights being *Atomic* (a strong hit in Australia), *Accidents Will Happen, Union City Blue* and *Living In The Real World.* The album was also released with the world's first accompanying video rock cassette. Debbie had appeared in various underground art movies and now appeared in her first big budget film *Roadie.* She also had a main role in *Union City,* as a New Jersey housewife and received critical acclaim for her performance.

In 1980 Blondie released the single *Call Me,* taken from the soundtrack of the film 'American Gigolo', and produced by Giorgio Moroder. With this record Blondie broke all remaining barriers and finally had a number one in America. Late that year they released *Auto-American,* which demonstrated a radical change in direction. Stein and Harry were flirting with calypso rhythms and one of the two smash hit singles from it, *The Tide Is High,* was a cover of a '60s hit by the Jamaican vocal group, The Paragons. The other hit was a white version of the black rapping style — *Rapture.*

Since that album Blondie's life seemed in jeopardy, fuelled by constant rumours of explosive demise. In 1981 Stein and Harry teamed with Chic members Bernard Edwards and Nile Rodgers to record Debbie's first solo album, *Koo Koo,* which despite a minor hit single with *Backfired,* was less than a success. Jimmy Destri also recorded a solo album, *Hearts On The Wall,* and Clem Burke played sessions. Late in 1981 *Blondie's Greatest Hits* was released and proved to be a platinum performer worldwide. Around this time Frank Infante took out a court injunction to prevent the band touring.

In 1982 Blondie released their sixth LP *The Hunter* and oversaw the publication of their biography of the band: "Making Tracks". They planned to tour England but it was cancelled after a poor response and low ticket sales. The group temporarily disbanded to allow members to focus on solo work and Chris Stein established his own record label, Animal Records, which boasts, Iggy Pop, John Cale, The Gun Club and James Chance. He produced Iggy's *Zombie Birdhouse* album, and he has also produced albums for avant-garde violinist Walter Steding and French duo Casino Music; as well as working on the scores to *Union City, Wild Style* (a television special about the rap style of South Bronx) and an animated feature *Drats.*

1983 opened with Chris Stein and Debbie Harry working on Debbie's second solo album.

BLUE RONDO
A LA TURK

Blue Rondo A La Turk

Blue Rondo A La Turk (a name inspired by a track by jazz pianist Dave Brubeck) became a physical reality in London early in 1981, though the idea had been fermenting and experiments had been conducted for some time before. The original thought had glimmered like a beacon across the vast uncharted regions of singer Chris Sullivan's mind. A legend after 11.00pm each evening, Chris was already a marked man following his involvement with clubs like Hell, which he co-hosted with Steve Strange, and the much-respected 'new funk' evenings at Le Kilt.

Their first official public performance was, on the eve of The Royal Wedding, an 'anti-loyalist' rally' held in the New Styles Art Gallery in the Barbican.

Subsequently they appeared at a Brazilian festival with real Brazilians, held (naturally enough) in Salisbury, England! They also played at a disused London theatre, and then a strip club in Birmingham.

These venues illustrate to some degree the A La Turk style of live performance. Not for them the constant drudgery of the English club and pub circuit. Their aversion to these rock mausoleums is not rooted in any misguided elitism either. Blue Rondo A La Turk simply hold the belief that the live experience should be just that — an experience. To this end, their shows can and will (and indeed do) feature any or all of the following: male and female strippers, festive on-stage decorations, dancing troupes, Northern Soul DJs, comics/clowns, cameo appearances by household names, and just about anything else they can think of.

Blue Rondo A La Turk's musical inspiration is Latin rhythms of the authentic kind, while their sartorial inspiration is Zoot suits, a brainchild of Chris Sullivan. Originally Zoot suits appeared in the United States during World War II, created by the youth of the day who wanted to display their contempt

for the laws applied to the rationing of everything, including cloth. Theirs was the most stylish rebellion of all time.

A unique multi-racial combination of Greeks, Brazilians, West Indians, Welsh and Englishmen, Blue Rondo A La Turk generated a great deal of interest in the UK and Australia with their 1982 singles *Carioca* and *Me And Mr Sanchez,* and their debut album, *The*

Heavens Are Crying.

The current lineup is Chris Sullivan and Chris Tolera (vocals), Moses Mount Bassie (sax), Mark Reilly (guitar), Kito Poncioni (bass), Geraldo D'Arbilly (drums), Mike Lloyd Bynoe (congas), Daniel White (piano), Tholo Peter Tsegona (trumpet) and Art Collins (saxophone). This configuration released a second album, *Chewing The Fat,* late in 1982, sporting a cover after the style of Dave Brubeck's classic *Take Five.*

Blue Zoo

Blue Zoo first came to attention late in 1981 with the engaging single *Love Moves In Strange Ways.* Denied reasonable airplay, the group had to wait until single two, *I'm Your Man,* before they breached the lower reaches of the British charts.

Strictly speaking, these discs were not the band's debut recordings. Under the odd monicker of Modern Jazz they had cut two flop singles for the Magnet label. At that point (1980/'81) the line-up comprised Andy O (vocals), Dave

BLUE ZOO

Woolfson (keyboards, sax), Mike Ansell (bass), Micky Sparrow (drums) and Tim Parry (guitar). Woolfson dropped out when Blue Zoo came into being.

Produced by the most able Tim Friese-Green (of Stiff Little Fingers, Tight Fit and other fame), Blue Zoo pursue a fairly natural rock sound, generally eschewing synthesizer dominance. Their crisp and striking sound has been best captured on single three, *Cry Boy Cry;* the first significant chart hit for this London-

THE BOOMTOWN RATS

based outfit.

Why Blue Zoo? According to Andy O, "It's our environment. Viewed from the inside, it's like a zoo. We feel like animals in a menagerie whenever we're on stage."

The Boomtown Rats

The Boomtown Rats were formed in 1975 in guitarist Garry Roberts's kitchen in Dublin, Ireland. Prior to the formation of the band its members had strenuously avoided other occupations. Roberts was a failed student and photographer, guitarist Gerry Cott and keyboards player Johnny Fingers were also failed students on the dole, drummer Simon Crowe had finished at art school, bassist Peter Briquette was working (!) and vocalist Bob Geldof had tried everything from meat worker to bulldozer driver, photographer, English teacher and journalist.

After constant gigging around Ireland and a venture to Holland in October 1976 The Rats signed with Ensign Records. Six months later they embarked on a full-scale English tour, including support dates for Tom Petty, and in August 1977 they released their debut single, *Lookin' After No 1,* which reached 11 on the English charts. In November they released their second single, *Mary Of The Fourth Form,* and their debut self-titled album.

March 1978 saw the release of third single, *She's So Modern* and in June their second album, *A Tonic For The Troops,* followed by another single, *Like Clockwork,* the same month. But their big breakthrough came in October 1978 with the release of *Rat Trap,* which went straight to No 1 on the UK charts.

While on a promotional visit to the States in early 1979, Bob Geldof heard the tragic story of Brenda Spencer, the girl who shot up her California schoolyard, which became the basis for a Boomtown Rats song, *I Don't Like Mondays.* When the single was released in July it went to No 1 in both the UK and Australia but was effectively banned from airplay in America. This was followed late in the year by their third album, *The Fine Art Of Surfacing.*

In the early months of 1980 The Boomtown Rats embarked on an ambitious world tour which took in Europe, America, the Far East and Australia. Their fourth album, *Mondo Bongo,* was released later that year with the single, *Banana Republic,* and it was the last record to feature guitarist Gerry Cott who departed in 1981.

The band continued on as a five piece and their fifth album, *Five Deep* came out early in 1982. Like *Mondo Bongo* it was co-produced with Tony Visconti, but the album failed to match the sales of its predecessors.

Also in early 1982 Bob Geldof completed work on the Pink Floyd feature film, *The Wall,* in which he played the lead role. The film was

directed by Alan Parker, renowned for his direction of *Bugsy Malone, Midnight Express* and *Fame* and was released worldwide late in 1982. Deliberate or not, The Boomtown Rats' profile is currently drastically low.

Bow Wow Wow

The roots of Bow Wow Wow go back to 1979, when ex-Sex Pistols manager Malcolm McLaren headed for Paris to buy porno films. While there, he collected a library of African ethnic music on tape. Soon after, Adam Ant approached McLaren for advice in getting his fledgling punk band, The Ants, off the ground. McLaren lent him his library to listen to and so introduced Adam to the jungle rhythms that became Ant Music.

McLaren became Adam & The Ants' manager but soon after persuaded the three member Ants to sack Adam. Drummer David Della Barbarossa, born in Mauritius, had been a star junior soccer player for Tottenham Hotspur before throwing it in to become a musician. Guitarist Mathew Ashman and bassist Leigh Roy Gorman had both grown up listening to jazz and had never played in bands before joining Adam & The Ants after leaving school. For a brief period Boy George filled in as lead singer, before going off to form his own group, Culture Club.

McLaren solved their search for a new singer when he discovered Burmese born Annabella Lu Win, a 14 year old working in a Kilburn launderette. Bow Wow Wow released their debut single, *C30, C60, C90, Go!,* late in 1980 on the EMI label. McLaren had composed the song in praise of home taping, a

> **"The press definitely tried to bury me, at one point, by presenting me as the most horrible person around."**
> — *Kevin Rowland, Dexys Midnight Runners*

cause McLaren believed would ensure the band's credibility. But the single failed to take off, as did the group's debut cassette-only EP. EMI later issued a cash-in album *The Original Recordings*.

In 1981 Bow Wow Wow changed to RCA Records and late that year they released their debut album, *See Jungle! See Jungle! Go Join Your Gang, Yeah! City All Over, Go Ape Crazy*. The group began touring extensively for the first time in both the UK and US and began to attract a considerable following through their dynamic shows.

In mid 1982 came an EP, *The Last Of The Mohicans*, which inspired

toy with 'scratch' records and score a hit with *Buffalo Gals*. Annabella admitted that she had submitted herself to a number of humiliations at her mentor's hands, all in the name of commercial advancement, but that such was in the past.

Certainly the focus of the band is now more on music than seedy exploitation and, to this end, master pop producer Mike Chapman was called upon to produce the second RCA album, *When The Going Gets Tough The Tough Get Going*. Under the direction of both Laguna and Chapman, Bow Wow Wow have shown themselves to be a formidable Eighties powerpop unit.

BOW WOW WOW

Bureau was complete.

A period of intense songwriting and rehearsing followed. Very much a group effort, they democratically write, arrange and play all their powerhouse R&B.

Early in 1981 The Bureau recorded their first single, *Only For Sheep,* with producer Pete Wingfield, who also produced the first Dexy's album. Released in

controversy through the discreet nude cover photograph of Annabella in the manner of the French impressionist painter Monet. Late that year, Bow Wow Wow released their second LP, *I Want Candy*, and the title track became their first major single, receiving chart action in the US, UK and Australia. The LP featured new recordings of some of their more promising early songs, this time crisply produced by veteran bubble-pop wizard Kenny Laguna, who at the time was spinning gold for Joan Jett.

By this point the group had severed their relationship with Malcolm McLaren, who went off to

The Bureau

The Bureau formed at the end of 1980 when five members of Dexy's Midnight Runners split from singer Kevin Rowland in violent disagreement with his decision to release the single, *Keep It — Part Two.*

Drummer Stoker Growcott, organist Mert Talbot, tenor/sax player JB Blythe, bassist Pete Williams and alto sax player Steve Spooner took out adverts in the English music press and held auditions for a singer and guitarist. Arch Brown (vocals) and Rob Jones (guitar), who had been members of The Upset and had supported Dexy's on tour, joined and The

"You put a group of people together and something unique is going to come of it — and it has nothing to do with art or German Experimentalists of the Twenties or Thirties, whom I've never heard of and don't care about."
David Thomas, Pere Ubu

THE BUREAU

March the single went Top 10 in both the UK and Australia. It was followed soon after by their first album, *The Bureau.*

Kate Bush ▬▬▬▬
Kate Bush, the daughter of a wealthy doctor, was born on July 30th, 1958 and established herself on the charts with her first single, *Wuthering Heights,* released in January 1978.

Kate's family were a strong musical influence and she studied violin before switching to piano which she taught herself to play, and now plays at live performances.

After leaving school at 16 Kate signed to EMI Records on the strength of a demo tape financed by Pink Floyd's Dave Gilmour. In the period between signing her contract and releasing *Wuthering Heights* Kate studied dance and mime, both of which were put to good use in the impressive videos that usually accompany her records.

Kate's debut album, *The Kick Inside,* was released in February 1978 and contained both *Wuthering*

Heights and her next single *The Man With The Child In His Eyes,* released May 1978. *Hammer Horror* followed in November.

In March 1979 Kate released *Wow,* following this with a live EP, *Kate Bush on Stage,* in September

KATE BUSH

1979. Two more singles, *Breathing,* and *Babooshka* were released in April 1980 and June 1980 respectively.

In December a second album, *Lionheart,* was released, this one containing *Wow* and *Hammer.*

Never For Ever, Kate's third album, was released in September 1980, and included *Delius,* her tribute to the composer, along with *Babooshka* and *Breathing.*

Aside from own recordings Kate found time to sing on sessions for Peter Gabriel and Roy Harper.

In September 1982 Kate released a new album, *The Dreaming.* Two singles, *The Dreaming,* and *Suspended In Gaffa,* were lifted from the album but neither made much impression on the charts. It seemed as if the intensely personal world of her music had now become inaccessible to her public.

THE BUSH TETRAS

Bush Tetras ▬▬▬▬
The Bush Tetras are Cynthia Sley (vocals), Dee Pop (drums), Laura Kennedy (bass), and Pat Place (guitar). Their sound has been compared to that of The Slits, Gang Of Four, and Delta 5, and the band has maintained its position as one of top new New York club bands, being associated with the likes of The Bongos, Raybeats, and dB's, as part of the Third Wave of bands from that city.

The band's recording career began with *Too Many Creeps,* a single released on the independent 99 Records which reached number 57 on the Billboard disco charts.

Too Many Creeps was followed by another single, *Boom,* and an EP titled *Ritual.*

Early in 1983, ROIR Cassettes released *Wild Things,* a tape of live performances recorded during 1982 at CBGB's, The Peppermint Lounge, and Hitsville.

C

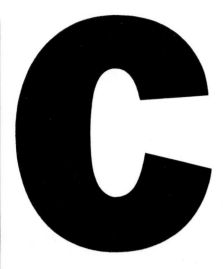

Cabaret Voltaire

Cabaret Voltaire (Chris Watson — electronics and tapes, Richard Kirk — guitar and wind instruments, Steven Mallinder —bass, electronic percussion and vocals) first came together in Sheffield in 1973. In those days they had no intention of playing live, but simply collaborated in a loft recording tapes.

In May 1975, they conned their way into a show and played their first performance. Cabaret Voltaire's unique instruments (a tape loop of a recording of a steamhammer as percussion and a clarinet covered in rubber with flashing lights) and their alienating music caused the audience to riot and they were beaten up and had their equipment smashed.

Punk's arrival made it easier for such an extremely experimental electronic group to get live work and they slowly began to find more acceptance.

Still, a cassette they made in early 1978 was rejected by every record label in England. Finally, Rough Trade invited them to make an album, *Mix Up,* released late in 1978. Since then they have released a live set in 1979, *Live At The YMCA,* and three studio albums, *The Voice Of America* in late 1980, *Red Mouse* in 1981, and *Hai!* in 1982, all of which received high praise from the UK music press.

John Cale

John Cale's career is one of the most remarkable in contemporary music. He has been a classical pianist, a prototype punk rocker, an A&R executive, a producer, an arranger and a film score composer. Almost every project for which he's been responsible has borne the unmistakable stamp of his brooding Celtic personality. His influence on young serious musicians might be viewed alongside that of Bowie, Eno and Fripp.

In the beginning, Cale armed

JOHN CALE

himself with a strong grounding in classical music, studying composition at London's Guildhall School of Music. He first arrived in the US in the early '60s on a Leonard Bernstein Fellowship. He continued his studies in New York and came increasingly under the influence of the avant garde composers such as Copland, Cage and LaMonte Young.

But in 1965 Cale met Lou Reed, and abandoned classical music for rock. They formed The Velvet Underground, which was initially a part of Andy Warhol's mixed-media show, The Exploding Plastic Inevitable. Playing electric viola, guitar and piano, Cale, more than any other, was responsible for the group's overall sound.

After two albums, Cale left The Velvet Underground early in '68 to pursue his own recording and production work. His first solo album was a collaboration with the avant garde pianist Terry Riley, *Church Of Anthrax,* which made Cale the only rock performer to record an album for Columbia's Masterworks classical division. In addition, Cale worked as a producer for Iggy Pop & The Stooges, Patti Smith, Jonathan Richman's Modern Lovers, Nico, Mike Heron, Nick Drake and Squeeze. For a while in the early '70s he held an office job as staff producer at Warner Brothers Records in California, all the while indulging his interest in motor racing and cocaine.

Cale's first true solo album was released in 1972, *Paris 1919,* a very

melodic, ethereal record. But it was the series of albums he made for Island from 1974 that established Cale as the high priest of screeching paranoia. *Fear, Slow Dazzle* and *Helen Of Troy* were direct antecedents of the late '70s punk movement. Cale established his reputation for extreme behaviour at a London concert in 1977, when he chopped off the head of a live chicken on stage and threw the remains into the audience.

Since the mid '70s, Cale's career has been very sporadic. In the late '70s he was without an American record company and a 1977 EP, *Animal Justice* and a 1979 live LP, *Sabotage,* were released on UK's Illegal Records. In 1981 A&M picked up his contract and he recorded the *Honi Soit* album, one of his best ever solo records. But the sales were disappointing and A&M dropped him soon after. In 1982, he was signed by New York avant garde independent label Ze Records, for which he recorded the *Music For A New Society* album.

Jim Carroll

Born and raised in New York City, Jim Carroll grew up in a working class Catholic background. At the age of 12, he began to write — certainly an unusual preoccupation for a street-wise kid. Carroll started out by writing a series of prose descriptions based on his experiences coming of age on the streets of New York — the drugs, the sex, the crime and the hustling to survive. And through it all, there was the thread of his devotion to basketball.

"The Basketball Diaries", as they were called, were written while Jim was between 12 and 15 (1963-66). Several years later, when excerpts from them were published in the Paris Review, they startled and impressed the current literary scene, gaining rave critiques from Jack Kerouac and William Burroughs.

Meanwhile, Jim's basketball talents, combined with his academic abilities, landed him a scholarship to a private school in the city. While there, the teachers interested him in poetry and at the age of 16, his first book of poems was published. It wasn't long before Jim was garnering acclaim as a bright young force on the literary scene, with numerous magazines running his work. After high school he went to Columbia University for one semester, then left to pursue his poetic ambitions exclusively. In the midst of all these literary developments, though, Carroll remained very much a New York street kid and was a junkie before he had even finished writing the "Diaries".

It was around the age of 19 that Jim first thought about writing songs. Through some literary involvement with the Andy Warhol scene of the late '60s, Jim became an avid follower of The Velvet Underground. At one point he did some poetry readings with Lou Reed, and in turn began to write lyrics, but purely for his own benefit. He continued to write poetry and at the age of 22, a collection of his poems, *Living At The Movies*, was nominated for a Pulitzer Prize.

In 1974 Jim finally reached a point when he had to get out of New York and away from heroin. He moved to California and for the next three years lived in seclusion in the country. During this period, Jim's only contact with rock was with his old friend Patti Smith, whom he had

known very well in New York and who had made the successful transition from poet to rock figure. Through Patti, Jim met Alan Lanier of the Blue Oyster Cult, who suggested they collaborate on some songs. Although none of their material was recorded at the time, it brought Jim ever closer to his own entry into rock'n'roll.

Having gradually emerged from his seclusion, Jim worked with Patti and some underground filmmakers in San Francisco, with Jim reading some prose poetry and Patti playing guitar and piano behind it. The next night, Jim went with Patti to her concert in San Diego. There was some disagreement with the scheduled opening act, and suddenly Jim was asked to start the show. So, in very spontaneous fashion, Jim got up and rapped his lyrics, with Patti's band playing behind him. That experience made determined Jim to get his own band.

Jim knew of a self-contained band that lived, as he did, in the country around San Francisco. Together they wrote and rehearsed six songs in a week and a half — with Jim half-talking/half-singing his words. And his next poetry reading turned into a musical introduction. They went over so well that Jim and the whole band were asked to come back next week and play later in the night, with the rock bands — not the poets. Suddenly, Jim Carroll was a rock'n'roller.

A few more shows followed, after which Jim and the band did a demo tape. Then the signing of a mass-market paperback deal with Bantam Books for the publication of "The Basketball Diaries" brought Jim to NYC for the first time in five years. Having previously met Earl McGrath (the President of Rolling Stone Records), Jim thought he'd bring him the tape "just to get an opinion". Instead, Earl liked what he heard so much that he offered to become fully involved in Jim's musical career.

Returning to California, Jim began to work on new songs, where there would be less rapping and more real singing. He used a basic knowledge of guitar to work out some of the song structures, working out the rest with the whole band. Then, finally, Jim was ready to go into the studio in 1981 to officially

embark on his new career as a rocker. With Earl producing (and Bob Clearmountain co-producing and engineering), the result was Jim Carroll's debut album, *Catholic Boy*, one of the most critically acclaimed LPs of the year. Carroll then went on the road with his band, which comprised Brian Linsley (guitar), Steve Linsley (bass), Terrell Winn (guitar) and Wayne Woods (drums). Every night the houses were filled with famous figures come to observe the 'next big thing', culminating with Keith Richards joining the band on-stage at the Ritz. This sort of attention was

JIM CARROLL

more damaging than helpful and Jim began to suffer from over-hype. This drew serious attention away from the second album, *Dry Dreams*.

Catholic Girls

Like England's Bananarama, Toto Coello and The Belle Stars, New York's Catholic Girls have surfaced in the wake of the Joan Jett/Go Go's explosion of 1982. A competent and at times exciting, rock unit they owe an obvious debt to the classic girl-group genre of the early Sixties. This is evident from their showcase track, the effervescent *Boys Can Cry*.

Lead singer and songwriter Gail Petersen and bassist Joanne Holland were in fact Catholic schoolgirls together in Staten Island. Moving to New Jersey, they fell in with guitarist Roxy Andersen and drummer Doreen Holmes. By early 1980 they were playing original material in local clubs and had adopted a school uniform garb. The obvious novelty of their outward appearance resulted in coverage in the New York Post, New York Daily News and other formidable publications.

Looking innocent but playing with considerable strength, the girls secured a deal with MCA Records and cut their first album with producer Evan Pace. Highlighted by the aforementioned *Boys Can Cry* and the ambitious *God Made You For Me,* the LP established the femme quartet as a credible music force. "We've started from scratch," explains Joanne Holland, "building

THE CATHOLIC GIRLS

everything around the songs; the kind of feeling, the arrangements which we feel are right. Not many people seem to work that way. Also, as opposed to many other bands, we play in a minor key, which gives our music a more haunting flavour, a darker and deeper feeling."

James Chance/White ■■■

James Siegfried (aka Chance and White) has recorded under a bewildering array of names, but he will always be remembered for being one of the first white musicians in the new music scene to be heavily influenced by funk.

Chance first surfaced in 1977 playing sax with the New York band, Teenage Jesus & The Jerks, which featured Lydia Lunch. In 1978, he formed the original Contortions with Don Christensen (drums), Jody Harris (guitar), Pat Place (slide guitar), George Scott (bass) and Adele Bertei (organ). They first attracted attention with four tracks on the *No New York* compilation album in 1978,

> *"I like synthesizers but I don't like synthesizers in The Church. That's a bit like putting Elizabeth I in a sports car. I want to keep the chime, it's such a lyrical sound."*
> — *Steve Kilbey, The Church*

produced by Brian Eno. Their debut album, *Buy The Contortions,* was released in 1979, along with a single, *Designed To Kill,* but it was under the name of James White & The Blacks that same year that he achieved immortality with the classic single *Contort Yourself.* In 1980, also under the name of The Blacks (a line-up that omitted Bertei), he released his second LP, *Off-White.*

Since the original Contortions line-up (who soon split, Christensen and Harris forming The Raybeats, Scott joining 8 Eyed Spy before dying of a heroin overdose in 1980, and Place forming The Bush Tetras), Chance has worked with an ever-changing backing group, which at times has included members of Defunkt. This has resulted in a major inconsistency in his live work, though there are two albums that document good nights. *Live Aux Bains-Douches* was recorded live in Paris and released in May 1980 by the French label Scopa, while *Live In New York* is an album-length, cassette-only release from May 1981 on the ROIR label. Both were issued under the name of James Chance & The Contortions. Also, in January 1981, Ze released a compilation of the *Buy* and *Off-White* records under the title *Second Chance,* though with an artist credit of James White & The Contortions (even he's confused!).

In mid 1982 James Chance released his first solo album, *Sax Maniac,* highlighted by a radical version of the Broadway standard *That Old Black Magic.*

Charged GBH ■■■

Locked in a time warp of their very own, Charged GBH are carrying on the dubious traditions of buzzsaw guitar and gobbin' on audiences.

The band emerged from a darkened rehearsal hall on FA Cup Final day in 1980, to play at a prostitutes' benefit. The first vinyl to bear their name was a 12" EP *Leather, Bristles, Studs And Acne,* followed by a 7" single, *No Survivors,* which managed to make its way to 63 on the BBC chart and bring them precariously close to a Top of the Pops appearance.

Like Clay Records stablemates Discharge, Charged GBH are one of the savage punk bands left in the land of New Romantics, as evidenced by their first album *City Baby Attacked By Rats.* This offering graced the world with such songs as *Slut, Big Women* and *Passengers On The Menu,* which seem almost pale when compared to earlier titles *State Execution, Necrophilia* and *DOA.*

The group comprises singer Colin, drummer Wilf, guitarist Jock and bassist Ross.

CHINA CRISIS

China Crisis ■■■

China Crisis are Eddie Lundon (guitar, vocals and occasional keyboard) and Garry Daly (keyboards, vocals and occasional guitar). The duo are augmented by: Mick Douglas (keyboards), Gary Johnson (bass), and Kevin Wilkinson (drums).

Eddie and Garry met while attending St Kevin's Comprehensive in Kirkby and quickly struck up a friendship based on mutual musical interests. These, at the time, centred around the collected works of David Bowie, Stevie Wonder and Brian Eno.

While Eddie passed time being an apprentice motor mechanic, Garry entered the more exotic realms of hairdressing, roof tiling, and making traditional beer pumps in a North of England factory. A sign of these harsh economic times, the pair began their musical career by making tapes on equipment they shared with three other friends. As part of this musicians' co-operative, the pair began composing music, not on the conventional guitar or piano, but by beginning with a drum machine pattern and building a song on this foundation.

First real steps towards public acceptance came on entering Jeremy Lewis's Amazon Studios and emerging with *African And White*. Originally on Lewis's Inevitable label, both record and band were snapped up by Virgin.

China Crisis' second single was called *Scream Down At Me,* and was followed by their debut album, *Difficult Shapes and Passive Rhythms: Some People Think It's Fun To Entertain.* Besides *African And White*, the album contained the band's third single, *Christian.*

The Church

The Church began in Sydney, Australia, in April 1980 as a trio. Steve Kilbey (bass and vocals) and Peter Koppes (lead guitar), before teaming up with drummer Nick Ward, had spent a few years writing and recording songs in Steve's bedroom studio. Steve had originally come from Canberra, where he had played in various bands with David Studdert, including Tactics.

Soon after formation The Church became a quartet with the addition of Marty Willson-Piper (guitar), freshly arrived from England where he had been an itinerant busker. After playing a few gigs in Sydney's smaller pubs, the group decided to pool their resources and record a four-track demo in Steve's bedroom. Eventually The Church's demo reached the hands of Chris Gilbey of ATV Northern Songs, who not only signed Kilbey to a publishing deal but also the band to a recording contract.

The Church's debut single, *She Never Said*, was released in November 1980, but it was their second single, *The Unguarded Moment,* released in February 1981, that broke the band. It went top 20 and suddenly The Church and their ethereal, Byrds-influenced Sixties-styled pop was the hottest sound in

THE CHURCH

THE CLASH

Australia. The debut album *Of Skins And Heart,* was released in March and reached the top 30. It had been recorded back in 1980 and produced by Chris Gilbey, who then sent the tapes to America for remixing by Bob Clearmountain. Soon after release, Nick Ward was replaced by Richard Ploog from Adelaide.

In late 1981, The Church released a five-track double EP, again produced by Gilbey and mixed by Clearmountain. The second LP, *The Blurred Crusade*, was released in February 1982 and the first single from it was *Almost With You*, which reached top 40. Following an Australian tour, the group journeyed to the UK and Europe to

tour and promote the release of their first album there, on which some tracks were replaced by EP songs. In late 1982 The Church released a 12 inch EP, *Sing Songs*, to mark their return to Australia. It was highlighted by a stunning version of Paul Simon's *I Am A Rock*. Album three, *Seance,* followed.

The Clash

The Clash's history began in May 1976, when a drummerless group rehearsed in a small squat near Shepherd's Bush Green in London. Guitarist and singer Joe Strummer, guitarist Mick Jones and bassist Paul Simonon were playing with a guitarist named Keith Levene (who was to leave soon after and eventually end up in PiL). In August 1976, The Clash moved their practice sessions to an abandoned warehouse in Camden Town, enlisting Terry Chimes on drums. They couldn't find work on the established pub circuit so manager Bernie Rhodes arranged gigs in unusual venues such as The Institute of Contemporary Art. Chimes left after having a bottle thrown at him on stage and was replaced by Topper Headon.

In late 1976, in the rush to sign punk bands by the major record companies, The Clash contracted to CBS, after only playing a few gigs. They recorded their debut album, *The Clash*, at CBS's studios in London in only three weekend sessions, their soundman acting as producer.

The Clash were bottom billed to The Sex Pistols on the ill-fated Anarchy tour in December 1976. They followed this by putting together their own legendary White Riot tour early in 1977, taking with them The Buzzcocks, Slits and Subway Sect. Early into the tour the band heard that their album had entered the charts at number 12. Their singles received virtually no airplay and only reached the low 30s on the charts. However, in retrospect *White Riot* is seen as a cornerstone song in the British punk/New Wave movement.

The Clash were one of the earliest English bands to experiment with reggae rhythms. Their version of the Junior Murvin song *Police And Thieves*, was included on their first album. Lee Perry (or Scratch the Upsetter), the co-author and producer of the original, visited London in mid 1977 and produced the *Complete Control* single. Following its release, the band toured England with America's Richard Hell as support and then worked throughout Europe.

During this time, various members of the band were repeatedly arrested and fined for petty theft and vandalism, culminating in an incident that took place on the top of the group's warehouse. A helicopter and armed police arrested two members and charged them with various gun offences and the shooting of some valuable racing pigeons.

While they were on remand, the band released *White Man In Hammersmith/I Don't Want To Be A Prisoner* and began a *Clash Out On Parole* tour with Suicide from New York and The Specials. Late in 1978 The Clash recorded and released a second album, *Give 'Em Enough Rope*, with American producer Sandy Pearlman. The album was released in November and entered the English charts at number two. It also gave them their first real single hit, *Tommy Gun*.

The Clash toured England on their *Sort It Out* tour, during which they parted company with Bernie Rhodes (though they were later to team up again). In February 1979, they set out on their first American tour, taking Bo Diddley along as support. Returning to England, The Clash rehearsed, wrote new material, worked on the film, *Rude Boy*, and recorded an EP, *The Cost Of Living*. Released on election day in the UK, it charted at number 22. From it, a raucous version of the

"I'd like to say that we're not boring University lecturers. We play great music and we're exciting. We jump about and wiggle our bums — we're not afraid to do that."
— *Joe Strummer, The Clash*

Bobby Fuller Four hit, *I Fought The Law*, was released as their first American single.

The band continued touring, playing their first date in Finland. On their return from Europe, they recorded a third album, *London Calling*. Produced by the late Guy Stevens, the double album saw them experimenting with new styles of rock'n'roll. In 1979 The Clash toured America, adding Blockhead keyboard player Mickey Gallagher. They were supported by various cult acts, including Sam & Dave, Screaming Jay Hawkins, Bo Diddley, Joe Ely, David Johansen, The Cramps and The Rebels. They persuaded Ely to return to England with them for further support work.

London Calling was released late in 1979, after the American tour, and proved to be the most successful and critically acclaimed album to date. Indeed, American acceptance was so strong that the once-reviled Clash were now placed on the cover of Rolling Stone. In Australia, the title track gave the group their first antipodean hit.

In June 1980, The Clash entered New York's Electric Ladyland Studios and recorded a triple album, *Sandinista!*, released early in 1981 after much bickering between the group and CBS over keeping the price down to less than a regular double album. The album was critically well received, but sales were disappointing and the single, *The Call Up*, was only a minor hit in the UK. Later that year the group planned to play seven nights in a row in New York, but early in the series, fans who could not obtain tickets rioted, causing the remaining concerts to be cancelled. Paul Simonon was also busted for possession of cocaine in England.

This began a series of calamities as amusing as they were disruptive. First, Joe Strummer disappeared off the face of the earth, immediately prior to a major tour and album launch. Finally located in Paris, he returned to the fold meekly, claiming he had needed a rest. Just when it seemed that the train was back on the tracks, drummer Topper Headon took his leave, claiming he was jealous over the amount of publicity afforded Strummer's midnight flit. He was later reported apprehended for "stealing a bus stop".

Having enticed original drummer Terry Chimes back into the group, The Clash returned to business as usual. A rap single, *Radio Clash*, made a strong impact and was followed by the 'breakthrough' album *Combat Rock*, which yielded up the international hit *Rock The Casbah*. This coincided with a wave of overwhelming popularity in America that saw them take out a number of major magazine polls, including Rolling Stone's. This attention was consolidated with a sweep through America with The Who on a farewell tour, which saw the support act steal a great deal of thunder from the headliner.

By their very survival and reasonable adherence to original principles, The Clash have emerged as the revered founding fathers of British new rock, whether they like it or not. Their undimmed energy and commitment levels have certainly placed them on a rung above the fashion and synthesizer bands who dominate British chart rock of the Eighties. In concert, they project an uncommon presence and therefore command a drawing power on par with many American 'dinosaur' bands. Their influence on American rock has been extremely positive.

Classix Nouveaux

Classix Nouveaux are Sal Solo (vocals, guitar, keyboards/synthesizers), Mik Sweeney (bass guitar and backing vocals), B.P. Hurding (drums, percussion), and Gary Steadman (guitar, guitar synthesizers). Steadman left in 1982 to be replaced by Jimi Sumen, a Finn who plays several instruments, sings and writes and has released three albums.

Early in their career the band was categorised by the media as New Romantics but they defended themselves, stating they were formed eighteen months before the advent of this latest teen cult.

As far as the mass populace were concerned, Classix Nouveaux came to prominence with their single, *Guilty,* which received extensive airplay in Britain.

During the early part of 1981 the band established their following with two major UK tours. The first was the much publicised 2002 Review which sprang from Sal Solo's idea of combining a number of promising new bands in one package. This tour gave national exposure in Britain to bands like Theatre Of Hate and Shock. A more extensive tour followed, ending at London's Hammersmith Palais in May and coinciding with the release of their debut album, *Night People.*

By this time Classix Nouveaux had charted in several territories and the overseas response resulted in them spending the remainder of the year away from Britain. They visited 11 countries including Sweden, Yugoslavia, and Portugal, where they received silver discs for sales of *Night People.* That album has been released in 27 countries including India, the Philippines, and Bolivia.

In November 1981 the band began work on a second album, *La Verite,* released the following year.

1982 saw the group touring extensively not only in England, but also Eastern Bloc countries such as Hungary and Czechoslovakia. They played India and also became the first western rock group to play in Sri Lanka.

The Comsat Angels

The group began as Radio Earth in 1977 in Yorkshire. Singer and guitarist Steve Fellows and drummer Mic Glaisher knew each other from schooldays in Rotherham, and Steve met keyboard player Andy Peake when they both attended Sheffield Art College. This original trio played together on a loose basis before deciding at the start of 1977 to recruit a bass player. After advertising in a local newspaper, Kevin Bacon from Derbyshire presented himself and the lineup was complete.

After lengthy rehearsals they embarked on a string of local gigs and by mid 1978 a demo tape of their work reached Radar Records. Radio Earth recorded a single with producer Clive Langer (now maestro of Madness), and the band prepared to sign with the label and record an album. But then WEA Records withdrew their finance from Radar, and although several Radar acts were 'transferred' to WEA, Radio Earth were not among them and the single was never released.

THE COMSAT ANGELS

In reaction to this major setback the group began to radically change their music and in consequence acquired a new name — The Comsat Angels, named after the communications satellite.

In early 1979 The Comsat Angels recorded and released the EP *Red Planet,* on their own label, Junta Records. Soon after, the group signed with Polygram and in May 1980 a three track EP, *Total War/ Waiting For A Miracle/Home Is The Range,* was released. Their debut LP, *Waiting For A Miracle,* followed in October and was warmly received by the English music press.

In October 1981, The Comsat Angels released their second album, *Sleep No More,* which saw the band's music developing in a more stripped down and stark direction. This was carried to an even more radical extent on album three, *Fiction,* of

which one British reviewer commented, "A relentless maudlin dirge so astonishingly dull that I find it hard to believe they actually sell records like this anymore." The Comsat Angels have experienced a great deal of difficulty using their name in America. The corporate entities in charge of America's communication satellite system have threatened to sue the band if they tour America under their current name, and have gone so far as to intercept telexes containing tour dates.

John Cooper Clarke

John Cooper Clarke, a leader in a field of one, takes the prize for the poet with the fastest live delivery and for the man who looks most like Bob Dylan, circa *Blonde On Blonde.*

Born in Salford, Manchester,

CLASSIX NOUVEAUX

JOHN COOPER CLARKE

John left school at 15 and began declaiming verse in local pubs and clubs. Inspiration came from the Italian Futurists and a spell spent at a devoutly Catholic school. Jobs included stand-up comic on the Northern club circuit, fire watcher, dishwasher, mortuary attendant and printer's apprentice. In the meantime, he married and divorced young.

In December 1977 John released an EP (which contained the acclaimed *Psycle Sluts*) on the independent Manchester-based Rabid Records, which led to a major record deal with Epic. In November 1978 his debut album, *Disguise In Love,* was released and it was followed in 1979 by *Walking Back To Happiness.* Clarke toured with Elvis Costello, Rockpile and Dr Feelgood in places as diverse as Ireland, Scandinavia and the USA.

In April 1980 Clarke's third album, *Snap, Crackle, Bop,* which contained his masterpiece *Beasley Street,* was released and he followed it in October with his first major British tour, co-headlining with Pauline Murray. With the release in May 1981 of a compilation album, *Me And My Big Mouth,* Clarke headlined another British tour.

In mid 1982 Clarke released his fifth album, *Zip Style Method,* which like all his previous LPs, was produced by Martin Hannett and Steve Hopkins with backing by The Invisible Girls. At the end of that year he embarked on his first tour of Australia with New Order, after previously touring Britain with Linton Kwesi Johnson.

John Cooper Clarke has had one book published, *The Cooper Clarke Directory,* as well as headlining the Oxford Poetry Festival in 1979 and

representing Britain in the very first Poetry Olympics held at Poets Corner, Westminster Abbey, in 1980. Clarke also featured in the *Urgh! A Music War* film and in 1978 was responsible for the only orange triangular single in the world — *Gimmix!* A second book of poetry is about to be published titled *Ten Years in an Open Neck,* also the name of a film Clarke recently appeared in.

Elvis Costello

Elvis Costello (real name Declan McManus) was born in Liverpool to a father who was quite a popular big band singer in England. Elvis grew up listening to his father's collection of jazz and MOR records and did not discover rock and soul music until his mid-teens, around 1970.

In the early '70s, after moving to

> "My relationship with rock is like Lenny Bruce's with modern jazz. I like the clothes and attitude."
> — *John Cooper Clarke*

London with a wife and child to work as a computer operator, he also began playing around the folk circuit with various groups. Around 1975 he met Nick Lowe and was turned on to the idea of playing rock music. But in 1976 he was still performing in folk clubs under the name of DP Costello, when Lowe introduced him to Jake Riviera of Stiff Records. He was immediately signed and with Nick Lowe producing, an album was recorded with an American group Clover backing him.

This debut album, *My Aim Is True,* was released in June 1977, two months after his first live performance as Elvis, at the Nashville Room in London. The album contained many of Costello's most enduring and masterful songs: *Alison, Less Than Zero, Welcome To The Working Week, Mystery Dance* and *(The Angels Wanna Wear My) Red Shoes. My Aim Is True* received enraptured reviews from all sections of the media, and this prompted Costello to leave his job in computers. Prior to his embarking on his first tour of England he formed The Attractions, comprising Bruce Thomas (bass), a former member of Sutherland Bros & Quiver, Pete Thomas (drums), ex-

Chilli Willi, and classically trained pianist Steve Nieve. Costello and The Attractions were part of the Live Stiffs tour through England and two tracks from those shows were released on Stiff's *Live Stiffs* album.

With The Attractions, Costello recorded his second album in 1978 with Nick Lowe producing again. *This Year's Model* contained another 12 strong Costello originals including the hits, *Pump It Up, (I Don't Want To Go To) Chelsea* and the classic *Watching The Detectives.* Reviews were once more of the ecstatic kind.

Late in 1978, Costello was back with his third album, *Armed Forces,*

around two to three minutes long, crammed onto one Nick Lowe-produced album. Elvis himself has admitted that the album was inspired by his love for the '60s soul sound of the Stax/Volt label. Many critics found 20 tracks difficult to digest, as most ended before they had an opportunity to state a definite theme.

Also late in 1980 all the non-album tracks of Costello's (limited edition singles and EPs and rare B sides plus alternative recordings) were compiled for a US-only album, *Taking Liberties,* which was released in cassette-only form in England and not released at all in Australia.

In early 1981, Costello released a

John McFee from the Doobie Bros sitting in) recorded an album of country standards, *Almost Blue.* The album received mixed reviews, but the single, *Good Year For The Roses,* was a major hit in the UK.

In mid-1982, just after his second tour of Australia, *Imperial Bedroom,* his eighth album (including *Taking Liberties),* was released. The record saw Costello picking up from where he left off with *Trust,* and is a remarkable affirmation of the continuing high creative level of his career and his ability to constantly keep developing.

Throughout his career, Elvis Costello has maintained a degree of aloofness and secrecy from the press, giving very few interviews. In part, this resentment is due to Costello's early bitterness at being rejected initially by every record company in England. It has been emphasised by such incidents as his bar room fistfight with Bonnie Bramlett (in which he came out second best)

ELVIS COSTELLO

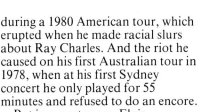

THE CRAMPS

again produced by Nick Lowe. It was an interesting departure from the previous efforts. The instrumentation and sound were more controlled and lush and Costello's songwriting was more oblique, less concerned with overt anger and frustration and more concerned with the subtle emotional deceit of relationships, laced with references to the world political situation. Interestingly, the album was originally to be called *Emotional Fascism.* It contained the savage single, *Oliver's Army,* which was a hit in the UK and Australia.

Get Happy, Costello's 1980 offering, presented yet another aspect of his songwriting and performing. Twenty tracks, all

new album, *Trust,* produced by Nick Lowe, which again showcased a change in direction. The album contained a wide range of styles and saw Costello refining his vocals and songwriting ability to a new peak. The single, *Clubland,* was a minor hit in England was also one of the critics' most favoured albums of the year.

One interesting aspect to Costello is his love of country music. This first surfaced in 1979 when he appeared on American C&W singer George Jones' album, *My Very Special Guests,* dueting on *Stranger In The House.* In 1981 Costello returned to Nashville and with Jones' producer, Billy Sherrill, and The Attractions (with steel guitarist

during a 1980 American tour, which erupted when he made racial slurs about Ray Charles. And the riot he caused on his first Australian tour in 1978, when at his first Sydney concert he only played for 55 minutes and refused to do an encore.

But in recent years, Elvis Costello's early petulance has softened, in tune with the growing maturity of his music. He has even threatened to return to his real name — which should please Dave Edmunds, who has always insisted on calling him "Costello".

The Cramps

Emanating from the bowels of the CBGBs Bowery punk scene in the late '70s, The Cramps have grown and festered to become one of the most talked-about musical and visual acts of the day. With a string of legendary and hair-raising concerts and two critically acclaimed LPs, the group have conquered European press and audiences alike, while remaining fairly unknown in their native America.

With an original line-up of Lux Interior (vocals), Poison Ivy Rorschach (guitar), Bryan Gregory (guitar) and Pam Gregory (drums), the group played their debut gig on audition night at New York's CBGB's club in January 1976. They instantly acquired a fanatical following and continued to play the New York club circuit. In April 1977 they branched out into acting to portray a gang of thugs in an Amos Poe film, *The Foreigner,* and in February 1978 received their first wide exposure by being featured in a CBS news special, *Raunch & Roll.* With new drummer Nick Knox, The Cramps released their debut single, *The Way I Walk,* in April 1978 on their own Vengeance label.

On Halloween 1978 the group released their second single, *Human Fly,* on Vengeance, accompanied by a horror promo film. In January 1979 Chris Spedding produced a five song demo for the band and the following month, while they were playing on the West Coast, the group signed to IRS. First product issued was a five track mini-LP of 1977 material recorded by ex-Box Top Alex Chilton at Memphis' Ardent Studio. *Gravest Hits* featured unforgettable versions of *Surfin' Bird, The Way I Walk, Lonesome Town, Domino,* and the original *Human Fly.*

In May 1979 the Cramps toured England for the first time, receiving rave reviews from the UK rock press, and on their return went once more to Memphis to record their debut album, again with Alex Chilton. In late 1979 the group embarked on their first headlining US tour, as well as supporting The Clash, Police and Iggy Pop, and in March and April of 1980 toured the UK and Europe to promote the album, *Songs The Lord Taught Us,* which hit top 10 in France. A single, *Garbage Man/Fever,* enjoyed some minor European success.

In June 1980 The Cramps embarked on another US tour, one performance of which was filmed for the *Urgh! A Music War* film. *Tear It Up* was included on the soundtrack album. In January 1981 the group with new guitarist Congo Powers (ex-Gun Club) replacing Bryan Gregory, entered A&M Studios in Los Angeles to record their second LP, *Psychedelic Jungle,* which was released in August. *Goo Goo Muck* was issued as a single. A year later, a three-track 12 inch EP was forthcoming, featuring *The Crusher, Save It,* and *New Kind of Kick.*

Such is the fervour of the band's cult following that two interesting bootleg albums have surfaced. *Transylvania Tapes* circulates in Europe, while *Tales From The Cramps Vol. 1* is an American production featuring Richard Robinson demos from 1977, two leftover Chilton productions, the Spedding demos and a live CBGB's cut. As well, the band made available a rare track to Australia's Fast Forward cassette magazine.

The Cramps parted company with the IRS label late in 1982, which whipped out the greatest hits album, *Off The Bone,* early in 1983.

CRASS

Crass

Anarchist inspired rock'n'roll band Crass were formed in 1978 by Penny Rimbaud and Steve Ignorant, but the band has its roots a decade earlier when Rimbaud opened his home to all comers. Crass are based around this country farmhouse, situated in North Weald, Essex, to the south-east of London, and the ten people who live there conduct all the activities under the Crass banner.

The original line-up was Steve Ignorant (vocals), Penny Rimbaud (drums). The original intention was that Crass would be just drums and vocals but the line-up evolved until it became: Ignorant (vocals), Eve Libertine (vocals), Joy De Vivre (vocals), Phil Free (lead guitar and backing vocals), G (backing vocals and piano), N.A. Palmer (rhythm guitar and backing vocals), Pete Wright (bass and backing vocals), Rimbaud (drums), and Mick (films).

The Crass debut was at a Squatters Free Festival, followed by gigs at the Roxy. In March 1979 the band released their debut EP, *5,000.* Other singles by Crass, on their own label, include *Reality Asylum/ Shaved Women, Bloody Revolutions,* and *Nagasaki Nightmare/Big A Little A. Rival Tribal Rebel Revel* was given away as a free flexi disc with Toxic Graffiti magazine.

Crass albums include *The Feeding Of The Five Thousand* (on Small Wonder Records), *Penis Envy, Stations Of The Cross* (which includes one live side), and *Bullshit Detector,* a compilation album of Crass orientated bands which includes an early Crass recording of *Do They Owe Us A Living?*

Other Crass involvements include Inter-National Anthem, the bands own 'Nihilist newspaper for the living', and The Eclectic, a magazine.

Evidence that the music and politics of Crass has spread far and wide is shown by the fact that an exhibition of the band's art was held in Australia early in 1983. Why, even British Prime Minister Margaret Thatcher has heard of them. She was truly touched when this lovable bunch dedicated their most recent single to her — *How Does It Feel To Be The Mother of 1,000 Dead?* the band's response to the Falkland Islands operation. Funnily enough, certain British politicians were less than impressed. Conservative MP Tim Eggar actually called it "the most vicious, scurrilous and obscene record ever produced". Doesn't anybody have a sense of humour anymore?

MARSHALL CRENSHAW

Marshall Crenshaw

Born and raised in Detroit, Marshall picked up guitar at the age of eight, his first full-blown influence being Buddy Holly. With his brother Robert pounding out rhythms on any available hard surface, Marshall began his apprenticeship picking out popular tunes of the day and eventually experimenting with amateur recording.

After a series of high school garage bands, Marshall graduated to playing the bars and clubs around Detroit. In 1973, he and his current band bought the remains of an old four-track studio and he found a new home for himself.

Three years later, the fledgling musician left Detroit and spent five weeks unsuccessfully circulating a four song demo of original material. He returned to the family home penniless and discouraged, and as an exercise with brother Robert, cut a note-perfect rendition of Lennon/McCartney's *I Should Have Known Better* and submitted it, along with a snapshot of himself in wire-rimmed glasses to the producers of *Beatlemania*, who had advertised for actors/musicians to perform in road companies of the long running musical. To his amazement, Marshall was hired to play John Lennon in the West Coast road company.

After two years, in early 1980, Marshall left the production and settled in New York with Robert.

> ***"If you don't have a bus and you're not paying a tour manager then you're not on tour, even if you're a couple of thousand miles from home."***
> *— Marshall Crenshaw*

They set about writing songs, putting a band together and recording demos. One such tape ended up in the hands of veteran producer Richard Gottehrer who was looking for material for Robert Gordon. As a result, Marshall eventually penned three songs — *She's Not Mine Anymore, But But* and *Someday, Someway* — for Gordon's fifth LP.

It wasn't long before the record companies began chasing him, but before Marshall was snared by Warner Bros he had a doubled A-sided single, *Something's Gotta Happen/She Can't Dance,* released in September 1981 on New York based Shake Records. In addition, a Crenshaw original, *Brand New Lover,* appeared on the debut album of Lou Ann Barton.

In early 1982 Marshall Crenshaw's debut self-titled album, produced by Gottehrer and Crenshaw, was released and received rave reviews from the US rock press, some dubbing him new artist of the year. Irresistible tracks such as *Someday Someway* and *Mary Anne* picked up strong airplay, though nothing broke through onto the charts. Inevitably, Shake Records marketed a 12" single of *Something's Gotta Happen.*

Cuban Heels

Long before Scottish rock'n'roll bands became this week's hip thing to sign, Cuban Heels had done the rounds of the major A&R offices in London and been rejected. It was in frustration at this rejection that drummer Ali Mackenzie decided to cease waiting in vain for interest from London and simply do things himself. Thus, the Cuba Libre label was formed.

Cuba Libre was set up simply to provide an outlet for the music that Cuban Heels wanted to make, as well as providing an opportunity for any other Scottish bands to release material.

Ali's ground level knowledge of both Glasgow and major record companies served him in good stead. Besides signing deals with The Shakin' Pyramids, Ali also produced the Cuban Heels' first single on Cuba Libre, *Walk On Water.*

Walk On Water did well enough to attract the attention of Virgin Records, who took over Cuba Libre's distribution and marketing. The band's first single under this arrangement was *Sweet Charity,* followed by *My Colours Fly.* In the summer of 1981 the band recorded their debut album, *Work Our Way To Heaven.*

The Cuban Heels line-up at this stage was: John Milarky (vocals), Laurie Cuffe (guitar), Ali Mackenzie (drums), and Nick Clark (bass).

Cuffe left the band after the album was released and did a stint with The Saints that included their Australian tour.

Culture Club

Culture Club was formed in April 1981 when Boy George (George McDowd) (vocals) met Jon Moss (drums and percusion), who advised him to restructure the band that had formed from the remnants of a unit called In Praise Of Lemmings. The member reshuffle saw Michael 'Mikey' Craig (bass) and Roy Hay (guitar and keyboards) make up Culture Club.

Boy George was born of Irish Catholic parents in Bexley Heath, Kent and began his flamboyant career by being thrown out of school at 15. He followed this with stints as

CUBAN HEELS

a fruit picker, milliner and printer before running a clothes store in Birmingham and later in London's legendary Kings Road. The jobs kept coming: one week he was a window dresser, then a make-up artist with the Royal Shakespeare Company, or modelling for TV and magazine advertisements.

Next, Boy George met with entrepreneur extraordinaire Malcolm McLaren and became a member of Bow Wow Wow, making his first appearance at The Rainbow Theatre. Apparently Boy George was being groomed to take over the lead vocal spot from Annabella but the reviews suggested otherwise and he wasn't a Bow Wow Wow member for long.

Jon Moss began playing in bands at school and like Boy George, had

CULTURE CLUB

worked in all areas of the music scene. A schoolboy rock concert promoter, he turned down the opportunity of a place at Cambridge University to become a tape operator at a London recording studio.

After a spell as an agent Moss replied to an ad in Melody Maker and landed a job with The Clash but left two months later after disagreements about policies. He then formed London, toured with The Stranglers, joined The Damned, turned down a drumming job with The Ramones and played with Jona Lewie, Kirsty McColl and Jane Aire, amongst others. He also played drums with the *Do It* period Adam Ant on *Car Trouble* and *Kick*.

Moss gradually became disillusioned with music and set about learning the rudiments of video production. Two years and a live date supporting The Jam later he regained his enthusiasm.

Roy Hay, a former hairdresser, was drafted in from the wilds of Southend and Michael Craig, a one-time Northern Soul disciple, reggae sessioner, sound system owner and father of two completed the Culture Club line-up.

According to Boy George, Culture Club aims to be ". . . creatively fluid. . . a bridge between the tremendous separation that still exists between white rock and black soul. It's not about being a part of anything but a part of everything."

Of the band's current look he continues: "It's basically workman's fabrics with provocative patterns. A very clean, very spiritual, very unsexy look. It comprises of symbols that represent all the peoples that are looked down on, Rastas, Pakistanis, Jews and tramps or hobos. It's not stagewear, however, it's my living

and we use it to advantage without making it pretentious."

Culture Club's debut album, *Kissing To Be Clever,* was released in 1982. The first single, *Do You Really Want to Hurt Me?*, went to number one, *Time* and *Church of The Poisoned Mind* followed.

The Cure

The Cure first came into being around 1976. The first incarnation saw them as a five-piece known as Easycure, hailing from and based around Crawley in Sussex. Later they abbreviated their name to The Cure and continued to play locally as a three-piece comprising Robert Smith (vocals and guitar), Lol Tolhurst (drums) and Michael Dempsey (bass).

In 1978, via the mailing out of a demo tape to various record

companies, they came to the attention of Chris Parry. Then an A&R man at Polydor, he was about to leave and form his own label, Fiction Records. This accomplished, he signed The Cure.

Their first single, *Killing An Arab,* was released in January 1979 to much critical acclaim. The record, leased to Small Wonder Records and then released on Fiction, sold well, and The Cure headlined their first UK tour. In May 1979 came the release of their first album, *Three Imaginary Boys,* and a second UK tour. Their next single, *Boys Don't Cry,* followed in June and though it was hailed by the critics, the record didn't become a hit. It did, however, gain the band their first interest from the US and Australia.

The Cure were then invited to tour the UK with Siouxsie and the Banshees. But two of the Banshees walked out on the eve of the tour. So Robert Smith not only played the support set with The Cure, but also filled in as guitarist for the headliners. At the end of the tour, bassist Michael Dempsey departed and Simon Gallup joined them on bass and keyboard player Mathieu Hartley was recruited at the same time. Their third single, *Jumping Someone Else's Train*, released in November 1979, was recorded with the original trio and coincided with the formation of the new line-up and their somewhat different musical direction.

The group embarked on their third UK tour and a highly successful series of European dates, and on their return began recording their second LP. *Seventeen Seconds* was released in April 1980 and gave them their first success, reaching the top 20 in England. The accompanying single, *A Forest,* did

THE CURE

almost as well.

Following their first US tour, the group toured the UK again and then embarked on their first trip to Australia and New Zealand where they were exceptionally well-received. Back in England, they reverted to a trio with the departure of keyboardist Mathieu Hartley.

Their third album, *Faith,* was recorded in London in early 1981 and the single released from it was *Primary.* They then commenced a world tour, *Picture Show,* in mid 1981 accompanied by a film commissioned from Ric Gallup called *Carnage Visors.* In August the group again arrived in Australia.

In October 1981 they released the single, *Charlotte Sometimes,* which was the last release until the album, *Pornography,* appeared in mid-1982, followed by the hit single *Let's Go To Bed.*

The Cure's first album was released in both the States and Australia under the title, *Boys Don't Cry,* and contained some different tracks to the original English release.

DAF

German made them the subject of great interest in their native Germany as well as throughout Austria, Holland and other European countries. Indeed, since their formation, many other German bands have begun to sing in their native tongue. In addition, DAF have been made the subject of the kind of 'cultural' attention not normally bestowed on 'rock' bands. They began their 1981 European tour as special guests of the Austrian government when they performed as part of a Culture Week in Vienna. Before that they played dates around Germany and prior to those dates they performed in London.

Also in 1981 they released their second album. Again produced by Conny Plank in association with DAF, *Alles Ist Gut* is the culmination of 18 months of ideas. Robert and Gabi consider that it is

D

Deutsche Amerikanische Freundschaft (DAF) ■

Gabi Delgado-Lopez and Robert Gorl are Deutsche Amerikanische Freundschaft (translated it means German American Friendship).

DAF have been developing into their current format for almost three years. They began when Robert met Gabi in Dusseldorf, where they were both living. Gabi had been singing with punk bands while Robert was completing formal music training. They elected to form a band and added three musicians in what was a straight format band. Their first single was *Kebab-Traume* which came out in 1980 on Mute Records. By the time they were ready to record a second single they had attracted the attention of legendary German producer Conny Plank. He contacted DAF and offered to produce their debut album, *Die*

THE DAMNED

Kleinen Und Die Bosen. Conny also produced their next single (with the assistance of DAF), *Tanz Mit Mir,* which also came out in 1980.

By this time Gabi's lyrics and voice and Robert's musicianship were very obviously the core of all DAF music. Robert's training at the Leopold Mozart Konservatorium in Germany and the Musikhochschule-Graz in Austria, and Gabi's experience as a singer in Dusseldorf stood them both in good stead, and having seen DAF reduce to a trio, they took the final step and began working as a duo.

Their electronic music (except for Gabi's voice and Robert's drums) and the fact that they sing in

in effect their first record and the single from it *Der Mussolini/Der Rauber Under Der Prinz* was their first record to make an impact in the UK.

At the end of the year they came up with album three, *Gold Und Liebe,* released in England on Virgin, from which the single *Goldenes Spielzeug* was lifted. 1982 saw the release of a UK single *Sex Unter Wasser (Sex Under Water)* and solo singles by both Robert and Gabi.

The Damned ■

The Damned were the first punk band to get a recording contract, the first to release an album and the first to tour the States. They were also the first to split up and then reform and one of the few bands to emerge from the punk era relatively unscathed.

Back in 1976 The Damned comprised Rat Scabies (drums), Bryan James (guitar), Captain Sensible (who played bass at the time) and Dave Vanian (vocals). Rat and Captain previously worked together as cleaners at The Fairfield Halls, Croydon; Bryan James had played with London S.S. as had Rat (while all three had played in the Subterraneans), and Dave Vanian had been a gravedigger.

Shortly after playing their first gig at London's 100 club, supporting The Sex Pistols, The Damned signed to Stiff and instantly hit the charts with their first two singles, *New Rose* and *Neat Neat Neat*. The band's debut album, *Damned Damned Damned*, did likewise and was produced, as were the singles, by Nick Lowe.

> **"Everybody still expects to hear us play three chords, poke the audience's eyes out and jump and down with no clothes on. I'd like to think that what we're playing now is a bit more sophisticated."**
> **— Rat Scabies, The Damned**

The Damned quickly built up an enormous live following before things started to go wrong. A second guitarist named Lu, of no previous musical experience, was recruited prior to the recording of the band's second album, *Music For Pleasure*, in 1977. The album, produced by Nick Mason of Pink Floyd, was hated by everyone, including the band.

Rat Scabies left during a European tour to be replaced by Jon Moss (who is now with Culture Club). The spark went out of the band, and in 1978 The Damned split up, playing a farewell gig at London's Rainbow Theatre.

Following various musical sorties, Rat and Captain (now playing guitar) reformed the band in September 1978 with Dave Vanian and played a couple of gigs as The Doomed, helped out by Motorhead's Lemmy on bass. A permanent new bassist (Henry Badowski) was found, The Doomed reverted to The Damned and signed to Chiswick Records early in 1979.

They found themselves back in the charts with a single, *Love Song,* before Henry Badowski was fired and replaced by former Saint, Algy Ward.

The band really put themselves back on the map with the November 1979 release of their third album, *Machine Gun Etiquette.* However in May 1980 Ward left to form Tank and was replaced by former Hot Rod Paul Gray, thus resulting in the present lineup. Around this time a fan club-only album, *Live Shepperton 1980,* was distributed to the loyal and fortunate few who had been paying their subscriptions since the beginning.

The band's most successful LP, *The Black Album,* was released in November 1980. The double album contained two sides of new material, together with a live side of oldies and a concept side entitled, *Curtain Call.* But then problems began to return for the band. Aside from an ill-fated liaison with NEMS Records —resulting in the release of one EP, *Friday The Thirteenth,* late in 1981 — there was no new product from The Damned until the issue of *Strawberries,* their fifth album and first on the Bronze label.

In mid 1982 Captain Sensible released his first solo single, a cover of Rogers and Hammerstein's *Happy Talk* from the *South Pacific* musical, which became a smash hit in England. It was produced by Tony Masfield of New Musik, as was the album *Women And Captains First.*

The good Captain was not the first member to record solo. Bryan James whipped out an interesting effort on his own BJ label in 1979 called, *Ain't That A Shame* (in 7 and 12 inch forms). Presently he is playing with Stiv Bators in the most recent formation of Lords Of The New Church.

Dance Exponents

Dance Exponents have been around for a little over a year, basing themselves in the South Island of New Zealand. Their first single,

Victoria, went to number six on the local charts and spent three weeks in the top twenty. The band are currently recording an album, and, as band member Jordon Luck says, "We want to get a New Zealand sound. A sound that typifies both urban and rural areas and gives a feel of the place."

Danse Macabre

One of the finest new music bands to emerge from New Zealand in recent years. Danse Macabre's line-up is: Nigel Russell (vocals and synthesizers), Roddy Carlson (drums), Ralph Crump (bass), and Wes Prince (guitar). They were formed in October 1980 and struggled for survival until March 1981 when an Auckland radio station began playing a demo of their song *Torch.* Suddenly the band began getting work offers, and in November 1981 *Between The Lines* was released to coincide with a first New Zealand tour. It made the New Zealand National Top 10 and stayed there for six weeks.

THE DANCE EXPONENTS

Between The Lines is a mini album that contains six songs — *Intro, Torch, Conditioner, Between The Lines, E.C.G,* and *Outro.*

The dB's

A few years back Chris Stamey, then fronting an outfit called the Sneakers, released an EP bearing the legend 'the definitive obscure American pop group'. Two obscure definitive pop EPs later — each a strange mixture of the likes of the Move, the Raspberries and the Byrds — and Chris went out on his own. He recorded a shamefully overlooked gem of a single, *Summer Sun,* for Ork Records in late 1977, produced by ex-Box Top, Alex Chilton, with whom Chris was gigging on the Manhattan club circuit at the time.

Chris then teamed up with journalist Alan Betrock to form the independent label, Car Records. He had long since left his North Carolina home behind him for New York but it was there that he met up with future dB Peter Holsapple — another refugee from North Carolina/Memphis — when Car Records released Peter's crazed modern rockabilly EP, *Big Black Truck.*

Thence, the dB's — completed by bassist Gene Holder and drummer Will Rigby — recorded one single for Car, *(I Thought You) Wanted To Know,* (written by ex-Television guitarist Richard Lloyd and recorded before Holsapple joined). Another single for Shake, *Black And White,* first brought the group to the attention of the UK and US public through a swathe of highly favourable reviews in the rock press (guaranteed to impede sales!).

Two singles, first *Dynamite* and then *Big Brown Eyes* came as the perfect appetiser for the group's overpowering debut album, *Stands For Decibels.* The album, a vivid combination of Stamey and Holsapple compositions, was greeted with rave reviews in the UK press and so they followed it up in February 1981 with their first UK tour. Audience response was initially cautious but they returned to Britain regularly, on one occasion supporting Dave Edmunds on a national tour.

The second album, *Repercussions* was even more fully-realised than its predecessor. Highlight tracks like *Ask For Jill, Living A Lie* and *Happenstance* offered a new, mature direction for power-pop — exhilaration without inanity. The album was issued in England with a free cassette edition that included two extra tracks — *Judy* and *ph Factor.* There are, in fact, bonus and rare tracks scattered all over the world. Australia's Liberation label issued a single of *Bad Reputation* with three tracks on the flip, including the rare *Baby Talk.* The Stiff live album *Start Swimming* sports two tracks, *Death Garage* and *We Should Be In Bed.*

Sadly, the dB's remain a fairly well kept secret. The only major distribution they have is on Albion in England and Liberation in Australia, America preferring to cast them into the 'too hard' void. Their day, be assured, will come.

D.D. Smash

One of New Zealand's most popular bands, D.D. Smash, were formed in mid-1981 by Dave Dobbyn, formerly of the very successful Dudes. As with most bands, the first months were spent running from gig to gig in Auckland building up a following. At the end of the year the band embarked on a national tour supporting the Pink Flamingos on their Alamo tour. D.D. Smash were promoting their first single, *Bull By The Horns.*

The band's debut album, *Cool Bananas,* was released early in 1982 with a single, *The Devil You Know,* being lifted from it. The album was the 29th best selling disc in New Zealand for 1982.

D.D. Smash have made a number of visits to Australia, where they're signed to Mushroom Records, but have failed to make much of an impact.

Dead Kennedys

Not many bands get as many death threats as fan mail. The Dead Kennedys do — it probably has something to do with their name.

The group were formed in San Francisco in early 1978 and the lineup comprised Jello Biafra (vocals), Klaus Fluoride (bass), East Bay Ray (guitar) and Bruce Slesinger (drums). The group first came to attention in America in 1979 when they released the single, *California Uber Alles,* a vitriolic attack on California's then Governor Jerry Brown (Linda Ronstadt's one-time beau), who was described in the song as a power hungry fascist posing as a trendy liberal. In early 1980 they

BIAFRA OF THE DEAD KENNEDYS

issued another single which caused almost as much controversy, *Holiday In Cambodia.*

The Dead Kennedys are one of the few punk bands in the world who have adopted an overt political stance. When San Francisco's mayor was assassinated in 1979 and his murderer later released, the band was outspoken in their criticism of the city's corruption. When elections for a new mayor were held, Biafra stood on a platform that included reforms such as all businessmen being required to wear clown suits and all motor vehicles except buses being banned. Out of the 10 candidates, Jello came fourth!

The group's debut album was released late in 1980, entitled *Fresh Fruit For Rotting Vegetables* and was accompanied by a single, *Kill The Poor.*

In early 1981 they created an international furore with the single *Too Drunk To Fuck,* released in a bold picture jacket. A worldwide airplay ban was effected and in Australia one specialist new wave dealer was hauled into court and fined for stocking it. After acquiring new drummer D.H. Peligro late in 1981, the Dead Kennedys released an EP, *In God We Trust, Inc.,* and another single, *Nazi Punks Fuck Off.* Not since the Sex Pistols and their

Belsen Was A Gas had a rock band been able to alienate and outrage the community to such a degree.

In late 1981 Jello Biafra released a compilation album of American punk bands, *Let Them Eat Jellybeans,* on his Alternative Tentacles label. Late 1982 saw a second Dead Kennedys' album surface, titled *Plastic Surgery Disasters.*

DECKCHAIRS OVERBOARD

Deckchairs Overboard

Deckchairs Overboard, one of the best Australian practitioners of the new minimalist funk, comprise Cathy McQuade (bass and vocals), Paul Hester (drums, vocal and guitar), Ken Campbell (guitar, vocal, drums) and John Clifforth (guitar, vocals, keyboards). Cathy came from Melbourne band The Ears while the others hail from Melbourne's Cheks.

The lineup formed and began rehearsing new songs in Melbourne during January 1982. As the Cheks they had been signed to Regular Records in August 1981.

Around May 1982 Deckchairs Overboard moved to Sydney and established a strong following amongst inner-city audiences.

While incorporating eastern influences in a sound based firmly on disco and rock traditions, the swapping on instruments and lead vocals allows each song an individual texture and atmosphere.

In November 1982 Deckchairs released a four-track 12 inch EP produced by Cameron Allan, best known for his work with Icehouse and Mental As Anything.

Depeche Mode

Depeche Mode, none of whom are over 21, came together while at different schools in Basildon, Essex. Originally a trio — Andy Fletcher, Martin Gore and Vince Clarke —

DEPECHE MODE

they featured two guitars and a synthesizer. Then David Gahan joined as singer. They discovered a new title while flicking through a French fashion magazine —Depeche Mode (Fast Fashion) — and then decided to ditch the guitars. All three instrumentalists then began playing synthesizers.

Their demo tapes stirred no interest with the London record companies, but while supporting Fad Gadget at the Bridge House in Canning Town they met Daniel Miller, founder of Mute Records. He was impressed, signed them, and issued the debut single *Dreaming Of Me* early in 1981.

Then came a year of dazzling achievement. Despite tempting offers from the major record companies, Depeche Mode stuck with Mute and *Dreaming Of Me* made the lower reaches of the UK charts. The second single, *New Life,* rose to number 11, and then the third, *Just Can't Get Enough,* cracked the top 10 late in 1981. This

> **"Devo deals with people who eat McDonald's hamburgers and wear Jordache jeans; that's our dilemma. I guess we're almost fed by the things we hate."**
> — *Jerry Casale, Devo*

single also broke the group in Australia where it also went top 10.

Depeche Mode's debut album, *Speak And Spell,* was released in November 1981 and made its way to the UK top 10, so they followed it with a short tour of England and Europe. It was during this time that Vince Clarke realised that he preferred the studio to the road and he left to form his own duo with Alison Moyet, Yazoo.

The remaining three members returned to the studio to record their fourth single, *See You,* which was released in January 1982 and reached the top 5 in England. With the addition of synth player and vocalist Alan Wilder, the group played their first US concerts at New York's Ritz club which preceded a tour of England early in 1982. Two further singles followed in 1982, *The Meaning Of Love* and *Leave In Silence,* and a second LP, *A Broken Frame.*

In October 1982 Depeche Mode embarked on an extensive and highly successful tour of the UK, confirming their position as one of the most popular synthesizer bands in Britain.

Devo

"The band evolved from a long line of brain-eating apes, some of which settled in Ohio, around Akron, where members of Devo eventually appeared, years after the A bomb ended World War II. By the process of natural selection they met and shared the habits of making electronic noise, watching TV and watching everybody else. They called what they saw around them De-evolution and called their music Devo. It made the sound of things falling apart.

"Spuds yelled and threw things like beer bottles at Devo when they played, but one day in 1977 the Spuds cheered and threw fits because Spudboys in the cities realised that 'We're all Devo!'. Boojie Boy had been telling everyone this for years. He told them in Devo's first movie, 'The Truth About De-evolution'. Now that nearly everyone is finding out, here is something else. The five Spudboys from Ohio are almost uniform in height and weight and their boot size is 8C. Alan provides the jungle style beats, Jerry emits debased pulses and Bob 2 adds precise robot rhythms. Bob 1 retaliates with sonic mutations and Mark sprays the entire mixture with alien synthesizer gases. Plus his voice is used more of the time than the other four.

"They are all following the commands of their genetic codes. They are suburban robots here to entertain corporate life forms. Devo says opposites and rebellion are obsolete. The fittest shall survive, yet the unfit may live. It's all the same."

Such is the original Devo story from the Spudboys' own mouths. For those who desire more down-to-earth facts, Devo first formed in Akron, Ohio around 1975 around a nucleus of singer/keyboardist Mark Mothersbaugh and bassist Jerry Casale. Mark's two brothers were in the first line-up — Bob (guitar) and Jim (drums). Jim left soon after and was replaced by Alan Myers, while Jerry's brother Bob was added on keyboards.

In December 1976 they independently recorded their first

DEXYS MIDNIGHT RUNNERS

single, *Mongoloid,* on a four-track in their garage, and followed it with a unique version of the Stones' *Satisfaction* in August 1977. That same year the group began playing in New York for the first time. But their real break came also in 1977, when Stiff in England decided to license the two singles for release there. The high praise and cult status immediately afforded them caused sudden interest from the major record companies. In early 1978 Devo signed with Warner Brothers and recorded their debut album, *Q: Are We Not Men?; A: We Are Devo.*

In 1979 Devo released their second LP, *Duty Now For the Future,*

DEVO

but it was not until their third album, *Freedom Of Choice,* that the group made an impression on the charts. The single, *Whip It,* became a dance floor favourite in America and eventually went top 20 in that country.

But their greatest popularity probably lies in Australia. In 1981 their *Devo Live* EP went to number one on the singles charts, while *Freedom Of Choice* and their fourth album, *New Traditionalists,* were both top 10 on the LP charts. In early 1982 Devo toured Australia and enjoyed sell-out concerts wherever they played.

In October 1982 Devo released their fifth LP, *Oh No It's Devo* and accompanying single *Peek A Boo.* They also have guest roles in the recently released Neil Young film *Human Highway,* performing *Out Of The Blue And Into The Black* with Mr Young himself, who has gained considerable mileage from his adoption of Devo-ology: "It's better to burn out than to rust."

Dexys Midnight Runners

Before Dexys Midnight Runners there were two other groups, Lucy And The Lovers and The Killjoys. The Killjoys were the only ones to record (*Johnny Won't Get To Heaven*) but were not the group vocalist Kevin Rowland had in mind.

In July 1978 he formed an

ambitious eight-piece unit called Dexys Midnight Runners. The line-up was Rowland, Stoker Growcott (drums), Mert Talbot (organ), JB Blythe (tenor sax), Pete Williams (bass), Steve Spooner (alto sax), Al Archer (guitar) and Jimmy Paterson (trombone). Disgusted and disillusioned by 1978's punk and 2 Tone, Kevin had returned to his '60s soul record collection and tried to transmit those feelings into his own music.

To tie in with the music, Kevin moulded the group's image around that of a tight-knit group. The inspiration came from American films such as *Mean Streets* and the clothes of New York's Italian-American dockers.

With the look, attitude and music complete, Dexys turned to former Clash manager Bernie Rhodes for help. In early 1979 the group embarked on a mammoth UK tour called Straight To The Heart and in August they signed a distribution deal with EMI for manager Rhodes' own Oddball record company. In November they released the debut

> *"I quite like the idea of sex being dirty. What's the point of me going on about how sex is beautiful?"*
> — *Kevin Rowland, Dexys Midnight Runners*

single, *Dance Stance,* which reached 40, and in March 1980 issued a second single, *Geno* — a loving tribute to '60s soul singer Geno Washington. A month later they saw it sitting at number one. By this time the group were recording their first album with producer/pianist Pete Wingfield. On the last day of recording, realising that they were now in a powerful position, they absconded with the master tape and refused to return it until EMI gave them a better contract, subsequently negotiating one of the best deals possible.

In July 1980 *There, There My Dear,* was released and reached seven on the charts. In the same month the debut album, *Searching For The Young Soul Rebels,* reached number four. The group then caused a massive stir by taking out full-page ads in the English music press calling them dishonest and stating that they would not undertake any more interviews, preferring to communicate with their fans by essays in the press and handouts contained within their records.

With the album's release, Dexys

undertook their long tour of the UK under the title, Midnight Runners Intense Emotion Revue. Tired from recording and badly under-rehearsed, the tour went poorly as the group struggled against hostile audiences. At the conclusion in November 1980 Kevin, against all advice, decided to release *Keep It Going Part Two* as the next single. The rest of the group disagreed, argued strongly against it, and in the middle of a European tour decided to leave, eventually to form The Bureau. Only Jim Paterson remained.

Kevin retreated back to Birmingham and began recruiting new members. When the new Dexys line-up — Seb Shelton (drums), Steve Wynne (bass), Micky Billingham (keyboards), Paul Speare (tenor sax), Billy Adams (guitar) and Brian Maurice (alto sax) along with Rowland and Paterson — returned to the public eye, it was amidst much confusion with their record company. In February 1981 the group asked that "recent recordings are not exploited". EMI went against their wishes and released *Plan B* as a single. In retaliation, Dexys left the company when they fortuitously discovered that EMI had unknowingly failed to take up their option in January.

In April 1981 the new look Dexys returned to the stage with a new look of pony tails, heavy-hooded anoraks, track suit trousers and boxing boots. The group's Projected Passion Revue tour of the UK caused another stir, with an edict banning alcohol at their shows.

Dexys signed with Polygram in June 1981 and the following month a new single, *Show Me,* produced by Tony Visconti, pu them back in the charts. Privately, Rowland had begun experimenting with violins and the first realisation of this new musical direction came with their seventh single, *Liars A To E,* released late in 1981.

Their next single, *The Celtic Soul Brothers,* featured the Emerald Express — fiddlers Helen O'Hara, Steven Brennan and Roger Macduff — replacing the familiar horns with an acoustic backdrop. Kevin also felt that a new image was needed. He dressed the group in American dungarees, neckerchiefs and leather jerkins and, when it was least expected, gave a spate of interviews to the English music press.

In July 1982 the group released their second LP, *Too-Rye-Ay,* and a new single, *Come On Eileen,* a number one hit in England, America and Australia.

The follow-up was an excellent cover of Van Morrison's *Jackie Wilson Said.* Their next single, *Let's Get This Right From The Start*

emphasised the group's affinity for acoustic instruments. However in late 1982, trombonist Jimmy Paterson left the group, followed by saxophonists Brian Maurice and Paul Speare.

In 1983, amid rumours of a lawsuit from EMI over alleged contract infringement, the company cut its losses with *Geno,* a compilation album of Dexy singles and oddities.

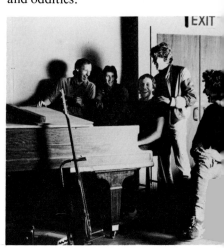

DIRE STRAITS

Dire Straits
1976 found Mark Knopfler (lead guitar and vocals), brother David (rhythm guitar) and John Illsley (bass) sharing a flat in Deptford, South London. Joined by drummer Pick Withers, they decided to form a group and started rehearsals. Mark, a former journalist, was teaching English at Loughton Technical College at the time, but gave it up to devote his time to the group. A friend of Pick's, seeing their financial plight, suggested the name Dire Straits.

The group practised intensely, played a few live gigs around Deptford, and scraped up enough money to pay for a weekend session in the eight-track Pathway demo studio. The result was a five-track tape which included *Sultans Of Swing.* They sent the tape to rock writer and DJ Charlie Gillett, who immediately began playing it on his *Honky Tonk* BBC radio show. The resultant interest led to a contract with Polygram and in early 1978 they embarked on a tour as support for Talking Heads. Upon their return they went into the studio with producer Muff Winwood to record a debut album. In June 1978 *Dire Straits* was released, quickly peaked at number 37 and just as rapidly dropped out of sight.

But by the end of 1978, though the UK was still unimpressed, the album had developed into a huge hit in America, Australia, New Zealand and most of Europe. In early 1979 they embarked on a sell-out tour of

DURAN DURAN

the States, where both the album and single had gone top five. The single was then re-released in England where it went top five.

In May 1979 Mark and Pick were invited to play on Bob Dylan's album, *Slow Train Coming* and two weeks later their second LP, *Communique,* recorded late the previous year with legendary producers Jerry Wexler and Barry Beckett in the Bahamas, was released and went gold on pre-sales in most countries. For the remainder of 1979 Dire Straits embarked on a lengthy tour of America and Europe.

In mid 1980 the group began recording their third album in New York with producer Jimmy Iovine and keyboardist Roy Bittan (from the E Street Band). But in the middle of recording David Knopfler decided to leave the band. *Making Movies* was released in October 1980 and repeated the phenomenal success of the earlier albums. With

IAN DURY AND THE BLOCKHEADS

DIVINYLS

the addition of guitarist Hal Lindes and keyboardist Alan Clark the group then embarked on a mammoth world tour from October 1980 until July 1981, which took in America, the UK, Australia, New Zealand and Europe.

After a long break, Dire Straits recorded their fourth album in New York in mid 1982 and *Love Over Gold* was released worldwide in September, to more platinum and gold success. An EP, featuring the throwaway song *Twisting By The Pool,* became an international hit early in 1983.

Though regularly tagged by the snotty British rock press as boring old farts, Dire Straits command an awesome following, particularly in the live area. Perhaps the answer lies in Mark Knopfler's capacity to arrive at a time when the humble electric guitar had been bled dry of its every marketable sound, and offer his own peculiar bent on the strings. An excellent example can be drawn from their 1981 visit to Sydney Australia, where they played to six sold-out adoring houses and one half-empty press conference.

Divinyls

The Divinyls first started performing in the sleazy bars of Sydney in September 1980. Christina Amphlett (vocals), Mark McEntee (guitar), Bjarne Ohlin (guitar and keyboards) and Richard Harvey (drums) all had a long history in the Australian rock'n'roll world without ever having been in a mainstream group. Only original bassist Jeremy Paul had such a credit; having been in the original line-up of Air Supply.

Soon after they began playing live, the group was spotted by film director Ken Cameron who was looking for a rock band to appear in his movie *Monkey Grip*. The group recorded the soundtrack and it produced their first single, *Boys In Town*. Released late in 1981 on the eve of Paul's departure, it immediately soared up the charts and hit top 10.

In mid 1982 the *Monkey Grip* mini-album was released and confirmed the growing popularity of the group in Australia. Around the same time they finally found a permanent replacement for Jeremy Paul in ex-Matt Finish bassist, Rick Grossman.

Although the Divinyls were signed to WEA, they swiftly fell into serious creative and financial disagreements and, having severed their relationship with the company, were swamped by offers from overseas labels. They eventually signed to Chrysalis and in September 1982 journeyed to New York to record their debut album with Australian producer Mark Opitz. After playing a few dates in America they returned to Australia late in 1982 to prepare for an extensive national tour.

A long-awaited album, *Desperate,* came out in January 1983, along with a third single, *Science Fiction.* The LP was highlighted by a passionate re-working of the Easybeats' classic *I'll Make You Happy* and the high velocity *Siren (Never Let You Go).*

One of the most dynamic live acts to have emerged from Australia, the Divinyls came close to stealing the show at the giant Narara rock festival near Sydney in February 1983, soon after which they departed

THE DUGITES

on an American tour to capitalise on the rave reviews being afforded the album internationally.

Dugites

The Dugites formed in Perth, West Australia in 1979 around the nucleus of Peter Crosbie (keyboards/ songwriter) and Lynda Nutter (vocals). Clarence Bailey (drums), Paul Noonan (bass) and Gunther Berghofer (guitar) completed the original line-up. After building a solid reputation in Perth, the band trekked to the East Coast in 1980 and almost immediately were signed to Deluxe Records.

With ex-Rumour keyboardist Bob Andrews producing, The Dugites recorded their debut self-titled album that year, and from it they scored a top 40 single with *In My Car.* In 1981 the group moved from Perth to Melbourne and recorded their second LP, *West Of The World,* again with Andrews producing. The single released from the album was *Waiting.*

Late in 1981 Berghofer left the band and he was replaced by ex-Sports guitarist Andrew Pendlebury. With the new line-up The Dugites recorded a mini-LP in 1982, appropriately entitled *No Money.*

Duran Duran

Duran Duran formed in 1978 when John Taylor (bass) and Nick Rhodes (keyboards) were playing together with another bassist, a clarinetist and a rhythm box. Roger Taylor (drums) joined shortly after from a local punk band, The Sex Organs, and the three realised they shared an interest in funk/disco music which the others did not. They started looking for a suitable guitarist and vocalist and took their name from a mechanical character in the Jane Fonda movie, *Barbarella.* Duran

Duran placed an ad in Melody Maker, resulting in guitarist Andy Taylor travelling from Newcastle to Birmingham for an audition. He fitted in well and joined the band in late 1979. A couple of months later, someone gave John Taylor the phone number of Simon Le Bon, a Londoner who was studying drama in Birmingham, and who had previously been a member of Dog Days. After rehearsing together, Simon joined Duran Duran as vocalist.

Duran Duran were helped during this formative period by their management team, Paul and Michael Berrow, two brothers running Birmingham's premier club, the Rumrunner. This club is a stylish melting pot of the city's youth cultures in which dance is the common factor.

By the end of 1980, Duran Duran had completed their first nationwide UK tour, supporting Hazel O'Connor, and had contracted with EMI Records after feverish competition. *Planet Earth* was the first single, peaking at number 12 in England and achieving top 10 in Australia in early 1981. Their debut album, *Duran Duran,* and two further singles, *Careless Memories* and *Girls On Film,* consolidated their success as the premier teen phenomenon in the UK and Australia. *Girls On Film* was accompanied by a highly provocative nine-minute video, produced by Godley and Creme, which generated enormous interest worldwide.

"Rock'n'roll is only 28 years old and it hasn't yet had time to realise how great it could be."
— Ian Dury

In September 1981 the group embarked on their first European tour and followed it later in the year with a series of dates in the US and Canada and a sell-out UK tour. After recording their second album, *Rio,* with producer Colin Thurston, Duran Duran journeyed to Australia for a very successful tour in April 1982.

The release of *Rio* in May, as well as two singles from it, *My Own Way* (top 10 in the UK and Australia) and *Hungry Like The Wolf,* consolidated their immense popularity in both the teen and more 'serious' spheres of fandom. A rather fortuitous combination of appealing looks seems to have cast them into the role of the Eighties Bay City Rollers, complete with mobbings, hotel sieges and fan magazine coverage.

Ian Dury

At the age of seven, the now 40 year old Ian Dury contracted polio, which left him with a withered left leg and arm. He spent his early years in an institution for the disabled, then became a grammar school boarder in his early teens.

At 17 he left to go to art college and from there to the Royal College of Art. It was while teaching art at Luton and then Canterbury in the early '70s that Dury became involved with rock'n'roll and formed a band. This became Kilburn and The High Roads, which despite a huge cult following on the London pub circuit, never achieved widespread record success. They recorded one album, *Handsome.*

After Kilburn and The High Roads finally fell apart, Dury spent 18 prolific months writing lyrics. During this time he also met up with keyboardist/guitarist Chas Jankel, who was to become his musical director. In early 1977 Dury became one of Stiff Records' first signings, and in October that year his first album, *New Boots And Panties,* began a residency in the UK charts of well over a year. This album was preceded by the legendary *Sex And Drugs And Rock And Roll* single, which though it never sold many copies, became one of the great rock anthems of the late '70s.

With his backing band The Blockheads — Jankel, Charley Charles (drums), Norman Watt-Roy (bass), Davey Payne (sax), Mickey Gallagher (keyboards) and John Turnbull (guitar) — Dury then went on the first Stiff Tour of the UK with Elvis Costello, Nick Lowe and Wreckless Eric to promote the album. Next, Dury toured the States as support for Lou Reed.

In 1978 he released two further singles, *Sweet Gene Vincent* and *What A Waste* (which was his first

UK top 10). This was followed in January 1979 by *Hit Me With Your Rhythm Stick,* a million-selling number one in England. Subsequently Dury and The Blockheads went on a huge European tour to promote their second LP, *Do It Yourself.* Another single, *Reasons To Be Cheerful,* gave them another huge UK hit late in 1979. After that exhaustive tour, the group took a long rest and Jankel decided to leave the band to record solo.

For most of 1980 Ian Dury devoted his time to getting himself fit by swimming almost every day. In late 1980 the Blockheads, with new member Wilko Johnson (formerly guitarist for Dr Feelgood), recorded their third LP, *Laughter,* and the singles, *I Want To Be Straight* and *Sueperman's Big Sister.*

This was Dury's last album for Stiff and he signed with Polygram. In early 1981 he again began collaborating with Chas Jankel and they travelled to Nassau to record a Dury solo album with Sly Dunbar and Robbie Shakespeare. A single, *Spasticus Autisticus,* was released in August and was subsequently banned from UK radio airplay because the subject matter of the song was deemed to be offensive. Since 1981 was the Year of the Handicapped and of course because of Dury's own personal history, he had every right to take grave affront at this decision. The Nassau recordings were released as the *Lord Upminster* album in early 1982.

Dury's musical director, Chas Jankel, also found time to record a solo album titled *Questionnaire.*

In late 1981, Ian Dury and The Blockheads embarked on their first tour of Australia which proved to be a huge popular success. A compilation of Dury's Stiff material was released with the delightful title, *Juke Box Dury.*

Dynamic Hepnotics

Within the space of a couple of years, The Dynamic Hepnotics have established themselves as Australia's sharpest and hottest soul R&B group.

The Dynamic Hepnotics formed out of a nucleus of vocalist/harp player 'Continental' Robert Susz and guitarist Andrew Silver. Susz, born in Hungary, migrated to Australia with his family and began playing in various blues and R&B bands around Sydney and Melbourne while still attending art college in the mid '70s. In 1977 he formed his own band The Rugcutters in Sydney, which remained fairly anonymous in their short existence. 'Continental' Robert contacted a friend and guitarist, Andrew Silver (ex-The Big Town Playboys and The Ravers), and together they began to put together The Dynamic Hepnotics.

By 1980, after many musicians had come and gone, the line-up was finalised. Robert Souter (drums) formerly with Gulliver's Travels, Lizard and The Living Legends, Bruce Allen (sax) formerly with Jeff St. John and Ol' 55, and Alan Britton (bass) formerly of Company Caine, Janie Conway Band, Rockhouse and countless others, were the three finally recruited.

In early 1981 The Dynamic Hepnotics released their debut vinyl, the EP *Shakin' All Over,* on the Mambo label and later that year came their debut single, *Hepnobeat,* on the Missing Link label. The single was picked up for overseas release by Statik Records and became a firm dance floor hit in Europe, England and America.

In mid-1982 the group went into the studio with Mondo Rock's Ross Wilson producing, and emerged with the *Strange Land* 12 inch EP.

THE DYNAMIC HEPNOTICS

JAPAN'S NEW MUSIC: THE HUMAN FACE OF TECHNOPOLIS

素顔のテクノポリス

BY RICK TANAKA & TONY BARRELL

The first thing to say about rock in Japan is the obvious: Japanese culture is very different from the western culture that produced the music in the first place. Yet, since none of the 'original' rock/folk/pop cultures, whether they be American, British, English or otherwise, produced the music single-handedly, Japan is no less involved in its evolution. Japan in many ways is another western country.

Since the middle of the last century the powers that ruled Japan have deliberately encouraged all contact with foreign culture. It was thought to be the way to modernise the nation. This policy was intensified after the disaster of the Second World War and encouraged not only from within Japan but from outside — by the USA and the great world corporations that have sponsored and encouraged the Japanese post-war economic miracle.

Since the war, Japanese culture has seized all foreign phenomena with great enthusiasm. Some say that Japan has no 'original' ideas at all, others go further to say that its real culture is the ability to improve on other people's culture — dubbed by some as "the art of improved copying".

It would be wrong to suggest that Japan has no culture or has everyone else's culture.

It's never been totally a simple matter of slavish imitation nor has it ever been a question of copying 'everything' either. Admittedly, to a certain extent what goes on musically in Japan has to be viewed in the context of it coming from an Asian outpost of the western, capitalist cultural conglomerate. Having said all that, it's still worth seeing how the process has produced what it has.

Language

It isn't what's the same, but what's different that makes the comparison interesting. First of all, youth culture itself has never had the same 'freedom', the western concept of self-expression, rebellion or liberation which has been associated with rock music for three decades. Rock and Roll certainly didn't hit Japanese youth in the way it rampaged through the west. The main reason is the most obvious one, the language barrier. The infectious beat, in the Fifties anyway, wasn't enough to cross the cultural gap. In the Sixties, pop and folk groups would copy foreign originals, but translate and sing the lyrics in Japanese. Except for the language, these versions were supposed to be as perfect a copy of the originals as the limited production techniques allowed. Often an original version would be copied to the point where every instrument would be duplicated, so, for every guitar track there'd be a guitar player, even though the original may have been multi-tracked.

As musicians and producers became more sophisticated and keen to explore their own musical ideas, new songs would be written, though they tended to be performed in English, with an American accent. It wasn't until the mid-Seventies that bands tried performing original Japanese material in Japanese. Nowadays albums tend to be a mixture of both languages. The first band to sing a single song with both English and Japanese lines was a rockabilly band called Carol in 1973.

Beat, Folk, Rock, Sugarpop, Enka

There's always been Japanese music without foreign influence. The original Japanese folk music itself still survives and so does a hybrid version called 'enka' which is original Japanese folk music with borrowings and influences from pre-rock music brought in from Europe during the 19th century. This is Japan's MOR, the staple diet of a nation of people that probably sing in public a good deal more than most westerners realise. Enka dominates the charts, radio and TV in Japan. However, during the Seventies its domain was challenged by

sugarpop, which is Japan's version of the Eurovision-song-contest type of music; and by the imitation 'laid back west coast' sound of groups like Alice. It should be understood that although the mainstream may be hooked on enka there's no longer a big time-lag between the 'new thing' in Europe and the appearance of a Japanese version. In fact, these days, although there are still many bands who are merely derivative, there are experimental noises coming out of Japan that don't sound like anything else, and in some areas, particularly electronics, the Japanese are well ahead.

To understand 'new music' in Japan it's necessary to look a bit further back than 1976 to see just how the various ingredients in the mix produced what's happening now.

Don't Be Confused, It's Only Confucius

By the end of the Sixties the process was established. A successful western music style was discovered and studied. Once understood to the point where it could be reproduced authentically it was then used as a medium, or genre, for original composition. This applied to every kind of western music whether it was folk, Beatles pop, R&B, jazz-fusion, hard rock or heavy metal. Before you run away with the idea that this kind of process is in some way indicative of an inferior or derivative culture, be aware that it took centuries for this theory to evolve to its present form. In fact, it probably started with Confucius, and as you probably realise, it applies to a lot more than music and explains a lot of Japanese political activity. It's also the classic way that other western countries like the UK and Australia discovered and absorbed American rock'n'roll in the first place — itself a fusion of all kinds of different music styles.

So the story of Japan's new music is the story of those artists and performers who have managed to make, or are in the process of making, the transition from derivative copying to original creative innovation. That then has been the criteria for the choice of bands and performers included in this essay.

Japanese Music Chronology

1868 The Meiji Restoration: In which the new government decides Japan is to look outward for its thrust toward modernity. Westernisation begins officially. Foreign culture including classical and popular music from France, Germany, Italy, Ireland and other countries floods in along with the rest of what the world has to offer.

1945 The Americanisation of Japan begins in earnest with the arrival of occupying forces and their culture following Japan's defeat in World War Two. However, over the next two decades Japan's own 'ethnic pop' known as enka develops strongly without much American influence.

1960 The art of the cover version attains supremacy in Japanese pop with singing groups rendering everything from *The Locomotion* to *Tie Me Kangaroo Down Sport* — usually translated into Japanese.

1963 *Sukiyaki* (original Japanese title *Ue o Muite Aruko*, meaning *Let's Walk With Our Faces Up So The Tears Won't Flow Down*) by Kyu Sakamoto reaches Number 1 in the USA, number 6 in the UK. This feat has yet to be repeated.

1966 The Beatles tour Japan, playing five consecutive nights at Budokan — the first time this great martial arts stadium was used for music of any kind. Subsequent Japanese beat boom doesn't last long but do make a mark with bands like The Tigers.

1967 Folk Crusaders' single *Kaette Kita Yopparai (Return Of The Drunk)* sells over a million, hits number 1 and begins widespread boom in folk-based acoustic music. This lasts until early Seventies and features many huge open air folk festivals. Folk 'guerillas' contribute a political anti-US, anti-war edge to this movement. Leading light is Nobuyasu Okabayashi — Japan's Bob Dylan, who receives similar treatment from folk fans when he goes electric in early 1970 with the band Happy End. Some antagonism between politically aware folk-bands and emerging rock-oriented bands develops.

1969 September: First Japan Rock Festival features survivors of the beat boom plus more hard rock and blues rock bands like Flowers (later Flower Travellin' Band) and Blues Creation (later Creation). Same month sees debut of Apryl Fool, first band for Haruomi Hosono.

1970 July: *Woodstock* movie released followed by free music event boom. November: First ever World Popular Song contest in Tokyo, at Budokan. December: First Rock Carnival features John Mayall and The Bluesbreakers.

1971 April: Hard rock blues style band Samurai returns from European tour where bass player Tetsu Yamauchi was asked to join Free (and later Rod Stewart and The Faces). Jazzrock becomes very popular, so Chicago and Blood, Sweat & Tears tour. So does Grand Funk Railroad in July — playing huge baseball stadiums, followed by Pink Floyd in August and Led Zeppelin in September.

1972 Sadistic Mika Band debuts in June led by Kazohiko Katoh (ex-Folk Crusaders guitarist) and vocalist Mika. August: Deep Purple hits Japan and records a live album at Budokan. September: Flower Travellin' Band gives free concerts all over Japan. Late in the year sees big boom in rockabilly and female singer-songwriters.

1973 January: Hosono's band Happy End breaks up. He starts pre-YMO solo career, with projects involving Caramel Mama. During this period 'New Music' appears — really a swing toward MOR by the old folk music movement. Leading the band in this move is Akai Tori featuring guitarist (and Ventures enthusiast) Kenji Omura. Album by singer-songwriter Yosui Inoue is long-term best-seller and changes habits of record buyers who are not used to buying domestic albums in large quantities.

1974 Despite being a big year for the blues, May sees the release of Sadistic Mika's debut album on Harvest in England, and a move by rock-oriented bands into big open air festivals hitherto dominated by folk. Sadistic Mika and Plastic Ono Band play One-Step Festival, a ten day event in August. November sees release of Sadistic's *Black Ship* album, produced by Roxy Music's producer Chris Thomas — also released in UK.

1975 In general much more Japanese product being released by record companies. Band called Son House releases single on an independent label known as D. New music/new folk move climaxes with mammoth sales for Yumi Arai album. Four folk biggies form their own record label — For Life. The blues and rock festivals keep coming. October: The Sadistic Mikas tour UK with Roxy Music, but break up in December.

1976 December: Bay City Rollers play eight nights at Budokan. Strong evidence of the musical preferences of the mass Japanese market.

1977 Bands from Okinawa begin playing mainland Japan including ethnic Shokichi Kina and Condition Green (heavy metal — there are a lot of Americans in Okinawa). This is the year that TV commercials start featuring pop, rock, MOR artists. October: Little River Band in Japan followed by Creation appearances in Australia. December: Alfa Records founded by Kuni Murai with jazz-fusion music and new folk acts including Yumi Arai.

1978 January: Girl crushed to death at Ritchie Blackmore's concert at Sapporo. This results in increasingly heavy tactics by bouncers. February:

Bob Dylan does eight nights at guess where. April: *Paraiso* album released by Haruomi Hosono and The Yellow Magic Band. May: S-Ken studio in Roppongi, Tokyo, opens, used by Tokyo Rockers Movement. Jazz-fusion and disco big in Japan. August: Solo concert by Eikichi Yazawa — Japan's first rock and roll millionaire — pulls 50,000 at baseball stadium in Tokyo that is bigger than Budokan. Yellow Magic Orchestra formed. November: First YMO album.

1979 The big split. The big bands get bigger thanks to all those TV commercials and it's another prime year for great open air concerts with plenty of open air bouncers PLUS the arrival of the small club venues featuring new bands like P-Model, Hikashu and The Plastics who are sometimes known as 'techno-pop'. YMO releases *Solid State Survivor* in September. December: Ten Japanese bands play Budokan — a different concert on ten different nights.

1980 January: Paul McCartney busted. Plastics first album. February: Anarchy's first album. April: Plastics tour USA. June: YMO have four albums in top 20. The big split continues mainly because there are no middle size venues, so the small bands join together to play the big venues. Plastics, RC Succession and Sheena & The Rokkets play one night at Budokan in August.

BOW WOW!

Bow Wow

Heavy Metal, Heavy Rock, Headbanging, Teutonic Warlord Rubbish, whatever you call it, it's been big in Japan ever since Deep Purple brought the one true riff to Japan's shores way back in 1972. Since then Japanese kids have welcomed everyone from Led Zeppelin to Van Halen, Ritchie Blackmore's Rainbow, Michael Schenker and Whitesnake. In fact, one of Japan's first successful exports was Flower Travellin' Band which specialised in the heavier rock approach and managed to gain a cult following in Canada.

Now armies of local guitar warriors are beginning to emerge from the mines and gorges of metal monster wonderland. One such band began life as a cynical, commercial realisation of this inevitability and goes by the name of Bow Wow (which would seem to preclude any real acceptance outside Japan due to its similarity to the Malcolm McLaren creation of almost the same name). They were formed in 1976 by singer/guitar hero and instant legend Kyoji Yamamoto, with Kenji Sano (bass), Mitsuhiro Saito (guitar) and Toshihiro Niimi (drums). A producer's formula band, they went on to record twelve albums in six years. Their lyrics don't demand or deliver much but their musicianship is tricky, amusing and enjoyable and much more likely to involve movements of parts of the body below the neck than most HM monstrosities. Bow Wow toured the world in '82, culminating in a performance at the Reading Festival. Among the albums (unavailable outside Japan) are: *Signal Fire* ('77), *Super Live* ('78), *Hard Dog* ('81), *Asian Volcano* ('82), *Warning From Stardust* ('82).

Chance Operation

One of the bands involved in the Tokyo Rockers Movement in 1978 was Mirrors, and the bassist/singer/leader of Mirrors, Hiroshi Higo, went on to found another very innovative outfit in 1980 — Chance Operation. Higo was also a founding member of an independent record label, Godzilla Records.

Since its formation, Chance Operation has released a five-track 12 inch EP ('81) and a four-track double 7 inch EP, *Spare Beauty* ('82).

Chance Operation's unique strength comes from its highly industrialised, repulsive, alienating, stark streets-of-Tokyo sound. The vocals are dry, the guitar inorganic, the rhythms effective. They remain strong because they have always stayed close to their origins.

After the first EP, the band lost the original drummer, who was replaced by a rhythm box for a while. *Spare Beauty* was recorded by original members Higo and Yoshiko (guitar, vocal), with assistance from Chiko-Hige from Friction and NON from the NON BaNd.

Now Chance Operation has acquired a new drummer (a real human being), and Takahiro Furusawa (keyboards, percussion), who was with Pressure and released an 8 inch LP before he joined up.

Friction

"Everywhere, anywhere, if there are human beings around I feel friction." This profoundly disturbing encapsulation of the post Nietzschean alienation sensibility is said to be the emotional theory behind the naming of Friction. Founding members Reck (vocals, bass, drums, guitar, percussion) and Chiko-Hige (drums, percussion, sax) deny that they got the idea from the Television song of the same name. However, both of them were living in New York at the height of the Punk Revolution, playing respectively with Teenage Jesus and the Jerks, and the Contortions. Having absorbed the One True Punk they returned to Japan and set about improving it in the time-honoured Japanese manner.

1978 was the time of the Tokyo Rockers Movement — bands who worked together in a series of the performances at the S-Ken studio in Roppongi. Friction's first product came out from the indie Pass label, in the form of a three track EP, *I Can Tell* ('79), followed by a self-titled debut album on the same label in '80. They also released a 10 inch mini-LP called *Friction Ed. '79 Live* but this was a self-financed operation. In '82 they made the great leap sideways into corporate wonderland and signed with CBS/Sony, who released their second album *Skin Deep*. The current line-up includes guitarist Emiko Mogi and

FRICTION

trumpeter-percussionist Scher-z Haruna. Toward the end of 1982, Chiko-Hige retired from live performances on the ground that he didn't see the point of performing. It still remains to be seen whether his move was a permanent split from Friction or a temporary rest from live performances.

If you know and like PiL or The Birthday Party you'll appreciate Friction's relentless but superbly produced angular anger. Its major attraction is that it doesn't come out of a New York loft or a basement in Islington, vinyl evidence of how the Japanese can absorb and re-define the essentially western language of raw rock'n'roll.

Hikashu

Hikashu is one of the bands thrown up by the massive 'techno-pop' eruption of '79. In June, 1978, an ex-Tokyo Kid Brothers actor and a scriptwriter, Koichi Makigami (vocals, bass, trumpet); son of a buddhist monk, Masamichi Mitama (guitar, vocals); Makoto Inoue (synth); Tetsu Tobe (sax, recruited by Makigami at a sex, not sax, shop in Shinjuku); and Ko Yamashita (synth, rhythm box) decided to form a band. None had previously considered a significant career in music. They played the first gig after only a week's rehearsal and got a surprisingly good audience response,

HIKASHU

which gave them the confidence to go and build a strong cult following, especially among people sick of sugarpop. Makigami's eerie vocals, the lyrics themselves and the band's tendency to improvise, emphasise this determined direction.

After the release of a self-titled debut album ('80), and the second *Natsu (Summer)* ('80), they replaced a rhythm box with a human drummer, Toshiro Sensui, and recorded a third album, *Human Being* ('81). One song each from both the first and the third albums are included in the sampler album, *Tokyo Mobile Music,* available in the UK. Makigami also released a solo album in '82 full of remakes of old Japanese popular songs from the pre-war period. Hikashu (it doesn't mean anything in Japanese or in any other language existing on this globe) do not use theatrical devices on stage, yet their music itself creates a kind of theatrical atmosphere.

HARUOMI HOSONO

Haruomi Hosono

Known as the leader/founder of the most successful contemporary Japanese rock group — Yellow Magic Orchestra (YMO), Hosono is perhaps THE most important person in the development of Japanese rock.

In the late Sixties he started his long career with Apryl Fool. Later came Happy End, who never achieved any commercial success, though critics and musicians saw them as influential, not so much for the music but for one very significant fact — they performed their songs in Japanese. Right through the Sixties and for most of the Seventies everything that came out of Japan was performed in English. The theory was that since rock music was American, everything had to be done the American way, which meant singing in English. Japanese folk artists of the time were the only others attempting to sing in their native tongue and there were intense arguments about what was the right thing to do. Happy End scored no hits but they definitely led the way. They broke up in '73 and Hosono made four solo albums: *Hosono House* ('73), *Tropical Dandy* ('75), *Bon Voyage* ('76) and *Paraiso* ('77). Before forming YMO he also performed with project-oriented groups such as Caramel Mama, (later known as Tin Pan Alley), with which he recorded one album in 1975. He also contributed one third of the *Pacific* album ('78) and in the same year recorded *Cochin Moon* with famous illustrator, Tadanori Yokoo.

To contrast with his pioneering work on behalf of the Japanese language Hosono has steeped himself in other music from other lands — all kinds of 'ethnic' sounds from China, the Caribbean and Latin America and perhaps, most significantly, Okinawa. The combination of these elements has produced in him something he has dubbed 'chunky music'. Hosono, probably the driving force of YMO, is one of the most prolific studio producers working in Japan, mainly working with artists signed to the Alfa and (his own) Yen labels. The Hosono touch (including chunky music elements) can be heard on Sandii & the Sunsetz albums and, most recently, with Test Pattern, as well as his own solo effort *Philharmony,* the first solo album to be made since he joined YMO.

Imitation

Another band to emerge from the ashes of The Sadistic Mika Band. Imitation was formed by keyboardist Yu Imai. After the breakup of the Mika band, Imai, with Yukihiro Takahashi and others, spent some years in The Sadistics.

Imitation came into being in October, '80. Their first album, *Original,* went almost unnoticed, but they were gathering audiences at their exciting live gigs which featured singer, Chee-Bo. They ditched their 'new wave' image and changed musical style for the second album, *Muscle & Heat* ('82). The band opened up to include Sandii and Makoto Kubota from the Sunsetz, and Steve Scales and Dollette McDonald of Talking Heads fame, with Chris

Mosdell contributing lyrics. *Muscle & Heat* is a fine collection of light jungle music sparkling with the charm of Chee-Bo and all manner of amusing percussion effects. Other Imitations are Osamu (guitar, chorus), Shigeru Inoue (drums, percussion, chorus) and Masanobu Hoshino (bass, chorus).

Ippu-Do

Ippu-Do, one of the very few bands exposed outside Japan, consists of three very competent musicians, Masami Tsuchiya (guitar, vocals, bass, synthesizers), Akira Mitake (synthesizers, keyboards) and Shoji Fujii (drums, percussions). Their third album *Radio Fantasy,* which was critically (but not commercially) successful everywhere in the world, is available in Australia and the UK. Apart from their extensive and subtle use of electronic gadgets, one of their attractive musical features is the diversity of influences they have absorbed and developed. Their debut album, *Normal* owes much to Sixties pop music. September '80 saw a style shift to German music with their second album, *Real,* which was aptly recorded at the Hansa studios in Berlin. Their third, *Radio Fantasy* ('81) recorded without their original bassist sounds more like electronic funk bands from the UK.

Masami Tsuchiya, a technically very versatile guitarist, was picked by (David Sylvian's) Japan for an Autumn tour throughout Europe in 1982. He also has his fingers in production. Not only has he produced all Ippu-Do's albums, he also produced other artists, such as Kim Wilde (actually her *Bitter Is Better* is Tsuchiya's composition, with the instruments played by him). He has one solo album (with help from Steve Jansen and Mick Karn from Japan), *Rice Music* ('82), to his credit.

Ippu-Do's first chart success in Japan came when Tsuchiya was touring with (the group) Japan in '82. The single *Sumire September Love* ('82), used for a TV commercial, brought the first big success to the band. As a group, Ippu-Do scarcely play live, which seems a bit odd, as they originally came to public attention in '79 backing a Japanese Mick Jagger clone. The most amazing thing about Ippu-Do is they are probably the only band ever to have released two 'best of' albums after having only released three original albums (though these 'best of' albums do include singles and some tracks from Tsuchiya's solo album).

KODOMO BAND

Shokichi Kina

It's important to appreciate the influence of Okinawa in modern Japanese pop. Administratively part of Japan, this string of islands in the South China Sea, half-way to Taiwan, are ethnically and historically independent and maybe would be again if it weren't for the presence of the huge US airbases that dominate the islands and give them their strategic importance. Okinawa has a very strong folk music base which is much more alive than that of Japan where folk music has been diluted over the years into the ever popular sentimental 'enka'.

Shokichi Kina is a native of Okinawa and comes from a family of folk performers involved in performing Okinawanese music. He started playing with them when he

MASAMI TSUCHIYA/IPPU-DO

was a student in 1977 and one of their performances, virtually live, appeared as an album *Shokichi Kina and Champluse.* In 1980 he made an album in Japan, *Blood Line,* which features that champion of ethnic causes, Ry Cooder, along with Haruomi Hosono, and Makoto Kubota (of Sandii and the Sunsetz). It's difficult to describe in words the exact nature of the Okinawanese sound but it's very beaty, sometimes jerky, certainly folky, often relying for its impetus on 'hup hup' type backing chants, usually by

SHOKICHI KINA

female singers. It appears to have had some influence, probably on YMO, (especially Hosono) and Ippu-Do (particularly on *Radio Fantasy* and *Rice Music,* the solo album by Ippu-Do's Masami Tsuchiya). Strangely, Kina himself seems to have wandered a bit on his new album *Celebration* ('82) and got hung up on writing lyrics. The album also features guitar playing by Kenji Omura.

Kodomo Band ▋

With three albums and as many mini LPs to their credit, Kodomo Band with the current line-up started gigging around Tokyo in 1978. The Kodomos won a Battle of the Bands quest in 1979. In the same year they managed to play an astonishing 203 gigs, which was long before the release of the record. Definitely one of the hardest touring bands in Japan.

The Kodomos feature two guitarists, Tsuyoshi Ujiki and Koichi Tanihei, Toben Yukawa on bass and Yu Yamato on drums. In '82 they won the support spot for Ritchie Blackmore's Rainbow's zillionth Japanese tour.

The Kodomos (which means Kids in Japanese) on stage can be highly enjoyable and are part of that quintessentially anachronistic obsession that the Japanese have for heavy metal.

Lizard ▋

To talk about Lizard is to talk about Momoyo (aka Yosuke Sugawara), its leader and originator. For it seems to exist for the sole purpose of expressing his perspective, his vivid almost lurid amalgamation of emotion, politics, paranoia and art. Since inception, the group has never had a fixed line-up.

Momoyo has been a cult hero in Tokyo's inner-city underground since the mid-Seventies. Like many others, he came to a wider audience through the Tokyo Rockers Movement of 1978 — a collective which included bands like Friction and Mirrors. It organised gigs in Tokyo, staged small tours of Western Japan and released the live compilation albums *Tokyo New Wave '79* (RCA) and *Tokyo Rockers* (CBS/Sony).

In 1979 Lizard supported The Stranglers' Japanese tour and so impressed Jean Jacques Burnel that he arranged a short UK tour for them — during which he produced their

first self-titled album. Other releases include an independent single about pollution called *SA-KA-NA (F-I-S-H),* a second album *(Babylon Rocker)* and a compilation album, *Keshi No Hana (The Flower Of The Poppy).* He also produced Zelda's debut album.

Momoyo was busted for heroin purchase in November 1980. He spent a month in jail and emerged to a huge reception at a big University gig in Tokyo. To express thanks for his fans' support, he released a special 7 inch Lizard mini-LP for a dollar a shot.

In 1981 came the third proper album, *Gymnopaedia,* which showcased the full Momoyo range — from Jim Morrison and the Velvet Underground to Joy Division. His songs are visions of armageddon and the apocalypse, strangely hymnlike. He sees the Babylonian side of Tokyo rather than the technopopular paradise.

HIDEKI MATSUTAKE

Logic System (aka Hideki Matsutake) ▋

It's hardly surprising that Japan has been producing so many synth/computer bands. One obvious reason is that Japan's advanced technology is relatively cheap at home. The other reason is the enormous influence and reputation of computer musician, Isao Tomita. However it was *Switched On Bach,* played by a computer at Expo '70 at Osaka that first got to Matsutake. He immediately decided to get into computer music and took up a course of electronic engineering in Tokyo. On graduation he became an apprentice to Tomita, who is still his master in the traditional Japanese sense. In those days Tomita allowed young Matsutake to play his newly purchased Moog 3-C at night, while during the day he worked as a roadie.

In 1972 Matsutake decided to buy the same machine and set up his own company. His work was mainly producing commercial jingles, until '77 when he helped keyboard player and singer, (and later YMO satellite) Akiko Yano make her third album. According to Matsutake, she was the first to use sequencers. He went on to work on Riuichi Sakamoto's first solo album, *Thousand Knives* ('78) (the title song appears in another version on YMO's *BGM* album). Ever since the inception of YMO, Matsutake has played an integral role in the programming of computers.

His own work has been released on three albums under the name of Logic System. The first album, *Logic* ('81) was released in the UK and Australia to high critical acclaim. In Sydney, it was discovered by the Nippi Rock Shop on 2JJJ-FM and became one of the cult records of the year. The second album, *Venus* ('82), also released overseas, was a disappointing effort made in Los Angeles with a number of American musicians, including Dave Grusin. The third LP, *Orient Express* ('82) was much more diverse and original even

THE MODS

though many of the tracks seem like computerised pastiches of film soundtrack and mood music.

According to the record covers, the consistent members of this outfit are Hideki Matsutake along with MC-4, MC-8, TR-808, Moog 3-C and other machines. All of whom are in big demand by other Japanese bands. As the techno-pop revolution makes its relentless way through mainstream culture, every sugarpop extravaganza wants that computer magic as part of the matrix. It remains to be seen whether Matsutake can keep his head above the great wave of synthesizer excess. One optimistic sign — Logic System is performing 'live' with some success, particularly in Hong Kong and for some strange reason the records sell better in South East Asia than in Japan.

The Mods

The Mods are one of the new bands that are capturing the hearts and minds of the new young audience in Japan.

Their popularity derives from the charisma of singer Tatsuya Moriyama (vocal, guitar), strongly accessible lyrics, fast, punchy, no-fifteen-minute-long-guitar-solo music, and strong stage presentation.

Moriyama started the band, then called Mozz, in 1974 when he was 18, in Hakata, one of the main cities on Kyushu Island — which is one of the four main islands of Japan.

After countless membership and name changes, the current line-up was established around '78 as The Mods. With this band Moriyama almost conquered the whole of Kyushu by the end of 1980, when they departed for Tokyo. Before their record debut in '79, they wrote and performed a fine sound track for a young film-maker, also from Hakata. This film *Thunder Road* was a classic tale of rebellious youth.

After a handful of gigs in Tokyo, The Mods flew to London to record their debut album, with Nick Bradford (of Jam fame) in the engineer's seat, at the Matrix Studio. This album *Fight Or Flight* ('81), sold reasonably well, though it was still live appearances that brought The Mods their big audience. Upon return from the UK, they supported The Jam's Japanese tour.

The second album, *News Beat* ('81), showed, among other things, a new maturity in the lyric department. At the end of '81, they made a second trip to London, playing three gigs at the Marquee Club under the name of News Beat. Their third album, *Look Out* ('82), produced by Ippu-Do's Masami Tsuchiya, transferred their live reputation into record sales at last.

Although they call themselves The Mods and they used to play typical mod music, they sound these days much closer to early Clash (although bassist Koichi Kitazato is a Sid Vicious lookalike!). The others in the band are Hiroshi Chisaki (guitar) and Masahiro Kajiura (drums).

Chris Mosdell

As the name may indicate, Chris Mosdell is a Gainsborough-born Englishman, a "gaijin" who's been living in Tokyo for the past six years. He is undoubtedly an interesting artist, but without having met Yukihiro Takahashi, Mosdell would not have been recognised in

Japanese rock. Conversely, without the contribution of this chemistry-graduate (pathology Masters degree holder) poet, it could have taken some more years for YMO and the rest of Japanese music to be recognised outside of Japan. For it is Mosdell who has helped 'Anglicize' rather than translate YMO's lyrics. He writes for other bands but his own work is also worthy of note. Alfa records spent a small fortune on the production and presentation of his solo album *Equasian,* which is full of what he terms as 'Visic' — a mixture of vision and music.

With The Javelin Opera (consisting of such names as Kenji Omura of YMO fame, Makoto Kubota, Sandii from The Sunsetz, Yu Imai, and Shigeru Inoue from Imitation), Mosdell created a strange cultural collection of sounds and words.

About the 'Visic' concept, Mosdell says ". . . I paint pictures with words, graphically, which can be understood visually, then gave it still another dimension with music. The project I'm taking up now has even more of a visual aspect. People tend to create their own visual image when listening to music, but I want to force them in a way to accept images closer to my own. Don't take me wrong — I don't intend to become a dictator. I just want to show one direction".

For all its beauty and intelligence *Equasian* suffers somewhat from over-attention to detail, certainly the opposite to the way his mentors YMO were moving on *Technodelic* (to which another Anglicizer, Peter Barakan contributed lyrics). Maybe now that he's got the colossus out of his system he'll revert to something more stripped-for-action; less poetry and more pathology perhaps.

RC SUCCESSION

R C Succession

There's no way this band can be accused of being 'new'. In one form or another it's been playing for sixteen years, having started as a folk trio in 1966 when founder Kiyoshiro Imawano was still at junior high school in Tokyo. As a singer-songwriter his great influence has always been black R&B and soul, and playing acoustic renditions of this music helped create RCS's early reputation in Tokyo folk clubs. Except for one single in 1972 RCS knew no commercial success until very recently, which is the one and only reason why they are considered 'new'. Toward the end of the Seventies they evolved and expanded, bringing in the electricity needed to establish them as a more conventional rock group, though still leaning towards R&B. By 1978 they'd achieved a big reputation on the live-gig circuit, still mainly in Tokyo.

However in 1982 they hit the national charts mainly through a combination of talent plus a peculiarly Japanese marketing device which enables singers and bands to get hits — the extended TV commercial in which a song is exposed (sometimes with a minor change of lyrics to fit the product name into the song) in its entirety on TV every night for a few weeks, paid for by the sponsor. Visiting artists have benefited from this exposure as well —namely Madness and Kim Wilde. RCS also had the good fortune to co-write and produce "Rouge Magic" with YMO's Sakamoto, a move which took them from the obscure Tokyo club scene to national pop star status more or less overnight.

The current RCS line-up is Yawao Kobayashi (bass) G-2 (keyboards) Reiichi Nakaido (guitar vocals) Kozo Niida (drums) and Imawano (vocals). Imawano has a knack for writing lyrics that seem to fit these times; despite his age and his strange, almost squeaky vocal style which makes him instantly recognisable. Live, the other main attraction is guitarist Nakaido who loves to play like Keith Richards, while looking a lot healthier.

In 1982 RCS performed at a jam-packed baseball stadium in Yokohama with black innovators Sam Moore and Chuck Berry, the concert was recorded and released as *The Day of R&B* — a perfect example of the Confucian ideal of respect-for-the elders.

By the way the name RC Succession has nothing to do with the RC Church. It's said to be a phonetic rendering of a Japanese phrase meaning "someday we'll form a band."

Riuichi Sakamoto

Like the other two YMOs, Sakamoto is an individual musician, spending considerable time outside the trio. He records solo and acts in movies. He is the most inquisitive and curious person in YMO with a history of political activity that goes back to the radical student movement which, when he was at high school, gave him the opportunity to enjoy the experience of physical confrontation with the Kido-tai, the notorious Japanese riot police. As his interest drifted from direct involvement in politics to art, Sakamoto went up to the Tokyo University of the Arts, where he studied at post-graduate level, majoring in musical composition. He is the only member of YMO with a formal education in music — hence the nickname, Professor.

However before YMO, Sakamoto had never been involved in what one could call a success, though he was well known as one of the few session keyboard players who could handle synthesizers. Through the recording of his first solo album, *Thousand Knives* ('78), he came to know Yukihiro Takahashi, and they struck up a mutual admiration which led to the birth of YMO.

Sakamoto's solo albums are much more experimental than those of YMO, (as indeed are the other members' solos). While Hosono explores the ethnic fringe and Takahashi the sleeker side of adult pop, Sakamoto expands the musical vocabulary of western music forms including classical and jazz. He recorded his second solo, *B2-Unit* ('80) with, among others, Andy Partridge from XTC, developing a strong feeling for using electronics with power and rhythm rather than for spacey mood effects. This was well developed on his third album, *Left-handed Dream* ('81), which was recorded with Adrian Belew, Robin 'M' Scott and Sakamoto. Both are available in the UK.

Sakamoto is one of very few Japanese musicians with chart successes in both Japan and the UK. Success in the UK came from his collaboration with David Sylvian on *Bamboo Houses/Bamboo Music* ('82). As well as success with YMO in Japan, he scored a hit with another single collaboration with the singer from RC Succession, which made Japan's top 10 in 1982. Sakamoto has also worked as a producer Akiko Yano, Friction (first album) and Phew (first single).

He has written a number of theme tunes for TV series and soundtracks for movies, and debuted as an actor in the recent Oshima movie, *Merry Christmas Mr. Laurence,* in which he co-stars with David Bowie. (He has absolutely no

SUSAN

SANDII & THE SUNSETS

connection whatever with Kyo Sakamoto who had a huge international success in the early '60s with the single *Sukiyaki).*

In 1979 Sakamoto won the best arranger of the year award in the prestigious annual Japan Record Awards (usually dominated by sugarpop and enka). His live performances outside YMO include appearances with free jazz entity Yuji Takahashi (said to be his mentor), Akiko Yano, Kazumi 'Kylyn' Watanabe, (YMO's original guitarist and another jazzer), RC Succession, Phew and Hajime Tachibana.

Sandii & The Sunsetz

This group is simply Sunsetz in its home land. 'Sandii &' was added when overseas record company executives saw strong commercial potential in the looks of the lead singer, Sandii. Sunsetz is a group of dexterous musicians: Sandii (lead vocals), Makoto Kubota (guitars, vocals, keyboards, percussions), Ken-Ichi Inoue (guitars, vocals), Takashi 'King Champ' Onzo (bass, vocals) and Hideo Inoura (drums, percussions).

Although the present Sunsetz lineup started in '80, both Sandii and her husband, Kubota, are no newcomers to the Japanese rock scene. Kubota debuted way back in '73 as a solo musician. Later the same year, he formed Yuyake Gakudan (Sunset Orchestra) and recorded three albums, *Sunset Gang* (featuring the ever popular Godzilla on the

cover) ('73), *Hawaii Champroo* ('75) and *Dixie Fever* ('77). A half Japanese, half Spanish/American singer, Sandii joined in 1977 and a transformation occurred. Sandii had won two top prizes in Yamaha's World Music Festival in Tokyo in 1976. She then released a single, *Mystery Nile.* Like Hosono of YMO, Makoto Kubota has absorbed many, essentially tribal, down-to-earth, ethnic musical influences from all over the globe — Bali to New Orleans, San 'Psychedelic' Francisco to Okinawa — creating an 'Atlas of Sounds'.

The Sunsetz have recorded three albums, including Sandii's solo album *Eating Pleasure* ('80). Both went on to bloom into full growth on *Heat Scale* ('81), the first true album for the group. This album is a clear indication of Sandii's versatile vocal ability and Kubota's pan-globalism. Like *Eating Pleasure, Heat Scale* was produced by Hosono who successfully realised the dynamism of the Sunsetz. Both albums are available in the UK and *Heat Scale* is available in Australia (with one extra track, *Alive,* originally included in Sandii's solo album). Their album, *Immigrants* ('82) is more than worth checking out. Remixed and co-produced by Dave Jordan of Fun Boy Three fame, and backed up by such names as Hosono and Takahashi from YMO, David Sylvian (chorus, contributing lyrics) from the group Japan, and Dollette McDonald and Steve Scales of the expanded Talking Heads, *Immigrants* sounds more accessible, partly because time is catching up with the band and partly because the production is more straightforward, without losing its distinctive elements.

The Sunsetz toured Europe as the special guest of (Sylvian's) Japan in 1982. Sandii's determined sex appeal is an essential part of the Sunsetz package as can be seen from this typical response from the Melody Maker's Adam Sweeting: "Sandii, of course is the major scene stealer, and I don't just mean her legs. She weaves gently at the microphone, exotic hair flaring around her face like a comet-trail, and sings with a rapt simplicity. She dances sinuous snaking figures as the rhythms twine and float, and if you don't mind, I'll head for the cold shower."

Susan

Susan is a creation, if not a confection, out of the head of YMO's Takahashi. Her first album was quite a hit across continental Europe — *Do You Believe In Mazik?* the title and the song originally coming from John Sebastian, the rest of the material coming from Takahashi, Haruomi Hosono, Hajime Tachibana and Kenji Omura. Most of the YMO extended family, including Sakamoto, play on the album. In 1981 Susan released *The Girl Can't Help It* using most of the same talent but without much development

CHRIS MOSDELL

beyond a fatal fascination for singing in such a high register she sounds like she's at 78 rpm. She obviously can sing but unfortunately it sounds like she's being manipulated, like a doll. Maybe she should stick with the lower registers and the less ickle-girl songs. She *can* do it, as you can hear on *Freezing Fish Under the Moonlight Eating My Backbone.*

Hajime Tachibana

What will Keith Richards do when the Rolling Stones finally implode? If he's got any sense he'll chuck his Les Paul into the Thames and pick up a saxophone. The analogy may seem stretched but even though they were nowhere as big as the Stones, The Plastics were in the late Seventies, Japan's only big modern international band that looked like making it.

Here's a quote from lead guitarist Hajime Tachibana, taking about the end. "July 1981, Los Angeles, The Plastics European and American tour ended after an exhausting three months; and everything seemed to end with it. After a spiritless two week stay in LA the only thing left in my hand was a saxophone. Basically, an enthusiastic interest in a reed instrument and in jazz music came back to me at a time when I had almost lost enthusiasm for music itself."

Says it all really. The results can be heard on an album released by Alfa in 1982 called *H* in which Tachibana and a band of mainly acoustic musicians play simple, almost amateurish Fifties music for the eighties without a tinge of rock and roll anywhere. However, you can't mistake this for Lounge Lizard or Joe Jackson pastiches, it really is modern music whose time has not yet come. *H* is a superb contrast to the mechanical white funk-pop that swept everyone up in the post-disco realisation that white kids could still dance. It's jerky and jokey but quite serious and 'free' in a very organised kind of way. Tachibana toured Japan in 1982 with a band which included YMO drummer Takahashi and bass player Hosono. A further quote from Tachibana reveals all: "When you think about music in this

IMITATION

modern society, in its long history ethnologically and innovatively, there has been a question of if it's art or non-art. I simply want to exist with the vinyl chloride that makes records, and to make that feeling mass productive." In other words, he has discovered the true essence of plastic music. An early release of *HM* internationally could do the same for the rest of us.

Yukihiro Takahashi

This Tokyo born (YMO) drummer is one of the best known musicians outside Japan. A former art student, he joined Sadistic Mika Band in the early 70s and, among a handful of others, was one of the earliest exports from Japan. With the Mika Band, Takahashi released four albums in Britain and scored the support on a UK Roxy Music tour in '75. This tour was supposed to ignite interest in Japanese music in Britain, but it didn't. Although the band received rave reviews from the media, it did not last long enough to capitalise on them. The split of the main component of the band, the Katohs, Mika, the singer and Kazuhiko (the founder, songwriter and guitarist), led to the breakup of the band immediately after this one and only British tour. The Mika band minus the Katohs formed a kind of jazz-fusion band, The Sadistics, which was nothing more than a group of skilled musicians without any clear direction or originality.

Since then Takahashi has not only contributed to the rise of YMO in the world market with solid, computer-like accurate and emotionless drumming, Ferryish vocals and poppy songs, but also extended his solo career at the same time. *Saravah!* ('77) was his first solo effort. *Murdered By Music* ('80), the second, was released in the UK and Australia. A third album, *Neuromantic* followed in '81 and *What, Me Worry?* in '82. On these albums he showcased his sense of pop with extensive help from his colleagues the YMO family (including Hosono and Sakamoto) and friends both from Japan and the UK and including Andy MacKay and Phil Manzanera from Roxy Music, Steve Jansen, Mick Karn and David Sylvian from Japan, Bill Nelson from Be Bop Deluxe and Tony Mansfield from New Muzik. Takahashi is also very active as a producer/session musician. He has produced various unique talents such as Susan, whose record *The Girl Can't Help It* is available in the UK, and played on albums by Robin Scott (M), Zain Griff, other YMOs and many more.

In 1982 Takahashi toured Japan with such names as Steve Jansen from Japan on drums, Hosono on bass and electronics, Tsuchiya (of Ippu-Do) on guitar and Hajime Tachibana (ex-Plastics guitarist) on sax. Takahashi concentrated on keyboards and vocals.

His robotic vocal and Harrison-influenced composition aside, he is also very interested in personal and visual style. A sartorial aesthete, his video clips of *Drip Dry Eyes* and *Something In The Air* display great taste, a studied manner and a romantic aloofness which invite obvious comparison with the empty posturings of Ultravox's *Vienna* but yet manages to retain a human distinction and charm. He also designs and sells clothes, some of which you can see on YMO album covers.

Yellow Magic Orchestra ████████████

Yellow Magic Orchestra is without doubt the most successful band ever to come out of Japan. They are bigger overseas than any other Japanese band have ever been and they're also bigger at home than any before them. YMO's history is the history of modern Japanese rock and pop because it involves so many people and so many talents. It's also the story of three incredibly talented individuals. (To see just how successful the three have been, check out the entries under Haruomi Hosono, Yukihiro Takahashi and Riuichi Sakamoto.) Hosono's early Seventies band Happy End was the first to use Japanese lyrics combined with essentially American rock. Takahashi was drummer for The Sadistic Mika Band which achieved a level of international fame through its involvement with Roxy Music. Sakamoto, an academically trained musician, was one of the first to understand the potential of the synthesiser, and has a close involvement with the free jazz movement.

Hosono had a strong solo career before YMO. However, the album *Paraiso* was released under the name "Haruomi Hosono and The Yellow Magic Band". (It may be pure coincidence that Captain Beefheart and his Magic Band's first album *Safe as Milk* included the track *Yellow Brick Road.*) It was during the recording sessions for this album that they decided to form a synthesizer-computer based band which released its first album as YMO in November 1978. It was very much a sign of its times. The album began and closed with the synthesized sounds of space invader games. Comparisons with Kraftwerk are unavoidable. In the great debate about whether computer music is really music let's just say that Kraftwerk have gone for melodies and YMO are more rhythm orientated, mainly because they've always had the services of Takahashi — a real drummer — rather than a rhythm box.

The first album surprised and delighted critics but didn't sell well until subsequent albums had devastated the Japanese music market. *Solid State Survivor* came out in 1979 and has sold 2 million worldwide. It stayed in the Japanese LP chart for a year. This was a great breakthrough for rock-based music, which had hardly dented domestic charts since The Sadistic Mika Band's *Black Ship* LP in 1974. The album was remixed and repackaged for the US market and YMO flew to LA in August '79 to open for The Tubes at the Greek Theatre. The line-up also included Akiko Yano (keyboards and vocals), Kazumi 'Kylyn' Watanabe (guitar) and Hideki Matsutake (computers).

YMO undertook a second world tour in October 1979, taking in Paris and London. The results were recorded and released as *Public Pressure* in 1980. The title is said to reflect contractual hassles involving Watanabe. His guitar was extracted and replaced in the remix by Sakamoto on synthesizer.

The prestige of these foreign tours meant that, on their return, YMO were greeted with doubled sales. In March 1980 the LP chart was inundated with YMO product. *Public Pressure* had gone straight to the top on release, *Solid State Survivor* was at 5 and the original YMO album at 27. The same month they set out on their first national major tour in Japan, it was called "Technopolis 2000-20" (two thousand *minus* twenty, ie 1980).

The next assault on the LP chart came in June 1980 with the release of a 10 inch mini-album which included all kinds of extraneous material, such as skits from a radio programme called *The Snakeman Show,* and a cover version of the Archie Bell classic *Tighten Up.* It was called *Multiplies* and shot to number 1, which meant YMO had four albums in the top 20 in June 1980. (Don't be confused if you've come across a 12 inch album under the title *Multiples* — this is in fact a compilation with material from *Solid State Survivor* and the original 10 inch).

It's on *Multiplies* that the band adds humanity to the technology, by singing. From then on they began to move beyond experimentation with gadgetry, and started to compose songs. Also, they began to develop the humour in their lyrics and titles. In 1981 we heard *BGM* (which is anything but 'Background Music') and *Technodelic* with the moving, almost spiritual *Pure Jam.*

Meanwhile YMO were still touring overseas. In the UK they played small gigs at pubs and clubs, as well as concerts. They were supported by The Comsat Angels and the tour's highlight was at the Hammersmith Odeon, where they played to an audience of the English rock establishment in all its diversity: Wings, Boomtown Rats, Japan, The Vapors and, of course, Throbbing Gristle. Perhaps most significant was the presence of Roxy Music's

YELLOW MAGIC ORCHESTRA

first producer Chris Thomas and his wife Mika from the original Sadistic Mika Band (which Thomas also produced).

1982 was quiet but saw one key development. Hosono at last produced a solo album — *Philharmony.* Up to this time he'd been totally engrossed in YMO, even though Takahashi and Sakamoto found time for solo efforts.

This could mean new directions for YMO, no longer seen by Hosono as the only outlet for his individual ideas. Throughout 1982 there was no YMO tour and no album. The 1983 album *People With Nice Smiles* once again has Matsutake performing computer programming duties, but with a guest guitarist, the first outside contributor (apart from Matsutake) to appear on a YMO album since *Multiplies.* He is Bill Nelson, formerly with British group Be Bop Deluxe.

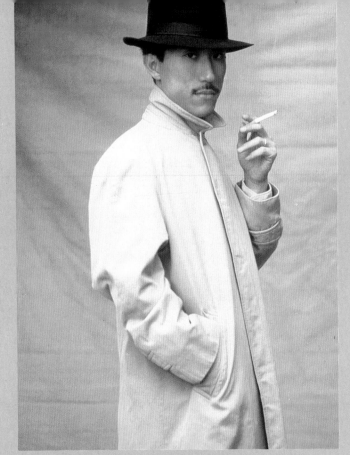

YUKIHIRO TAKAHASHI

ZELDA

Although Momoyo's influence is obvious, the album exhibits Zelda's unique charm; mixing seemingly contradictory terms, such as masculinity and feminity, darkness and light, hope and despair, innocence and foxiness.

The Japanese Joy Division envelops the Go-Go's!

Coming, Going, Gone

The Plastics, one of the only Japanese bands that ever toured overseas or released records outside Japan. They split in Los Angeles but live on with Hajimi Tachibana's solo career and Chika Sato, who, with Toshi Nakanishi, has released some sophisticated pop funk under the name of **Melon** in *Do You Like Japan?* on Hosono's Yen label. Other Yensters include synth-pop duo **Test Pattern**,

CHICA OF THE PLASTICS

produced by Hosono, and **Guernica**, "directed" by himself. Guernica manage to engender a different kind of Japanese fusion on their 1982 *Kaizo Eno Yakjudo (Intimations Of Reformation)* album. Traditional Japanese singing style, modern electronics and a 1930s European cabaret sound.

Interior produce something they call "hard ambience". Also produced by Hosono but from the Kitty label comes "tin rock" from the **Virgin Vs** on two albums very definitely opposed to heavy metal.

P Model looked like making it in 1981 after four albums. **The No Comments** did Japanese ska in a cover version of *Under the Boardwalk* on their self-titled album. **Five X** have produced three albums with lead singer Carmen Maki claiming the title of queen of heavy metal. **Phew** is a lead singer in her own right, but she was originally with a band called **Aunt Sally.** She records with the Pass independent label.

The leading Tokyo Indie label is Telegraph. One of its most adventurous releases is a dense 10 inch from the **NON BaNd.** Another big little Indie is Ylem, who put out an amazing double, clear-plastic compilation album in 1982 called *Foam.* It featured around 20 bands, was a limited edition of 5000 and came with ready-printed cassette labels for the inevitable pirates, a high-gloss cut-out cover, a brown paper bag, a bay leaf and a stick of chewing gum.

Also of interest is the TRA cassette Indie, who produce regular soundscapes plus a fashion mag to read along. It comes (and goes) for US$8 and you get it from: TRA PROJECT, 603 Azabu Palace Building, 2-25-18 Nishi Azabu, Minato-ku, Tokyo 106, JAPAN.

Zelda

Formed in March 1980 by the editor of a Tokyo fanzine *Change 2000,* Sachiho 'Chiho' Kojima, Zelda are one of the very few all-female new rock bands in Japan. Named after Zelda Fitzgerald, wife of Scott and notorious American beauty of the Twenties, Zelda are equally beautiful and talented. The Zelda of the Eighties consists of Sayoko Takahashi (vocals), Yoko Suzuki (guitar), Kuniko 'Maru' Nozawa (drums) and Chiho (bass, keyboards). Soon after their first appearance at The Loft in Shinjuku, Zelda became the darling of the Tokyo club scene. Their first independent single, *Ash-La* sold 2,000 copies immediately after release.

Their second release was a flexi-disc of a live performance. They spent most of '81 gigging around Japan, then went into the studios with producer Momoyo, a new wave wiz and leader of Lizard. Their self-titled album was completed in June '82 and finally picked up by Phonogram Records.

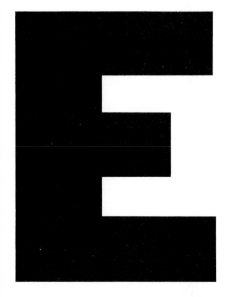

Echo And The Bunnymen ■

Ian McCulloch put together Echo And The Bunnymen in October 1978, one month after he'd departed from A Shallow Madness (a five piece affair who rehearsed themselves into obscurity before ever having played a gig) and 14 months after the finish of The Crucial Three: a four-man line-up which drew Ian together with Julian Cope (now of The Teardrop Explodes), Peter Wylie (now of Wah!) and Steve Spence (now at college).

Ian met up with Will Sergeant, who'd been working with Industrial Domestic, and together they began writing the songs, with the aid of a drum machine, which were to form the basis of The Bunnymen repertoire. On November 15 at Eric's Club in Liverpool, Echo And The Bunnymen — Ian McCulloch (guitar and vocals), Will Sergeant (guitar), Les Pattison (who'd turned up on Ian's doorstep four days before on bass), and a drum machine called Echo — played their first show.

This initial configuration remained unchanged for the best part of a year, during which time the band played some dozen-and-a-half shows and recorded one single, *Pictures On My Wall/Read It In Books* on Zoo Records, released March 1979. Another song, *Monkeys,* from this period has also surfaced on the *Street To Street* compilation of then proliferating Liverpool bands.

In October 1979, Echo the drum machine was laid off and Pete De Freitas became The Bunnymen's drummer. By the end of the year, after further live work in Liverpool and London, they were signed to the newly formed Korova Records.

Echo And The Bunnymen's first single for Korova, *Rescue/Simple Stuff,* was released in April 1980. Three months later their debut

album, *Crocodiles,* was made available and, in keeping with its release, the band made a 20 date tour of clubs and colleges across the country. Both the album and single made indentations on the UK charts, with the album peaking in the top 20.

In October 1980 The Bunnymen completed a highly successful UK tour which saw the group grow in confidence and ability. With a newly recorded single, *The Puppet,* The Bunnymen unwittingly became the champions of camouflage gear on the tour — both the group and the crew adopted the camo look — playing amidst an impressively lit stage set which was likened to something out of the film *Apocalypse Now.*

In January 1981 the Bunnymen made a 30-minute film, *They Shine So Hard,* based around a mysteriously divulged date at Buxton Pavilion, and for which distribution is currently being sought. A 12 inch live soundtrack EP has already appeared, featuring the title track, *Crocodiles, Zimbo, All That Jazz* and *Over The Wall.*

The filming complete, The Bunnymen spent the whole of March at Rockfield Studios with producer Hugh Jones to record their second album, *Heaven Up Here,* released in June 1981. The group then embarked on an ambitious world tour for the remainder of the year, which took in the UK, Europe, the States, Australia and New Zealand.

Apart from the single *The Back Of Love,* The Bunnymen were relatively quiet until early 1983 when the *Porcupine* album and *The Cutter* single appeared.

Dave Edmunds/Rockpile ■

Dave Edmunds' musical career began in the early '60s when he formed The Raiders, a band who played solid rock'n'roll in his home town of Cardiff. By 1968 he had a top 10 hit, *Sabre Dance,* with his group Love Sculpture. After the demise of that group, Edmunds helped set up Rockfield Studios in Wales and launched his own solo career in 1970 with *I Hear You Knocking,* which sold over three million copies worldwide.

In the early '70s he concentrated mostly on production, working with The Flamin' Groovies, Brinsley Schwarz, Man, Del Shannon and Dr Feelgood among others. He also performed in and was musical director for the film *Stardust.*

In 1975 Edmunds re-activated his

ECHO AND THE BUNNYMEN

own career with a solo album, *Subtle As A Flying Mallet,* and in the following year signed with Led Zeppelin's company, Swan Song Records. He then formed a new band, Rockpile, with Nick Lowe (bass) Billy Bremner (guitar) and Terry Williams (drums).

During 1977 and 1978 Dave Edmunds released two further solo albums, *Get It* and *Tracks On Wax,* and toured extensively through the

DAVE EDMUNDS

UK and US with Rockpile. By the summer of 1979, he had managed to split his time between Rockpile commitments, playing on Nick Lowe's solo albums and his own career. *Repeat When Necessary* was released under Edmunds' name and he scored a large hit single in both the UK and Australia with Elvis Costello's *Girl's Talk.* After tours of Australia, America and Britain in 1980, Rockpile finally released a bona fide album, *Seconds Of Pleasure,* but by early 1981 had issued a joint statement announcing their demise.

In 1981 Edmunds released another solo album, *Twangin,* and also produced most of the first Stray Cats album and The Polecats single, *John I'm Only Dancing.* Later that year Edmunds left Swan Song for Arista and in 1982 released the album, *D.E. 7,* which featured his new band, Dave Charles (drums), John David (bass), Geraint Watkins (keyboards) and Mickey Gee (guitar). This was followed by *Information* and the Jeff Lynne-produced hit *Slipping Away.*

Edmunds has a startling capacity to faithfully reproduce the classic original rock strains, such as Sun, the Everly Brothers and even Girlgroup.

Accordingly, he enjoys a strong cult and critical following. As one scribe wrote, "Edmunds is a rare artist who knows not only where his music is going but also where it came from."

Eurogliders

The Eurogliders were formed in Perth, West Australia in mid 1980. Guitarist/singer/songwriter Bernie Lynch, former social worker turned professional musician, left Perth band The Stockings and began to collect the various musicians who would become Eurogliders.

Lead singer Grace Knight had come to Australia from her native Scotland a few years before and was looking for a band to sing with. Crispin Akerman (lead guitar) and Amanda Vincent (keyboards) both came from a classical background. Geoff Rosenberg (bass guitar) joined in July 1981 after a long stint with Canberra garage bands and then with Melbourne's Stockley See & Mason. Drummer John Bennetts had worked with Lynch in The Stockings and when the drummer's stool became vacant in November 1981, he was asked to join.

Eurogliders spent most of 1981 working the traps of Perth and in December 1981 signed with Polygram Records. They then took the unusual step of travelling to Manila in the Philippines to record the debut album with English producer Lem Lubin. In early 1982 the group moved permanently to the east coast of Australia and in March and April gained significant exposure through supporting Teardrop Explodes on their Australian pub tour.

To coincide with the tour their debut single, *Without You,* was released and shot into the top 40. Their first album, *Pink Suit Blue Day* came out in May and after the success of the single, its sales were surprisingly disappointing.

The Eurythmics

When the Tourists exploded after a shaky 1980 Australian tour, members Annie Lennox and Dave Stewart elected to work together on a new project — not a band but a partnership which would draw upon the assistance of other musicians where required.

The Eurythmics was born out of a jam at Conny Plank's Cologne Studio New Year's Eve party at the end of 1980. Participating were DAF members Robert Gorl and Gabi, and former Can members Holger Czukay and Jackie Liebezeit. Signed by RCA on the same favourable conditions as the Tourists, the new 'group' cut the single *Never Gonna Cry Again,* followed by *This Is The House* (which featured Blondie drummer Clem Burke), and *Love Is A Stranger.* The album, *In The Garden* appeared in 1982, followed by *Sweet Dreams* in 1983.

The philosophy of the Eurythmics is best explained by Annie Lennox: "For us the old concept of rock'n'roll is dead, and we don't want to go on using this dead old formula of a group playing all around the world just to flog its flamin' albums. We want to create something new which is flexible and can grow. People can work it for six months or two weeks, it won't matter."

EUROGLIDERS

THE EURYTHMICS

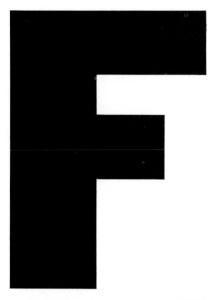

Fad Gadget

Fad Gadget is the alias of 25 year old Londoner Frank Tovey, one of the brightest lights in electronic music.

Tovey began taping noises in his teens and by the time he enrolled in a Fine Arts course at Leeds Polytechnic he was obsessed by electronic sound. At Leeds he became acquainted with fellow hopefuls Green (Scritti Politti) and Marc Almond (Soft Cell).

With the aid of a drum machine, electric piano and tape recorder, Tovey prepared demo tapes which came to the attention of the independent Mute Records label. For Mute he recorded the single *Back To Nature* in 1979 and the album *Fireside Favourites* the following year, along with two more singles. He also commenced live appearances in 1979, which consisted of standing motionless on stage, eyes directed at the floor, operating a keyboard and tape recorder.

In time, Tovey recruited musicians and eventually toured America with bassist Peter Balmer, keyboards player Dave Simmonds and percussionist Nick Cash. This lineup recorded the second Fad Gadget album, *Incontinent,* in 1981, along with the single *Saturday Night Special.* Although none of this quirky product cracked the pop charts it all featured prominently on the independent listings.

Considerably more successful was album three, *Under The Flag,* which yielded the hit *For Whom The Bells Toll.*

Marianne Faithfull

As a child, the eldest and only surviving of four, Marianne lived with her mother in Reading after her parents' divorce. Her mother, Austrian-born Baroness Erisso (in full, Eva Baroness Sacher Masoch of Appollonia and Erisso), was not a wealthy woman but arranged for Marianne to attend a convent school as a charity boarder.

At the age of 17, while still at school, her student boyfriend, John Dunbar, took her to a party in Cambridge, being held to launch the career of actress/singer Adrienne Posta. Present at the party were Mick Jagger, Paul McCartney and a number of other "names", although Marianne does not recall actually talking to any of them at the time.

The Rolling Stones' then-manager, Andrew Loog Oldham, spent the evening talking to Dunbar and eventually stated that he wanted to record Marianne. Her first single was custom-penned by Jagger and Richards. *As Tears Go By* became a top 10 hit in the UK in 1965 and Marianne became an instant star,

MARIANNE FAITHFULL

going on the road with The Hollies, Gerry and The Pacemakers and Freddie and The Dreamers.

A string of hits, including *Come Stay With Me* and *This Little Bird,* followed and meanwhile Marianne and Dunbar married and had a son. Marianne continued to work, but eventually the strain of being a mother, wife and pop star took its toll and the marriage failed. It was soon after that that Marianne teamed up with Mick Jagger to form one of the most tempestuous and publicised love affairs of the '60s.

By this time Marianne had given up singing and was pursuing an acting career instead. She appeared in the films, *I'll Never Forget Whatshisname, Girl On A Motorcycle* and *Hamlet* as well as stage productions of *Three Sisters* and *Hamlet.* During this time Marianne began suffering breakdowns and in July 1969 in Australia, while Jagger was filming *Ned Kelly,* suffered a barbiturate overdose which almost killed her.

Returning to England, she parted from Jagger and had a number of well-publicised romances as well as a heroin addiction, which she finally kicked in 1973.

Marianne returned to a recording career in 1978 with a single for NEMS, *Dreamin' My Dreams,* which stayed on the top of the Irish charts for 10 weeks. She followed it with an album of countryish material, *Faithless.*

In late 1979 Marianne Faithfull's career was re-established with a stark vital new album, *Broken English,* on the Island label. The single *The Ballad of Lucy Jordon* was a mild hit. Due to the profanity of

FAD GADGET

the lyrics on *Why'd Ya Do It,* a musical adaptation of a Heathcote Williams poem, the album caused a sensation and, in Australia, the offending track was deleted.

In 1981 she released her second Island album, *Dangerous Acquaintances,* a less volatile offering, from which the singles *Intrigue* and *Sweetheart* were lifted.

During 1982 Marianne embarked on a series of well received live concerts in England and America. Her only record for the year was a 12 inch EP containing an uninspired remake of *Sister Morphine* (which she wrote with Jagger & Richards) backed by an extended version of *Broken English.* The Australian release included Marianne reading *The Letter,* a 16th Century poem by Laclosse.

The Fall

The Fall were formed in Manchester in January 1977 and played their first gig in May. In their lifetime the group have earned the reputation for being totally uncompromising in their music and attitudes to the music business, record industry and ultimately the world. In that time they also must hold the record for the most fluctuating membership of any band. Only vocalist Mark E. Smith has been constant through the ever-changing line-ups.

The group first recorded for the independent Step Forward Records in 1978, releasing an EP, *Bingo Master's Break Out,* in August and a single, *It's The New Thing,* in November. Their first album, *Live At The Witch Trials,* came out in March 1979 and was followed by a second, *Dragnet,* in November. In between came the single, *Rowche Rumble.*

After a final EP for Step Forward, *Fiery Jack,* The Fall signed to Rough Trade. For that label they recorded a single, *How I Wrote Electric Man,* and a third album, *Grotesque (After The Gramme),* in 1980, as well as a live album, *Totale's Turn,* and an EP, *Slates,* to round off a very productive year.

After a final single for Rough Trade, *Totally Wired,* their classic song which came out early in 1981, The Fall left the label to sign with Kamera. A single was released late in 1981, *Lie Dream Of A Casino Soul,*

THE FALL

to be followed by an album, *Hex Enduction Hour,* in March 1982. In 1982 also Cottage Records in America issued *The Fall In North America* and a limited edition cassette, *Live In London,* came out in the UK on Chaos Tapes. Step Forward have also released an album entitled, *Early Years 77-79.*

In August 1982 The Fall (who have always rated highly in the UK music press readers' polls) toured Australia for the first time with a line-up that comprised Mark E. Smith (vocals), Marc Riley (guitar), Steve Hanley (bass), Paul Hanley (drums) and Karl Burns (drums), an original member who rejoined the group in 1982.

Fashion

In 1978 John Mulligan was making videos for the Stranglers/Steel Pulse tour. He later became involved with drummer Dik Davis while getting together a one-off art performance with the concept of the *Zero Zero* Samurai theme. This incorporated video screens and live drums, but further instruments were needed so Mulligan bought a bass and learnt the basics. This was the birth of Fashion.

Fashion began to play around Birmingham as a trio (with guitarist Luke). They formed their own label, Fashion Music, and secured distribution through Miles Copeland's IRS label. In late 1978

FASHION

came a debut single, *Steady Eddie Steady*, followed in 1979 by *Citinite*, and first album, *Product Perfect*. Two more singles, *The Innocent* and *Silver Blades*, eventuated; then, following an American tour, Luke quit and for a while, the band rested.

By 1980 Fashion were ready to re-emerge but, with various line-up juggles, it was not until 1981 that the membership was stable, with bassist Martin Recchi (ex-Dance) and guitarist and vocalist Dee Harris (ex-Ferrari and the Italians) joining Mulligan and Davis. The new members brought new influences and the band began moving towards an electronic jazz/funk style.

In November 1981 the group signed to Arista and released *Move On*. Another single, *Street Player-Mechanik*, followed in March 1982, as well as the album *Fabrique*.

Fingerprintz

Two Scots, a Pole and an Englishman is usually the start of a joke. But in this case, the above describes the nationality of the four members of Fingerprintz — Jimme O'Neill (guitar, songs and voice), Cha Burnz (lead guitar), Kenny Alton (bass) and Bogdan Wiczling (drums).

Fingerprintz have been together since 1977, when they played the London pub circuit before coming to the attention of Virgin Records. After supporting Bill Nelson and Lene Lovich (for whom Jimme wrote *Say When*), the band went into Alvic Studios and recorded *The Very Dab*, their first album, which was released in October 1979 in the UK. It was very much a Fingerprintz project, with the band producing themselves as well as designing the sleeve, and with Jimme writing all the songs.

Despite Ms Lovich's success, the songs of Jimme O'Neill and Fingerprintz have yet to receive the appreciation they deserve. *The Very Dab* boasted material that was occasionally enigmatic, as in *Wet Job*, a song about the "mysterious" death of Bulgarian defector and broadcaster George Markov; sometimes funny as in *Beam Me Up Scotty*, and always interesting.

Early in 1980 Fingerprintz toured the US for several weeks, sometimes supporting XTC and also playing headline dates of their own. Their reception was such that they returned on completion of their second long-playing record, *Distinguishing Marks*. Throughout October and November of 1980, Fingerprintz toured the American East Coast and Canada. On their return to the UK they were special

guests on a series of dates with Split Enz.

In August 1981 Fingerprintz released their most successful single, *Bohemian Dance*, full of ethnic, catchy riffs. Their third and undoubtedly best album, *Beat Noire*, was released soon after. *Bullet Proof Heart*, from the second album, was a strong FM radio favourite in Australia and America.

Although as The Portraits they supported Simple Minds on a UK tour, and as The Fixx they have built up a steady following on the London circuit, by and large the group has ignored the call of the road, preferring to concentrate on writing

FINGERPRINTZ

"There are more clowns than good guys in music. Rock'n'roll is simply an attitude — you don't have to play the greatest guitar."
— *Johnny Thunders, The Heartbreakers*

The Fixx

Based in London, The Fixx have been together in their present form since early 1980, first as The Portraits, then as The Fixx.

The decision to change the band's name and approach came when Jamie West-Oram, the last man in, joined after seeing an ad in Melody Maker. His addition made such a difference to the group — both musically and personally — that they decided to make a fresh start.

Giving up their jobs to concentrate on writing and rehearsing, The Fixx released a single, *Lost Planes*, on the independent 101 label. Around this time they sent a demo to producer Rupert Hine, whom they admired for his polished sound. With Hine

they recorded their debut album, *Shuttered Room*, and the singles, *Some People* and *Stand Or Fall*, released mid-1982.

THE FIXX

and rehearsing. They want to build up their following via their records before they go out on tour, though in late 1982 they intended setting up a UK tour on the strength of *Shuttered Room*.

The current line-up of The Fixx is Cy Curnin (vocals), Jamie West-Oram (guitar), Rupert Greenall (keyboards), Charlie Barrett (bass) and Adam Woods (drums).

Flaming Hands

Flaming Hands in their short two and a half year existence were one of the most respected and popular live bands in Sydney, with their intense '60s soul influenced music with early Jefferson Airplane overtones.

The group was formed by guitarist/songwriter Jeff Sullivan and singer Julie Mostyn (ex-Kamikaze Kids) in early 1980 with a line-up that included sax player Sluggo, keyboardist Steve Harris, bassist Richard Allen and drummer Michael Hiron. This line-up continued until late 1980 and recorded two singles for the independent Phantom label, *I Belong To Nobody* and *Wake Up Screaming*. In late 1981 there was a major split and only Sullivan, Sluggo and Julie Mostyn remained from the original line-up. The new recruits were New Zealanders Peter Bull (keyboards) and Grant Conner (bass, from Idiot Savant), and ex-Proteens drummer Allan Brown.

Flaming Hands recorded a third single, *Go Or Stay/It's Just That I Miss You,* in early 1982. Soon after, they supported The Clash on their Sydney dates and in May made their first tour interstate. Clash manager Bernie Rhodes became a Flaming Hands fan, expressing admiration for their "Voodoo Music". Later that year the group were dissatisfied with their progress and inability to gain a major record contract and broke up. Jeff Sullivan and Julie Mostyn are at present collaborating with other musicians on the formation of a new group, Tunnels and Trains.

Flash & The Pan

Flash & The Pan is the latest (and most durable) in a long line of alter-ego identities for master rock producers/songwriters/performers Harry Vanda and George Young. Since 1976 the pair have been responsible for three albums of inventive, illuminating, progressive rock, marked by a heavy emphasis on spoken-word vocal tracks. One major American reviewer said of the earliest Flash & The Pan efforts: "They sound like they've visited music in the Eighties and are ready to lead us across the threshold." This sentiment is obviously shared

JULIE MOSTYN OF FLAMING HANDS

by the Scandinavians, who have sent all three albums instantly to number one.

Originally intended as an engaging sidetrack while producing albums for AC/DC, Angel City, Rose Tattoo and Cheetah, the Flash & The Pan concept spread from two top three Australian hits to strong international acceptance and a moderate UK hit with *And The Band Played On (Down Among The Dead Men* in Australia).

Vanda and Young were members of Australia's most sensational hit act, the Easybeats. Their songs have been recorded by David Bowie, Grace Jones, Rod Stewart, Mott The Hoople, Peter Frampton, Suzi Quatro, Bay City Rollers, Divinyls, Sports, Plimsouls and many others.

For the third Flash & The Pan album, *Headlines,* Easybeats vocalist Stevie Wright was brought into the group to share vocal chores with George Young. With a working partnership going back almost 20 years, the three have struck up an exceptional level of empathy and security. The 1982 album sees the overt synthesizer sound of its two predecessors moved slightly to the left to accommodate a more basic rock approach, fleshed with layered vocals, dynamic structuring and some exhilarating music power. Tracks such as *Psychos On The Street, Love Is A Gun, Hey Jimmy* and *Waiting For A Train* surge with purpose, definition and a truly original style.

FLASH AND THE PAN

Fleshtones

In 1975 Marek Pakulski was making three dollars an hour inoculating sick fowl on a chicken farm in his home state of Maine, USA. One weekend he went to New York to visit old friend Keith Streng and the pair went on a bar crawl with Keith's high school friends Peter Zaremba and Brian and Gordon Spaeth. Keith suggested that Marek move to New York and he agreed immediately.

Shortly thereafter Keith and Marek were living in Queens in New York, and Marek discovered an old bass guitar in the basement. Keith

Fleshtones performed *Shadow Line* for the movie cameras in New York as one of the new music bands featured in the film, *Urgh! A Music War,* and that song appeared on the accompanying soundtrack album. They also played *Shadow Line* and *F-F-Fascination* for Thau's and Jimmy Destri's *2X5* album/concert, released in 1980.

Shortly after the *Urgh!* filming, The Fleshtones signed with IRS and rushed out to the West Coast for a whirlwind series of appearances, after having settled in with drummer Bill Milhizer in January 1980. In November 1980 IRS released a five-

THE FLESHTONES

soon dropped his former passion for the drums and took up guitar, and Peter dropped by one day with a handful of harmonicas. Inevitably, the trio decided to form their own band and The Fleshtones were born.

For three years the band struggled their way through a spate of drummers and ancillary musicians, although Brian and Gordon, playing tenor and alto saxes respectively, floated in and out of gigs with more freedom than any of the other one-time members. In 1978 Suicide's Alan Vega brought The Fleshtones to Marty Thau's attention and Thau signed the band to his adventurous but ill-fated Red Star Records. Red Star released The Fleshtones' first and only record of the '70s in mid 1979 — the single *American Beat.* The record captured the fuzzy reverb, tambourine and oohing backups that epitomise The Fleshtones' rootsy pop sensibilities.

The band continued to pack houses in New York and build their repertoire, and in March 1979 they won the first New York Battle of the Bands. In September 1980 the

> *"Synthesizers have bullied music into a kind of cold place. So much of the music that's being made at the moment is very earnest. It's enthusiasm that I'm looking for."*
> *David Bowie*

song 12 inch EP entitled *Up Front,* from which two cuts, *The Girl From Baltimore/Feel The Heat,* were released as a single early the following year in the UK.

After a debut US single for IRS in June 1981, *The World Has Changed,* The Fleshtones released their debut album, *Roman Gods,* in January 1982. In February ROIR released an LP-length cassette of material the group had recorded in 1978 under the title, *Blast Off!*

THE FLYING LIZARDS

The Flying Lizards

David Cunningham studied art in his native Ireland with a Dadaist teacher who would throw his paintings in the bin if he didn't like them. Interested in elements of chance — of which mistakes and incongruities are an essential part — and in the subordination of "ability" to "curiosity", Cunningham applied his sense of inquiry to theatre, film and experimental music. He performed with a 13 piece band, Les Cochons Chic, and made a solo album, *Grey Scale,* distinguished principally by its uneventfulness.

Having chosen The Flying Lizards as the name of a group unlikely to succeed, in early 1979 he disinterred Eddie Cochran's *Summertime Blues,* enlisted a former college friend, Deborah, on vocals and proceeded to disembowel it in the converted slaughterhouse which served as his studio. After it had been rejected by over a dozen record companies, Virgin finally decided to release it.

The British public loved it. For a followup, Cunningham chose *Money.* He began by throwing objects like rubber toys, cassettes, sheet music and telephone directories at the phone in order to achieve the banjo effect. This was recorded in the piano player's front room. Then he took the tape to the slaughterhouse and added the rest, using a borrowed drum kit. The recording costs were £6.50. The single was a huge hit in both the UK and Australia in 1979.

An album followed in 1980 and The Flying Lizards released another single, *Move On Up* (originally recorded by Curtis Mayfield) with Patti Palladin on vocals.

In 1981 The Flying Lizards' second album, *Fourth Wall,* was issued and featured guest appearances by Robert Fripp, Steve Beresford, Michael Nyman and Julian Marshall.

David Cunningham has worked with the Electric Chairs, (with and without Jayne/Wayne County), This Heat, The Pop Group, The Mo-Dettes, The Passage and Tony Sinden.

Ellen Foley

When Meat Loaf and his collaborator, Jim Steinman, were looking for a female singer for his band in 1977, they remembered Ellen Foley, whom they'd met a few years earlier when all three were part of the touring company of the National Lampoon Show. Ellen became the co-star of Meat Loaf's live show, adding her vocal chords to several songs on the million selling *Bat Out Of Hell* album.

Born and raised in St Louis, Ellen moved to New York in 1972 to pursue an acting career, working in off-Broadway and Public Theatre productions, and singing with a rock'n'roll band called Big Jive. After joining the National Lampoon Show (and meeting Meat Loaf and Steinman), she moved into television, sharing the lead in the NBC-TV mini-series, *3 Girls 3*, with Debbie Allen and Mimi Kennedy. That 1977 variety series led to more TV work, including appearances in soap operas, such as *Search For Tomorrow* (in which she played a deranged Nurse's Aide reject) and *One Life To Live* (a student radical).

In 1978 Ellen returned to the stage, appearing at the Kennedy Arts Centre in Washington, DC in Jim Steinman's play, *Neverland*, a rock'n'roll Peter Pan. Next came the lead role of Sheila in the Broadway revival of *Hair*, which led to a different role in the film version directed by Milos Forman.

While undertaking these myriad activities, Ellen was collecting material and planning her first solo album, *Night Out*, produced by Ian Hunter and Mick Ronson. Released in August 1979, the album saw her supported by an ensemble of notable musicians, including Ronson and Hunter. The material was all covers (including the Stones' *Stupid Girl*, Parker's *Thunder And Rain* and Rambow's *Night Out*) except for one song, *We Belong To The Night*, which was co-written by Ellen.

In early 1981 Ellen Foley released her second solo album, *Spirit Of St Louis*, which marked a radical change in direction for her. Gone was the powerhouse rock and in its place was a bizarre mixture of European cabaret and pop/rock balladry. The album was produced by Ellen's then-boyfriend, Mick Jones of The Clash, and half of the 12 songs were written by Jones and Clash cohort Joe Strummer. The album was recorded in England, where she lived with Jones, and featured The Clash and Ian Dury's Blockheads in various permutations as the backing musicians. *Spirit Of St Louis* was simply not what people expected from Ellen Foley and critical reaction and sales were disappointing.

ELLEN FOLEY

JOHN FOXX

John Foxx

John Foxx was born in Chorley, an industrial town in Lancashire, and attended school in the area. Having become interested in music by fooling around with tape recorders, he moved to London in 1974 and began writing material. He then formed Ultravox, with whom he toured extensively and made three acclaimed albums, *Ultravox, Ha! Ha! Ha!* and *Systems Of Romance*.

Foxx left the group in 1979, after deciding that it was easier to work with synthesizers alone than in a group. They replaced him with Midge Ure and achieved much greater success. Foxx formed his own label, Metal Beat, and arranged a distribution deal with Virgin Records. According to Foxx, his intention is "to put out records by people I like, usually on a one-off basis so that they have freedom to move on to another label if they choose to".

Foxx's first solo album, *Metamatic,* was released early in 1980 and contained 10 originals. A single, *Underpass,* was released with moderate success. *Metamatic* was produced by Foxx, engineered by Gareth Jones and recorded at Pathway Studios in London. Foxx played synthesizers and rhythm machines, alongside two other musicians, John Barker (synthesizers) and Jake Durant (bass).

During 1980 two further singles were released — *Burning Car* and *No One Driving* — and Foxx realised a dream by buying and fitting out his own recording studio. In early 1981 John Foxx recorded a new single there, *Miles Away,* which oddly featured a real drummer Edward

Case, and in late 1981 he released his second solo album, *The Garden,* which featured his own lavish colour booklet and prose poem.

Fun Boy Three

The Fun Boy Three story began in January 1981 when three members of The Specials — Lynval Golding (guitar), Terry Hall (vocals) and Neville Staples (vocals) — took the opportunity of an enforced break from recording, rehearsing and touring, to finish four demos with producer Dave Jordan. Among the tracks were Lynval's *Why,* later to appear on The Specials' *Ghost Town* EP, and an early cut of *The Lunatics.*

The Specials split up in mid 1981 after *Ghost Town* had gone number one in the UK singles charts. The internal tensions in the band that had always existed, eventually, almost inevitably, pulled them apart. The three Fun Boys took a calculated gamble in leaving such a successful group, but their first single, *The Lunatics Have Taken Over The Asylum*, rewarded them with a UK top 20 hit at the end of 1981.

From the outset The Fun Boy Three strove for a sound that was a world away from the pop ska and eerie mosaics of The Specials. Stripping the studio process down to

its most basic, they build their songs in layers over a rhythm box base, recording and mixing each track in a single take.

For a followup single in early 1982, the trio teamed up with the London based all-girl trio, Bananarama, on a cover version of swing bandleader Jimmie Lunceford's '30s standard, *It Ain't What Yo Do, It's The Way That You Do It,* which repeated the success of their debut.

The Fun Boy Three were attracted to Bananarama after hearing their debut Deram single, *Aie A Mwana,* and they have established a long-term working relationship with the girls. Almost half of the tracks on The Fun Boy Three debut album, *Fun Boy Three,* released early in 1982, feature the vocals of the Banana bunch. While The Fun Boys

sang backup vocals and played on the second Bananarama single, *He Was Really Saying Something.*

The *Fun Boy Three* LP was recorded in London with producer Jordan, the band commuting from Coventry every day, yet another example of their unorthodox way of working. The final two tracks had to be completed by Terry and Neville alone after the senseless and unprovoked knife attack in a club fracas on Lynval which almost cost him his life. The attack was sadly and savagely ironic, for both The Fun Boy Three and The Specials had always been vehemently opposed to violence, racism and repression. In 1983 Fun Boy Three were able to keep the momentum of their career going with the single *Tunnel Of Love* which jumped straight into the UK charts.

FUN BOY THREE

G

Gang Of Four

Jon King (vocals), Hugo Burnham (drums), Andy Gill (guitar) and Dave Allen (bass) met in Leeds in 1977. Dave waited for the others to graduate from college two years

group were invited to play Top Of The Pops. But when they were asked to drop an oblique reference to contraceptives in the lyrics to *Tourist,* they refused and so were dropped from the show.

Gang Of Four's debut album, *Entertainment,* was recorded in July 1979 and following its UK release the group embarked on a marathon US tour, headlining all but seven dates where they supported The Buzzcocks. Back in the UK, a national tour was lined up immediately to maintain momentum. They returned to tour America in March 1980 on completion of a deal with Warners to distribute *Entertainment* in North America.

The second album, *Solid Gold,* was recorded early in 1981 at Abbey Road Studios with New York producer Jimmy Douglass. The critical and public reception of the album was very disappointing and

Howlett producing, and it was preceded in May by the single, *I Love A Man In Uniform.*

THE GO-BETWEENS

Girlschool

Girlschool are Kim McAuliffe (vocals, guitar), Enid Williams (vocals, bass), Kelly Johnson (vocals, guitar), and Denise Dufort (drums).

If anyone still thinks heavy metal is an all male domain and something that only the lads can play properly, one listen to Girlschool will destroy that illusion.

In 1977 the nucleus of the band, McAuliffe and Williams, were playing under the name Painted Lady, and by March 1978 the name Girlschool, and the present line-up was established.

The band's debut single, *Take It All Away,* was released on the independent City Records label. Soon after, Girlschool supported Motorhead on a major British tour, and in 1979 they signed a worldwide contract with Bronze Records, working with producer Vic Maille on their second single, *Emergency,* released in February 1980. *Demolition* was the band's debut album, released in June 1980.

Constant touring paid off for the band when Sounds' Readers Poll had them at number two in the New Band section, and Kelly Johnson at number three in the Female Vocalist section.

With Motorhead the band recorded the *Saint Valentine's Massacre* EP in February 1981. The record went to number five in the English charts two weeks after release.

Hit And Run, Girlschool's second album, was released in 1981 and consolidated their position as one of the world's top heavy metal outfits. A third album, *Screaming Blue Murder,* appeared in late 1982.

GANG OF FOUR

later, before they committed the first of their ideas to vinyl on an EP released through the Fast Product independent label. It contained *Damaged Goods, Armalite Rifle* and *Love Like Anthrax.* Combined with two hot sessions on John Peel's show on Radio One and increasingly enthusiastic reviews and interviews, Gang Of Four signed a deal with EMI early in 1979.

A new single, *At Home He's A Tourist/It's Her Factory,* cracked the mid-reaches of the charts and the

the group encountered further problems in July of 1981 when in the middle of a US tour, Dave Allen walked out of the band. Sometime Talking Heads bassist, Busta Cherry Jones filled in for the remainder of the dates. Later in the year, Sara A Lee (formerly of Robert Fripp's League Of Gentlemen and Jane Aire And The Belvederes) became the permanent replacement.

This line-up recorded Gang Of Four's third album, *Songs Of The Free,* in February 1982, with Mike

Vic Goddard & The Subway Sect

Though Vic Goddard has always moved against the current musical trends, he has been able to retain credibility and a measure of popularity in his endeavours. In 1976 when he first formed The Subway Sect, in contrast to the prevailing punk scene, Vic developed an off-beat melodic sound, preferring to sing proper songs with proper tunes.

The original line-up of The Subway Sect which Vic formed in Bristol, England, comprised Paul Myers (bass), Robert Miller (guitar) and Paul Smith (drums), who was followed by Mark Laff and Rob Ward. After a move to London they rehearsed in The Clash's warehouse in Camden Town and when Clash manager Bernie Rhodes started his own Braik Records label, the first single he released was *Nobody's Scared*, in March 1978. In November of that year, Rough Trade released Vic's second, *Ambition*. In 1980 he released *Split Up The Money*, and his debut LP, *What's The Matter Boy*, both on MCA Records. In January 1981 Rough Trade released his fourth single, *Stop That Girl*.

In 1981 Vic disbanded The Subway Sect and set up a club called Club Left. Later that year though, he came across a band in a rehearsal studio who, with another singer, were doing covers of Goddard's songs. Vic immediately hired them (minus the singer!) and began playing regular dates at his own club. They had a single released on Club Left Records, *Stamp Of A Vamp*, late in 1981 and soon after signed to London Records. In May 1982 a single, *(Hey Now) I'm In Love*, and an album, *Songs For Sale*, were released.

> ## "Artists everywhere steal mercilessly all the time and I think this is healthy."
> — Peter Gabriel

The Go-Betweens

Brisbane's Go-Betweens' debut single, *Lee Remick*, was released on the independent Able label and attracted the interest of influential British DJ John Peel, and America's oddball Beserkley Records.

Although offered a trip to London the band stayed in Brisbane until a second single, *People Say*, was released, again on the Able label.

November 1979 saw bass player and vocalist Grant McLennan, guitarist and vocalist Robert Foster, and drummer Bruce Anton travel to England. There they recorded for independent Scottish label Postcard Records. The single, *I Need Two Heads*, was voted 'Single Of The Week' by Sounds, the same paper that praised The Saints' *I'm Stranded*, creating the interest for them to tour England.

Upon returning to Australia Lindy Morrison became The Go-Betweens' new drummer. The new trio released two singles — *Your Turn, My Turn* and *Hammer The Hammer* plus the superb *Send Me A Lullabye* album which was released in Australia by Missing Link Records and in England, with the addition of four tracks, by Rough Trade.

The band's second album, *Before Hollywood*, was recorded in England during October 1982 whilst the band were living in London. On the album the band were augmented by Bernard Clarke's organ/piano playing. The band recently added a fourth member, bass player Robert Vickers, a former member of The Riptides who had been living in New York. In May/June 1983 the group undertook a return Australian tour.

VIC GODDARD

GIRLSCHOOL

GO GO'S

The Go-Go's

When Charlotte Caffey, Belinda Carlisle and Jane Wiedlin formed the Go-Go's in 1978, few people, themselves included, would have predicted that they would become one of the top phenomena of the '80s. The Go-Go's are the first all-female band who write and play their own material to hit number one on the Billboard album charts. Their debut IRS album, *Beauty And The Beat,* sold over two million copies in the States and their single *Our Lips Are Sealed* went top 10 in the US, UK and Australia.

The Go-Go's struggle to establish themselves would have broken the spirit of lesser women. They honed their instrumental talents on the LA club scene, but for three years were virtually ignored by major record labels, who felt that an all-female line-up would not sell records.

By 1980 the current line-up was established. To counter the relative inexperience of vocalist Belinda Carlisle and guitarists Charlotte Caffey and June Wiedlin, they recruited bassist Kathy Valentine, who had previously joined

Girlschool on a short sojourn to England before illness forced her to depart, and drummer Gina Schock, a young veteran of Baltimore New Wave bands.

In April 1980 the band quit their day jobs to commit themselves totally to the group they'd been playing with during evenings and weekends for nearly two years. Forgoing a regular pay-cheque was a risky step — the group's manager, Ginger Canzoneri, even took out a loan on her car and pawned her jewellery to keep the band going. The risk was justified. Shortly

> **"A lot of people thought we were a punk band but that was the last thing we wanted to be. We just couldn't play our instruments that well."**
> — *Belinda Carlisle, The Go-Go's*

afterwards the band was invited to tour the UK with The Specials.

A single for England's Stiff Records, *We Got The Beat,* started a buzz in LA on the band and they were welcomed home as conquering heroines. Assured they would now get a new record deal, the band played a showcase at the Starwood in LA for record execs, but still encountered corporate resistance. Through their ability to sell out any club in LA, they eventually attracted the interest of IRS Records and the band recorded *Beauty And The Beat* for the label.

On the album's release, radio programmers were resistant to the idea of an all-female band, so the Go-Go's set out across America on a lengthy tour. By the end of 1981, *Beauty And The Beat* was climbing the US charts and the band landed the opening slot on The Police tour. Suddenly playing before 20,000 people a night, the Go-Go's made a lot of new fans. *Our Lips Are Sealed* took off on the singles charts, followed by *We Got The Beat.* Airplay finally boosted *Beauty And The Beat* to the number one spot on the album charts after an arduous seven-month climb.

In 1982 the Go-Go's embarked on a world tour to follow up on the huge international success of their debut album. They also released their second album, *Vacation,* which did not match the success of the first, despite featuring their re-make of The Olympics' soul classic, *Cool Jerk,* which was a live favourite.

Grandmaster Flash & The Furious Five

Grandmaster Flash is a 25 year old DJ, part of a young generation of disc jockeys who have radically changed the art of spinning records into the art of break-mixing, the science of montaging bits and pieces of different songs to create an entirely new sound. Equipped with two copies of a record, the DJ can concentrate on the "break" — that portion of a dance track usually 30 to 60 seconds long where the bass and percussion work out — and extend it indefinitely, dropping in fragments of other songs for melodic flash.

In the mid-'70s when Flash first began spinning in New York, there was a strong dichotomy between break music and disco. Flash was spinning for kids who preferred the tough funk not heard in adult-oriented discos. Rapping evolved out of the same milieu: the echo-chambered patter of the emcees who worked with break-mixing DJs provided cover for the jocks when they switched records. As young DJs moved away from the conventional blend-mix style toward the more revolutionary break-mix, emcees developed the elaborate rhymes and ensemble work which characterise rap on record today.

Flash developed his style by studying the top DJs in the New York clubs — names such as Cool Herc, Pete "DJ" Jones, Maboya, and Grandmaster Flowers. After he had acquired a big enough system (1100 watts, which was considered small) he gained his first emcee, Cowboy, and the two began playing in the New York parks to the kids. Soon after, Melly Mel and his brother Kid Creole (no relation to August Darnell) joined and the three emcees began developing their rap style, based on trading phrases like horn players.

The group were persuaded to take their act into the clubs and they soon proved to be a smash success. By the time the fourth emcee, Mr Nees, joined, the rappers had developed elaborate choreography and Flash had perfected his technique of spinning records so that he could make synthesizer-like noises as well as repeating phrases over and over at dizzying speeds.

In 1977 Raheim completed The Furious Five, but even though rapping had acquired large street popularity, they hesitated to visit the recording studio.

But in 1979 the success of the Sugarhill Gang's *Rapper's Delight* single, coerced them to record and they released two singles, *We Rap More Mellow* (under the pseudonym Younger Generation) and *Superrappin',* on the Brass and Enjoy labels, respectively.

In 1980 the group switched to the Sugarhill label and released the *Freedom* single, which garnered them a gold record. The group then toured extensively throughout America and released a second single on Sugarhill, *The Birthday Party.* On both of these records Grandmaster Flash & The Furious Five, in contrast to their live work, were backed by a studio band. But for his next release, *The Adventures Of Grandmaster Flash On The Wheels Of Steel,* released 1981, he chopped up a number of hits — including *Rapture, Good Times* and *Another One Bites The Dust* — to produce his own effects.

In early 1982, *Showdown* by The Sugarhill Gang Meets The Furious Five, was released and it was followed mid-year by his biggest hit, *The Message.* Later that year the group's debut album, *The Message,* was released.

GRANDMASTER FLASH AND THE FURIOUS FIVE

The Gun Club

The original Gun Club line-up was virtually a Fan Club presidents convention. Lead vocalist Jeffrey Lee Pierce was president of the Blondie fan club while guitarist Kid Congo (now with the Cramps) ran The Ramones fan club in Los Angeles. The band's first drummer headed a Mumps appreciation society, and his replacement. Terry

THE GUN CLUB

Graham, managed LA band The Weirdos.

Pierce had also worked as a record reviewer for LA fanzine Slash, which is affiliated with the record label of the same name, which in turn released the Gun Club's debut record, *Fire Of Love*, (issued elsewhere on New Rose Records).

Besides original material, *Fire Of Love* contained Pierce's arrangement of Robert Johnson's *Preaching The Blues,* and *Cool Drink Of Water.*

The Gun Club were one of the first signings to Chris Stein's Animal Records, along with Iggy Pop, John Cale, and Panther Burns.

Stein produced the band's second album, *Miami,* which featured backup vocals from Debbie Harry on one track. Besides the traditional *John Hardy,* the Gun Club tackled Creedence's *Run Through The Jungle.*

The next release was a five-track, 12 inch EP titled *Death Party,* produced by Stein and Pierce, and recorded at Blank Tape Studios in 1983.

The Gun Club's line-up at this stage was: Pierce (vocals, piano, guitar, and bass), Jim Duckworth (lead guitar), Dee Pop (drums and percussion).

Pierce has recently been spotted around New York clubs doing solo gigs.

NINA HAGEN

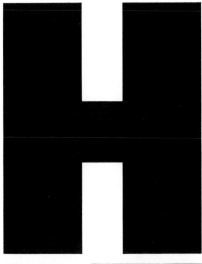

HAIRCUT 100

Nina Hagen

Nina Hagen was born in East Berlin on March 11, 1955, to actress Eva Marie Hagen and writer Hans Hagen. Her parents divorced when she was two and in 1965 the dissident poet/songwriter Wold Biermann entered her life as stepfather.

In 1972 Nina failed her entrance examination to the government-controlled East German Actors' School and she went to Poland for a few months, where she sang for the first time with a band. In 1973 she graduated with outstanding honours from the Studio fur Unterhaltungsmusik (Studio for Popular Music), and as part of her training toured East Germany for two months.

A few more years were spent touring East Germany with the Alfons Wonnberg Orchestra but, tiring of this, Nina decided to change her act and started her own band, Automobil. From then on she did full-scale concerts, often lasting as long as eight hours, with five hours of singing and three of dance music. Nina worked so hard she was forced by her doctor to take a break, but reappeared a few months later with a new band, Fritzens Dampferband (Fred's Steamboat Band).

Desiring a tougher sound, Nina left this band after a few months. After Wold Biermann was expelled from East Germany in 1976, Hagen decided to exit as well. She renounced her East German citizenship and received approval for her exit application in a record four days. On 9 December, 1976, Hagen arrived in West Germany and quickly signed a recording contract with CBS Germany.

She flew to London to get in touch with the music scene there, met The Slits and wrote some songs with Ari Up. On 10 August, 1977, in West Berlin she met the nucleus of her first band, guitarist Bernhard Potschka. He arranged for her to meet what became the original Nina Hagen Band: Manfred Praeker (bass), Herwig Mitteregger (drums) and Reinhold Heil (piano). This line-up recorded Nina Hagen's first two LPs in 1978 and 1979, which were best sellers in Europe and Japan. The second album, *Unbehagen (Ill At Ease),* sold more than a quarter million copies in Germany alone.

When Nina Hagen moved to the United States in 1980, Columbia Records released a four-song EP of the best cuts from her two German albums, including the classic *African Reggae.* A performing tour followed, but was cut short when she found she was pregnant. Nina moved to Los Angeles, where she prepared for the birth by doing yoga exercises and watching for UFOs. Cosma Shiva Hagen was born on May 17, 1982.

After the birth of Cosma, Nina felt the need for a spiritual cleansing and cut off all of her brightly coloured hair. She made a number of videos at this time and, in keeping with her shorn locks, she performed as a man.

At the end of 1981 Nina moved to New York where she recorded her first American album, *Nunsexmonkrock,* with Mike Thorne producing. The musicians on the album were Allan Schwartzberg (drums), Karl Rucker (bass, synthesizer), Chris Spedding (guitar), Paul Shaffer (synthesizer), Paul Roessler (piano, synthesizer) and Axel Gothe (sax and clarinet).

In conjunction with the release of the album, Nina Hagen did a US tour beginning May 1982. The touring band included Paul Roessler and Karl Rucker, as well as Steve Schiff (lead guitar), Pat Bulsara (rhythm guitar) and Paul Baker (drums).

Haircut 100

Haircut 100 was formed by singer/guitarist Nick Heyward, guitarist Graham Jones and bassist Les Nemes one Sunday afternoon in 1980. Nick hit on the name, when the three were sitting around trying to think up the silliest name they could for a group. Nick, Les and Graham had been friends since schooldays, they all had girlfriends who knew each other and they'd all been chucked by their respective ladies in the same week. This unfortunate event threw them more into each other's company, they started rehearsing and the band began to take shape.

With an unknown drummer, they played their first gig early in 1981 at a private pop concert in the Ski Club, a London gentleman's club. Soon after, Blair Cunningham, an American session drummer, was prised out of his band Shake, to become a permanent member. The first Haircut tape was made in early 1981, courtesy of engineer Karl Adams, later to become the band's manager. Sax player Phil Smith was working in the studio at the time and got drafted into the session. Soon after he was invited to join full time. He invited percussionist and conga player Mark "Ilford" Fox to a rehearsal and in December 1981 he also became a permanent member.

The demo tape which Adams took around the record companies took them by storm and in late 1981 Haircut 100 finally signed with Arista Records. The first single, *Favourite Shirts (Boy Meets Girl),* produced by Bob Sargeant, shot straight into the charts and by November 1981 reached top five in Britain. The group's second single, *Love Plus One,* released January 1, 1982, was a number one in the UK and top 10 in Australia, and even broke top 40 in the US. The release of their ambitious debut album, *Pelican West,* in February 1982 confirmed them as the top teen band in the UK, while also directing a great deal of serious critical acclaim toward them.

Visually, the group represented another tangent in the style cacophony known loosely as New Romantic.

Their collegian pullovers, generally wholesome appearance and cultivated naivety cast them into a realm of their own.

In January 1983 British teeny boppers were shattered by the news that heart-throb vocalist Nick Heyward was leaving for a solo career. The band had been recording a new album but it had been in a shambles since the previous November with only three vocal tracks completed. Percussionist Mark Fox stepped forward to take over the microphone.

HAYSI FANTAYZEE

Haysi Fantayzee

What Spandau Ballet began, Culture Club and Haysi Fantayzee have taken to outrageous extremes. As fashion standard bearers, Kate Haysi (Katherina Maria Garner), Jeremiah, and (manager/third member) Paul Kaplin have the rare capacity to still be able to turn heads in British public places.

"Our visual influences are along similar lines to our musical influences — very Dickensian, Hillbilly, Huckleberry Finn, style clothing. We like that sort of imagery," explains Kate, adding for good measure, "Was (Not Was) and the Tom Tom Club are probably the only '80's style music that's happened so far."

Haysi Fantayzee came to notice in 1982 with the quirky single *John Wayne Is Big Leggy*, followed by *Holy Joe* and *Shiny Shiny*. Their debut album, *Battle Hymns For Children Singing* (complete with booklet) appeared in 1983, by which time Police manager Miles Copeland had engaged them to compere a video programme for American cable TV featuring Spandau Ballet, Anti-Nowhere League, Wide Boy Awake and Steve Strange.

Kate and Paul live together on the top floor of an old underwear factory and devote most of their free time to developing their White Rasta dreadlocks and devising new clothing absurdities from any old junk they can lay their hands on. Occasionally they get around to playing some music.

Hitmen

The Hitmen formed in 1978 out of the charred ruins of Australia's legendary Radio Birdman. When that band broke up in England after an abortive tour, guitarist Chris Masuak and bassist Warwick Gilbert returned to Sydney and teamed up with singer Johnny Kannis who had previously performed on an irregular basis with Radio Birdman as Master Of Ceremonies.

In March 1979, after establishing a cultish following, The Hitmen signed to WEA Records and released their debut single, *Didn't Tell The Man*, in July 1979. Around this time the drumming position was stabilised when Mark Kingsmill joined.

Later that year Kannis released his only solo single, *King Of The Surf*, on RCA Records.

I Want You, The Hitmen's second single, was released in March 1980, and was well received although some critics thought they'd nicked more than a few ideas from Kiss. The band toured Australia supporting Tom Petty and The Heartbreakers.

The Hitmen went into the studio with producer Mark Opitz in late 1980 but during the sessions more member changes ensued. Second guitarist Tony Vidale left and was replaced by Brad Shepherd who hailed from Brisbane, where he'd played with the Fun Things and the 31st.

In April 1981 the band's third single, *I Don't Mind*, was released, followed in June by their self-titled debut album.

Warwick Gilbert left in September to pursue his career in graphic design, still maintaining his association with the band by creating the artwork for their posters and record sleeves. He was replaced by Tony Robertson who'd played with Shepherd in the 31st.

In March 1982 The Hitmen's WEA contract expired and they signed with RCA, releasing a single, *Everybody Knows (I Don't Like Love)* in April on RCA's Black label. Soon after, they recorded a second album, *It Is What It Is*, but suffered more changes prior to its release in November when Shepherd decided to leave and join Le Hoodoo Gurus. The Hitmen decided to continue as a four piece.

Holly And The Italians

In January 1979 Holly And The Italians were playing, to general approval, in Los Angeles. Phil Spector complimented them on their splendid version of *Chapel Of Love*. Kim Fowley, then aspiring to be the local punk Svengali, paid traditional lip service. Everything appeared to be all right.

However, Holly Vincent wasn't happy. Born in Chicago, bred in Las Vegas and matured in Los Angeles, she had no special interest in sun and beaches — in fact, she went to considerable lengths to avoid them. Feeling more affinity with events in London than those in California, and rapidly running out of interesting places to perform, she and Italians drummer, Steve Young, took off for London.

Once there they recruited a new bassist, Mark Sidgwick, and set about the complex business of finding work and building a reputation. By playing their demo tapes to booking agents, they managed to secure the first crucial engagements. Next they met rock writer Charlie Gillett, who helped them to record a single, *Tell That Girl To Shut Up*, released on his label Oval.

Their hard work on the London circuit, just as restricted in its way as

THE HITMEN

the one they had fled, and perseverance in the face of poverty, began to pay off. Courted by media and moguls alike, the group signed with Virgin.

Their first recording for the label was the single *Miles Away,* which lots of people liked but hardly anyone bought. To coincide with its release, they accepted an offer to be second-on-the-bill in a three-group tour with Selecter and The Bodysnatchers. Sandwiched between two ska bands, and foolishly assuming that they'd be given a fair hearing, they eventually retreated bruised and dispirited from small pockets of violent fans who were unwilling to have their diet upset by anything as presumptuous as a pop group.

Reeling from their first encounter with British fandom, they defiantly arranged their own tour under the banner *The Right To Be Italian.* That was also the title of their debut album recorded in 1981 in New York with Richard Gottehrer producing. In 1982 Holly dismissed Sidgwick and Young and recruited new Italians Kevin Wilkinson (drums), Bobby Collins (bass) and Bobby Valentino (violins, mandolin) for the recording of the heavily electronic second album *Holly Beth Vincent.*

Radalj (guitar, vocals), and Kimble Rendall (guitar, vocals).

Faulkner, Baker, and Radalj all came from Perth where they'd played in cult bands like The Scientists, The Victims, and The Mannikins. Rendall was a founding member of Sydney's XL Capris.

This line-up recorded a single — *Leilani/Leilani II,* for the independent Phantom label. After selling 1,000 copies the single was re-released through an arrangement between Phantom, and Big Time Records.

Hoodoo Gurus then suffered a major member change with Rendall and Radalj leaving, the latter to form cowboy rock'n'roll band The Johnnys.

The pair were replaced by Brad Shepherd (ex-The Hitmen), and (when the band decided to add a

> **"I'm the Gerald Ford of guitar playing. It's really terrible; every time we do a video or television I fall over."**
> — *Holly Vincent, Holly & The Italians*

HOODOO GURUS

Hoodoo Gurus
Hoodoo Gurus (at that stage prefacing their name with 'Le') made their first appearance on *Simon Townshend's Wonderworld,* an Australian kids' TV program. This was followed by another TV appearance, backing Phil Latterly and His Singing Dog on the national *Don Lane Show.* Not long after this they got serious about their rock'n'roll — a curious mixture of rockabilly, Merseybeat, psychedelia, Glitter, punk, and straight pop.

Hoodoo Gurus' initial line-up was: Dave Faulkner (guitar, lead vocals), James Baker (drums), Rod

bass player) Clyde Bramley (ex-The Other Side) was recruited. Hoodoo Gurus toured Australia with Gary Glitter and The Troggs and signed a long term recording contract with Bit Time Records (former home of Air Supply!).

Human League
The central nucleus of The Human League came together in June 1977 when Ian Marsh and Martyn Ware, two computer operator shift leaders, believed the world of synthesizers posed a more stimulating challenge. The right vocalist proved a critical

factor in their ambitions and after an agonising search, they finally found Philip Oakey waiting to be rescued from employment as a plastic surgery theatre porter. As The Human League, none were trained musicians, but they were single-mindedly united in the pursuit of electronics in music and their future application.

The final chapter in The Human League's initial evolution came with the recruitment of Adrian Wright in March 1979, who continues to function as the band's visual director by providing a constantly changing slide commentary from his huge collection of pop and comic artifacts to complement the music's visual energy.

Once Philip joined the band they were able to start playing around their hometown of Sheffield. They were one of the first entirely electronic bands to do successful live performances. They were brought to the attention of Bob Last of Fast Product in Edinburgh by a tape produced by the band in their living room on a two-track Sony tape-recorder. Two tracks were lifted from this to be released in June 1978. The Human League's first release, entitled *Electronically Yours,* featuring *Being Boiled/Circus Of Death,* garnered reviews and alternative chart entries in the USA, Belgium, Japan, Greece, France, Australia and Finland.

In April 1979 a 12 inch single entitled *The Dignity Of Labour* was released on Fast Product and was made single of the week in several UK music papers. Soon after, they signed to Virgin and toured Europe with Iggy Pop, taking in France, Spain, Germany, Italy, Holland and Belgium.

The Human League recorded the rhythm tracks of the debut album at the group's own studio in Sheffield on a TEAC four-track, before being taken to Red Bus Studios where, with the help of Colin Thurston, final overdubbing and mixing were completed. The resultant album, *Reproduction,* was released in October 1979 and met with considerable critical acclaim. *Reproduction* rightly established The Human League as one of the more futuristic and pioneering electronic pop/New Wave bands in Britain.

Soon after the band's fortunes took a temporary setback when, after Talking Heads leader David Byrne had expressly sought The Human League as special guests for their UK tour, they were pulled from the tour due to a misunderstanding by the promoter. What The Human League conceived for the tour was to pre-tape their live performance which would have resulted in the band appearing in the audience but

THE HUMAN LEAGUE

released an all-instrumental version of *Dare* under the name of The League Unlimited Orchestra which was an enormous success in the New York discos. This was followed by another hit, *Mirror Man*.

Hunters and Collectors

Melbourne-based new funk exponents Hunters and Collectors are: John Archer (bass), Geoff Crosby (keyboards), Doug Falconer (drums), Martin Lubran (guitar), Robert Miles (live sound), Greg Perano (percussion), and Mark Seymour (guitar, vocals).

The band first performed in May 1981, spending at least six weeks as the hippest outfit in Melbourne. Their music is unconventional, most notably in the way it is conceived and written. Usually in a rehearsal situation, songs are built on a basic rhythmical idea or theme, producing a fused sound where each player's contribution meshes and builds the sound and atmosphere to a peak of energy and mood. The band's lyrics are written by Perano, Seymour, and Crosby.

Hunters and Collectors' self-titled debut album was recorded between October 1981 and April 1982 at AAV studio in Melbourne, and produced by the band with engineers Tony Cohen and Jim Barton. Included with the album was a two-track EP. The album's single was *Talking To A Stranger*, which performed respectably on the Australian charts. The band's next release was a four track EP titled *Payload*.

These records came to the attention of Virgin records in England, who signed the band, prompting them to move to London for an extended period. Their second album is presently underway in Cologne, Germany, under the direction of Conny Plank.

not on stage. The promoter baulked at this and replaced them with a safer proposition. This eleventh hour withdrawal left the band without a tour to promote the album.

But after recording the second album, *Travelogue,* which was released in May 1980, the band undertook a headline tour of the UK and Europe, which saw their popular and especially, critical stocks soar.

Just before Christmas of 1980 The Human League suffered a split which at first was thought to be a terminal blow. Martyn Ware and Ian Marsh quit the band to form B.E.F. and work on their Heaven 17 project. Philip Oakey and Adrian Wright were left to pick up the pieces with only a week remaining before they were to undertake a European tour. Synthesizer player Jo Callis was recruited from Shake and The Rezillos, while Ian Burden was taken on because his girlfriend shared a house with Oakey. The final two members, 18 year old vocalists Joanne Catherall and Suzanne Sulley, were found by Oakey in a Sheffield disco and had never sung professionally before.

The Human League's new line-up exceeded all hopes with the release in October 1981 of their first album, *Dare,* produced by Martin Rushent. The record was a huge seller in the

UK, Europe and Australia as well as breaking the group in America, and spawned a rash of hit singles such as *Love Action, Don't You Want Me?* and *Open Your Heart.* The Human League had moved a long way from their original pioneering sound and it amply conveyed the group's intention to be an electronic Abba. The British daily popular press began to feature them on the front page, in the manner of Rod Stewart and Princess Diana (who hasn't had a decent hit in ages).

In 1982 The Human League

HUNTERS AND COLLECTORS

ICEHOUSE

Icehouse

Iva Davies (guitar and vocals) spent his late teenage years in Sydney with the ABC National Training Orchestra playing the oboe. But by the mid-'70s, he had been seduced by rock music and particularly the glam rock of Marc Bolan and David Bowie.

Iva taught himself to play the guitar and formed a number of garage bands which seldom got out of the garage. In 1977 he formed the first Flowers line-up with bassist Keith Welsh and keyboardist Michael Hoste. Davies and Hoste co-wrote a number of songs, some of which were to appear much later on the debut album, but Hoste left the group to complete his musical studies and was replaced by Anthony Smith. The line-up was completed in 1979 when drummer John Lloyd came up from Melbourne where he had played with Paul Kelly & The Dots.

By 1979 Flowers were still essentially a cover band — playing material by Lou Reed, Bowie, Bolan, Sex Pistols, Iggy Pop, Kinks,

Easybeats, etc. — but Davies' material was coming more to the fore and in early 1980 they signed to the independent Regular Records. The first release was the single, *Can't Help Myself*, an immediate top 10 hit in Australia. The second single, *We Can Get Together*, did even better, and in October 1980 the debut album, *Icehouse*, produced by Davies and Cameron Allan, was released and went instantly into the top 10. It became one of the biggest selling Australian albums of the year.

A third single, *Walls*, was released

early in 1981, going top 40, and soon afterwards the group were signed internationally by Chrysalis. Since a Scottish band already had the rights to the name Flowers, Davies and Co. changed their name to Icehouse. The album plus the singles, *We Can Get Together, Icehouse* and *Can't Help Myself*, were released in England, Europe and the US, and Icehouse spent most of 1981 touring those territories.

In late 1981 the group released a new single, *Love In Motion*, which gave them another top 10 hit in Australia, and then toured the country, with Scotland's Simple Minds supporting. By this time it was obvious that Icehouse as a group existed in name only. It was later revealed that Davies recorded *Love In Motion* all by himself and early in 1982 Icehouse ceased to exist as a formal group.

For the first six months of 1982 Iva Davies recorded the long-awaited second album in both Sydney and Los Angeles with co-producer Keith Forsey (Giorgio Moroder's drummer and production assistant). With the aid of a Linn drum computer, synthesizers and guitars, Davies recorded the album unassisted by other musicians.

The first single was *Great Southern Land* and it too became a top 10 Australian hit. When the album, *Primitive Man*, was released in August 1982 it immediately went

> "Initially I hated rock'n'roll. The fascination was that it had so many things wrong with it that I couldn't work out why it even existed... I ended up really liking all these people who sang out of tune, wrote simple songs that were clumsy, and had really bad production."
> — *Iva Davies, Icehouse*

BILLY IDOL

top 5. The second single, *Hey Little Girl* also went top 10.

In late 1982 Davies formed a new Icehouse line-up for touring, consisting of original Flowers keyboardist Michael Hoste and drummer John Lloyd, plus Melbourne guitarist Bob Kretschmer, and two musicians recruited from England: Guy Pratt (bass) a 20 year old veteran of Funkapolitan, Sylvain Sylvain and Killing Joke, and a founder of Children Of 7 (who had a UK top 30 hit with *Solidarity*). The other English musician was Andy Qunta (keyboards).

After Australia, the group embarked for tours in the UK, Europe and the States to support the release of *Primitive Man*. 1983 opened with *Hey Little Girl* climbing rapidly into the British charts and with Icehouse doing a series of UK TV dates to promote it, followed by some European support stints with David Bowie in May/June.

Billy Idol ▰▰▰▰▰▰

Billy Idol's career began with Generation X, one of the pioneering British punk outfits.

Billy, and bass player Tony James, came together in 1976 with Gene October and John Towe in a band called Chelsea. After three gigs Idol, James and Towe left October, who kept the name Chelsea for his new band.

Even before they completed their new line-up Billy and Tony had a name for their next band —

Generation X — the title of a mid-Sixties paperback on youth. Guitarist Bob 'Derwood' Andrews was discovered by Idol and joined the band immediately.

Generation X played their first gig in December 1976 and opened the Roxy Club in the same month. Towe left in April 1977 and Mark Laff replaced him as drummer in June.

Generation X made a number of albums, a tidy pile of singles and very little money before subsiding at about the same time as the punk boom. Idol re-appeared in 1982 under the management of Kiss Svengali Bill Aucoin with a self-titled album that has spawned two hits — *Hot In The City* and *White Wedding*. His band on the album, produced by Keith Forsey (who scored his own hit with *Take Me To The Pilot*), comprised Steve Stevens (guitars), Phil Feit (bass) and Steve Missal (drums).

INXS ▰▰▰▰▰▰

INXS began in early 1979 when vocalist Michael Hutchence visited Perth from his native Sydney and met up with the Farriss brothers — Tim (guitar), Andrew (keyboards) and Jon (drums). The three had been playing in various groups around Perth since their recent school days. Kirk Pengilly (guitar and sax) had gone to school with the Farriss brothers and soon joined to be followed by Garry Beers (bass), a friend of Hutchence.

After rehearsing for a few months, INXS decided to move to Sydney and began playing around the small pubs on the North Shore. The energetic music and presence of frontman Michael Hutchence soon attracted a large following and in early 1980 the group signed with the independent Deluxe Records.

INXS's debut single, *Simple Simon,* was released in June 1980 and was followed by their first album, *INXS,* produced by veteran rock musician Duncan McGuire, late that year. The single released from it, *Just Keep Walking,* was their first top 40 hit.

Their constant touring throughout 1981 in Australia caused a marked rise in their popularity and a common belief that they were the most promising young band in the country. In mid-1981 they released a cover of the Australian '60s rock classic, *The Loved One*, which gave them their first top 20 single. In September 1981 came their second LP, *Underneath The Colours*, which was produced by rock singer-songwriter Richard Clapton. The single from it, *Stay Young,* gave the band their second top 20 success.

For the first half of 1982 the group remained invisible, doing no live work, preferring to concentrate their energies on songwriting, particularly from the Michael Hutchence/ Andrew Farriss partnership which was proving to be the most productive. In August 1982 they released their first single on their new label, WEA, and it gave them another top 20 hit. A month later their third LP, *Shabooh Shoobah*

produced by Mark Opitz, came out and shot straight into the top 10. Their next single from the album was *Don't Change*. Their old label, Deluxe, released a compilation of greatest hits, un-issued out-takes, and non-album tracks entitled *Inxsive,* no doubt motivated by the band's defection to the powerful WEA conglomerate.

INXS

J

Joe Jackson

Joe Jackson was born in Burton-on-Trent and raised in Portsmouth, where he taught himself to play piano. After winning a place in the Royal Academy of Music he became a professional musician. Three years later Jackson began working in the cabaret circuit with his own band, Arms And Legs, in order to finance an album. He took his demo to London and received a publishing contract. The demo was brought to the attention of David Kershenbaum (then house producer for A&M), who produced the debut album, *Look Sharp*. A recording contract was not actually signed until August 1978, after the album was completed but before the band had ever played a live show.

Although Jackson had built up a degree of popularity in England, it was in America that his major success came. During April/May of 1979, the Joe Jackson Band — Graham Maby (bass), Dave Houghton (drums) and Gary Sanford (guitar) — embarked on

> "Groups like Genesis and Yes are about as exciting as a used Kleenex. It might as well be Tony Bennett. The Dead Kennedys, that sort of thing, sounds tame to me. It's like having a lot of damned noisy children misbehaving all over the house. You feel like telling them to go play in the garden."
> *Nick Lowe*

their first tour of America. At the end of June, *Look Sharp* entered the US top 20 and went gold. Meanwhile back in the UK, a stunning debut single, *Is She Really Going Out With Him?,* finally began to make an impression and peaked top 20.

In early 1980 the second album, *I'm The Man,* was released and charted high all over the world. As the band continued its extensive touring of Europe and America, Joe released his second UK single *It's Different For Girls.* It went top 5. The third album, *Beat Crazy,* released late 1980 showed a marked change from the earlier Spiv Rock, with its reggae influences, and consequently was not as successful as the previous albums.

Jackson broke up the Joe Jackson Band in early 1981 in order to do something completely different. The original idea was to put together a swing combo, play a few gigs around London and maybe record a single, but the concept became more enduring and in June 1981 the *Jumpin' Jive* album was released. After successful tours of America and Britain, and a top 20 album in the UK he broke up the band and moved to New York.

In June 1982, Joe Jackson's fifth album, *Night And Day,* was released. It was recorded in New York with David Kershenbaum and was reflective of the time he spent in that city. It proved to be one of his most successful albums yet and the first single from it, *Real Men,* was a worldwide hit. The other musicians featured on *Night And Day* were original bassist Graham Maby, drummer Larry Tolfree and percussionist Sue Hadjopoulos. For the remainder of 1982 Jackson toured Europe and America, augmenting his band with two keyboardists, Al Weisman and Joy Askew. *Night And Day* has had an astounding effect on Joe's career, transforming him from occasional New Wave hitmaker to mass-appeal AOR superstar. Critics have dubbed him "a new age Duke Ellington" and the song *Steppin' Out* was actually nominated for a dreaded Grammy.

The Jam

The genesis of The Jam, one of the pioneering bands in New Wave music, goes back to the Surrey schooldays of lead singer/guitarist Paul Weller and drummer Rick Buckler. These two would meet during lunch breaks and jam with other school musicians. The band's name was inspired by these jams.

In time guitarist Steve Brookes and bass player Bruce Foxton joined and The Jam began playing youth/social club gigs. Eventually

they became popular enough to land work in London. During those early days Steve decided to leave and The Jam opted to remain a three piece line-up, pounding out rock'n'roll inspired by the first English mod movement of the early '60s — vibrant, catchy and concise power rock in the vein of Weller's heroes The Who.

In February 1977 a representative of Polydor arranged the recording of a demo tape and eventually a recording contract. The Jam's first single, *In The City,* made the lower reaches of the British charts and was followed by their debut album of the same title, which remained in the charts for four months. Next up was the single, *All Around The World,* which went to number 13 and later in 1977 came *The Modern World,* and a second album *This Is The Modern World.*

News Of The World, The Jam's first single of 1978, was followed by a cover of The Kinks' *David Watts* and the Springsteenish *Down In The Tube Station At Midnight.* All three

JOE JACKSON

singles charted. Then came the critically acclaimed third album, *All Mod Cons,* which is still considered one of The Jam's finest moments.

If The Jam weren't already popular enough, 1979 saw their following increase even more. A revived interest in Mod culture and music, courtesy of the movie *Quadrophenia,* saw the band's popularity skyrocket overnight. Two more singles, *Strange Town* and *When You're Young,* fared moderately well on the charts, but the next release, *Eton Rifles,* shot to number three. A fourth album, *Setting Sons,* debuted on the album charts in the same position.

1980 was just as good a year for The Jam. Their next single, *Going Underground*, went straight to number one in March as did *Start* in September. At one point early in 1980, The Jam had five singles at once in the top 50.

It was a long wait for *Sound Affects*, the fifth album which displayed a sophisticated redefining of The Jam sound. Through 1981 Jam-mania continued on the pop charts, with the hits *That's Entertainment, Funeral Pyre* and *Absolute Beginners* — the latter manifesting the trio's growing obsession with brass sections.

The phenomenal success of The Jam had, until 1982, been confined

The final album, *Dig The New Breed,* was an excellent value 14-track live anthology, featuring performances

> **"I think that punk and new wave and new new wave and no wave and Adam & the Ants all have a certain place and have a certain part of people's lives that they're gonna influence."**
> — *Southside Johnny*

"punk funk" scene, has a very long and obscure history in the music business, including a stint playing bass with Neil Young.

But it was not until the release of his first Motown album, *Come Get It* in 1978 that he achieved notoriety. Hailing from Buffalo, New York, James emerged sporting shoulder-length braids, leather gear and a posture as the new super stud. Hailed as the new successor to George Clinton and Parliament/ Funkadelic, James released two more albums in the late '70s, *Bustin' Out Of L. Seven* and *Fire It Up,* which boasted impressive sales.

Rick James moved to California in 1980 and lived in one of Randolph Hearst's old mansions. But the laid-back lifestyle of the West Coast did not agree with him and the album he produced there, *Garden Of Love,* was a disappointment. James moved back to Buffalo the next year and the change did him good, because his fifth album, *Street Songs,* soared into the mega-league, remaining on the top of the US charts in 1981 for 22 weeks. The album garnered two smash hit singles, *Give It To Me Baby* and *Super Freak,* the latter becoming his signature tune. *Throwin' Down* was slightly less of a success, spawning two moderate hits, *Dance With Me* and *Standing On The Top.* Late in 1982 Rick produced and guested on tracks for a Temptations reunion album.

Japan

Japan endured the full range of critical reactions after their formation in 1976 after schooldays in Lewisham, South London. David Sylvian (vocals and guitar), Mick Karn (bass), Richard Barbieri (keyboards), Steve Jansen (drums)

THE JAM

to England. This situation was effectively altered by a sixth album, *The Gift,* and the double-sided hit *Precious/A Town Like Malice.* The former track made strong impact on the US disco charts and the latter became the group's first ever Australian hit. This hit was followed by *The Bitterest Pill* and its twin-track flipside *Pity Poor Alfie/Fever.* The international breakthroughs were not to be pursued. In October 1982 The Jam announced that it was disbanding, insisting that the unit had attained all possible success and that they were all (read Weller) disillusioned by the deceit that was rampant in the music industry. As a farewell gesture, they undertook a final British tour, culminating in early December with a series of concerts at London's Wembley Stadium. The final single, *Beat Surrender,* was marketed as a limited-edition twin disc set, with a remake of the Edwin Starr hit *War.*

from the 100 Club in 1977 through to the Glasgow Apollo in 1982.

During August 1982, original Jam member Dave Weller, co-writer of *This Is The Modern World* and *In The Streets Today,* died of acute heroin poisoning. His poetry collection, *Tales From Hostile Street,* has been published by Riot Stories, Paul Weller's book publishing company.

Paul Weller, once voted by the readers of New Musical Express as "the world's most wonderful human being", signed a solo recording deal (reportedly for £200,000) with one arm of the deceitful music industry. In March 1983 he released his first solo single *Speak Like A Child,* calling his new line-up Style Council. It was top three within a matter of weeks.

Rick James

Rick James, who with Prince has been labelled a prime mover of the

RICK JAMES

JAPAN

DAVID JOHANSEN

and Rob Dean (guitar) were heaped with scorn when they appeared at the fag end of the glam period in satins, long hair and stacked boots. The group's three albums for Ariola in the late '70s — *Adolescent Sex, Obscure Alternatives* and *Quiet Life* — were ignored by the public and critics alike, and not even an attempt at white disco in 1979 with a single, *Life In Tokyo* produced by Giorgio Moroder, could improve their popularity. Guitarist Rob Dean left at this point due to the dominance of synthesizers in the group's sound.

In 1980 Japan left Ariola and signed with Virgin and their debut album and single for the label were both titled *Gentlemen Take Polaroids.* In tune with the group's new musical style, based on the white disco sound of producer Giorgio Moroder, they also changed their image to coincide more with the new emerging Romantic look. Surprisingly, both moves worked and the band suddenly found themselves in favour.

In May 1981 Japan released another single, *The Art Of Parties,* which became a hit in Britain. They then embarked on their first tour of the UK in over two years though in that period they had had three sell-out tours of Japan, where they are now one of the country's biggest foreign bands — Sylvian's androgynous appearance being the stuff that Nippon teenybop dreams are made of.

In late 1981 Japan released their fifth album, *Tin Drum,* and the *Vision of China* single which even won them critical raves. To coincide

with it, Mick Karn held his first major sculpture exhibition which was widely acclaimed.

Other members have also made advances outside the group. David Sylvian recorded a single with Yukihiro Takahashi of Yellow Magic Orchestra, and Jansen took photos and wrote poetry for Karn's exhibition catalogue.

Before the split, Ariola/RCA issued a compilation of the first three albums, titled *Assemblage.* The American market also has an interesting compilation — an album containing half of *Gentlemen Take Polaroids* and half of *Tin Drum.*

The group was inactive for most of 1982, until they commenced a British tour in October which was inspired by the huge success of the *Tin Drum* album. However, on completion of the tour, the group disbanded. A double live LP, *Oil On Canvas,* followed.

David Johansen

In the early '70s The New York Dolls were being hailed as the best chance America had of producing a band with the style, power and rock'n'roll spirit of The Rolling Stones, but owing to numerous personality clashes within the band, The Dolls never fulfilled their early promise. However, lead singer David Johansen has emerged as one of the most impressive vocalists in the New Music, while his old Dolls cohorts, Sylvain and Johnny Thunders are still making tough, urban rock'n'roll records.

Johansen hails from Staten Island, New York. His earliest musical memories involve, besides singing along with songs on the radio, demolishing his older sister's record collection. As he remembers: "I used to put her records in the oven, melt them down and make things out of them. I'd say, 'Hey look at the neat potato chip tray I made and she'd yell, 'Oh no!, not 'Johnny B. Goode'."

During the mid '60s, David started listening to records instead of destroying them. The earliest influence was British rock'n'roll from The Stones, The Animals, The Pretty Things and Them. After playing with a few small-time bands, Johansen was involved in the formation of The Dolls, who had a brief, much-mythologised career, centering around The Mercer St Arts Theatre and the Manhattan club scene, that spawned two albums in 1973 and 1974: *New York Dolls* (produced by Todd Rundgren) and *Too Much Too Soon* (produced by Shadow Morton).

Four years after The Dolls' demise, David returned to the studio with producer Richard Robinson to record his first solo album, *David Johansen*, an effort which received unusually high praise. At this stage the Johansen band included Thomas Trask (guitar), Frankie La Rocka (drums) and, for a short period, former Dolls member Sylvain Sylvain (guitar).

Johansen spent the early part of 1979 touring before disappearing into the studio to record *In Style* which he co-produced with Mick Ronson. There was a two-year gap before David re-entered a studio and produced his third solo album, *Here Comes The Night*. Co-produced by David with Barry Mraz, it was his most rock-oriented album to date. It also marked the first recorded collaboration with former Beach Boys sideman Blondie Chaplin, who, as well as co-writing most of the material was also a member of Johansen's touring band. The other musicians featured on *Here Comes The Night* were Ernie Brooks on bass (formerly with the Modern Lovers), Tony Machine on drums (ex-Machine and The Dolls) and Tommy Mandel on keyboards (formerly with Ian Hunter).

1982 saw the release of the dynamic *Live It Up* album, recorded at Boston's Paradise Theatre on February 4-5. With an almost entirely new band, comprising Machine, Huw Gower (ex Records) on guitar, Charlie Giordano on keyboards, Brett Cartwright on bass and David Nelson on guitar, Johansen tore through a fiery Animals medley, the Foundations' *Build Me Up Buttercup,* the Cadets' *Stranded In The Jungle*, the Four Tops' *Reach Out,* the Ronettes' *Is This What I Get For Loving You?* and a number of his own "classics", including *Melody* and *Frenchette.*

Johansen commands a fiercely loyal following and a number of bootlegs of his live performances are in wide circulation, particularly of a CBS radio-only live promo disc which was distributed early in his solo career.

Linton Kwesi Johnson

Linton Kwesi Johnson was born in rural Jamaica in 1952 and moved to Britain in 1963 with his mother, settling in Brixton, London, where he has lived ever since. On leaving school he worked for a local tailor's

LINTON KWESI JOHNSON

"I didn't want to be a singer. No, I wanted to be an air stewardess and still do. . . I'm not really cut out for this business."
— Annabella Lwin, Bow Wow Wow

firm and later for the civil service, while at night he studied and finally obtained an honours degree in sociology from the University of London.

During this time, Linton became involved with the British Black Panthers, who were to have a profound effect on his career. The Panthers introduced him to established political thought, disciplined political action and the growing American black power movement with its compelling literature and personalities: Bobby Seale, Huey P. Newton, Eldridge Cleaver, Malcolm X and others.

It was not long before Linton felt compelled to flex his own literary muscles. He has been writing since 1971, his work gaining ever increasing attention and respect, and is the author of two widely-acclaimed volumes of verse, *Voices Of The Living And The Dead* (1974) and *Dread Beat And Blood* (1975). The main musical source of creative energy for Johnson's poetry was reggae. "Whenever I wrote I had a reggae bassline in my head," he stated. Besides the reggae rhythms which permeate his poetry, Linton took much from the style and language of the reggae DJ lyricist, artists like Big Youth, U Roy, Dillinger and their many counterparts.

In November 1977 Linton Kwesi Johnson — at that time alias Poet And The Roots — made his recording debut with a four-track 12 inch EP for Virgin Records, featuring two poems from *Dread Beat And Blood* intoned over powerful reggae rhythms. It was the start of a unique synthesis of poetry and music.

In August 1978 Poet And The Roots' first album, *Dread Beat And Blood,* was released to unanimous acclaim from the British music press. Produced by Johnson and engineered by British club maestro Dennis Bovell, the album was a landmark in British reggae. In 1979 he switched to Island Records and the first release was the *Forces Of Victory* album. Musically, it was more sophisticated and melodic than his previous work and featured some innovative dub effects.

In 1980 Johnson released his second Island LP, *Bass Culture.* Again the themes were police oppression, racist politics, the inevitable confrontations between the authorities and black youth in a Britain which prefers to ignore its ethnic minorities.

Grace Jones ▋

Hailing from Jamaica, Grace came from a family which enjoyed great social status. Her great uncle had been a bishop and most of his descendants were either ministers or local politicians. Her father was a preacher who emigrated to America while Grace was still in her infancy, leaving her behind to grow up running loose in a small army of siblings, cousins and unspecified relations.

In her teens Grace rejoined her father, who was then preaching in Syracuse, New York. Grace found herself swamped by the rampant consumerism of America after the rural paradise of Jamaica, and at school, this manifested itself in her behaviour. She railed and swore,

wore Afros before they were fashionable, showed off her breasts and spat blood. In her report card she was described as socially sick. She was always more of a tomboy, something she believes is a result of a biological tangling at birth when she believes she and her twin brother were born with each other's chemistry.

Grace toyed with respectability long enough to enter college, but soon rebelled. She joined the roster of the prestigious Wilhelmina Modelling Agency and at the same time as pursuing her acting career,

GRACE JONES

she enjoyed New York's social life. She haunted fashion shows, polysexual baths, multimedia studios, salons, fist bars and openings and was seen with anybody that mattered in that city.

By this time Grace's brother was in Paris. She decided to join him and, with friend Jerry Hall, they soon became the two hottest models in Paris. Grace was on the covers of Elle, Vogue and Stern. She travelled through Europe taking advantage of her fluency in French, Italian and Spanish. A cardinal in Milan offered her unofficial marriage, and when she refused he shot himself. While mourning his passing, she advertised hair spray, canned peas and

tampons and tried jumping from a cliff, but only succeeded in spraining her ankle. Healed, she travelled to Africa, Japan and South America on modelling assignments and in Buenos Aires, she made a movie.

Singing has always ranked among her obsessions and, disillusioned with modelling, Grace set her sights on music — acquiring a manager, a publicist and a record label, Island. Tom Moulton, the master of the disco mix, was hired as her producer and *I Need A Man* was unleashed on the public to instant acclaim. She began performing at Les Mouches and was the first performer to appear at a live concert at New York's Studio 54 — the mecca of disco.

Grace released three albums in the late '70s — *Portfolio, Fame* and *Muse* — but it was when she was teamed with the hot reggae producers, Sly Dunbar and Robbie Shakespeare, for 1980's *Warm Leatherette* that she received true musical respect from the critics rather than the fashion designers. This album was followed by *Nightclubbing* in 1981 and *Living My Life* in 1982 (both with Sly and Robbie). The former was highlighted by a compelling version of Vanda & Young's Flash & The Pan song *Walking In The Rain.* Grace Jones' shows have been described as both a "total extravaganza" and a "sinister spectacular". She is a mixture of comic-strip fantasy and jungle book myth and she parlays this into one of the most theatrical performances in contemporary music. For one show she wore a leopard skin leotard and climbed into a cage with a live tiger!

IGNATIUS JONES

Ignatius Jones

Ignatius Jones reached legendary status in Australian rock by fronting the outrageous and often obscene shock/horror group, Jimmy and The Boys, who pioneered the use of theatrical trappings for Australian bands. Their act featured S&M, transvestism, self-mutilation, drug abuse, inebriation, simulated sex and mock rape in a blisteringly-paced tribute to cultural degeneracy.

Since formation in 1976, the central duo of Ignatius and transvestite keyboards player Joylene Hairmouth was surrounded by various combinations of backing musicians.

Though the group only recorded two studio albums, *Not Like Everybody Else* from 1980 and 1981's *Teddy Boys Picnic*, they were one of the most popular live acts in Australia. In 1981 they scored their only top 10 single with *They Won't Let My Girlfriend Talk To Me*, written by Split Enz leader, Tim Finn.

In January 1982 Jimmy and The Boys broke up and, shortly after, Ignatius moved to the theatre stage, playing the dual roles of Eddy and Dr. Scott in the Australian revival of *The Rocky Horror Show*. This wasn't the first time Ignatius, born of Spanish parents in Manila, had been

involved with non rock'n'roll areas of performance. From an early age he'd been involved with drama and at the age of 16 he joined a major ballet company, but unfortunately he broke both his ankles shortly after, which somewhat curtailed his dancing career, though it did not dull a stunning evil wit.

In early 1982 Ignatius released his first solo single, *Like A Ghost*, which was penned by The Church's Steve Kilbey. This has become a hot dance club favourite on the American west coast. At the end of 1982 Jimmy and The Boys temporarily reformed for a national tour, which resulted in a live album, *In Hell With Your Mother*. At last report, Warner Bros had signed him to a six-album American recording deal.

Joy Division

As a group Joy Division only lasted three years, but their importance

and influence on the contemporary English music scene cannot be overestimated.

Joy Division began life in 1977 in Manchester under the name of Warsaw. The line-up was Ian Curtis (vocals), Bernard Albrecht (guitar), Peter Hook (bass) and Stephen Morris (drums). By 1978 they had changed their name to Joy Division and recorded an EP, *An Ideal For Living*, on the independent Enigma label. In 1979 they signed to Factory Records and released their first single, *Transmission*, and the debut LP, *Unknown Pleasures*, which received rave reviews from the English music press (no mean feat).

In April 1980 a second single, *Love Will Tear Us Apart*, garnered great critical acclaim and was closely followed by their second album, *Closer*, hailed on all sides as a masterpiece. On the eve of the album's release, Ian Curtis committed suicide by hanging,

JOY DIVISION

"Ariola signed us for our appearance. They didn't hear the music, they weren't that kind of company. We'd take tapes to them and they'd sit there with stopwatches. If a song didn't reach the chorus in the first 30 seconds it wasn't right."
— David Sylvian, Japan

leaving behind a wife and child and a reputation for making intensely emotional music that time has not dimmed.

In August 1981 Factory released a double retrospective album of the band, *Still*, which contained two sides of studio material (some new and others released on obscure issues) and two sides recorded live at Joy Division's last gig at Birmingham University on May 2, 1980.

After Curtis' death on May 18, 1980 the remaining three members decided to continue on under the name of New Order. The amazing popularity of Joy Division can be measured by the great number of bootleg albums that have appeared since their demise.

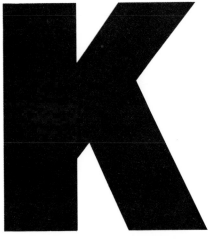

K

(keyboards), Steve Askew (guitars), Nick Beggs (bass) and Jez Strode (drums, electric percussion). Vocalist Limahl happened by a little later, having answered a classified ad, and entered into a songwriting partnership with Nick Beggs. His diverse background had embraced a number of stage roles and even pantomime.

Citing influences as diverse as Frank Zappa, Kate Bush, The Tubes and Bill Nelson, Kajagoogoo recorded their debut single, *Too Shy,* late in 1982. As can only seem to happen in the British Isles, it stormed to number one, staying there for two weeks. A follow-up, *Ooh To Be Ah,* entered the charts in the 20 spot at the beginning of April 1983, fanning the flames of their scream-teen popularity.

Kajagoogoo

Any claims by Kajagoogoo to the effect that they are not trying to bite off a little of the gigantic Duran Duran teenybop audience, no matter how sincerely expressed, should be disregarded entirely. In fact, it's amazing that it has taken so long for the British rock marketing machine to come up with a viable challenge.

Hailing from Leighton Buzzard, the group first assembled as a quartet, comprising Stuart Neale

KISSING THE PINK

KAJAGOOGOO

The first Kajagoogoo album, containing both their hit singles, is titled *White Feathers.*

Paul Kelly & The Dots

In his late teens, Paul Kelly began writing and publishing poetry and short stories, at the same time writing songs inspired by a long-standing involvement with the music of Bob Dylan. But nothing much was happening for him in his hometown of Adelaide in regards to music, so in 1977 he moved to Melbourne and drifted into the inner-city rock scene. He assembled a loose-knit outfit called The High Rise Bombers and they quickly became one of Melbourne's major underground live attractions.

Despite their powerful and innovative attack, the Bombers began to feel the strain of having three top writers in the one band and broke up without releasing any vinyl. Guitarist Martin Armiger (formerly of the legendary Bleeding Hearts) left to join The Sports, while drummer John Lloyd split for Flowers (now Icehouse). Paul Kelly went on to form The Dots, who featured a stripped-down guitar sound that's been a feature of the band ever since. They recorded an independent EP early in 1980 and on the strength of this they were signed to the Mushroom label.

PAUL KELLY AND THE DOTS

Their first single, *Seeing Is Believing,* was released in May 1980 and throughout that year they recorded their debut album with three producers (Martin Armiger, Joe Camilleri and Trevor Lucas) and a succession of changing line-ups. The second single, *Billy Baxter,* was released in October 1980 and reached top 40 status. The album *Talk* emerged in March 1981 and the band's line-up at that stage was Paul Kelly (guitar and vocals), Tim Brossnan and Mick Holmes (guitars), Alan Brooker (bass) and Tony Thornton (drums).

In late 1981 The Dots journeyed to the Philippines and recorded their second album, *Manila.* The completion of the album was long delayed by line-up changes and the time Kelly needed to recover from a severe beating he received in Melbourne. The album was finally released in September 1982.

Though Paul Kelly's career has been very sporadic, he remains one of the most respected songwriters in Australia, receiving heavy praise from such peers as Joe Camilleri, Iva Davies, Don Walker, Doc Neeson and Paul Hewson. He regularly writes songs with Joe Camilleri from Jo Jo Zep and occasionally appears on stage with the band. One of his "guest" performances was captured on the *Mushroom Evolution* triple concert album.

Kid Creole & The Coconuts

The Coconuts' roots stretch way back. Brought up in the New York Bronx, August Darnell (alias Kid Creole) cites this cross-cultural centre as one that has most affected him, musically, throughout his career.

It was not until the mid '60s that Darnell first put these influences into any kind of shape. Together with guitarist-keyboardist Stony Browder he formed The In Laws. At this stage they were merely rearranging Beatles and Motown

tunes, but in essence, this was the blueprint for what was to become Dr Buzzard's Original Savannah Band in the early '70s.

At first The Savannah Band were resisted by audiences unwilling to accept their particular sound — a mix of soul meets big band at the gates of the rock garden. But they scored almost immediately with their first single, *Cherchez La Femme,* and their debut self-titled album. People had decided, quite wrongly, that they were a disco band. August and Stony, together with vibes player and orchestrator, Andy Hernandez, vocalist Cory Daye and drummer Micky Seville, scooped up the loot and left for the West Coast to start work on their second album.

When the record was released in 1977 August returned to an empty apartment in New York. His live-in lady had upped and left — for good. To cap it all the record flopped. When the third album went the same way, The Savannah Band called it a day late in 1977. From there Darnell threw himself into numerous projects — there was Gichi Dan's *Beachwood No 9,* a combination of calypso and disco, then a meeting with Ze Records supremo Michael

Zilkha resulted in work on Cristina's album as well as the James Chance/Black/White connection; and Don Armando's Second Avenue Rhumba Band and a near hit single in Britain with *I'm An Indian Too.*

Meantime he was still working on tunes for Chappell Music along with Andy Hernadez. But Chappell were not impressed with their output and disparagingly called them Banana Boat songs. Nevertheless, the indefatigable Darnell along with Hernandez put together The Coconuts to perform these songs.

The first Kid Creole & The Coconuts album, *Off The Coast Of Me,* was released in 1980, and met with muted enthusiasm. But their second, *Fresh Fruit In Foreign Places,* released in 1981 was unanimously acclaimed and they became the darlings of the English music press. Their third LP, *Tropical Gangsters,* released in 1982, was helped by a media blitz organised by their record company — a series of showcase gigs, TV shows and videos firmly established them in the UK.

Darnell's sidekick, Andy Hernandez, had a big English hit in 1981 with the single, *Me No Pop I,* under the name Coati Mundi.

Greg Kihn Band

In seven years, Greg Kihn has grown from scrambling for loose change on the Berkeley campus to leader among San Francisco-based rock'n'roll bands.

Kihn arrived in Berkeley from Baltimore late in 1974 and joined the Berserkley label early the next year. Kihn contributed two songs to the infamous *Berserkley Chartbusters* album (released in 1975) in addition to handling other utility recording chores, such as helping out with the backing vocals on Jonathan Richman's classic, *Roadrunner.* His onstage appearances at first were limited to vocalising with

KID CREOLE AND THE COCONUTS

KILLING JOKE

Berserkley rockers Earth Quake. Kihn formed his own group soon after crossing paths with bassist Steve Wright and his longtime rhythm section partner, drummer Larry Lynch. The Greg Kihn Band began holding down regular Sunday night gigs and Kihn's material began to take shape.

The first full Greg Kihn album, released in '75, featured Earth Quake guitarist Robbie Dunbar, a role he also played in the clubs until early '76, when Kihn drafted Dave Carpenter, a veteran of numerous Berkeley bands. With Carpenter, the unit gelled. The second LP, *Greg Kihn Again* (released in '77) contained Kihn's reworking of Bruce Springsteen's *For You* with an arrangement Springsteen himself eventually adopted (giving Kihn due credit), as well as a handful of memorable Kihn originals such as *Madison Ave Man* and *Real Big Man*.

By the time the band's third LP, *Next Of Kihn*, was released the following year, Berserkley action

Kaufman reached its fullest expression with the release of their seventh LP, *Rockihnroll*, in 1981. album remained in the US top 40 for over six months, peaking in the top 20, and it spawned the worldwide hit single, *The Breakup Song (They Don't Write 'Em)*.

A second single, *The Girl Most Likely*, did almost as well. His next hit, *Happy Man*, came from album eight —*Kihntinued*, which features a fine cover of the Jackie Wilson/ Rita Coolidge hit *Higher & Higher*.

Similarly, album nine, *Kihnspiracy*, includes a version of the 1961 Patsy Cline hit *I Fall To Pieces*. The first hit from this album seems likely to be *Jeopardy*.

Are You Receiving; and in 1980 a 12 inch EP, *Requiem*, and the single, *Psyche*, all of which stayed on the alternative charts in England for some months.

Prior to the release of their debut self-titled album late in 1980, Killing Joke signed a management deal with E.G., which resulted in Polygram distributing their records, with artistic control remaining firmly in the hands of the group and Malicious Damage.

In April 1981 *Amost Red* (plus tracks from their debut EP) was released in both 12 inch EP and single form and the following month *Follow The Leaders* was also released as both a 10 inch EP and a single. In October of that year came a second LP, *What's This For!*.

In early 1982, on the eve of the release of their third album, *Revelations*, Killing Joke suddenly split in two. Jaz Coleman and Geordie, without any notice to the other two members, decided to go to Iceland and join local band Peyr, about which very little will no doubt be hard.

GREG KIHN BAND

shifted to Europe, where acceptance of the label's new sound ran far ahead of the States. The Kihn Band made several jaunts across the Atlantic for concert and club tours. During that period the band still found time to take its distinctive sound to most major US cities several times.

The group's fourth album, *With The Naked Eye*, and 1980's *Glass House Rock*, fuelled the expansion of their following among the industry and public alike even without any hit singles. The quartet became a quintet late in 1980 when keyboardist/vocalist Gary Phillips joined after previously working with local bands like Copperhead and Earth Quake. *With The Naked Eye* featured another deft Springsteen cover, *Rendezvous*. An interesting bootleg issue of this song features Greg and Bruce performing it on stage together.

The collaboration between Kihn, the band and producer Mathew

Killing Joke

Killing Joke began in June 1979 when Jaz Coleman (vocals and keyboards) called around to manager Brian Taylor's house and met Paul Ferguson (drums). Musical ideals and common interests (especially astrology and tarot) brought the two together to form a band.

Bass and guitar were the next requirements, procured by ads in the UK music press. Guitarist Geordie had been playing for several years but had never been in a band, and he didn't even turn up to the audition with a guitar. But an instant argument with Jaz earned him a place. Bassist Martin 'Youth' Glover escaped the life of a penniless artist in Earl's Court to join the group.

After moving to Gloucestershire to rehearse, Killing Joke finally emerged to play a few support dates with The Ruts and Joy Division. In late 1979 they issued a debut 10 inch EP on the Malicious Damage label,

Kissing The Pink

As one British music magazine candidly admitted: "It's not exactly street credible to admit it, but Kissing The Pink boast no fewer than five ex-students of the Glasgow College of Music."

Peter Barnett (bass violin), Steve Cusack (drums), Jo Wells (sax, clarinet, percussion), Sylvia Griffin (vocals, percussion), Jon Kingsley-Hall (keyboards), and George Stewart (assorted instruments) came together early in 1982 to play hard-edged jazz-funk/punk in the vein of Pigbag. Their first single, *Mr. Blunt* on the Magnet label, was produced by Colin Thurston of Bowie/Duran fame. He returned to the studio with them later in the year to work on the second and third singles *Watching Their Eyes* and *The Last Film*. Kissing The Pink (a name with myriad connotations) are presently finalising their debut album, *Naked*.

L

Legionnaires

If ever there was a resident New Zealand "super group" then Legionnaires could lay strong claim to being just that.

Graham Brazier has a reputation as New Zealand's most dynamic lead singer. Brazier is a veteran of Hello Sailor, a rather legendary outfit, that had a hit with *Blue Lady* and released two albums.

successful on the live circuit in New Zealand but are yet to make a record.

Jona Lewie

Of all the artists who have recorded for Stiff Records, Jona Lewie seems to be the one of whom least is know, even though his career has been long and varied.

As a sociology student in the late '60s, Lewie met Dave Brock and they played two or three gigs together while Brock was putting a band together (which was later to become Hawkwind). Next he

JONA LEWIE

THE LEGIONNAIRES

Guitarist Harry Lyon, another former Sailor, was also with Coup D'Etat and wrote their hit, *Doctor I Like Your Medicine.*

Former Pink Flamingo member, Paul Woolwright, play bass, while drummer is Lyn Buchanan, ex-Blind Date. Guitarist, and second vocalist is Dave McCartney who led the Pink Flamingos, recorded two albums, and toured Australia.

Legionnaires are extremely

recorded an album with veteran American bluesman, Arthur 'Big Boy' Crudup, (who wrote Elvis Presley's first hit. *That Alright Mama*), called *Roebuck Man.* During this period Lewie, who was still at college, played on a number of other blues albums and supported himself playing piano around London clubs.

After a brief stay as a camp counsellor in the States, Lewie returned to England where he joined Brett Marvin and The Thunderbolts, who toured as support for Eric

Clapton's Derek & The Dominoes. Under the alias of Terry Dactyl and The Dinosaurs, the group had a number two smash hit in Britain with *Seaside Shuffle.* The mid '70s saw Lewie playing with a succession of London-based groups as well as supporting himself working as an all-night car park attendant, part-time masseur and sociology lecturer.

Never too far away from rock'n'roll, Lewie impressed with a new group, The Jive Bombers (which lasted six months), followed by a few one-off independent singles that charted in Europe. Late in 1977 he signed to Stiff Records and spent the next nine months in the studio. His first Stiff single, *The Baby She's On The Street,* was followed by an album, *On The Other Hand There's A Fist,* and Lewie joined the Be Stiff tour of England and New York in

> **"My real name is Preliminary Drawing but most people find that a bit of a mouthful."**
> — *Sketch, Linx*

94

mid-1978. These were his last live dates.

In 1979 Stiff released another single, *God Bless Whoever Made You,* written by Nick Lowe and Ian Gomm and produced by Bob Andrews of The Rumour. In early 1980 *You'll Always Find Me In The Kitchen At Parties* was a hit in England and also gave him some prominence in Australia. Late in 1980, *Stop The Cavalry* became a top five hit in both England and Australia and sold over five million copies worldwide. The next year, the quirky *Louise (We Get It Right)* became another Anglo-Antipodean smash. Both it and *Stop The Cavalry*

were featured on the album *Heart Skips Beat,* which also gave the world the essential *Rearranging The Deckchairs On The Titanic.*

Linx

Singer Dave Grant and bassist Sketch (real name Peter Martin) were raised in Hackney and Plaistow, two working class areas of East London. Dave's first musical influences were Motown, some mid '60s English pop and, later harder American funk. Sketch was weaned on rock, then funk.

Dave got some idea of how a record company worked during a spell as an employee of Island Records, while Sketch, who came to bass late in his short career, worked in jobs as diverse as a filing clerk in Somerset House, the British register of births and deaths, and a shop assistant in a West End hi-fi store. It was then that he and Dave met and decided to write together.

They wrote what they thought was a strong, commercial song and took a tape of it to every record company in London. None were interested so they formed their own production (The Solid Foundation) and publishing (Solid Music) companies, recruited producer/keyboard player Bob Carter and drummer Andy Duncan, and cut *You're Lying.* They had a thousand copies pressed and distributed it through one specialist shop. City Sounds. A fortuitous spin on the air led to it selling out early the next week.

Linx signed with Chrysalis and when *You're Lying* was re-released it became a UK top 20 hit. By Christmas 1980 *Rise And Shine,* their second single, had been a disco hit and in June 1981, *Intuition* was top 10 in the UK and soon after was a minor hit in Australia.

The debut album, *Intuition,* was released mid-1981 and was quickly followed by two more singles: *Throw Away The Key* (re-recorded in Los Angeles with producer Ollie E. Brown) and *So This Is Romance.* Their second LP, *Go Ahead,* came out early in 1982, and confirmed their status as a top British black pop group.

In October 1982 Sketch left the group, though the name Linx will continue to be used in David Grant's future projects. Their final single, *Don't Hit Me With Love*, was released soon after the announcement of the break-up.

Lords Of The New Church

The Stiv Bators story goes back to the early days of American New Wave and a band called The Dead Boys, with a lineup of Bators (vocals), Johnny Blitz (drums), Jimmy Sero (guitar), Cheetah Chrome (lead guitar) and Jeff Magnum (bass).

LORDS OF THE NEW CHURCH

The Dead Boys were based in Cleveland, Ohio but in 1976 moved to New York to take advantage of the greater possibilities for punk bands in that city. After acquiring a reputation in Gotham's punk clubs

LENE LOVICH

LINX

album on I.R.S. Records. Two tracks from the album. *Open Your Eyes* and *Holy War,* were issued as a 12 inch single.

The Lords undertook a European jaunt at the end of 1982. Stiv demonstrated his high-diving technique into an orchestra pit in Bordeaux, France, and played the last half of the tour in a wheelchair.

Lene Lovich

Born in Detroit during the '50s to a Yugoslav father and an English mother, Lene moved to England when she was 13 with her mother, but ran away two years later and worked selling hotdogs and calling Bingo games. She developed an interest in art and enrolled at the Central School of Art in London, where she studied sculpture. While there, she set off to Spain on a pilgrimage to meet Salvador Dali.

After becoming interested in theatre, Lene learnt saxophone from Bob Flag, a musical director of many small circuit theatre shows. Next, she sang in an all-girl trio before meeting Les Chappell, another art school student. They joined the soul/funk band The Diversions and attracted the interest of French disco king, Cerrone. The two began composing songs together, many becoming hits for Cerrone in France.

When The Diversions broke up, English DJ and writer Charlie Gillett helped Lene record a version of the Tommy James classic, *I Think We're Alone Now,* which was released by Stiff Records in 1978. Soon after, her debut album *Stateless* was recorded and to promote it she went out on the 1978 Be Stiff tour followed by sold-out dates in New York.

During 1979 Lene embarked on her first headlining tour and had a top 10 UK and Australian hit with *Lucky Number.* Later that year she and husband Chappell journeyed to Holland to appear in the film *Cha Cha,* with Herman Brood and Nina Hagen. This was followed by the release of her second album *Flex,* in early 1980. Later that year a double EP, containing a new single *What Will I Do About You?,* and some live material emerged.

In early 1981, Lene Lovich released another EP, *New Toy,* the title track of which was a hit in both England and Australia.

After numerous disagreements with her record company, her third LP *No Man's Land* was finally released late in 1981, along with the single *It's You, Only You.*

Outside of recording, Lene's activities have included appearing in and scoring the London West End musical *Mata Hari,* as well as a role

particularly CBGB's they eventually became popular enough to tour America. The Dead Boys recorded two albums, *Young, Loud And Snotty* in 1977 and *We Have Come For Your Children* in 1978, both for Sire. In 1977 they toured England with The Damned.

Bators disbanded The Dead Boys early in 1979 to concentrate on his own career. Before the break-up they recorded a farewell concert at CBGB's, eventually released in October 1981 on Bomp under the title *Night Of The Living Dead Boys.*

Leaving New York, Bators moved to California where he teamed up with long-time friend, bassist Jeff Jones, formerly of Blue Ash. They recorded a single for Bomp, a killer version of the Choir classic. *It's Cold Outside,* followed early in 1980 by *Not That Way Anymore.* Another single, *Too Much To Dream,* and an LP, *Disconnected,* appeared late in 1980 and Bators began touring with a new Dead Boys line-up that included Frank Secich (bass).

Georgie Harrison (guitar) and David Quinton (drums).

In early 1982 Bators broke up that band and moved to England where he formed a new group with ex-Damned guitarist Bryan James. The rhythm section of Lords Of The New Church is Dave Tregunna (ex-Sham 69) on bass and Nicky Turner (ex-Barracudas) on drums. The group toured England and in mid-1982 released their self-titled debut

> **"Love is what you feel for a dog or a pussy cat. It doesn't apply to humans and if it does it just shows how low you are. It shows your intelligence isn't clicking."**
> **— Johnny Rotten, Sex Pistols**

in a French TV movie *Rock*. In May 1983 she undertook her first Australian concert tour.

Lydia Lunch

Lydia Lunch was born in Rochester, New York, in 1959. She formed her first group when she was 17 and her Catholic upbringing led her to name the group Teenage Jesus And The Jerks. She could barely play guitar and the music was minimalist in the extreme. Although the sets sometimes only lasted for seven minutes, even that was too much for

> "People keep talking about the death of rock'n'roll. It probably has died, but music and songs, performance and image, none of that has stopped. If you can throw some of that out in the forms that are available to you then it's exciting to be an artist."
> — *Peter Garrett, Midnight Oil*

most people, as Lydia stood immobile and screamed in anguish. *Orphans/Less Of Me* was released by LustUnlust records in April 1978 and followed in March 1979 by *Baby Doll/Freud In A Flop/Race Mixing*. Just as this record came out she disbanded Teenage Jesus and Lust-Unlust released all these tracks plus two more as an EP. She signed with Ze Records and they released the *Pre-Teenage Jesus* EP: three tracks recorded in 1977 when James Chance played sax with her (she appears on his *Off White* album). Just before the group broke up, Brian Eno produced four tracks with them for his *No New York* compilation album released in 1978. Lydia hated them because they made the band sound "nice".

Next came Beirut Slump, a short-lived line-up which produced one single, *Staircase,* released on Lust-Unlust in March 1979. Around this time she got married to someone she met two weeks previously. She said she was happy because he was as horrible to her as she was to him.

In 1980 she cut an album under her own name for Ze, called *Queen Of Siam*. It surprised people by being very mild and bland, though still retaining that very American sleaziness that characterises her work.

A new band followed. 8 Eyed

LYDIA LUNCH

Spy's first self-named album was released on Fetish in October 1981 and was followed by a single, *Diddy Wah Diddy,* in February 1982. A good example of 8 Eyed Spy's live work was released in cassette-only form by ROIR in 1982. The concert dated from 1980, shortly after the group had formed, but it shows how Lydia fits perfectly into the

> "When we get letters saying 'We want to start a Crass Army,' it's hard not to write back, 'Don't be such a bloody arsehole.' That's how the music business has always exploited people."
> — *Steve Ignorant, Crass*

minimalist/sleaze/art/punk world of downtown Manhattan. 8 Eyed Spy fell apart when bass player George Scott died of a heroin overdose.

Lydia next surfaced in late 1981 in London as support for a UK tour by Australia's Birthday Party. A live album followed (Lydia on one side, Birthday Party on the other): *The Agony Is The Ecstasy/Drunk On The Pope's Blood.* During this visit she met the people from the British Independent label Fetish, which is why the 8 Eyed Spy records came to be released in Britain rather than the US,

Back in the US, Lydia ran through another short lived line-up called Devil Dogs then assembled musicians to cut a self-named album: *13.13.* Not content with the music scene, Lydia meanwhile collaborated with Exene Cervenka from X to write a book of poetry. Called *Adulterers Anonymous,* it was published by Grove Press in late 1982.

M

Machinations

Guitarist Tim Doyle and keyboardist Tony Starr first started writing songs, with a drum machine, in the sumer of 1979, soon after both had left high school in Sydney. During that year they began rehearsing this material and writing new material with Fred Loneragan, an old school friend, who had just returned from a year overseas.

This original nucleus of the band had their first gig at Garibaldi's in Sydney in March 1980. For the next six months the trio confined their live work to the inner city venues and acquired a bass player, Nick (Nero) Swan, another old school friend. in 1981 the group began to expand their operations out into Sydney's suburban venues and recorded for the first time, using producer Lobby Loyde.

The results of these sessions were first released on the Phantom label in September 1981 in the form of a 12 inch EP. With Loyde's assistance,

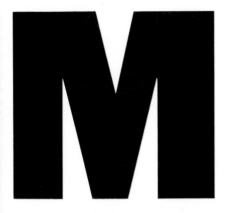

MACHINATIONS

the group then signed with Mushroom's White Label off-shoot and in March 1982, Machinations released their debut single, *Average Inadequacy.* For most of 1982 the group were off the road while Fred journeyed overseas, but they found time to record their second single, *Jack,* and lay the groundwork for a first album. *Average Inadequacy* was re-issued in a revised form by White Label, prompting Phantom to capitalise on their product by

releasing a four-track 12 inch EP.

The first Machinations album, *Esteem,* was issued in May 1983. It was again produced by Loyde, with the exception of the single *Pressure Away,* produced by Brown & Dunlop.

Malcolm McLaren

"Rock'n'roll had three things if it had anything, in terms of popular youth culture in the '50s — sex, style and subversion. Elvis Presley had those three elements. The Sex Pistols were England's answer to Elvis Presley."

So speaketh Malcolm McLaren, claimant to the title of The Man Who Invented The Sex Pistols. Coming from an art school and fashion background, McLaren had some dubious involvement with The New York Dolls before opening a clothes shop in Kings Road, which became a focal point for the punk movement in the mid-'70s.

After the Pistols' saga, McLaren was involved with the making of *The Great Rock'n'Roll Swindle,* the movie that gave his version of the band's explosive career.

McLaren released a single in France from the soundtrack, *You Need Hands,* while he was living in Paris.

Somewhere along the line he had something to do with the early career of Adam Ant but McLaren's next major association was with Bow Wow Wow. Under his managerial guidance, the group explored the use of African rhythms blended into a pop formula, coupled with his ideas of the destruction of the work ethic and cassettes as the way of the future.

McLaren's most recent project supposedly combines the mountain music of rural Tennessee with the urban street beats of 'scratch' DJ's of New York in the song *Buffalo Gals.* Accusations of plagiarism were levelled at him over this hit, and repeated when the follow-up, *Soweto,* appeared in early 1983.

Madness

Madness call their ska/reggae-influenced dance music the "nutty sound". This description was coined by saxophonist Lee Thompson, who explains: "It's a sort of happy fairground sound with jokey lyrics. Almost like Steptoe and Son music!"

Madness were originlly known as Morris And The Minors, and later The Invaders, and have been together in one form or another since 1976. The first members were Thompson, keyboards player Mike Barson, and guitarist Chris Foreman. There were then several drummers, with present compere/dancer Chas Smash, and manager John 'Tin Tin' Hassler trying their hand at different times. Smash also tried the bass, but wasn't much good at that either, and now acts as Master of Ceremonies.

Early in 1978, Graham McPherson (stage name Suggs) came along as lead vocalist. He was sacked on stage for going to a football match instead of band practice, but reinstated soon after. September 1978 saw drummer Daniel 'Woods' Woodgate and bass player Mark 'Bedders' Bedford join and the Madness line-up was complete.

Madness started playing gigs to unenthusiastic audiences and even dropped the blue beat numbers from their set at one point because of lack of interest. About this time The Specials, a band with similar roots, started attracting attention and Madness members fell in with Specials' keyboards player Jerry Dammers, who kindly mentioned in interviews that Madness were the

> **"I'm all for sociological lyrics. . . I just can't be bothered to write them."**
> — *Suggs, Madness*

MALCOLM McLAREN

only other band he liked.

When The Specials began their own record label, 2 Tone, they released Madness' first single, *The Price.* The song, written by Lee Thompson, was a tribute to original ska king, Prince Buster, whose song *Madness* had inspired the band's name. (Up till then, Madness had been working as The Invaders but had to change as there was another band working in England with the same name).

The Prince Buster song appeared on the B side of Madness' first single and was also featured on their *One Step Beyond* album (although it's not credited on the sleeve) as an extra track.

After Stiff's Dave Robinson had used Madness at his wedding reception, the band signed to his label. Their follow-up to *The Prince, One Step Beyond,* went to number seven on the English charts. The song was an instrumental, · occasionally featuring Smash on shouting vocals.

Madness then embarked on an English tour as part of the 2 Tone package with The Specials and The Selecter, before going to America to play venues such as Hurrah's in New York and The Whiskey in Los Angeles.

The band's next release was a special four-track EP, *Work Rest And Play* featuring *Night Boat To Cairo, Deceives The Eye, The Young And The Old* and *Don't Quote Me On That.* This was followed by the *Baggy Trousers* single and an album *Absolutely.*

In 1981 Madness released their seventh single, *Return Of The Los Palmas Seven,* before filming *Take It Or Leave It,* a film produced by Stiff detailing the Madness sage.

April of that year saw the release of *Grey Day,* followed by a tour of New Zealand, Australia, Japan and America.

Next came *Madness 7,* released in

1981, and in the following year came the *Complete Madness* album.

By this time Madness could do no wrong. Their concerts were sell outs and they moved into the top echelon of British groups.

The next album of studio material was *Rise And Fall,* which was released early in 1983.

Magazine

Magazine, as much as anyone, were acquainted with the outrageous slings and arrows of good fortune. The band — who were originally assembled by former Buzzcocks vocalist Howard Devoto in his hometown of Manchester in 1977 — released a debut single which was eulogised by Rolling Stone as "the best rock'n' roll record of 1978, punk or otherwise".

But while Magazine went on to consolidate the enormous critical success of the single *Shot By Both Sides* with an equally devastating and enthusiastically received first album, *Real Life,* it was inevitable that no band, particularly one so new, could expect such continued universal acclaim. The second

album, *Secondhand Daylight,* received a critical mauling — despite the obvious growth and maturity of the new music.

From July to September 1979 the band embarked on a coast-to-coast tour of the States and Canada. The tour proved not only commercially successful, but more importantly, it reinforced Magazine's belief in themselves. Soon after, they took a two month break to write new material.

In January 1980 they recorded their third album. It was eventually hailed by the UK rock press as one of the albums of the year, and once more Magazine were firmly back in favour. *The Correct Use Of Soap* was an album replete with great songs and sensitive, articulate playing, topped by sympathetic production by Martin Hannett. It also spawned a single that was voted a contender as one of the singles of 1980, the wonderfully riffy *A Song From Under The Floorboards.* A successful UK tour followed by impressive tours of America, Europe, New Zealand and Australia continued Magazine's solid comeback after the disappointing response to *Secondhand Daylight.*

It was while touring Australia in September of 1980 that they recorded a concert that formed the basis for the release in December of the live album *Play.* Critics were in total agreement that Magazine had released one of the finest live albums of the past few years and a more than fitting testament to their dynamic live sound.

When original guitarist John McGeoch left Magazine to pursue a number of different projects, ultimately ending in his joining Siouxsie and The Banshees, his temporary replacement was former Ultravox guitarist Robin Simon, who after being featured on *Play,* parted company with the band. After searching for a permanent replacement for McGeoch, the band

MAGAZINE

finally settled on an old friend of Howard Devoto's, vocalist-turned-guitarist Ben Mandelson. Joining with the rhythm section of drummer John Doyle, bass guitarist Barry Adamson, and keyboard player Dave Formula (who has also been a key member of the studio band Visage), the band embarked on a solid schedule of writing and rehearsing for the next album.

During March and April of 1981 Magazine went into the studio and recorded *Magic, Murder And The Weather,* an album that proved that Magazine were one of the most influential bands to emerge in the UK in the last decade. But in July 1981 Howard Devoto dropped a bombshell when he decided to leave the band just three weeks before release of *Magic, Murder And The Weather.* He left in order to pursue solo interests (which so far have not appeared) and was quoted as saying that he was very happy with the album and wished all the members well. The remaining musicians decided against using the name "Magazine", preferring instead to keep Magazine special, as it was.

At the end of 1982 Virgin Records issued the *After The Fact* anthology, featuring album cuts, single-only tracks and illuminating liner notes by NME's Paul Morley.

CAROLYNE MAS

Carolyne Mas

New York native Carolyne Mas was introduced to music practically at birth by her guitarist father and pianist mother. She played piano from the age of six, guitar from the age of II and also that year began voice lessons for opera singing. In her early teens she joined a bunch of rock'n'roll bands, being the only girl around who played electric guitar.

After failing high school, Carolyne ran away to Pennsylvania with her electric guitar and after a few trips across the country settled in New York again, where she attended the American Music and Dramatic Academy in Greenwich

THE MEMBERS

Village. Next stop was the Light Opera of Manhattan, where she sang Gilbert and Sullivan, and then the Pennsylvania Folk Festival in 1974. She returned to New York and began playing with rock'n'roll bands, at first the Last Chance Blues Band, which led to a gig in a piano bar, and then with her own backup band.

Some demo tapes she recorded found their way to various radio stations and the response was impressive. In 1978 Carolyne met up with producer Steve Burgh and guitatist David Landau (who had toured with Jackson Browne and Warren Zevon) and they persuaded her to concentrate on rehearsing. In 1979 her first serious exposure came when she opened for Sonny Terry and Brownie McGhee in New York. A subsequent headlining show at New York's Bottom Line led to a flurry of offers from record companies and she eventually signed with Mercury Records.

A self-titled debut album was recorded in May 1979 and hailed as one of the finest debut albums from a female rock singer in many years. Her second album, *Hold On* (again produced by Burgh), came out in early 1980, to be followed in June 1981 by her third, *Modern Dreams,* both of which have further enhanced her reputation as one of the best of the new breed of female singers in rock.

The Members

The Members were formed in 1977 by student and insurance salesman Nicky Tesco, who had spent considerable time recruiting musicians from around his hometown of Camberley. The Members initially were Tesco (vocals), Adrian Lillywhite (drums),

Gary Baker (guitar) and a nameless bass player. After a few gigs this line-up expanded into a five piece with the addition of Jean-Marie Carroll (rhythm guitar), a former bank clerk who could write songs.

In October 1977, the bass position was taken by British Airways technician Chris Payne. The band then recorded the track, *Fear On The Streets,* which appeared on the Beggars Banquet label's *Streets* sampler album.

By the end of 1977, The Members had moved away from crashing two-chord English Punk and developed the reggae side of their music, which became obvious in songs like *Stand Up And Spit, Chelsea Nighclub* and *Solitary Confinement. Solitary Confinement* was released by Stiff Records in 1978 and Nigel Bennett replaced Gary Baker. In November 1978, The Members changed record companies, signing with Virgin, and 48 hours after inking their contract were on the road supporting Devo. By the end of the year they had recorded the song that had become their anthem, *Sound Of The Suburbs,* and an album, *At The Chelsea Nightclub.* They toured Australia, playing pubs and clubs, in November 1979, promoting their album and two singles, *Offshore*

Banking Business and *Killing Time.*

The Choice Is Yours, a second album produced by Rupert Hine, was released in 1980 and featured a guest appearance by Joe Jackson. Their career went into virtual limbo until mid-1982 when they released a new single, *Radio,* top 10 in the UK and Australia, also issued in a 12 inch dub version. This was followed by the *Working Girl* single late in 1982 and a third, self-titled album, both produced by Martin Rushent.

Men At Work

Australia's Men At Work are a success story that comes along once a decade — in any country. Early in 1983, a little over three years after final formation, the group were holding down the number one single and album position in both England and America — a grand slam only achieved in the past by the likes of Rod Stewart and Barbra Streisand. The nucleus of the band — Colin Hay, Greg Ham and Jerry Speiser — came together at Melbourne University in the mid-'70s though

Firmly entrenched as the house band at the Cricketer's Arms pub in the Melbourne suburb of Richmond, Men At Work attracted the remarkably loyal attention of young CBS employee Peter Karpin, freshly returned from a posting to New York. Against considerable opposition, Karpin persuaded his company to sign the group and record them with American producer Peter McIan. The rest is rather startling history.

MAW's debut single, *Who Can It Be Now?* when to number one, as did the follow-up *Downunder* and the album *Business As Usual* — all for marathon numbers of weeks. Singles three and four, *Be Good Johnny* and *Dr. Heckyl & Mr Jive* performed a little less spectacularly but by that point it hardly mattered, as exactly the same chart process was being repeated in America. *Business As Usual* remained at number one on the Billboard charts for 15 weeks, shattering The Monkees' record for a debut album.

After touring America as support to Fleetwood Mac, Men At Work

Work have racked up almost unbelievable success by the age old virtue that shall never be replaced — they sound *different* from the rock mainstream. The difficulties they face in trying to better their international debut are terrifying to contemplate. They have begun their formidable task with the *Cargo* album and *Overkill* single.

Mental As Anything

In 18 months Mental As Anything progressed from playing on top of a pool table in a small Sydney pub to securing an international deal with Virgin Records and having their debut album released in England.

The Mentals are Martin Plaza (vocals and guitar), Reg Mombassa (vocals and lead guitar), Greedy Smith (vocals and keyboards), Peter O'Doherty (bass) and Wayne DeLisle (drums). The band was formed at art school by Plaza, Mombassa and DeLisle in June 1976, their name coming from the first show they played in September that year at Sydney University. They

MEN AT WORK

not for musical reasons. It was not until singer Hay transferred himself to Sydney to join the chorus of the rock opera *Heroes* that the musical links began to join together.

Hay came back to Melbourne with guitarist Ron Strykert, intent on forming an acoustic duo. In time, bassist John Rees joined up, as did old friend Speiser, a drummer. The quartet then became a quintet with the addition of woodwinds teacher Greg Ham.

suddenly found themselves a hot headlining act and swung through around 50 North American dates commencing late in 1982; some with compatriots Mental As Anything. England managed to hold out longer than most countries but succumbed early in 1983, sending *Downunder* and *Business As Usual* to the top of the singles and albums charts respectively.

Oft-criticised for sounding a little too much like The Police, Men At

were billed without a name and asked the promoter to come up with one. He decided on Mental As Anthing.

As this stage Smith was playing in another band but was spending so much time playing with The Mentals that in December, 1976, they decided to make him a permanent member. Mombassa's brother, Peter, took over on bass in August 1977 and the line-up was finalised.

Throughout 1977 the band's

MENTAL AS ANYTHING

residency at the Unicorn Hotel (playing on top of the legendary pool table) in Paddington became so popular that they cajoled the publican of the Civic Hotel in the city to allow them to play on Thursday nights. In September 1978 Regular Records was formed by two ardent fans wanting to record the band and in December of that year the group's debut EP, *Mental As Anything Play At Your Party*, was released and became a cult classic. In July 1979 Festival Records took over distribution of Regular and a song from the EP, *The Nips Are Getting Bigger*, produced by Cameron Allen, was re-released as a single and became a top 20 hit.

Mental As Anything's first album, *Get Wet*, again produced by Allen, was released in November 1979 in Australia, and with a support slot on Rockpile's national tour, was soon top 20. The album was released in England on Virgin in January 1980 and received rave reviews, while the single, *The Nips Are Getting Bigger*, reached number one on the UK alternative charts.

A second album, *Expresso Bongo* appeared in July 1980, produced by Allen, and though its sales were disappointing, the single, *Come Around*, stayed in the Australian charts for 26 weeks. Another smash single, *Just Like Romeo And Juliet* was released in early 1981, but the biggest success came with their third album, *Cats & Dogs*, produced by Bruce Brown and Russell Dunlop, which emerged in September, 1981.

> "It's really hard to be a Midnight Oil fan. You don't see us on TV, we don't put out a lot of records, we don't tour as much as some of the other bands and when you can see us it's in an over-crowded nightmare. I mean I only joined the band so I could go along to a Midnight Oil gig and get out of the crowd."
> — Rob Hirst, Midnight Oil

The album went top 10 as did the first two singles taken from it, *If You Leave Me, Can I Come Too?* and *Too Many Times*, while a third, *Berserk Warriors*, went top 40.

In May 1982, the group held a painting and art exhibition of their own individual works, which attracted a good response. Buyers included Elton John, Mary Travers and Australian novelist Patrick White. The following month, while Elvis Costello was touring Australia, he was easily persuaded to enter a Sydney studio with Mental As Anything and produced their single, *I Didn't Mean To Be Mean*.

In September, 1982 a compilation album, also entitled *Cats and Dogs*, was released in America and Canada, and in the latter country has proved quite popular. They toured with Men At Work in both countries to promote the record just after its release, by which time *If You Leave Me. . .* had made 20 in the Canadian charts. On returning home in late November, they released a new single, the waltzy *Close Again*, the 12 inch version of which came with two free dance lessons from Arthur Murray Studios. This was followed early in 1983 by the *Creatures Of Leisure* album and hit single *Spirit Got Lost*.

Mental As Anything remain one of the most popular bands in Australia, due in most part to their almost constant touring throughout the country and their ability to initiate a raging party wherever they play. They have the honour of being the first band signed to the new A & M Oz label, established in America for the release of Australian product.

Midnight Oil

Midnight Oil are one of Australia's most popular live bands, though they consistently baulk at tours outside New South Wales (with rare exceptions) and shun many aspects of the hype-bound rock business — generally refusing to grant interviews or appear on television.

The band developed from an association struck up in 1974 between drummer Rob Hirst, bassist

Andrew James and guitarist/keyboards player James Moginie. The three found shavened head vocalist (and law graduate) Peter Garrett two years later, and the line-up was completed in 1977 by the addition of guitarist Martin Rotsey. First gigs were around the northern beaches of Sydney.

All members of Midnight Oil contribute to the writing and arranging of the howling, roaring original material. In September 1978 they recorded their debut album on the Powderworks label, produced by the band and radio 2JJ's Keith Walker and mastered in LA. The LP was recorded and mixed at Alberts Studios and included songs the band had made Sydney-wide favourites through their white-hot live performances. *Run By Night,* released as a single, picked up scattered airplay.

Midnight Oil's second album, *Head Injuries,* was recorded during July/August 1979 at Trafalgar Studios in Sydney with producer Les Karski and engineer Peter Walker. A tighter and more proficient effort, it made solid chart impact and approached gold status.

At the end of 1980 the group released an EP, *Bird Noises,* which got them onto the singles chart by virtue of the instrumental track *Weddingcake Island.*

Early in 1981 they travelled to

they turned down a lucrative offer to support the disbanding group on a number of American dates.

Back in Australia they initiated the novel release of a 12 inch single *(Armistice Day)* with a free t-shirt, giving rise to the jibe that it was the first t-shirt to ever chart on the top 40.

After a sell-out national tour, capped by a series of amazing shows before small audiences at a classy Sydney theatre, the group saw the fourth album, *10-9-8-7-6-5-4-3-2-1* and single *US Forces* storm into the charts, proving that success can be achieved on their own strict terms.

The Mighty Guys ▆▆▆▆

Though lumped for convenience under the Rockabilly banner, Australia's Mighty Guys are no Stray Cats. They render an intriguing blend of rockabilly, r&b, beatnik rhythms and pure rock'n'roll that has been described as "Maynard G. Krebbs Beatabilly" The national Juke magazine said: "Their effortless precision, intuitive understanding and sheer vivacity place them well to the fore. The Mighty Guys have got that something extra, an EDGE. Their roots-boogie rock'n'roll sizzles lean and taut with humour, personality and lots of shoulder shakin' flash. To boot, it's loose limbed, opened, a little wiry and very raunchy.

begun playing professionally in 1959 with early rock combo Dig Richards and the RJ's and, over more than twenty years, had developed an awesome skill and musical knowledge. Guitarist Mick Hamilton was not far behind, having made his mark in the mid-'60s in legendary Melbourne garage beat bands the Moods and Vibrants. Bassist Phil Eisenberg was a relative newcomer, his first chart success being a 1977 number one single by The Ferrets.

THE MIGHTY GUYS

THE MIGHTY GUYS

The chemistry among the three was perfect. Their early performances became a wonderful spiritual communion with the body, substance and soul of rock'n'roll. Audiences were beset with gooseflesh, prickled hairs and sweaty brows as the three delivered raw, frantic, explosive energy, overlayed with surging, rolling rhythm; then dropped into a lower gear altogether for a sprinkling of twee, twangy teen ballads in the Johnny Tillotson mould.

Signed by independent Rivet Records, The Mighty Guys were introduced on record with a 10 inch album *Rockin' All Thru The Night,* highlighted by an up-tempo version of *Old Shep.* In 1982 came the first 'proper' album, *Be Cool Be Smart;* the title track of which was produced by John 'Cool For Cats' Woods. That release has resulted in strong Japanese and Asian interest in the band. It was followed by the single *Hang On Sloopy* mid-year.

MIDNIGHT OIL

London to record a third album, *Place Without A Postcard,* with producer Glyn Johns. As well, they performed two sell-out concerts at the Marquee.

During early 1982 the Oils played selected showcase gigs in Australia and then returned to England to record a fourth album under Nick Launay. During this visit they were invited to support The Who on the farewell UK concert, in Birmingham. Characteristically,

Occasionally, when it's truly firing, it also gets just a little mean and when it does, believe, the Mighty Guys are formidable."

The seasoned trio came together in Sydney around the middle of 1980. Each was looking for a means to escape the inherent boredom of a career as a backing or session musician and stretch out some talents that were in danger of being buried.

Drummer Leon Isackson had

Ministry ▆▆▆▆

Ministry are Al Jourgenson (vocals, guitars, synthesizers) and Stephen George (percussion/synthesizers).

After teaching himself synthesizer, Chicago-born Jourgenson was approached by the owner of independent Wax Trax Records, who was interested in releasing some of his material. This resulted in a three-track EP containing *I'm Falling, Cold Life* and *Prymental,* recorded with the assistance of drummer George.

The EP engendered enough interest for Ministry to be offered a contract with Arista Records, whereupon Psychedelic Fur Vince Ely left his band to become production partner with Jourgenson. The two co-produced (with Ian Taylor) Ministry's debut album at the Cars' Syncro-Sound Studio in Boston.

Jourgenson, George and Ely intend basing themselves in Chicago, and becoming involved with recording other artists.

As for Ministry's music, Al Jourgenson has this to say: "Nothing about our sound is sweet; I'm constantly jabbing at everything I can get my sticky hands on, so the vocals alone and the lyrical content will make something that isn't pop. We try to write catchy tunes that have a meaning, not just airhead pop songs. From the beginning, I've considered myself a perfectionist; I've grown fascinated with the controlled circumstance of the studio. Yet the cynicism will be there — like sugar-coated poison, cyanide candy."

Mink DeVille

In 1971 New York born Willy DeVille emigrated to London with the intention of forming a band. Unable

MINK DE VILLE

to find suitable musicians, he ended up playing solo in clubs and discovered that though English musicians might be respected in America, the reverse wasn't necessarily true.

DeVille returned to New York to look for more sympathetic

musicians but ended up in San Francisco, where various early versions of Mink DeVille were tested. Out of this period came a core trio of DeVille (vocals, guitar and harmonica) drummer Thomas R. Allen (who's played with John Lee Hooker and other blues performers), and bass player Ruben Siguenza. At this stage De Ville's aim was clear — he wanted to bring romance back to rock'n'roll.

Venues in San Francisco were limited and the band ended up playing anywhere they could, from lounges to leather bars. Eventually DeVille went back to New York with Siguenza and Allen and they went through a succession of lead guitarists before settling on Louis X. Erlanger. Mink DeVille became a mainstay of the legendary punk haven, CBGB's. Unfortunately, Willy and company were hardly punk rockers, though they became routinely lumped with the burgeoning New Wave movement. And, while the inclusion of three of their songs on the 1976 *Live At CBGB's* compilation album helped them to get a recording contract with Capitol, it did little to help defend their unique musical approach, which owed more to New York's Latin strain of '60s rhythm and blues (a la Ben E. King), than punk.

With the addition of keyboards player Robert Leonards, the group recorded their debut album, *Cabretta,* produced by the legendary Jack Nitzsche, in 1977. The album contained such classics as *Mixed Up, Shook Up Girl,* the Crystals' *Little*

Girl and the single, *Spanish Stroll,* which was a hit in Europe, reaching number 12 in the UK and number three in Belgium and Holland.

Deville's second album, *Return To Magenta,* released in 1978, was again produced by Nitzsche but the sales were so disappointing that Capitol refused to release his third album, *Le Chat Blue.*

THE MODELS

For this album, Willy had journeyed to Paris and recorded with Elvis Presley's rhythm section (Ron Tutt — drums and Jerry Scheff — bass), noted string arranger Jean Claude Petit (who had worked with Edith Piaf) and producer Jack Douglas. The album was an eclectic selection of DeVille's influences and included songs co-written with Doc Pomus, who had composed hits in the early '60s for the Drifters and Dion and the Belmonts. The album was released in England and Europe in mid-1980 to rave reviews, but Capitol only finally released it in the US after import copies had garnered critical acclaim and radio airplay. Three Mink DeVille songs, *Heat Of The Moment, Pullin' My String* and *It's So Easy* were included on the *Cruisin'* soundtrack LP at this time.

Willy then set about forming a totally new Mink DeVille, citing the old band's unsympathetic attitude to his drug problem as the reason for their sacking, and also signed to Atlantic Records. DeVille's fourth album, *Coup de Grace* (again produced by Nitzsche), was released in mid-1981 and featured his new band: Kenny Margolis (keyboards), Ricky Borgia (guitar), Louis Cortelezzi (sax), Joey Vasta (bass) and Tommy Price (drums).

When Capitol lost Mink DeVille to Atlantic they rushed out an excellent value compilation called *Savoir Faire,* featuring such standards as *I Broke That Promise* and *Just To Walk That Little Girl Home.*

The Mockers

"We appear directionless but that is our predetermined direction. The music we play is diverse because the songs reflect the different moods we are in when we write them," says Andrew Fagan of New Zealand's The Mockers.

The band was formed in May 1980 at Rangotai College from the

> "People feel the need for a certain sort of order in their music and the way it's played and presented. That reassures them, just like it does in life and relationships."
> — *Jah Wobble, Public Image Limited*

remnants of The Ambitious Vegetables.

In October 1980 the band's first single, *Good Old Days,* was released, followed in July 1981 by *Trendy Lefties,* and early in 1982, *Woke Up Today.*

The Models

The Models formed in Melbourne in 1978 from the remnants of a couple of punk bands. Guitarist and singer Sean Kelly had been in Teenage Radio Stars with James Freud while drummer Johnny Crash (aka Janis Friedenfelds) and keyboardist Ash Wednesday had been members of JAB. Late that year bassist Mark Ferrie joined, after playing in a succession of Carlton bands in the mid-'70s, including pioneering rockabilly outfit, The Leisuremasters.

The group quickly attracted a following in Melbourne and in 1979 supported shows by Dr Feelgood and The Stranglers. Early that year, Ash Wednesday departed to pursue solo projects and he was replaced by Andrew Duffield, who had formed the highly acclaimed electronic group, Whirlywirld.

In mid-1979 The Models released their first record, a giveaway single, *Early Morning Brain.* The band were far from happy with their recorded

product and late in 1979 the internal conflicts came to a head and they announced they were breaking up.

But soon afterwards an invitation arrived from producers Harry Vanda and George Young to record some demos in Sydney and The Models were suitably encouraged to reform. The group returned to gigging and supported The Ramones on their Australian tour in 1980 while an intense bidding war began between the record companies. In July 1980 they began recording a self-financed album and shortly afterwards announced a contract with Mushroom Records.

Their debut album, *AlphaBravo-CharlieDeltaEchoFoxtrotGolf,* was released late in 1980 to critical acclaim and in February 1981 they supported The Police on their Australian tour. Derek Green, Vice President of A&M Records, saw the band and offered them an international recording contract which was duly signed. In the meantime Janis Friedenfelds left and was replaced by Buster Stiggs, ex-The Swingers from New Zealand.

In early 1981 The Models recorded some demos to send to an English producer, but the sessions were so successful that they were released on a 10 inch mini-LP, *Cut Lunch,* in July. In June the group

travelled to England and recorded their second LP with producer Steve Taylor at the Farmyard Studios. *Local &/Or General* was released in October 1982 and received disappointing sales. Soon after Buster Stiggs left and he was replaced by drummer Graham Scott with John Rowell also joining on guitar.

In 1982 The Models experienced further disruptions. First, Mark Ferrie quit and was replaced by James Freud from Berlin. Then, both Andrew Duffield and John Rowell departed. The group recorded a single *On/The Whole Story* as a trio and then recruited drummer Barton Price, formerly with the Proteens.

Modern English

In the first two years of their 'collective existence', Modern English, Robbie Grey, (vocals); Gary McDowell, (guitar); Michael Conroy (bass); Richard Brown (drums); Stephen Walker (keyboards) have kept a fairly low profile. Committed as they are to a group format, their development has been a slow process. Originally formed in Colchester, the group have rarely performed outside London in their

MODERN ENGLISH

own right. Touring experience has been gained the hard way, via support to Wasted Youth and Japan on their national tours in '80 and '81, respectively — though in early '82 the band did briefly tour Europe and the US.

Modern English released their debut single *Drowning Man* on Limp Records in 1979 and in 1980 signed to 4AD. Their first release on that label was a single, *Swans On Glass,* in April 1980 followed by a second, *Gathering Dust,* in October. The group's first album, *Mesh And Lace,* came out in April 1981 and was followed in August by another single, *Smiles And Laughter.*

After nine months of preparation and recording, Modern English's second LP, *After The Snow,* produced by Hugh Jones at Rockfield Studios, was released in mid-1982. The lengthy rehearsals for

Modern Romance ████

Known for crisp, danceable rhythms and stylish, witty lyrics, Modern Romance have emerged as one of the more interesting British singles acts of the past two years. The outfit was formed in 1980 by bassist David Jaymes and vocalist Geoffrey Deane, who in turn recruited drummer Andy Kyriacou, keyboards player Robbie James, and guitarist Paul Gendler.

The new group found their feet swiftly and by 1981 had entered the charts with the highly danceable *Everybody Salsa.* With the addition of trumpeter John Du Prez, Modern Romance racked up a string of chart hits — *Ay Ay Ay Ay Moosey, Queen Of The Rapping Scene, Cherry Pink And Apple Blossom White, High Life,* and the top five silver disc winner, *Best Years Of Our Lives.*

Late 1981 saw release of the

Adventures In Clubland album, which enjoyed success in both South and North America, earning a Venezuelan gold album. In September 1982, vocalist Deane departed and was replaced by Michael J. Mullins, who sings on the second album, *Trick Of The Light,* produced by Tony Visconti and released early in 1983. *Don't Stop That Crazy Rhythm* followed.

Mo-Dettes ████

All-female group The Mo-Dettes have a fascinating involvement with the early punk scene. Guitarist Kate Corris was born in New York, but a broken marriage sent her fleeing to London in 1974. She got involved in the music business almost immediately through 101'ers members Joe Strummer and Palmolive. The latter had been

MODERN ROMANCE

the LP resulted in a much sparser group sound. To coincide with the release, Modern English embarked on their first headlining tour of Britain, followed by their third tour of Europe. Exposure on the MTV network in America prompted release of *After The Snow* on the Sire label stateside and strong radio attention for the single *Melt With You.*

"I don't know if prison is good for everybody, but it did me a lot of good."
— *Hugh Cornwell, The Stranglers*

thrown out of Sid Vicious' Flowers Of Romance and persuaded Kate to form The Slits with Ari Up. Kate soon split and in quick succession played with The Passions, The Raincoats (one gig) and Vincent Units. Through getting involved in the *Great Rock'n'Roll Swindle* movie she met drummer June Miles.

June was born in the East End of London and after dropping out of

THE MO-DETTES

art school went through a succession of menial jobs, including a two year stint in a mortuary. Through meeting Julian Temple she got to work on the *Swindle* movie where she met Kate, who badgered her into buying Paul Cook's old drum kit.

Bassist Jane Crockford (who is now married to Madness' Don 'Woody' Woodgate) left school at 15 and ran away from London to Edinburgh, where she ended up in a hostel. She drifted back to London, where she became immersed in the emerging punk scene and shared a squat with Johnny Rotten and Sid Vicious. In mid-1979 Jane began to learn bass and was invited into Bank Of Dresden by ex-PiL drummer Richard Dudanski. On the side she was secretly rehearsing with The Mo-Dettes.

The final member of the group is vocalist Ramona Carlier, born in Geneva, Switzerland, where she studied ballet until the age of 20 before being introduced to the world of rock'n'roll by her brother, who played in a French band called Electric Chaos. After starting a controversial Swiss fanzine called Lola's Tits, she decided Geneva was too stultifying and used her savings to flee to London, where she soon met the other three Mo-Dettes.

The Mo-Dettes' debut single, *White Mice*, released on Rough Trade in 1979 (then reissued as the flipside to *The Kray Twins*), received positive reviews and in June 1980 the group signed to Deram. Their first single for the label, *Paint It Black*, went top 40 in the UK and was followed late in 1980 by *Dark Heart Creeping* and their debut album, *The Story So Far*, which stiffed. The group released a fourth single, *Tonight*, in July 1981 after which

MONSOON

Ramona left the group. She was replaced by Sue Slack and then Melissa Ritter took over from Kate Corris. With this accomplished, the group then disbanded.

Monsoon

Monsoon was a brave and pioneering attempt to blend traditional music from the Indian sub-continent with '80s British rock. Led by 17 year old Sheila Chandra, best known for her role in the BBC production *Grange Hill*, Monsoon originated late in 1980

> *"When you're successful things appear mundane, just like a job, really. . . We've been lucky, we came along at the right time. We haven't done that much work."*
> — *Martin Gore, Depeche Mode*

THE MOODISTS

when keyboards player/producer Steve Coe developed an interest in Indian music through an Asian girlfriend. Hoping to form a band to pursue this direction, he discovered Sheila via some demo tapes which she had forwarded to Hansa Records when she was 14. Sheila joined Monsoon in March 1981, three months before she left school.

The Eastern music basis was reinforced by Dari Mankoo and his mastery of sitar and tabla. Rooting for the West was guitarist Martin Smith. The textured combination attracted the attention of would-be record mogul David Claridge, who signed the outfit to his Mobile Suit Corporation after a great many major labels had turned them down.

Monsoon's first single, distributed through Rough Trade, was *Ever So Lonely/Sunset Over The Ganges.* Ignored upon original release, it was reissued as a 12 inch disco remix, with the extra tracks *Shout* and *Mirror of Your Mind.* Second time around, *Ever So Lonely* was heavily supported by John Peel on the BBC. Two subsequent singles, *Shakti* and (The Beatles') *Tomorrow Never Knows,* were issued in 7 and 12 inch forms. However, sales and attention were only moderate and the group called it a day at the end of 1982.

The Moodists

The Moodists began playing around Melbourne in late December 1980. That line-up featured a bass player who departed six months later, complaining the sound was too rough. According to the band, this roughness can be detected on that particular Moodists' single, *Where The Trees Walk Downhill,* if the disc is rubbed with heavy duty sandpaper before playing.

The Moodists proper began with

the arrival of bass player Chris Walsh in July, 1981.

The band promptly recorded the much less inhibited single *Gone Dead/Chad's Car* which was released in April 1982. The single was "almost single of the week" in New Musical Express (pipped at the post by Bucks Fizz).

Next, The Moodists recorded a six-track mini-album called *Engine Shudder,* for Melbourne based independent label Au-Go-Go Records. Guest appearances on the record are People With Chairs Up Their Noses' saxophonist David Palliser on *This Road Is Holy,* and Feral Dinosaurs' sax player Nick Danyi on *Kept Spectre.* The mini-album was released in England on Record Flame Records.

The current Moodists line-up is: Steve Miller (guitar), David Graney (vocals), Clare Moore (drums), and Chris Walsh (bass).

Morrissey Mullen

Dick Morrissey learned his art working out of the jazz circuit built around Ronnie Scott's Club in London. He played sax opposite many visiting jazz greats and this introduced him to the world of sessions. Dick toured with Cannonball Adderley, made an album with Jimmy Witherspoon, and did session in the late '60s for the likes of Georgie Fame and John Dankworth. Having developed a taste for recording, he decided to branch out and formed If. If made seven albums in the four years they existed in the early '70s, and they toured the US continuously. It was while Dick was in New York that he was introduced to guitarist Jim Mullen by the Average White Band.

Jim Mullen originally played double bass on gigs and radio work in Glasgow and then moved to London in the early '70s, where he

MORRISSEY MULLEN

played with Vinegar Joe, and Brian Auger's Oblivion Express before joining Kokomo. After touring the States opposite AWB, Jim found himself in New York working on sessions with Herbie Mann and Ben E. King, before going to Montreux with Dick and the Atlantic Family.

Morrissey Mullen really came into existence as a partnership in those days in New York, working with Herbie Mann. They recorded their first album, *Up,* for Atlantic with their long-time companions AWB, and it was followed by another album, this time for EMI, called *Cape Wrath.* Since then, Morrissey Mullen have been extensively working London clubs, building up a large following. Morrissey has also played on hit albums for Peter Gabriel, Jon Anderson, Gino Vanelli and Georgie Fame.

With the current boom in British jazz funk, Morrissey Mullen began to appeal to a wider audience and they were signed to Beggar's Banquet. Their first album for that label, *Badness,* was released in 1981 and was followed by *Life On The Wire* in 1982, which charted in the UK.

> *"We played the Liverpool Warehouse the other night and nearly every girl in the audience looked more like a pop star than I did!"*
> — *Mari Wilson*

The Motels

The Motels finally found a workable line-up in July 1978 when lead singer/songwriter Martha Davis and lead guitarist Jeff Jourard assembled a band to play at The Whiskey in Hollywood. Other members of this makeshift line-up were Michael Goodroe, a classically trained guitarist who had switched to bass and played with jazz artists and rock'n'roll bands, and keyboard/sax player Marty Jourard. Rumour has it that The Motels rejected 85 drummers before deciding on Brian Glascock, a veteran of British band Toe Fat and contributor to sessions for Iggy Pop, Bee Gees and Joan Armatrading.

Martha Davis, the central figure in The Motels, began singing and playing guitar when she was eight, mostly music derived from her mother's collection of jazz, classical and blues records. She was writing songs at 15 but it was not until her late teens that she began playing around the coffeehouses of her

THE MOTELS

native Berkeley. In the early '70s, Martha formed the first of many versions of The Motels. The group relocated to Los Angeles in the mid '70s and spent a few years arranging and rearranging personnel and musical direction.

The Motels' new line-up began regular live work in January 1979 and within six weeks had attracted a great deal of record company interest. They eventually signed with Capitol and their first LP, *Motels,* produced by John Carter, was released in September 1979. The single *Total Control* was taken from the album but Australia was the only country in which it charted.

To promote the album, The Motels toured America, Canada, Britain and Europe. On their return to LA in late '79, a leadership rift

developed between Martha Davis and Jeff Jourard, with the latter leaving. His replacement on guitar was Tim McGovern, formerly of The Pop.

This new line-up recorded The Motels' second album, *Careful,* released in July 1980. They successfully toured Australia late that year, but then there was a long two year gap before the next album. In that time the band again changed guitarists, with Guy Perry (at one time a member of Elephant's Memory) replacing Tim McGovern. The group's new album, *All Four One,* and the singles, *Only The Lonely* and *Take The L Out of Lover,* again sold well in Australia, encouraged by a second tour. The group have yet to really break in the US or Britain.

AUSTRALIAN NEW MUSIC: FERTILE AND FORTHRIGHT

BY STUART COUPE

*"The Oz-rock establishment rejects the Inner City Sound, probably because to them, it is without commercial potential. Bands like Models, Riptides and Serious Young Insects may have made some inroads. And yet while the Birthday Party are applauded loudly in England and now America (and ditto the Go Betweens in England), Australia at large remains unaware of them simply because without major support they receive little exposure. And given that exposure to their music couldn't fail to connect because it's not second-hand; it's fresh and vital. Just because they're obscure is no reason to continue to ignore them. These bands — and more, like Bad Poets, Dead Travel Fast, David Chesworth, End, Equal Local, Essendon Airport, Hugo Klang, Hunters & Collectors, Laughing Clowns, Laughing Hands, Lounge, Machinations, Nervous System, Nuvo Bloc, Out Of Nowhere, Pel Mel, Popular Mechanics, Sardine, Scapa Flow, Sekret Sekret, Severed Heads, Singles, Slugfuckers, Sunday Painters, Systematics, Tactics, Triffids, Wild West, Wildlife Documentaries, Xiro, (Tchtchtch) and *** *** are making the true Australian rock (if indeed 'rock' is stll an issue) of the 80's. That's all there is...".*

(Clinton Walker, Inner City Sound, Wild & Woolley Press 1982).

That observation is taken from the introduction to Clinton Walker's essential *Inner City Sound*, a detailed chronicling of what's happened in the non-mainstream areas of rock'n'roll since the mid-Seventies when Australian kids first started hearing about the Sex Pistols, Damned, Ramones, etc. and their philosophies of telling everything to do with the superstar system exactly where to get off and doing something about it, ie: start a band, a fanzine, an independent label or just plain get along and support those who *were* doing it.

Without any doubt, Australia has a thriving new music scene that's on a par with anything that's happened overseas. Unfortunately not too many people outside the Southern Hemisphere get to hear what's been produced.

At present four of Australia's most innovative 'new' bands are making a go of it in Europe — The Saints, Go Betweens, Birthday Party, and Laughing Clowns.

As there's a whole pile more where they came from, this should serve as a beginners guide to Australian new music. Everything you should know that no-one has told you — starting with those assertive bands who have made the forbidding trip overseas.

THE BIRTHDAY PARTY started a few years back as The Boys Next Door and seem hell bent on creating some of the most aggressive, abrasive, psychotic music ever to come from this, or any country; their manic excess frequently descending/rising to the ridiculous.

Vinyl wise, The Birthday Party are best captured on their 12" single, *Nick The Stripper,* the single *Release The Bats,* or their most recent album, *Junkyard.* They've got a live set out with Lydia Lunch — a side of each recorded at The Venue in London during 1981.

The present day SAINTS contain only one founding member, lead guitarist/songwriter Chris Bailey. The original line-up recorded three albums — *(I'm) Stranded, Eternally Yours,* and *Prehistoric Sounds* — before disbanding in London. Drummer, Ivor Hay went on to form a jazz inspired combo called Wild Life Documentaries (now disbanded), while guitarist Ed Kuepper started up The Laughing Clowns.

Bailey put the new Saints together, then with Hay still drumming. They've since released an EP and two albums — the excellent *Monkey Puzzle* and the patchy *(I Thought This Was Love But This Ain't) Casablanca.* The Saints work regularly in England and Europe, the latter being the band's strongest region. Overseas they're signed to New Rose Records.

Like The Saints, THE GO BETWEENS come from Brisbane. The trio, featuring guitarists, Grant McLennan and Robert Forster, and female drummer Lindy Morrison, have struggled hard on the underground Australian pub

THE GO-BETWEENS

circuit, in between spending time overseas where they've had singles released by Postcard Records.

The band has been compared to Talking Heads because of their unique rhythms and vocal sound. They've recorded two albums — *Send me a Lullaby* and *Before Hollywood.* The overseas edition of the former contains four more songs than the Australian version on Missing Link Records.

LAUGHING CLOWNS, a heavily jazz influenced outfit, formed by guitarist and would-be singer Ed Kuepper after The Saints disbanded, in many ways extends the sound The Saints were developing on *Prehistoric Sounds.* Before moving to England for an indefinite period the Clowns established a reputation as one of the most innovative bands in the country. Forget James Chance and his pseudo Albert Ayler meandering, *this* is the real thing. However it may have to be enjoyed in retrospect, as the group give every indication of dissolving in the near future.

Anyway, there's two 12" EP's, a single, an album that combines 'em all called *Throne Of Blood,* and an album of new material called *Mr. Uddich Smuddich Goes To Town.* Get 'em all and be amazed.

On the more commercially successful and viable front Mental As Anything, The Church, and Icehouse have all toured overseas in the past twelve months.

Latest to go are the radical Melbourne-based

Hunters and Collectors, superb practitioners of the new funk, who've scored a deal with Virgin Records and intend supporting the release of their debut album with outstanding live performances in Europe and Australia.

But the real story lies with what's going on at home — the young bands taking the chances, trying for something new, or simply making great, passionate rock'n'roll.

Situated as it is, almost equidistant from England and America, Australian rock'n'roll has always absorbed influences from both countries, and with the advent of the new music, nothing changed.

As an example, let's take a typical night in Sydney. At the Southern Cross Hotel in inner-city Surry Hills, The End will be performing a Velvet Underground inspired set, whilst four blocks away, at the Sydney Trade Union Club, ska exponents The Allniters will be playing to 800 Rude Boys. At the tiny Sussex Hotel there'll be 20 vespas parked in the street and inside 200 Mods will be dancing to Division 4 or The Sets, doing their best to re-create the atmosphere of London circa 1964 and the days of The Who and The Small Faces. Over the Harbour Bridge at the Mosman Hotel, The Hoodoo Gurus, a curious amalgam of The New York Dolls, Cramps and Modern Lovers, will be playing with tough, Detroit inspired Fifth Estate or maybe new psychedelic band Suicidal Flowers. Reggae fans will be gathered at the Haymarket to see Big 5, at The Stranded Nightclub you'll be able to see Mad Room do the best version of Joy Division going, and at the All Nations Club the sublimely seasoned Mighty Guys will be churning out a spine tingling blend of rockabilly, r&b and beatnik rhythms.

MENTAL AS ANYTHING

ALLNITERS

THE SAINTS

THE HOODOO GURUS

On and on the list could go. The point is that Australia does have a *very* diverse new music scene, and its influences largely come from overseas.

As Walker points out in *Inner City Sound*, the early days of Australian new music were very similar to those overseas and this wasn't necessarily a good thing:

"As in America, punk/post-punk music was forced to fend largely for itself. Bands played their own gigs, made their own records. Fans wrote fanzines. Not even the rock press was particularly moved. The only real early support — and then there was resistance — came from student, public-subscription and occasionally ABC (Government) radio, and these sources have continued their support, to varying degrees, to this day.

"Slowly the influence of the new wave infiltrated the Oz-rock establishment. But the ridiculous part of it was that it didn't look in its own backyard first, to its own new wave. It looked overseas, and then tried to duplicate in Australia what it saw happening there. Never mind that there was Australian punk/post-punk music in its own right; Australian old wave bands of any persuasion dressed up as English or American new wave bands, and that was the Oz-rock new wave."

However, things did improve and during the last few years of the Seventies Australian new music changed, diversified, and took on much more of a distinctive character. Sure, everyone listened to what was coming from overseas but the ideas from there were assimilated with original ideas from Australian bands. As things developed more and more, people realised there wasn't so much point copying from overseas because bands in this country were

WILDLIFE DOCUMENTARIES

creating as much that was new and original, as that emanating from overseas — at the same time, and often earlier.

A thriving independent record scene developed, spearheaded by labels like Missing Link in Melbourne, and Doublethink in Sydney. The latter also acted as a booking agency for most of its bands.

Some of the better fanzines developed into magazines with a wide readership. Roadrunner, which had evolved from the fanzine Street Fever, was a prime example. Magazines like Vox appeared, and arguably the world's first new music cassette magazine, Fast Forward, was started in Melbourne.

But still, things could have been better. As in many other countries, a great number of great and not so great bands were lost to the passing of time without getting the recognition they deserved. Walker's random list of Australian bands is indicative — Broken Toys, Crime and City Solution, Filfth, Leftovers, Mannikins, Passengers, Poles, Primitive Calculators, Scientists, Terminal Twist, Thought Criminals, Two Way Garden, Voigt/465, Whirlywirld, X, Young Modern, and Young Charlatans.

The majority of those bands had loyal followings in their own cities and cult status elsewhere. They released independent records but that was as far as it went.

Australian new music is extremely diverse, both in terms of specific cities, and again within those cities.

Melbourne has traditionally produced a more English styled music, a colder, more austere, avant-garde, fashion conscious rock'n'roll, that some deride as arty and pretentious. Melbourne's other dominant strain is a healthy pub rock'n'roll scene that's spawned bands like The Sports, Jo Jo Zep And The Falcons, Paul Kelly And The Dots, and The Models.

Sydney, on the other hand, has always been associated with tough, hard, American-styled rock'n'roll. Running through the list of popular inner city bands over the past five years and listening to their music you could be excused for thinking that the only records Sydney bands listened to were by Iggy Pop and The Stooges, The MC5 and a zillion obscure Sixties American punk bands, with an occasional dash of The Kinks, Searchers, and other British Invasion Bands thrown in.

Radio Birdman started it all, an unashamed Detroit and surf music (!!!) influenced band who established a following with a degree of fanaticism that has never been equalled in this country. All of Birdman's records are excellent hard

THE INTROVERTS. CELIBATE RIFLES (BELOW)

THE SCIENTISTS

rock'n'roll but in no way capture the fervour and intensity of their live shows.

For Australians, seeing Radio Birdman was probably akin to seeing the Pistols at the 100 Club or The New York Dolls at The Mercer Art Centre.

Birdman's demise whilst touring England and Europe with The Flamin' Groovies saw the members splinter into three bands — The Visitors, The Other Side, and The

THE JOHNNYS

Hitmen. Later bands like The Kamikaze Kids, The Passengers, Sunnyboys, Lime Spiders, Fifth Estate and Midnight Oil carried on the tradition of tough Sydney rock'n'roll. Some tried to imitate Radio Birdman, others were simply inspired by their spirit, and the same music they'd listened to.

From other major cities comes a diverse mixture of rock'n'roll, the band's usually orientating themselves towards 'making it' in Sydney or Melbourne, a stepping stone to going overseas.

Go Betweens, Saints, Riptides, Scientists, Victims, Speedboat, Mannikins, Fun Things, Screaming Tribesmen, Nuvo Bloc, and The End are just some of the extremely talented bands to come from Perth, Brisbane and Adelaide.

Australian bands aren't slow about discovering what's hip that week in London and getting involved. Two weeks after the airmailed copies of New Musical Express have arrived announcing this week's fashion, there's a couple of Australian clones about to start work.

Maybe it's Dorian Grey's version of new romanticism, or Strange Tenants, No Nonsense or Naughty Rhythms' ska. During the Mod revival both Sydney and Melbourne had thriving Mod scenes, whilst numerous bands like Pel Mel have 'discovered' funk.

Others are much less derivative. . . and some are totally unlike anything else. Take The Johnnys, a trio dressed in cowboy gear who've been seriously described as a cross between Merle Haggard and The Sex Pistols.

PEL MEL

115

Bands like Sunday Painters, Cough Cough, Tch Tch Tch, Kill The King and Great White Noise, the music coming from the experimental bases at Melbourne's Clifton Hill Community Centre, and the tiny studio/booking agency/label called M Squared in Sydney are as varied, and innovative as anything you'll hear in any other country in the world — despite the constant immature cynicism of adolescent English rock writers who carry on the tiresome British attitude of Australia being a penal colony.

There's little Australian new music that takes influence from aboriginal culture, the exceptions being politically-inspired aboriginal reggae (for want of a better word) band

KILL THE KING

SWINGERS

GREAT WHITE NOISE

No Fixed Address, and Us Mob who lean towards heavy rock. Both bands are featured on the soundtrack of the movie *Wrong Side Of The Road,* while No Fixed Address have released a mini-album. With few exceptions, the non-bandwagon hopping Australian new music is released on independent labels. In the last few years the number of independents has shrunk, largely due to the economics involved with regularly releasing records that will generally sell less than 2,000 copies.

The significant Australian independents are Missing Link, Au Go Go, Regular, White, Green, Phantom, Rivet Monash, and Larrikin. Virtually all of them suffer traditional distribution problems and are forced into a situation of relying on major companies to get their releases to a wide variety of stores — Australia being considerably larger than Great Britain (which could fit into the state of Victoria).

It's rare that independent releases get programmed on major AM and FM stations though there's an alternative radio network that constantly supports independents. The most visible of these are 2JJJ-FM, 2MBS-FM, and 2SER-FM (Sydney), 3RRR (Melbourne), 4ZZZ (Brisbane) and 5MMM (Adelaide).

These stations, although small, have a great deal of influence and consistently break newer bands. No-one doubts that 2JJJ was programming the B-52's for six months before most other stations knew they existed.

Australian television has an abundance of rock'n'roll video — a record was attained during the middle of 1982 when six weekly shows were vying for ratings. Any newer bands that have the resources to make a video have a strong chance of having it shown on a number of programs.

COUGH COUGH

MICHAEL TRUDGEON, ANDREW MAIN & BRUCE MILINE/FAST FORWARD.

Fast Forward, the cassette magazine, is an excellent outlet for demo tapes and information about new music bands, whilst rock oriented publications like RAM, JUKE, Roadrunner, Virgin Press, (Australian) Rolling Stone, and a variety of fanzines give constant coverage in varying degrees to young bands.

The fact that there is a large audience for overseas new music bands is obvious when looking at a sample of the bands that have had successful pub, club and concert tours of Australia in recent years. Human League, The Cure, The Fall, XTC, New Order, The Teardrop Explodes, Simple Minds, John Cooper Clarke, The Strangers and Elvis Costello are just some of the performers who've attracted large crowds.

It's not being overly nationalistic to repeat that some of the most exciting rock'n'roll happening anywhere in the world is to be found in Australia. It's coming from small pubs, labels and bands throughout the country and deserves a place in more hearts than it's currently finding.

You want it, well here it is. Ya just gotta look. . . and listen. . . and feel.

MOTORHEAD

Motorhead

Heavy metal giants Motorhead were formed in 1975 by lead vocalist and general loudmouth Lemmy Kilmister, who also played bass. The other original members were guitarist Larry Wallis and drummer Lucas Fox. This line-up broke up after they'd recorded one album, *On Parole,* which was released in 1980.

The new line-up had Philthy Animal Taylor drumming and Fast Eddie Clarke playing guitar. The band signed to Chiswick Records and released a self-titled album.

The band moved to Bronze Records in August 1978 and released a single, *Louie Louie* which dented the bottom of the charts. It was followed by the very successful *Overkill* album.

Since then Motorhead have had a steady stream of singles and albums, each selling better than the previous one. Their LP's include *Bomber, Ace Of Spades,* and the live set *No Sleep Till Hammersmith.* The band also recorded *Please Don't Touch,* an EP combination with Girlschool.

Motorhead's live album contains ear-splitting versions of the band's standards — *Overkill, Motorhead, Bomber, Capricorn,* and *Ace Of Spades.* It was recorded over three nights and prompted Sounds magazine to describe it as "The most gruelling mind garrotting metal excess ever unleashed on humankind to date."

Melody Maker stated: *"No Sleep..* has set the standard for Heavy Metal in the Eighties; it's a yardstick by which everything will be measured."

The live set was followed by *Iron Fist,* a new studio album released late in 1982. Soon afterwards Fast Eddie Clarke left the band because he objected to Lemmy recording a duet version of the old Tammy Wynette hit *Stand By Your Man* with Wendy O. Williams of The Plasmatics. He was replaced by Brian Robertson.

Motorhead then entered the studio to record yet another album.

Pauline Murray

Pauline Murray was born in Durham, England, on March 8th, 1958. Leaving school at the age of 16, she went to art college for a year, before leaving in 1976 and working various short-term jobs. In 1977 she formed Penetration with guitarist Gary Chaplin. Robert Blamire (bass) and Gary Smallman (drums) were drafted in to complete the line-up.

In April 1977 Penetration played their first gig — supporting Generation X at London's Roxy, and in October they released their debut single on Virgin, *Don't Dictate* one of the best punk singles of 1977 though sadly overlooked. Early in 1978 Gary Chaplin left the group to be replaced by Neale Floyd and in May they released their second single, *Firing Squad.* The band went on tour with The Buzzcocks and in June an additional guitarist, Fred Purser, joined the line-up. Their debut album, *Moving Targets,* came out in October 1978 and shot to 21 in the UK charts. A major tour of Britain followed, with visits to Europe and the States taking up the early part of 1979. Their second LP, *Coming Up For Air,* emerged in September 1979 and also made the UK top 10. But by that time musical differences had begun to divide the band and in November they disbanded.

Pauline continued to write with bass player Robert Blamire and with his help embarked on a solo career. Her first single, *Dream Sequences,* was released in mid-1980 and was followed later that year by her debut album, *Pauline Murray And The Invisible Girls.* Produced by Martin Hannett, it featured John Cooper Clarke's sometime group, The Invisible Girls.

Outside a string of 1980 singles, including *Mr. X* and *Searching For Heaven,* little has been heard from Ms Murray for the past couple of years.

Musical Youth

An unrivalled highlight of chart rock in 1982 was the sheer exuberance

> "Classic record company quote. When we were beginning The Hunter they said, 'Well, we hope this isn't another album like Autoamerican.' What do you mean? You hope there's not gonna be two number one singles on the album?"
> — Clem Burke, Blondie

and infectious joy of *Pass The Dutchie,* the first official recording of five black Birmingham schoolboys known as Musical Youth. The single achieved gold status on day of release, selling a staggering 115,000. Within a month it was near the million mark. By the time it had exerted its charm on America, Australia and other territories, collective sales were around four million.

The origins of Musical Youth can be traced back to 1980, when former Jamaican hit singer Freddie White started a group with his sons Junior and Patrick, and enlisted Michael and Kelvin Grant. In time, Freddie stepped down as vocalist and Dennis Seaton was recruited as lead singer. With the assistance of the Saltley Print & Media Workshop, the very young group recorded some demos and forwarded them to John Peel at the BBC. Peel was entranced by the performances, playing them often and directing as much attention as possible toward the five lads at Dudgeston Manor School in Nechells, Birmingham.

After slogging away for a couple of years in Birmingham youth clubs, the band landed a spot at the Notting Hill Carnival in London, where they were seen by MCA Records. Handed over to ace hit producer Peter Collins, Musical Youth reworked an old Jamaican reggae ganga song called *Pass The Kutchie.* The basic melody had featured in a number of recent reggae songs, including the Mighty Diamonds' *Full Up.* Altered to *Pass The Dutchie* (a dutchie being a communal cooking pot), the song

> **"We only know about four chords but we arrange them pretty well."**
> **— Lemmy, Motorhead**

was fashioned by Collins into an irresistibly commercial track. With the loyal assistance of John Peel, it proved to be one of the fastest selling charting hits in British pop music history.

When the record exploded in September 1982, Dennis and Junior were 15, Patrick 14, Michael 13 and Kelvin 11. Granted a month of school leave, with the stipulation of an on-the-road private tutor, the five starry-eyed kids hit the promotional trail all over England and then went out on the road with Kid Creole & The Coconuts.

Far from being one-hit wonders, Musical Youth went back into the studio to create the excellent *Youth Of Today* album, from which a second hit, *Never Gonna Give You Up,* was lifted. All instrumentation on the album was handled by the five young musicians and all songs were originals — somewhat more than might have been fairly expected.

MUSICAL YOUTH

N

NUCLEUS OF NEW ORDER, JOY DIVISION

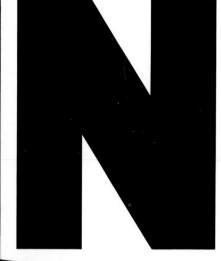

NAKED EYES

Naked Eyes

Jumping on the synthesizer duo bandwagon before its wheels fall off is Bath couple Pete Byrne (vocals) and Rob Fisher (electronic wizardry), known collectively as Naked Eyes.

The two first came together at the end of 1979, having both recently departed obscure local bands. Initially they recruited other musicians but by the end of 1981 had reverted to a duo configuration.

Signed by EMI UK in May 1982, Naked Eyes entered the famed Abbey Road Studios with producer Tony Mansfield and came up with an ultra-commercial version of the Sandie Shaw/Dionne Warwick classic *(There's) Always Something There To Remind Me.* The single became a sizeable international hit and Messers Byrne and Fisher duly received the 15 minutes of fame to which Andy Warhol claims we are all entitled.

The Narcs

The Narcs hail from the New Zealand city of Christchurch and have been playing for three years. A year into their career they released

Narcs EP, a four-track EP. *Over My Head* was lifted as a single but failed to receive much attention from radio, despite rave reviews from the country's active music press.

The next Narcs' disc was a three-track 12 inch single titled *No Turning Back.*

The Narcs, as drummer Steve Clarkson explains, are "just a rock'n'roll band; no pretence; just energy and a determined attempt to give an audience a good time".

NATASHA

Natasha

Natasha first came to light as the European balance between two American girls in the 1979 British 'girlgroup' act The Flirts. A forerunner of the Belle Stars/Bananarama phenomena, the unit was quie literally ahead of its time, leaving behind the charming single *The Kind Of Boy You Can't Forget,* a cover of the Raindrops' 1963 American hit.

Natasha went solo in 1980 and broke through onto the charts in 1983 with a version of the 1965 Dixie Cups' hit *Iko Iko,* beating out a rival rendition by the Belle Stars for top 10 honours. This was followed by *I Can't Hold On,* written and produced by Richard Hartley of *Rocky Horror Show* fame, who also played every instrument on it.

Natasha's debut album, *Captured,* was an impressive effort, featuring musical contribution from Mel Collins, Phil Rambow and Snowy White. Amongst a number of strong originals lurked versions of the Jaynettes' *Sally Go Round The Roses,* the Kinks' *All The Day And All Of The Night* and Sam Cooke's *Bring It On Home To Me.*

New Order

Following the suicide of singer Ian Curtis on the 18th of May 1980, the remaining three members of Joy Division — Bernard Albrecht (guitar), Peter Hook (bass) and Stephen Morris (drums) — decided to continue on under the name of New Order, with a new keyboardist Gillian M. They are not to be confused with a Detroit savage-rock band of the same name.

The new group released their first single, *Ceremony,* in April 1981 and followed it with another single, *Procession,* in August. A three-track 12 inch EP containing *Everything's Gone Green/Mesh/Cries And Whispers,* came out in October 1981. Their debut album, *Movement,* appeared in November 1981 to great acclaim and in early 1982 their third single, *Temptation,* was released.

Although dubbed "the new Pink Floyd" by cynics, the group have built up large followings in both the UK and USA through extensive touring. After an Australian tour with John Cooper Clarke, 1983 saw the release of their best-selling single, *Blue Monday,* followed by their second album *Power, Corruption And Lies.*

New Race

When Radio Birdman split up after a tour of England in June, 1978, all the members returned to Australia and formed other bands. Pip Hoyle (keyboards), Deniz Tek (guitar) and Ron Keeley (drums) formed The Visitors, Rob Younger (vocals) The

Other Side, and Chris Masuak (guitar) and Warwick Gilbert (bass) The Hitmen.

Both The Visitors and The Other Side were short-lived and in August 1979, Birdman (minus Younger) reformed for a one-off reunion gig. Following that appearance, Deniz Tek (who had found time while playing with Birdman to complete a medicine degree) returned to his native America where he has worked in hospitals, mostly around the Detroit area, as a resident physician. While there, he met and became friends with former Stooges guitarist Ron Asheton and when time permitted, sat in with his band, Destroy All Monsters.

In 1981 WEA Records released Radio Birdman's long-lost third album, *Living Eyes,* which had been recorded in 1978 at the Rockfield Studios in Wales. To coincide with the release, Deniz Tek invited Asheton to form a band for a one-off tour of Australia. Former MC5 drummer Dennis Thompson joined and in Australia they recruited former Birdman members Younger and Gilbert. In April 1981 New Race (named after an old Birdman song) played a short series of hotel and club dates with a repertoire that included Birdman songs, plus Stooges and MC5 material, as well as a couple of originals. For some dates Masuak and Hoyle appeared with the band. At the completion of the tour the members went their separate ways, and Tek returned to the States with Asheton and Thompson, to begin training as a fighter pilot. In mid-1982 WEA released a live album recorded on tour, *The First and The Last,* featuring Birdman/Stooges/MC5 classics and just one new song — *Columbia*, written especially for the tour.

No Fixed Address ■■■■
Since its inception in Adelaide in

1979, Australian Aboriginal reggae band No Fixed Address has pursued an unparalleled career through a number of near insurmountable racial problems, financial hardship, line-up changes and public notoriety.

Across Australia, No Fixed Address has made its name as the classic touring band: preferring life on the road to an urban existence; making a name with rock audiences as a support to Cold Chisel, Ian Dury and The Clash, among others. The experience of No Fixed Address, however, was no more pointedly stated than in the 1981 award-winning film, *Wrong Side Of The Road.* A quasi-documentary, it portrayed the trials of two Aboriginal bands on the road and the experiences relevant to them and their people.

Lyrically, the band is very serious about its stance and proudly sings the deep-rooted convictions of the Aboriginal people. The reggae-flavoured songs *We Have Survived, I Can't Stand And Look, Stupid System* and *Pigs* leave no illusion as to how No Fixed Address see their people's situation in Australia.

Powering the band is young drummer and founding member Bart Willoughby — who writes and sings the majority of the band's songs — Les Graham on lead guitar and Chris Jones on rhythm guitar. Together they have provided the core through various line-ups. Now solidified as a five-piece, No Fixed Address has recruited bassist Joe Hayes, and percussion and didgeridoo players Joe Geia and Billy Inda.

No Fixed Address' recording debut was on the soundtrack album to *Wrong Side Of The Road,* which they shared with another Aboriginal band, Us Mob. In mid-1982 the band signed with the independent Rough Diamond label and released a mini-LP, *From My Eyes.* Billy Inda provided the eerie didgeridoo sound

on the late 1982 number one Australian single *Solid Rock* by Goanna.

NEW RACE

Gary Numan ■■■■
Gary Numan's rise to fame was relatively quick. He formed his Tubeway Army in 1977 with bass player Paul Gardiner and recorded a demo album, with his uncle Jess Lidyard sitting in on drums. In January 1978 he was signed to Beggars Banquet Records and a first single, *That's Too Bad,* was released from the demo. With drummer Bob Simmonds the trio began playing around the clubs of London, but Simmonds soon left and the line-up was expanded with the addition of Sean Burke (guitar) and Barry Benn (drums). This line-up recorded the second single, *Bombers,* but after becoming disillusioned with live appearances, Numan broke up the band in July 1978.

With Gardiner and Lidyard, Numan recorded demos for his debut album in August 1978 and Beggars Banquet were so impressed with the quality of the tapes that they released them intact under the defunct group name, *Tubeway Army.* In January 1979 Numan recorded

NO FIXED ADDRESS

GARY NUMAN

his second album, *Replicas,* and introduced Christopher Payne (keyboards) and Ced Sharpley (drums) to the group.

Down In The Park, Numan's third single, was released in March and the *Replicas* album came out the following month. *Are Friends*

> "If you were a normal person, walking down the street, people wouldn't come up to you and say, 'Cor, I think you're ugly'. But if you're famous, then they think it's alright."
> — Gary Numan

Electric was released in May and within seven weeks was at number one on the singles charts. Three weeks later *Replicas* held the same position on the album charts. The name Tubeway Army was finally dropped for the release of Numan's fifth single, *Cars,* and his third album, *The Pleasure Principle,* which was released in October 1979.

With the addition of guitarist Russell Bell, Numan embarked on his first UK tour in September and in early 1980 he toured North America, Japan, Australia, New Zealand and Europe to wide acclaim. *Cars* went top five in America and in mid-1980 the new single, *We Are Glass,* continued his success in England by going top five.

Numan released his fourth album, *Telekon,* in September 1980, plus the single, *I Die, You Die,* and then embarked on extensive touring of the UK and USA for the remainder of the year. In 1981 Numan retired

indefinitely from live and recording work and devoted his time to his new passion of flying. Later that year he went on an around-the-world-flight in his small plane and en route crash-landed with only minor damage in India.

In early 1982 the double live album *Living Ornaments* appeared (released as two single albums in some territories) and later in the year, Gary bounded back into action with the solo album *I. Assassin.*

The Numbers

Brother and sister Chris (guitar and vocals) and Annalisse (bass and vocals) Morrow began playing in bands together on Sydney's North Shore in the mid '70s, while Chris was attending art college and Annalisse was working for a fashion house.

In January 1979 drummer Simon Vidale replaced Marty Newcombe and The Numbers' original line-up was complete. Using Sydney as a base, the group toured extensively interstate supporting XTC and in September 1979 released their debut EP, *Government Boy,* on the independent Local label.

Late that year The Numbers were signed with Deluxe and in March 1980, *The Modern Song* single was released and peaked just outside the top 40. In May they went into the studio with Icehouse/Mental As Anything producer, Cameron Allen and July saw the single *Five Letter Word* released, followed by a debut self-titled album in October.

In early 1981 the trio decided to add a fourth member, keyboards player Russell Handley (ex-Popular Mechanics). But after only a couple of months of live work, the Morrows realised that the new line-up was not working out and Handley was sacked. Soon after, Vidale departed of his own accord. Two new members — a returning Marty Newcombe (drums) and Gary Roberts (bass) — were added and Annalisse now concentrated on singing. This line-up released the *Jericho* single late in 1981.

The Numbers then went into the studio to record their second album, but it was soon apparent that the band was not ready, so Newcombe and Roberts were discarded. With Annalisse again taking up bass and former-Angel City drummer 'Buzz' Bidstrup assuming that role as well as producing, they proceeded with recording. The result, *39:51,* was released mid-1982. It was so titled to counter criticism over the shortness of the first album.

To coincide with the album's release, The Numbers went back on the road with a new line-up that included former Reels Colin 'Polly' Newham (keyboards) and John Bliss (drums). But in late 1982 both Newham and Bliss left the group without having recorded with the Morrows. The future of The Numbers, the only original signing to the independent Deluxe label that has not defected to another company, remains uncertain.

THE NUMBERS

O

OINGO BOINGO

Hazel O'Connor

Hazel O'Connor left school in 1971 and dropped out of art school in April 1972. For the next year she travelled the hippie trail around Europe and Morocco, eventually landing a job as a dancer in Tokyo.

After a year in Japan, Hazel moved to Beirut, where she danced for another six months before taking off for Africa. By late '74 she had made up her mind that she wanted to sing and over the next three years did just that with various groups in Germany and France, returning to London in 1978 to play around the traps with various punk bands.

After one gig in April 1979 Hazel O'Connor was approached to play the lead in a new rock film. *Breaking*

Glass turned out to be one of the major English films of 1980 and the soundtrack album by Hazel, produced by Tony Visconti, went gold in the UK and spawned three hit singles, *Give Me An Inch, Will You,* and *Eighth Day,* the latter going top five.

Soon after the film came out, Hazel formed her own backing band, Megahype, the personnel being Ed Case (drums), Steve Kinch

HAZEL O'CONNOR

(bass), Andy Qunta (keyboards), Wesley Maggogan (sax) and Neil O'Connor (guitar). Throughout late 1980 and early 1981 they toured extensively throughout the UK and America with the likes of the Stranglers, Iggy Pop and XTC.

In early 1981 Hazel O'Connor recorded her debut solo album, *Sons And Lovers,* with producer Nigel Gray. Tony Visconti was brought in to re-record *D-Days* from the album and it became a top 10 single in Britain. Also in 1981 she published her autobiography *Uncovered Plus* and followed it with her second album *Cover Plus.*

Oingo Boingo

The history of Oingo Boingo is as unusual as their moniker (which incidentally has absolutely no meaning — or none that the members will admit to).

They seem to have existed for almost a decade in various incarnations. Originally called The Mystic Knights Of The Oingo Boingo, they started as an avant-garde musical theatrical troupe in L.A. They became well known for their absurd, colourful (and occasionally obscene) appearances which occurred randomly — on streets, in backyards, movie lines and makeshift stages.

Some years later, they moved indoors exclusively to produce elaborate fast-moving, multi-media musical shows. These were described in one article as "brilliantly paced, high-energy, dark, surrealistic cabaret which puts time-warped pieces of pre-war Berlin into a schizophrenic, modern format".

ORANGE JUICE

Between 1978 and 1979 the band's constant evolution and transmutation took firmer shape. Dropping the huge sets and concentrating on the music, they switched entirely over to rock'n'roll.

Basically starting from scratch, Oingo Boingo built up a new power base over this period and developed into one of the top live draws in southern California, selling out virtually all of their shows.

In 1979 they recorded *I'm Afraid* for a Rhino Records sampler. This brought them to the attention of the International Record Syndicate which released their self-titled four song EP in September 1980. The EP's release further demonstrated the band's popularity by scoring as a national breakout in Billboard only a short two weeks after its release, literally jumping out of the box onto scores of radio stations nationwide. The EP featured *Only A Lad, Violent Love, Ain't This The Life,* and *I'm So Bad.*

The band's first major exposure in their present incarnation was as the backbone of the maniacal and irreverent film *Forbidden Zone* which premiered to an SRO audience at the Los Angeles Film Exposition. Their first album, *Only A Lad,* appeared in

> **"Giving synthesizers to the Europeans was like giving whisky to the Indians."**
> **Will Rigby, The dB's**

1981, produced by Pete Solley. This was followed by *Nothing To Fear,* produced by O.S. & Joe Chiccanelli and the single *Little Girls,* a sublimely salacious ditty.

With their synthesizer based input and far from subtle overtones of kinky sex and black humour, Oingo Boingo are one of the more interesting new American bands. In 1980 they were, along with X and the Go Go's one of three L.A. bands

regularly packing out the Roxy and Whisky. Like those two acts, they have broken through nationally, helped along by a memorable appearance in *Urgh! A Music War.*

Oingo Boingo's present line-up is Danny Elfman (singer, writer and rhythm guitar), Steve Bartek (lead guitar and co-arranger), Richard Gibbs (keyboards), John Hernandez (drums), Sam Phipps (sax), Leon Schneiderman (sax) and Dale Turner (trumpet).

Orange Juice

Formed near the end of 1977 in Glasgow, Orange Juice have developed a style that owes much to the basic sensibility of pop music, especially that of Britain in the mid-'60s. Yet the approach they have adopted exudes a freshness (the word which inspired their name) and also a primitiveness which marks them as a distinctive and exceptional band.

Guitarist/vocalist Edwyn Collins, lead guitarist and vocalist James Kirk and drummer Steven Daly came from a punk outfit called the Nu-Sonics, then when Edwyn met bass player David McClymont at art school, Orange Juice was complete.

The band helped Alan Horne form the Postcard label (which they still retain an interest in), a small Scottish independent which released four Orange Juice singles — *Falling and Laughing, Love Sick/Blue Boy, Simply Thrilled Honey,* and *Poor Old Soul.*

Following the release of *Simply Thrilled Honey* the band toured with The Undertones, a move which bought them to a far wider audience.

After four singles the band decided their next would be through a major company. *L.O.V.E...Love* was released by Polygram Records, and was followed by Orange Juice's debut album, *You Can't Hide Your Love Forever.*

The band continued touring in 1982 to support the album, including a number of dates with Australia's

Go-Betweens, who have also recorded for Postcard.

Robert Ellis Orrall

Compared alternatively to Genesis, Elvis Costello, Fleetwood Mac, Joe Jackson, Nick Lowe, and a number of ska and funk acts, Robert Ellis Orrall is a difficult man to get a fix on.

Born in Boston, Orrall was infatuated with '60s pop, notably the output of The Swinging Medallions, Monkees, Nazz and Dave Clark 5. A member of teenage bands JB4 and The 2 Plus 2's, he worked through to the mid '70s writing songs and playing in a dozen unknown duos, trios, bands and ensembles. He also spent two years at the Berklee School of Music.

This grounding culminated in the obscure 1978 album *Sweet Nothing,* which he wrote, produced, distributed, designed and financed. The following year a single, *How Can She Even Like That Guy?,* appeared on the Sail label.

Substantial progress did not occur until 1980, when Orrall drew together a number of seasoned Boston musicians to form the Robert Ellis Orrall Band: Kook Lawry (guitar), David Stefanelli (drums), Don Walden (bass) and himself (vocals, keyboards). The following year he came to the attention of Sire Records U.K. chief Paul McNally, who was in the process of establishing his own Why-Fi label. Through McNally's patronage, Orrall was able to record the highly acclaimed *Fixation* album. Solid, hook-laden, intelligent and

ROBERT ELLIS ORRALL

THE ONLY ONES

due to their lack of success and disillusion with the music industry the group decided to break up and in March 1981 they played a farewell concert at London's Lyceum Ballroom.

Orchestral Manoeuvres In The Dark

Orchestral Manoeuvres In The Dark are Andy McClusky and Paul Humphreys, both from West Kirby, Wirral, Cheshire near Merseyside.

ORCHESTRAL MANOEUVRES IN THE DARK

adventurous, Orrall's stylish pop earned him considerable respect at radio level in America.

1982 saw release of a 10 inch EP, *Call The Uh-Oh Squad,* and early in 1983 an impressive five-track album, *Special Pain;* issued in America by RCA. Recorded at Rockfield Studio in Wales and produced by Roger Bechirian (of Elvis Costello, Lene Lovich, Squeeze, Nick Lowe fame), the record featured appearances by Carlene Carter, Virginia Astley (from The Ravishing Beauties), Troy Tate, and members of Blanket of Secrecy.

The track *I Couldn't Say No,* recorded as a duet with Carlene (wife of Nick Lowe, daughter of Johnny Cash — for those who don't read the gossip columns), was issued as an American single and performed respectably.

Like his hero Nick Lowe, Orrall is alarmingly prolific, claiming to have 290 'spare' songs on hand. Effusive, optimistic and undeniably talented, he is best summed up by his own words: "Personally, I like pop songs, but I also like songs that grab you, and I like songs that don't. I like songs that are smooth and slick, and I like songs that are irritating".

Only Ones

After several years of on-off bouts of singing and playing his songs, both in groups and solo, South London-born Peter Perrett finally assembled what threatened to be a permanent ensemble in 1972. The combo's name was England's Glory. Perrett chose not to approach record companies with the usual demo tape but with a properly pressed demonstration LP. Despite initial enthusiasm from record companies,

England's Glory broke up after only a couple of gigs.

Perrett then began forming a new band and through auditions recruited bassist Alan Mair, a refugee from Scottish teen bands, drummer Mike Kellie, who had played with Spooky Tooth, and guitarist John Perry, who had recorded with Grateful Dead writer Robert Hunter and Ratbites From Hell.

The Only Ones first recording release was on their own Vengeance label, a 12 inch single entitled *Lovers Of Today* released in a plain wrapper which quickly sold out its 500 copies in mid-1977. Soon after, the group signed with CBS. After their 'proper' single debut in April 1978 with *Another Girl, Another Planet,* The Only Ones released their self-titled debut album in May 1978. Over the next year the group made their first sojourn to the US and prepared for a second LP, which was released in March 1979 entitled *Even Serpents Shine,* and was accompanied by a single, *You've Got To Pay.*

After a second tour of the States in late 1979, a compilation of the first two LPs, *Special View,* was released in the US and Australia. In June 1980 The Only Ones released their third LP, *Baby's Got A Gun,* and another single, *Fools.* However,

Following their debut show at the late-lamented Eric's in Liverpool in October 1978, they elected to send a tape to Tony Wilson, who worked for a local TV channel on which they hoped to make an appearance. Tony, however, had other plans. He had recently formed Factory Records, and offered to release *Electricity* as a single on his label. The first of several versions of that song was recorded in a garage and the pressing of 5000 sold out in a fortnight.

The name the duo chose for themselves, Orchestral Manoeuvres In The Dark, was derived from one of the early VCL XI songs. These were recordings based on a hybrid of radio clips and 'war noises' taken from television.

September '79 saw the completion of a major deal with DinDisc and their first extensive series of UK dates supporting Gary Numan. They

THE ORIGINAL MIRRORS
OUR DAUGHTER'S WEDDING

promptly built their own studio in Liverpool calling it The Gramophone Suite and it was there they recorded their debut album *O.M.D.* The album was greeted with fascination — generally followed by enthusiasm, and the group entered 1980 preparing for their first headline tour of the UK. The tour marked the introduction of Dave Hughes (keyboards and bass) and Malcolm Holmes (drums, electronic percussion and rhythm unit control) as part of the live show, replacing the pre-recorded tapes that O.M.D. had previously used in concert.

Mid-1980 found O.M.D. once again buried in the studio, this time with Mike Howlett producing. The music that emerged included the British top 10 hit *Enola Gay* — a title taken from the name of the plane that dropped the A-Bomb on Hiroshima. *Organisation*, O.M.D.'s second LP, was released that same month, October 1980, and it too entered the UK top 10.

1981 saw O.M.D. emerge as one of the most consistently fresh and musically accessible of the British synthesiser bands. By the beginning of that year, their British success was consolidated, but perhaps more remarkable and relevant is their subsequent conquering of Europe. They have had number one singles in several countries, including

massive success with *Enola Gay* in France, Italy and Portugal.

The release in early 1982 of *Architecture And Morality,* their third LP, and the single, *Maid Of Orleans* (top 10 in the UK again), provided evidence that their popularity and reputation are far from a momentary fad. This was confirmed by the early 1983 charting of album four, *Dazzle Ships.*

Original Mirrors

Original Mirrors spent most of their first year together without a name — they couldn't find one they all liked.

Vocalist Steve Allen and guitarist Ian Broudie met in January 1979 and developed a songwriting partnership. Allen had come from Deaf School, one of the last of the early '70s English art rock bands, while Broudie had worked originally with Big In Japan. They were joined by drummer Pete Kircher (who had served his apprenticeship with Mick Green of the legendary British beat band The Pirates) and together the trio recorded some demos which earned them a contract with Polygram. After two auditions for a bass player they found Phil Spalding, who had worked with heavy metal guitrist Bernie Torme. Keyboardist Jonathan Perkins (ex-punk outfit Stadium Dogs) joined

just before the band's first live shows in June 1979.

Come the end of that year, no name had been decided on but eventually, for no real reason, they went with Original Mirrors.

In November 1979 came a debut single, *Could This Be Heaven?*, produced by Bill Nelson. It was followed in February 1980 by the release of their debut self-titled LP, which received enthusiastic reviews but failed to capture the public imagination. Undeterred, the band departed for a three month tour of Europe supporting Roxy Music.

In late 1980 they went into the studio with producer Mike Howlett and new bass player Jimmy Hughes (Spalding had split to join Toyah's band) to record their second album. *Heart-Twango And Raw-Beat* was released in early 1981 and garnered a minor British hit with the single, *Dancing With The Rebels.*

Our Daughter's Wedding ∎

Taking its name from a section marker in a greeting card rack, Our Daughter's Wedding came together early in 1980 at the hands of three veterans of the 1977 San Francisco punk explosion — Keith Silva (string synthesizer, vocals), Layne Rico (electronic Synare synthesizer) and Scott Simon (bass synthesizer, sax). The unit does not qualify as a rock band except in the most general sense. Although they play live, they do not use guitars or drums on stage. However, they insist they have nothing at all to do with the "New Romantic" synthesizer school out of England. "There are synthesizers," says Simon, "but it's not a science lab like Gary Numan." To preserve a human ingredient, the three musicians do not employ automatic triggering devices or sequencers — they actually *play* their synthesizers. "When times change you want to change with them," says Silva. "We approach our instruments as songwriters, not technology fiends."

Our Daughter's Wedding debuted with an independent label single, *Nightlife/Raincoats & Silverware,* which swiftly sold out a first pressing and landed them club dates in New York and Philadelphia. The rock-disco follow-up, *Lawnchairs/Airline,* became a full-scale breakout, making number 31 on the Billboard disco chart and selling 40,000 copies in England. 1981 saw the trio tour Canada with Orchestral Manoeuvres In The Dark and England with Classix Nouveaux. While in England, they recorded their first mini-LP for EMI America under producer Colin Thurston of Duran Duran/Bowie/Human League Kajagoogoo fame — *Digital Cowboy.*

Parker went into the studio to record some demos, which eventually found their way onto the radio show of influential DJ Charlie Gillett. Robinson then introduced Parker to the Rumour: Brinsley Schwarz (guitar) and Bob Andrews (keyboards) from the old Brinsley Schwarz line-up, ex-Ducks Deluxe guitarist Martin Belmont and the rhythm section of Andrew Bodnar (drums) and Stephen Goulding (bass).

Graham Parker and The Rumour started playing the English pub circuit in 1975 and then ventured forth on major tours with Ace, Kokomo, and Thin Lizzy. They

album followed early in 1979, *Squeezing Out Sparks,* produced by Jack Nitzsche. Another sell-out Australian tour followed late in 1979, where by now they were more popular than in their homeland. This time the horn section had been dropped and the sound was even tougher and harder.

Following *Sparks,* Parker has fallen increasingly out of favour in England. Not only is he now unfashionable but the two albums he has made since have been well below his best. The Rumour (minus Bob Andrews) split after recording *The Up Escalator* in 1980 to team up with Garland Jeffreys. *Another Grey Area*

Graham Parker

Early in 1975 a classified ad appeared in Melody Maker, reading "Singer/songwriter needs tasteful musicians for Stones/Dylan band." The ad had been placed by one Graham Parker, a Surrey petrol pump attendant and songwriter. The ad didn't help Parker discover the world's best rock'n'roll band but it did put him in touch with Dave Robinson, former manager of British pub rockers, Brinsley Schwarz, and a partner in a recording studio.

GRAHAM PARKER

"All I want to do is send a shiver up people's spines."
Graham Parker

THE PAYOLA$

released their first album, *Howlin' Wind,* in 1976 and began solid touring through the States, England and Europe. Touring was briefly interrupted in 1977 for the recording of a second album, at the legendary Rockfield Studios in Wales. *Heat Treatment* broke the band in America, winning them Rolling Stone's "Critics' Best New Band" award at the end of that year.

Next came the famous *Official Live Bootleg,* a limited edition live album from the Marble Arch show. It is much sought after by collectors and has been bootlegged a number of times. A pink vinyl 12 inch EP called *The Pink Parker,* contained the magnificent *Hold Back The Night.*

1978 saw a support stint to Southside Johnny on a sold-out UK tour, an offer to support Bob Dylan at the Blackbush outdoor festival, a solo album from The Rumour, the addition of a brass section, and the release of the third album, *Stick To Me,* again produced by Nick Lowe.

In late 1978 Parker and The Rumour undertook a highly successful tour of Australia, coinciding with the release of a live album, *Parkerilla.* A fourth studio

was recorded in America late in 1981 and Parker toured with an American pickup band early the next year. Critics lamented the absence of The Rumour, who were then off playing with Carlene Carter and Garland Jeffreys.

Apart from tempestuous singing, Parker also dabbles in literature and has one novel to his credit, *The Great Trouser Mystery* (Wyndham Books).

Early in 1983 Graham entered the studio with American producer David Kerschenbaum to begin a new album and drew up plans for an international tour.

Payola$

The Payola$' story is full of fairy tale fortunes, liberally spiced with embarrassments and disappointments. Their self-released *China Boys* single brought instant underground notoriety in hometown Vancouver in 1979 and an unexpected call from A&M Records, Canada. Paul Hyde (vocals) and Bob Rock (guitar) figured they'd better scratch together a band real fast and write more songs, as they only had three.

127

A&M released a four-song mini-LP on their Debut Series, then Miles Copeland's IRS Records released it in the US and Britain, and included *Jukebox* on IRS' *Greatest Hits Volumes 2 & 3*. The only thing that kept the band going was a nine-song demo which excited A&M enough to allow them to record an album and the time to form a proper band.

That same demo tape went to a few 'name' producers, but no one was available, so Bob Rock put his own studio engineer/production skills to work. *In A Place Like This,* released in 1980, was high charged aggressive rock'n'roll, tinged with reggae, calypso and bold melodies.

PERE UBU

After some local dates in 1981, the Payola$ were selected to open for ZZ Top in Vancouver, and then played support to The Police in Ontario.

Ex-Bowie sidekick Mick Ronson had some spare time and energy, and on a visit to Toronto popped into A&M's office looking for a production project. Mention of the Payola$ reminded him of a demo tape he'd received the year before and in February 1982 Ronson and the Payola$ recorded their second LP, *No Stranger To Danger.*

The Payola$ are now trimmed to a quartet with Bob Rock, Paul Hyde, Larry Wilkins (bass) and Chris Taylor (drums).

Pel Mel

Pel Mel are one of the few significant groups to emerge from the industrial city of Newcastle in Australia. The group formed in that city in 1979 as a means of escaping the stupefying atmosphere of their hometown.

Their predilection for the avant-garde earned them universal scorn in a metropolis renowned for its love of hard rock, so early in 1980 they journeyed down the coast to establish themselves in Sydney.

After gigging around that city's inner-city venues, and finding a far more receptive audience than they had in Newcastle, Pel Mel released their debut single, *No Word From China,* on their own Primate label early in 1981. The line-up at this stage was Judy McGee (vocals, keyboards and sax), Graeme Dunne (guitar and vocals), David Weston (drums), Jane McGee (guitar) and Glen (bass).

> "We're definitely the most fashionable group to have a go at. But that doesn't matter. At least getting numbered means that people are still paying attention to us."
> — Paul Simonon, The Clash

The single gave Pel Mel instant respect in Australian music circles and in June 1981 Gap Records signed the group and released a re-mastered version of the song. By the time their second single, *Head Above Water,* came out in December 1981 the line-up had undergone some changes. Jane McGee and Glen split and were replaced by Craig Robertson on bass.

As a four-piece the group continued to play constantly around Sydney and in mid-1982 had recorded a debut album, *Out Of Reason,* with producer Tony Cohen. The album was released late in 1982 along with the single, *Blind Lead The Blind.*

Pere Ubu

Pere Ubu hail from Cleveland, Ohio and are further evidence of the remarkable musical culture of that area. The first line-up was formed in 1975 by singer David Thomas with the idea that the specific grouping of talent might result in a 'unique music'. Certainly Pere Ubu remain at the forefront of American avant-garde music. They began before punk, they existed through the rise and fall of that period, and they continue to exist. They aren't post-punk, they are more post-rock.

David Thomas was originally a writer for a Cleveland teen paper, and together with rock critic, the late Peter Laughner, he formed a Stooges type band, Rocket From The Tombs, in 1974. Other members included Cheetah Chrome and Johnny Blitz, who later joined the Dead Boys. Rocket soon broke up due to musical differences.

Thomas then put a band together to record the single *30 Seconds Over Tokyo*, and was so encouraged by the result that he decided to continue the group under the name of Pere Ubu, a name taken from the Alfred Jarry character. They spent the next year playing around the Cleveland area and recorded a second single, *Final Solution,* released on their own Hearthian label. By early 1977 when Pre Ubu released *Street Waves,* the line-up had stabilised as Thomas (vocals), Tom Herman (guitar), Tony Maimone (bass), Scott Krauss (drums) and Allen Ravenstine (synthesizer).

In early 1978, after a fourth single, *Modern Dance,* came a debut LP of the same title. The second album, *Dub Housing,* came out at the end of that year, and in September 1979 after the release of their third LP, *New Picnic Time,* Tom Herman left the group. He was replaced by Texan Mayo Thompson who also remained a member of the reformed Red Crayola. This line-up recorded the fourth LP in 1980, *The Art Of Walking.* Since then a live album, *390⁰ Of Simulated Stereo,* has been released, along with a new studio effort, *Song Of The Bailing Man,* in 1981.

Tom Petty & The Heartbreakers

Though a forerunner in New Wave

Music, Tom Petty is in fact doing nothing more than reinterpreting traditional rock'n'roll for an '80s audience. Like The Rolling Stones, Yardbirds and others in the '60s, Petty is drawing on the groundwork laid by such pioneers as Chuck Berry and Bo Diddley, transforming basic rhythm patterns into a fresh, compelling sound.

Petty, the son of a Florida insurance salesman, quit high school at 17 to join local hot group, Mudcrutch, whose ranks later included Heartbreakers Mike Campbell (guitar) and Belmont Tench (keyboards). By the early '70s Tom was in Los Angeles hustling a record deal for the band, and from an array of attractive offers he chose Shelter, a company owned by Leon Russell. Thrust straight into the studio, Mudcrutch cut a single, *Depot Street/Wild Eyes,* which did absolutely nothing. The group changed its name to Tom Petty & The Heartbreakers and forged ahead with a self-titled album in 1976 which was critically acclaimed and criminally overlooked as was its 1977 successor, *You're Gonna Get It.* Then, just as Petty appeared to be breaking down the barriers, cruel fate struck in the form of a huge legal battle with MCA Records, new owners of Shelter after it went bankrupt. For almost two years, Petty was unable to record, suffering much the same problem as Bruce Springsteen in his famous battle

TOM PETTY

against manager Mike Appel. Though financial disaster loomed, Petty kept his sense of humour, naming a string of live performances permitted by the court The Law Suit Tour.

When a final agonising compromise was reached, Tom Petty

and The Heartbreakers descended on the recording studio with a fierce determination. The fruits of those sessions, released late in 1979, as the *Damn The Torpedoes* album, elevated the scrawny blond guitarist/singer/songwriter to the mega-platinum league. Only Pink

> "If I see one more rock video I'm gonna scream. I can't even tell who the musicians are. Is this guy the bass player? Is he an actor? Is he the French chef?"
> *Tom Petty*

Floyd could keep him out of number one in the American LP charts.

In early 1982 Petty released his fourth album, *Hard Promises,* which was just as successful as its predecessor. Meanwhile Petty and Campbell co-wrote *Stop Dragging My Heart Around* for Stevie Nicks' solo album, *Belladonna,* and the song was a smash hit worldwide when released as a single. Tom also went into the studio with hit veteran Del Shannon, producing his *Drop Down and Get Me* album, which

yielded up *Sea Of Love,* Del's first American chart entry since 1966.

1982 was a prolific year for Petty. Apart from his outside activities, he delivered his fifth album, *Long After Dark* late in the year, following another bitter battle with MCA over list pricing. Co-produced with Jimmy Iovine, it offered another high voltage surge of Petty Power and Petty Passion.

For the avid fan, there are a number of live tracks on single flips, 12 inchers and samplers, including *Stories We Could Tell, Something Else* and *Don't Bring Me Down.* Tom has also been extensively bootlegged.

PH.D

PH.D were one of the first British synthesizer duos to crack the pop

PH.D

charts, significantly in advance of Yazoo, O.M.I.D., Wham, The Quick and B.E.F. PH.D comprises Jim Diamond and classically trained pianist Tony Hymas.

The pair collided with each other fruitfully early in 1981. Diamond had arrived back in London from extensive stints in Germany and America, playing with nondescript bands. Hymas was more gainfully employed as a session musician, having been conductor of the Ballet

PiL

Rambert for three years.

The first single from the duo was *I Won't Let You Down,* which made number one in France, Austria, Belgium, Italy, Holland and Switzerland, top five in Britain and Australia and top 20 in Germany and South Africa. Two albums, *PH.D* and *Is It Safe?* and subsequent singles failed to match the dramatic impact of their debut. The derivation of the duo's name is worthy of note. The letters stand for Polyphemus (many themes of) Hymas, Diamond.

Pigbag ▮▮▮▮▮▮

Pigbag was formed in late 1980 by a number of people who enjoyed just playing together and had no real intention of actually forming a group. Eventually, in early 1981, a gig was arranged at Bristol's Anson Rooms where the nucleus of Pigbag, plus friends, played what was to become a legendary night.

The power was cut off by irate porters who objected to the free funk madness being perpetrated on the stage. The group, however, carried on acoustically until forcibly removed. The audience enjoyed the frolics and a near riot ensued.

Eventually Pigbag came to play in London and Y Records boss Dick O'Dell was invited to see the group. He was impressed and arrangements were made to record a single. The record, *Papa's Got A Brand New Pigbag,* was released in the UK on May 1, 1981 and rapidly gained momentum. From an initial NME Single Of The Week review, it sold upwards of 100,000 copies and was in and out of the UK charts for nine months, finally reaching the number one position in April 1982. The record became a dance floor favourite in the US as well, and after selling very well as an import, Y Records signed a licensing deal with Stiff America.

In early 1982, Pigbag's debut

album, *Dr Heckle And Mr Jive,* was issued and it continued the group's chart success in England. The line-up of the band is Simon Underwood (bass), Ollie Moore (percussion), James Johnstone (guitar and sax), Roger Freeman (percussion and trombone), Chris Leigh (trumpet) and Chippie Carpenter (drums). They all come from Bristol and Cheltenham in the West Country. The youngest is 18 and the eldest is 23. All are relatively unknown

In June 1983 they announced their disbandment, following release of the album *Lend An Ear.*

> **"I don't give a shit about any other outfit; they're all wankers and wallies."**
> — *John Lydon, Public Image Limited*

Public Image Limited ▮▮▮

Public Image Limited (PiL) was formed by Johnny Rotten in mid-1978 following the demise of The Sex Pistols. They released a debut single, *Public Image,* in October 1978 and a debut self-titled album in December. PiL played a few shows in early 1979 with a line-up of Johnny Rotten (Lydon) (vocals), Keith Levene (guitar), Jah Wobble (bass) and Jim Walker (drums), but dates were isolated and there was no conventional tour.

In June 1979 the second single was released in both seven inch and 12 inch formats. *Death Disco* was followed by *Memories* in October. In November PiL's second album was released in two forms: in the UK *Metal Box* came in a unique metal box (naturally),in a configuration of three 12 inch 45 rpm discs. In the rest of the world it was released as a double album titled *Second Edition.*

In the summer of 1980 PiL toured America for the first and last time. On their return they declared their intention never to perform live again and shortly afterwards Jah Wobble split.

Paris Au Printemps, a live album recorded in Paris March 1980, was released in November that year and was designed to counter the vast number of PiL bootlegs. *Flowers Of Romance* was released in May 1981 and the title track as a single in June. The line-up for this album was Johnny Rotten, Keith Levene and Jeanette Lee, with Martin Atkins playing drums on some tracks.

Late in 1981 the three members agreed to appear in a New York club, The Ritz, despite their prior avowal never to play live again. But

PIGBAG

THE POLECATS

the performance, which consisted of the group standing on stage obscured by screens while tapes played, caused the large audience to riot, resulting in extensive damage and police cordoning off the area. PiL have not appeared live since, nor released any records. Lydon now lives in New York permanently.

So far, the far-reaching concept of Public Image Limited, as a creative organisation capable of involving themselves in all spheres of communication, has only produced a handful of records in over four years.

Jeanette Lee quit the group in 1982 for obscure reasons, leaving Lydon and Levene to continue what one writer dubbed as "the band when they feel like it". A new album has been scheduled for 1983 — *You Are Now Entering The Commercial Zone,* though when it will actually be bestowed upon a breathless world is anybody's guess. Two new corporate identities have been established: Multi Image Corporation (MIC) and Public Enterprise Productions (PEP).

The most immediate plans for the intrepid duo involve providing the soundtrack for an Italian film, *Cop Killer,* starring Harvey Keitel and, in his first dramatic role, Mr Lydon.

The Plasmatics ▬▬▬

The Plasmatics are New York based and have established a cult reputation for their outrageous stage presentation, built around singer Wendy O. Williams' contortions, distortions and disrobing. As one critic said, "Wendy Williams' blatant exhibitionism stands eroticism on its head, turning sexual pleasure into a castrating horror show."

In early 1980 The Plasmatics recorded a three track 12 inch EP on

the Vice Squad label, produced by Stellar Axeman. Stiff Records moved swiftly to sign the act and late in 1980 their debut LP, *New Hope For The Wretched,* produced by former Stones producer Jimmy Miller, was released. It was previewed by a live/studio 12 inch EP.

As a visual act, The Plasmatics take rock theatre to a new extreme. Wendy Williams, topless except for gaffer tape over her nipples, systematically destroys all manner of objects on stage — including motor vehicles. It was for this stunt that in August 1980 the Greater London Council used safety regulations to ban the group from playing their first ever show outside America.

Wendy O. Williams' mammary exposure also troubled the band in many places and in 1981 the group's concert in Milwaukee was stopped by the police, who arrested Wendy for offensive behaviour and allegedly beat her up.

The Plasmatics were formed by manager Rod Swenson around Wendy, who was working in live sex shows in New York's Times Square area. Guitarist Richard Stotts joined soon after to write the songs with Swenson. The remaining members of The Plasmatics are recruited when needed.

In 1981 The Plasmatics released their second LP, *Beyond The Valley Of 1984,* followed by *Coup d'Etat* late in 1982 and a single of Tammy Wynette's *Stand By Your Man* sung as a duet by Wendy and Lemmy from Motorhead. Wendy's other activities included posing for an American hard core porn magazine.

Polecats ▬▬▬

The Polecats grew out of the nucleus of singer Tim Worman and guitarist Martin 'Boz' Boorer around 1975 when, at the tender age of 12, they

began strumming rockin' numbers (Bill Haley's among other favourites) in the living room of Tim's home in North-West London. By 1977 they had been playing in youth clubs for a year and had poached bassist Phil Bloomberg, who had been playing in a rival suburban band. The trio then gigged anywhere they could, to get money for new equipment.

In early 1980 the last of the line-up joined — drummer Neil Rooney who they also copped from a rival gang. By this time The Polecats were gaining a rapidly growing following around the pubs and clubs of London, and this led to the band's first breakthrough: a support gig to Matchbox at the Music Machine. Later that year they filled the support slot on a Rockpile UK tour which gained a tremendous reaction, both from audiences and the headliner.

Wendy O. Williams of THE PLASMATICS

1980 was a year of solid gigging throughout Britain, including supporting The Cramps on their UK tour. The Polecats signed to Polygram in early 1981 and first made vinyl in February with the release of their debut single *John I'm Only Dancing,* an energetic cover of this David Bowie classic, produced by fan Dave Edmunds. This was followed by their debut album *Polecats Are Go.*

The rise of The Polecats has been part of a recognisable rockabilly surge that has focused attention on the Stray Cats, Levi & The Rockats, The Mighty Guys, The Blue Cats, The Crackajacks, Jets and many others.

The Police

The Police, along with Blondie the most commercially successful New Wave group to emerge, were formed in 1977 by drummer Stewart Copeland, the son of an ex-CIA agent. Brought up in Lebanon, he had lived in England since the early '70s and spent some time drumming with progressive art-rock band Curved Air. Copeland discovered Sting (real name Gordon Sumner), an ex-school teacher, living in Newcastle, playing bass in the local jazz band No Exit (with long, dark hair and beard). Guitarist Andy Summers, whose past included stints with Zoot Money, The Animals, Kevin Coyne and Soft Machine, joined just before original guitarist Henry Padovani left to join the Electric Chairs. The new trio appeared on an obscure album and a tour of European Opera Theatres with classical composer Eberhard Schoener late in 1977.

The first Police record was the single, *Fall Out,* released on manager

POOKIESNACKENBURGER

Miles Copeland's Illegal Records. It sold out all picture-sleeved copies. Subsequent sessions with American producer John Cale proved unproductive and no output was issued. At this time the group, desperate for money, agreed to appear in a TV chewing gum commercial, and to look like a genuine punk band each member had to dye his hair blonde.

The band's breakthrough to mass popularity came in America. The Police financed their first American tour with the profits from English club performances. They took a cheap Laker flight in 1978 and toured in a second hand station wagon (with one roadie). This way they actually made a profit as well as opening up a new market for their records.

Roxanne and *Can't Stand Losing You,* the first singles released after

THE POLICE

the signing of a contract with A&M, were included on the band's debut album *Outlandos D'Amour,* which wasn't slated for release in America until March 1979. However The Police generated such interest through their live work that *Roxanne* gained extensive radio exposure, and the album was rush-released. Soon after, *Roxanne* soared into the US top 20 and was a major hit in the UK as well.

Although Sting wrote the majority of songs on *Outlandos D'Amour,* Copeland and Summers contributed extensively to the band's second album, *Regatta de Blanc,* which went to number one in England and broke the band internationally. The first two singles from the album, *Message In A Bottle* and *Walking On The Moon,* went to number one in England and were top 10 in Australia. Early in 1980 the group first toured Australia, after playing in South-East Asia, and then went on to appear in concerts in Bombay, Cairo, Nairobi and Athens.

In between recording the second and third albums, the group engaged in solo projects. Sting indulged his acting aspirations with a major role in the film *Quadrophenia* and also portrayed an Eddie Cochran fan in *Radio On.* Stewart Copeland recorded a solo album under the name of Klark Kent.

In 1980 and 1981 The Police continued their phenomenal international success with two further albums, *Zenyatta Mondatta* and *Ghost In The Machine.* The former yielded *Don't Stand So Close To Me,* worldwide hit in 1980. The latter, a concept album written by Sting and influenced by the philosophical writings of Arthur Koestler, contained another two hits — *Every Little Thing She Does Is Magic* and *Spirits In The Material World.* The first single lifted from the album, *Invisible Sun,* was banned by the BBC because of its alignment

> **"I think that rock stars let people down in many ways. It's not that they're not intelligent, it's just that they don't think, and that is disgraceful."**
> — Sting, The Police

with the anti-nuclear lobby.

Andy Summers realised a long-standing ambition during 1982 by recording an experimental guitar album with Robert Fripp, *I Advance Masked.*

In 1982 Sting performed solo at Amnesty International's *The Secret Policeman's Other Ball,* appearing on the resultant live album. He also acted the major role in an English film, *Brimstone and Treacle,* which included songs by Sting and The Police.

Two amusing Sting tracks appear on the soundtrack album of the movie *Party Party.* Mid 1983 saw release of the group's fifth LP *Synchronicity* and the huge global hit *Every Breath You Take.*

Pookiesnackenburger ■■■■

Based on the street/Metro bands of Paris, Pookiesnackenburger came together on the beach at Brighton in May 1981. So successful was their busking that their fame spread beyond the southern shores of merry England to the ever-alert ears of Stiff Records in London.

Nurtured by the Cliffhanger Theatre Group, who incorporated the band into a presentation at the Edinburgh Festival, and by Madness, who hired them to play in the foyer at the London premiere of the *Take It Or Leave It* movie, The Pookies soon had very near the world at their grimy feet.

The Pookies formed their own record company, Hebnote, and released *Just One Cornetto,* which they signed to Stiff in Australia. It went lead. Undeterred, The Pookies hurtled back into the studio to devote their not inconsiderable talents to the creation of a landmark seven-track mini-LP (maxi-EP?), *Pookie Beach Party.* Served up for discriminating consumption were the sidewalk standards *I Built The Pyramids, Shish Kebab* and *Happy Cajun.*

Inmates of this particular asylum are Steve McNicholas (violin, mandolin, guitar, vocals), Luke Cresswell (drums, vocals), Paul Clark (accordion, vocals), Sue Bradley (violin, vocals), John Helmer (guitar, vocals) and Gabby Dwyer (saxes, vocals).

Iggy Pop ■■■■■■■

James Jewell Osterberg (aka Iggy Pop) was born in 1947 in Ann Arbor, Michigan, the son of school teacher parents. Having spent his first 18 years in a trailer camp, James was ready to bust out and in the mid-'60s he formed his first band, The Iguanas.

He drummed and sang lead with The Iguanas but they soon folded. A

> **"It's a very tragic thing, but in England they just won't forgive me for being an American."**
> **— Iggy Pop**

brief sojourn to Chicago introduced Iggy to Sam Lay of The Paul Butterfield Blues Band, and this led to another short-lived exercise, The Prime Movers. By Halloween 1967 Iggy was back in Ann Arbor, for the premiere performance of his newest ensemble, The Stooges.

The Stooges were one of the seminal outfits for the '70s punk movement. Their adrenalin-charged power rock and Iggy's demented showmanship and penchant for on-stage self-mutilation were the models for what was to come almost 10 years later. The group signed to Elektra and in 1969 their self-titled debut album, produced by John Cale (ex-Velvet Underground), was released. Club dates, concerts and festivals followed, as did *Fun House,* the second Stooges album, which in its own searing way equalled the first.

IGGY POP

The group then went through a long period where personal and drug problems, compounded by the overkill of success, put their career on hold. But in 1973 they signed to Columbia and issued *Raw Power.* But by January 1974 The Stooges were history. A final performance, at Detroit's Michigan Palace, was recorded for the *Metallic K.O.* album.

Iggy Pop then disappeared for a couple of years, caught in a drug crisis, until David Bowie came to his rescue. After relocating in Germany, he released two albums on RCA, both produced by Bowie, *The Idiot* in 1976 and *Lust For Life* in 1977. Iggy toured extensively to support the records with Bowie playing piano in the band, and a live LP, *TV Eye,* was released in 1978. That same year an album, *Kill City,* recorded with guitarist James Williamson, which had sat in the can for a couple of years, was also released by Bomp.

In 1979 Iggy signed to Arista and late that year *New Values,* produced by Williamson, came out. In 1980 he formed a new band with Ivan Kral of The Patti Smith Group on guitar, bassist Glen Matlock of The Sex Pistols, ex-Tangerine Dream drummer Klaus Kruger, lead guitarist Steve New from The Rich Kids, and ex-XTC keyboardist Barry Andrews. They recorded an album at Rockfield Studios in Wales, *Soldier,* and toured England, Europe and America.

CHRISSIE HYNDE OF THE PRETENDERS

The group disbanded soon after and in 1981 Iggy recorded his third and last album for Arista, *Party.* In 1982 he signed to Blondie guitarist Chris Stein's new label, Animal, and with Stein producing, recorded the *Zombie Birdhouse* album, released late in 1982.

Pretenders

In 1974 Chrissie Hynde moved to England from her native America and was employed on a freelance basis by New Musical Express. Soon after, she recieved a phone call from Paris asking her to be the singer in a band. Chrissie visited a few record companies, scrounged as many free records as she could, and after selling them, left for Paris. After six months, the language problems of working with French musicians overcame her and she fled to Cleveland, USA, to join a R&B group, Jack Rabbit.

They soon broke up and Chrissie was lured back to Paris to join the French Rockets. Six months later she returned to London and began

working with the musicians who later became The Damned, Mick Jones later of The Clash, and she played guitar in Johnny Moped's rhythm section. At this time she was managed by infamous Tony Secunda, former manager of The Move, who in a brilliant career

move, forced her to reject an offer to play guitar and sing backup vocals for Nick Lowe on the 1977 Stiff Tour.

A demo tape of one of Chrissie's originals led to a recording contract with Dave Hill's Real Records, so she set about forming a band, filling in time singing backup vocals on albums by Johnny Thunders, Chris Spedding and Mick Farren.

Eventually The Pretenders came together as Peter Farndon (bass), Martin Chambers (drums) and James Honeyman-Scott (lead guitar). In January 1979 their debut single produced by Nick Lowe, the Ray Davies composition *Stop Your Sobbing,* was released and immediately hailed as one of the best debuts in years.

The second single, *Kid,* was produced by Chris Thomas and increased the band's fortunes by going top 30 in the UK.

In October 1979, *Brass In Pocket,* was released and their success was assured. The record went to number one on both the UK and Australian charts and was a top 10 hit in the US. The group's self-titled debut album, produced by Thomas, was released in January 1980 and achieved the rare feat entering the British charts at number one. The group embarked on an extensive tour of the UK, Europe and America to promote it. Their appearance at

PRINCE

134

the Concerts For The People Of Kampuchea over Christmas 1979 was a triumph, placing them on the same stage and by association, in the same league, as The Clash, Specials, Ian Dury and The Blockheads and Rockpile.

The Pretenders toured constantly for almost a year, issued *Talk Of The Town* in March 1980 and *Message Of Love* in March 1981, as well as the *Extended Play* EP in April 1981. All were proof of massive international popularity. Meanwhile in the early months of 1981 the group finally recorded their second album with Chris Thomas again producing.

Pretenders II was released worldwide in August 1981 and the band immediately set out on another gruelling world tour, concentrating particularly on America but also taking in the UK, Australia and the Far East. The months on the road appeared to take their toll on the band, with Chrissie Hynde especially presenting a very disillusioned face to the rock media.

In June 1982, just as Pete Farndon left the band less than amicably, James Honeyman-Scott died tragically in London. This rent the already debilitated group right down the middle and, for some months, it ceased to exist. Chrissie pulled herself together with the assistance of new husband Ray Davies and the advent of motherhood, and reassembled The Pretenders with Rockpile's seasoned Billy Bremmer temporarily taking over on guitar. This fresh line-up made an instant mark, with their *Back On The Chain Gang* single going top ten in both Britain and Australia.

> **"I never think what I do is good enough. I'm analytical, critical, fastidious. . . a perfectionist."**
> — *Chrissie Hynde, The Pretenders*

Prince

Prince, a native of Minneapolis in the US Midwest, was still in his teens when he recorded his first album, *For You,* in 1979. A year later, *I Wanna Be Your Lover* from his second self-titled album became a hit in the US soul charts. Then in 1981 *Uptown,* from the *Dirty Mind* album, became his first major crossover hit in the States and he toured for the first time in the UK and Europe.

1982 was the year that Prince achieved his breakthrough. *Controversy,* like all his albums, was composed, performed and produced totally by himself. The record, and its two hit singles — *Controversy* and *Sexuality* —established Prince as *the* new black star in America. Within three years, his uninhibited sensuality and unique musical finesse had taken him from total obscurity to recognition as a major artist and a leading light in the 'new funk' style. He is being hailed as the "Sly Stone of the '80s".

In late 1982 Prince, still only in his early 20s, released his fifth album, the double *1999.* Like its predecessor, it was banned by a number of public institutions in mid-western America for its explicit sexual references.

The Psychedelic Furs

The Psychedelic Furs came into existence in January 1977, formed by four beginners from south of London — Richard Butler (lyricist and singer), Tim Butler (bass), Roger 'Dog' Morris (guitar) and Duncan Kilburn (sax). From the very outset this band was a blend of unusual influences and active imaginations.

At a gig in September, 1978, John Ashton asked to play guitar on one number and promptly found himself the fifth permanent Fur. Early in 1979 drummer Vince Ely came along. Within the course of an hour his audition had evolved into a full rehearsal. The Psychedelic Furs were the six-piece band that remained for years.

The Furs signed with CBS in September, 1979, and November saw the release of their exceptional single debut, *We Love You.* The Furs also began to build up a national following with their first dates outside the capital. In February 1980, *The Psychedelic Furs* album found instant favour, entering the UK charts at 18.

In May 1981 The Furs released *Talk Talk Talk*, again produced by

THE PSYCHEDELIC FURS

Steve Lillywhite, which repeated the chart success of the former. By this album they had expanded their sound, with Duncan Kilburn doubling on saxophone and keyboards.

The Furs' third album, *Forever Now,* produced by Todd Rundgren in America and featuring Flo & Eddie backing vocals, came out in late 1982 and the single *Love My Way,* was a minor hit in the UK. By this time the group had reduced to a four-piece with Phil Calvert, ex-Birthday Party, as the new drummer.

Q

THE QUICK

Q Tips

Q Tips first got together in the late '70s through their common love of '60s soul music. The members are Paul Young (vocals), Ian Kew (keyboards), Mick Pearl (bass), Garth Watt-Roy (guitar), Steve Farr (sax), Stewart Blandamer (sax), Tony Hughes (trumpet) and Barry Watts (drums). All are in their early 20s, except for Mick Pearl who is approaching 50.

The group initially attracted attention in England in 1980 with two singles, both soul classics — *Tracks Of My Tears* and *The Letter Song.* Both songs made the UK charts and they followed it up in August 1980 with their debut album, *Q Tips.*

The group have toured constantly throughout England in the last three years and have played in Europe several times, including the Montreux Jazz Festival. In consequence of their great live reputation, Hannibal Records released *The Q Tips Live* album.

> **"I'm sick of pop music. Most of it is just crap. It's sick, really sick. Every now and then you get a new face who becomes The New Face of Rock Rebellion. Ah, it just pisses me off."**
> — *Paul Weller, The Jam*

THE Q-TIPS

The Quick

Although both members of The Quick are English born, they first met at a party in Los Angeles in 1978 where George McFarlane (bass/keyboards/synthesizers) had been doing session work. George heard the dulcet tones of a fellow Brit, Col Campsie, and soon The Quick were formed.

On their return to London, the duo went into Basing Street Studios with Roxy Music producer Rhett Davies and recorded a demo which immediately gained them a contract with Epic Records. Their debut single, *Sharks Are Cool, Jets Are Hot,* was released in September 1979 and was followed by *Ship To Shore,* in April 1980.

A third single, *Hip Shake Jerk,* stiffed in England but became a monster hit in Australia. Accordingly, an album titled *On The Uptake* was rush-recorded at the CBS London studios and pushed out on the Australian market only. It included the follow-up singles *Young Men Drive Fast* and *Zulu* —both of which were relative failures.

When it came time to prepare a debut album for the rest of the world, The Quick remixed some tracks from *On The Uptake,* recorded a few fresh titles, and released it all as *Fascinating Rhythm,* produced by New Yorker John Luong. *Zulu* eventually broke out in American discos and became number one on the Billboard Disco Top 100. *Rhythm of the Jungle* became a top 20 Australian hit during the second half of 1982.

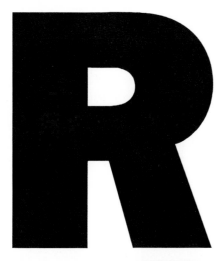

R

Radio Birdman

Radio Birdman are probably Australia's most legendary band from the late '70s (excluding glam rockers Skyhooks). Radio Birdman and The Saints were the first groups to give Australia a sense of punk. Though in Birdman's case, it had very little to do with the English punk scene, and everything with the late '60s Detroit punk of Iggy Pop and The Stooges and MC5.

Guitarist Deniz Tek, who formed Radio Birdman, had in fact grown up in nearby Ann Arbor, Michigan and been immersed in the Detroit sound during that time. In the early '70s he moved to Sydney, Australia, with his parents and began studying medicine at Sydney University. In his spare time he played with a small group called TV Jones.

In November 1974, Tek teamed up with three members of another seminal punk band, The Rats: Rob Younger (vocals), Warwick Gilbert (bass) and Ron Keeley (drums). Tek also introduced a fellow medicine student, Pip Hoyle (keyboards), to the line-up. Hoyle's relationship

with the band was undertaken on a part-time basis, depending on the restraints of his university course. So another guitarist, Canadian-born Chris Masuak (ex-Jackals) was added.

Radio Birdman got their first regular gig at the Excelsior Hotel in Sydney, playing some originals along with covers of songs by The Stooges, MC5, Ventures, The Dictators, Blue Oyster Cult, The Remains and The Doors. Due to their aggressive music and uncompromising stand with promoters and the Australian music business in general, the group had a lot of trouble finding places to play. Finally, they established their own regular gig at the Oxford Funhouse and they quickly became the loudest and most menacing band in Sydney.

It was from this point that Radio Birdman began to attract a large, loyal band of followers. The group encouraged this attitude with their paramilitary stage clothes, the parading of their own prominent symbol, and the promotion of the group as a solid enclave against the world. Some people thought of them as highly paranoid. Others considered them Nazi sympathisers.

After an independent EP, *Burn My Eye,* and an independent album, *Radios Appear,* Radio Birdman accepted a contract with Sire Records in America.

In early 1978 they (plus Hoyle) went to Britain to record an album at Rockfield Studios. The band then toured England and Europe with The Flamin' Groovies. They received poor support from Sire and went down badly with critics and audiences alike. After a final show in Oxford in June, the group

acrimoniously split and all soon returned to Australia.

Radio Birdman had a further album (again called *Radios Appear)* released globally by Sire, containing tracks straight from the Australian album, some new material and re-recorded versions of others from the first album. In 1981 the album they recorded in Wales was finally released under the title of *Living Eyes.* But that is far from the end of the Birdman story. Looming larger in death than in life, the group has become almost a religion.

A well-packaged bootleg album (a

THE RAINCOATS

first for Australia) appeared, titled *Eureka Birdman.* Captured at the Eureka Hotel in Geelong on November 30 1977, it featured such stage favourites as *Kick Out The Jams, L.A. Woman* and *California Sun.* In 1982, former RAM magazine editor, Anthony O'Grady prepared a one-hour Birdman audio documentary album for WEA Records, *Soldiers Of Rock'n'Roll*

Devotees have patronised well the subsequent bands of the Birdmen. Chris Masuak and Warwick Gilbert formed The Hitmen, which Masuak leads to this day. Gilbert then recorded with garage band the Lime Spiders, while working as an animator. Rob Younger formed The Other Side and the New Christs. He also participated in the New Race tour (see: New Race). Tek and Keeley played as The Visitors for a time, recording a 12 inch EP for the independent Phantom label.

Tek is a fairly phenomenal creature. He laid aside his advanced medical studies to train in America as an astronaut/fighter pilot, briefly breaking his training for the New Race tour.

The Raincoats

The Raincoats were formed in London in 1978 by ex-Slit Palmolive (drums), Portuguese-born Anna Da

RADIO BIRDMAN

Silva (vocals), Gina Burch (bass) and Vicky Aspinall (violin and guitar). After one single for Rough Trade, *Fairytale In The Supermarket,* released in April '79, Palmolive left the group. She did stay long enough to play on their debut album, *The Raincoats,* which came out in November of that year.

The remaining trio have searched for the last three years for another female drummer, but have been unable to find one suitable. In the meantime they have worked live with ex-PiL drummer Richard Gudanski, This Heat member Charles Hayward, and Derek Goddard. For the recording of their second LP, *Odyshape,* released mid-1981, The Raincoats utilised a number of seasoned musicians including Robert Wyatt, formerly of Soft Machine.

In early 1982 the group released a new single, *No One's Little Girl,* which demonstrated well their combination of pop with feminist sentiment.

Smith, Talking Heads, and Television — all of whom played to a market created by the seminal New York Dolls.

The Ramones signed to Sire Records in 1976 and recorded what many considered to be the best album of that year, containing a stack of classic Ramones material like *Now I Wanna Sniff Some Glue, Judy Is A Punk, Beat On The Brat,* and *Blitzkreig Bop.*

A second album, *Ramones Leave Home* was issued in 1977 and, surprise surprise, didn't sound all that different to the first album.

In New Musical Express Charles Shaar Murray best summed up the band's appeal: "They're simultaneously so funny, such a

Legendary producer Phil Spector was enlisted to produce *End Of The Century* in 1980, an album containing an extraordinary marriage of the Spector/Ramones style in their version of *Baby I Love You,* the song Spector produced with The Ronettes in 1964. The project, while not entirely a success, had some undeniably high moments, notably *This Ain't Havana* and, the gungy ones' first true ballad, *Danny Says.*

Thus was born a pattern for future albums — the securing of interesting but unlikely producers. Graham Gouldman of 10cc and '60s hit-writing fame was called upon for album seven, *Pleasant Dreams;* a surprisingly lacklustre and poorly focused effort.

The situation was improved dramatically with 1983's *Subterranean Jungle* album, produced by pop/bubblegum wizard Ritchie Cordell and containing fine versions of the Chambers Brothers' *Time Has Come Today* and the Music Explosion's *Little Bit O' Soul.*

The Ramones of today have evolved into a precise, pulverising powerpop unit, without losing their intrinsic neanderthal charm. The songs are now generally exceeding two minutes in length and contain considerably more than five or six words. Like all pesky brats, Joey and the boys have been tempered a little by the passing of time.

THE RAMONES

The Ramones

Until recently, The Ramones persisted with the notion that they were four brothers — first it was Joey (vocals), Johnny (guitar), Dee Dee (bass), and Tommy (drums). Then, in 1978 Tommy left and was replaced by former Voidoids drummer Marc Bell, who traded under the name Marky Ramone. With his recent departure, The Ramones recruited new drummer Richie Beau and stated definitely that he is not and will not be a Ramone.

Conceived as cartoon punks, The Ramones hail from Forest Hills, a New York suburb. Formed around 1974, they worked the same New York club circuit that spawned Patti

cartoon vision of rock and roll, and so genuinely tight and powerful, that they're just bound to enchant anyone who fell in love with rock'n'roll for the right reasons."

Rocket To Russia was the third Ramones album, yielding an American chart entry in *Sheena Is A Punk Rocker.* Early in 1978 they were back in the charts with *Rockaway Beach.*

Album number four, *Road To Ruin,* was an obvious indication that The Ramones were broadening their horizons. Next came *It's Alive,* a double live album recorded at London's Rainbow Theatre on New Year's Eve 1977 — 28 songs in not many more minutes — the archetypal Ramones performance.

The Raybeats

The Raybeats were put together as a hobby in October 1979 by four musicians with impressive credentials on the New York scene. Guitarist Jody Harris and drummer Don Christenson played with James Chance and the Contortions, and guitar/keyboard/ sax player Pat Irwin and original bassist George Scott (who had also been a Contortion) had played with Lydia Lunch in 8 Eyed Spy.

The group's popularity around New York persuaded them to continue on a permanent basis, but in mid-1980 Scott died of an overdose. He was replaced by Danny Amis in September and they

THE RAYBEATS

THE REVILLOS

signed with the British label Beggars Banquet's new subsidiary Don't Fall Off The Mountain. In late 1980 they recorded an EP, *Roping Wild Bears,* and in early 1981 journeyed to England to record their debut album, *Guitar Beat,* with Human League producer Martin Rushent.

In keeping with the group's kitschy matching uniforms — double-breasted cowboy shirts or electric-blue suits and bow ties — their original music is a panoply of '60s instrumental music: Link Wray, Junior Walker, The Mar-Kays, Dick Dale and B-movie theme music.

The Reels

The Reels are the only Australian rock band of any note to emerge from a New South Wales country town. David Mason (vocals), Craig Hooper (guitar and synthesizer) and John Bliss (drums) had gone to school together in Dubbo in the early '70s and formed a band called Native Son, which played around that area for three years. Along the way they picked up Colin 'Polly' Newham (keyboards) who had been playing in cabaret bands around the nearby Bathurst/Orange district.

In 1978 the group moved to Sydney and acquired a new bass player there, Paul Abrahams, as well as a new name, The Brucelanders. The group attracted a lot of notice in the city with their quirky, XTC influenced music and in 1979 they signed to Polygram. Late that year they returned to Dubbo to record their debut album on a mobile recording unit on the verandah of a country property. The album, *The Reels,* was produced by Mark Opitz

and contained two singles that were minor successes, *Love Will Find A Way* and *Pre Fab Hearts.*

Soon after the LP's release in early 1980, The Reels recruited a sixth member, synthesizer player and costume designer, Karen Ansell, who had been playing with a Melbourne group, The Romantics. The new line-up recorded a third single, *After The News,* and then embarked on a tour of Australia by train.

At Christmas 1980 The Reels released an EP, *5 Great Gift Ideas,* from which they achieved a minor hit single with their surprisingly faithful cover of Jim Reeves' C&W classic, *According To My Heart.* By this stage they had become a predominantly synthesizer-based group and the tempo of their music had slowed markedly.

In early 1981, after recording the second album, John Bliss left the group and was replaced by Stephan Fidock, who had played with Karen Ansell in The Romantics. A fourth single, *Shout And Deliver,* was released and just failed to make top 40. In mid-1981, just as keyboardist Colin Newham was leaving the group, their second LP, *Quasimodo's Dream,* produced by Bruce Brown and Russell Dunlop, was released and received disappointing sales. The title track was also released as the group's fifth single — another flop.

The Reels carried on as a five-piece group and released *No. 3* late in 1981, which had been recorded in New Zealand as part of an aborted 'heavy metal' EP. In early 1982 the group suffered further changes when both Paul Abrahams and Karen Ansell departed. The Reels have carried on as a trio since then with

the adition of a tape recorder for live work.

In late 1982 The Reels demonstrated that they have changed direction yet again with a new single, *This Guy's In Love With You,* a straight cover of the old Burt Bacharach song, which by going top 20 has given them their biggest hit to date. In December 1982 they released their third LP, *Beautiful,* which emerged by special license on the K-Tel label. The record continued their flirtation with synthesized MOR and 'Beautiful Music'. Undoubtedly The Reels are the most commercially adventurous group in Australia — which may be a nice way of saying that they have absolutely no direction.

The Revillos

Following the demise of The Rezillos in 1978, two of the founder members, Eugene Reynolds and Fay Fife, began plans for a new group which would continue and expand the ideas of the first. In 1979 the zappy seven-piece Revillos were formed, greatly inspired by the more off-beat elements of the early '60s when pop was brash, inventive and unpretentious.

The original line-up for the group was Fay Fife (vocals), Eugene Reynolds (vocals and keyboards), Robo Rhythm (drums), Hi Fi Harris (guitar), Felix (bass) and The

RICCI

Revettes (Babs and Cherry) on backing vocals.

Former art students Fay and Eugene design their own unmistakable style of clothes which are worn as much off stage as on. The band appear on their own label, Snatzo, in a distribution deal with Dindisc, recording most of their songs in a friend's kitchen; and

THE REELS

design their clothes and art work in their front rooms in Edinburgh. The Revillos don't believe in tours, instead they prefer to play somewhere in Britain every weekend.

Their first single, *Where Is The Boy For Me?* released in October, 1979, was followed by the equally

> **"Style is bullshit, very overrated. Content is more important than style. I've never had a style and I still don't."**
> *Joe Jackson*

jovial *Motor Bike Beat*. Their first and only album, *Rev Up*, was released in 1980.

The singles *Scuba Scuba* and *Hungry For Love* followed in late 1980 with little success. The group was dropped by Dindisc soon after and it was not until late 1981 that the next single, *She Fell In Love With A Monster Man,* appeared on the band's own Superville label. In 1982 The Revillos continued to play weekend gigs in Britain and released one further single, *Bongo Brain*.

Ricci

Ricci is a fascinating young Manchester performer whose beginnings can be traced back to the Rum Runner Club in Birmingham, home of Duran Duran. Unable to achieve anything significant in England he moved to Hollywood early in 1982 and began recording while working by day for an X-rated film company.

His mentors became Alan Howarth (synthesizer programmer for *Raiders Of The Lost Ark, Star Trek — The Movie,* and the band Weather Report) and Cinema Eagle Award winner Tony Geufen. Under these two talented gentlemen he recorded an adventurous techno-pop remake of the Frank Sinatra chestnut *Strangers In The Night*. A bizarre film clip for the song was directed by rock guru Kim Fowley. Released in Europe and Australia, the single and clip became somewhat of an underground sensation.

An unabashed devotee of Joel Gray, Sinatra, Minelli, Bowie and Presley, Ricci (pronounced Reesey) dabbles in experimental film-making and at 17 was the youngest stock market dealer in England. In 1982, old friends Duran Duran invited him to guest on some West Coast dates of their summer tour of America.

Rip Rig & Panic

Like Pigbag, the roots of Rip Rig & Panic can be traced back to The Pop Group, a 1978-'80 hard-edged British funk rock outfit which included within its ranks multi-instrumentalist Gareth Sager, drummer Bruce Smith and bassist Sean Oliver who formed RR&P, and Simon Underwood, wh formed Pigbag. Sager recruited singer Neneh Cherry (daughter of famed jazz trumpeter Don Cherry), pianist Mark Springer nd singer/dancer Andrea Oliver for his new group in 1981; with the aim of further exploring the back lanes of wild'n'woolly jazz-rock improvisation. He, however, sees his pursuit in far more lofty terms: "We're anti-logic and definitely anti-culture. . . walking a tightrope between desperation and hope. Everybody's all tied up in the horizontal and vertical, when really

the lateral is more interesting. All this stuff about getting down and dancing on the disco floor is just like waltzing — it's the old world. We go where the groove takes us."

The groove first took Gareth and his comrades to a debut album, *God* and later the single *Storm The Reality Asylum.* The relative lack of success of both issues was almost welcomed by Sager, who haughtily tossed off, "No real soul music ever gets into the charts. Nothing with feeling ever gets played on the radio."

Late in 1982 Smith and Cherry sojourned in Sweden, preparing for the birth of their child. During their absence, veteran jazz drummer Louis Mahalo was recruited.

RIP RIG AND PANIC

Around this time, the second album, *I Am Cold*, appeared, featuring session sax work by Don Cherry and David DeFries. This LP included the aforementioned single. 1983 saw the release of album three, *Attitude;* produced by Sager and Alan Kidron, and featuring the single *Do The Tight Rope*.

Tom Robinson

Tom Robinson's musical career began in 1974 under the guidance of the Kinks' Ray Davies, who signed an unknown band called Cafe Society to his Konk label. Their debut album came out in 1975 and was spectacularly unsuccessful — selling a worldwide total of 650 copies. The group consisted of three singers — one of whom was Tom Robinson.

In late 1976, Robinson quit to

TOM ROBINSON

form a group of his own with guitarist Danny Kustow, which shortly became known, playing in pubs and clubs around London, as the Tom Robinson Band. The line-up was Robinson (bass and vocals), Kustow (guitar), Mark Ambler (keyboards) and Brian Taylor (drums). This unit were captured live on the *Rising Free* EP which contained Tom's signature song, *Glad To Be Gay*.

In August 1977, they signed to EMI and in September released their first single, *2-4-6-8 Motorway,* a huge British hit that also charted well in Australia. This was followed by two further UK hit singles and debut album, *Power In The Darkness,* which carried forth Robinson's strong pro-homosexual stand.

Their second LP *TRB-2* and single *Bully For You* produced by Todd Rundgren, fared somewhat worse and in June 1979, after extensive touring in England, Europe and America, the band broke up, due to Robinson's growing hatred of touring and Kustow's fear of flying. Robinson suffered a nervous breakdown and disappeared from view for nearly a year. His only

ROMEO VOID

activities were an occasional solo benefit performance and a stint writing lyrics for fellow confessed gay, Elton John, on his *21 At 33* and *The Fox* albums.

In June 1980, Tom Robinson formed a new band, Sector 27, of which he insisted he was only one equal member. The group recorded a self-titled album with Steve Lillywhite, of songs co-written by Robinson with bassist Jo Burt (ex-Troggs) and guitarist Stevie B. Sector 27 toured as support for The Police on their US jaunt in early 1981 and then embarked on a tour of Europe on their own.

But in June 1981, amid drastic financial problems, Tom Robinson was sacked from the band by the other three when he demanded that they include his older material in their live set and bill themselves under his name. He moved to Hamburg and recorded a single in German called *Tango On The Wall*, and also produced Ingeburg

> **"I don't agree with the right to work anyway. I agree with the right not to work."**
> *Simon Underwood, Pigbag*

Thomsen and Christian Lunch.

In October and November 1981, Tom played small club dates in Japan with Richard Mazda and the Cosmetics and also returned briefly to England to play a few benefit concerts including Amnesty's second *Secret Policeman's Ball*. In early 1982 he returned to Hamburg and recorded the *North By North-West* album, a collaboration with producer Richard Mazda. A unique record, it was recorded on semi-professional equipment in a demo studio, using the cheapest technology and instruments they could find.

During 1981, EMI allowed Tom to compile and annotate the *Tom Robinson Band* LP, which comprised ten tracks not previously released on an album — including *2-4-6-8 Motorway*. Also included was a stirring version of Dylan's *I Shall Be Released* and three tracks from the rare *Rising Free* EP.

Romeo Void

Romeo Void, a band of relatively reserved, art-minded musicians who hail from San Francisco, are one of the few West Coast punk-related bands to move beyond the region's obsession with artful nihilism. They are trying to forge an American equivalent to the English post-punk music.

Singer and lyricist, Deborah Iyall, a Cowlitz Indian, grew up in Fresno, California, and as a teenager harboured aspirations to become a poet, but became enamoured of rock music after seeing a Patti Smith concert in 1975. In 1977 she was studying at the San Francisco Art Institute where — after a brief stint singing for the Mummers and Poppers, a '60s style pop revival

ROUGH TRADE

and former Labelle member Nona Hendryx. Once more, themes of brutal sexuality, homosexual murder, masturbation, masochism, drug addiction and mental instability prevailed throughout.

Ruts DC

In the summer of 1979, The Ruts had a UK top 10 hit with the pile-driving single, *Babylon's Burning.* They were in the eye of the punk rock maelstrom then, and perhaps it was the pressures of that position that led to the demise of singer Malcolm Owen, who died of a heroin overdose during the summer of 1980. So, after just one album, *The Crack,* The Ruts were faced with an uncertain future.

It was decided to tie up all of the loose ends with a final album as The Ruts. *Grin And Bear It* was a compilation of previously released material and rare items, such as a John Peel session and a live cut recorded in Paris. It also contained the group's last single with Malcolm on lead vocals, the prophetic *West One (Shine On Me).* The album symbolised the end of The Ruts and the beginning of Ruts DC. DC stands for Da Capo which translates from the Latin as a "new beginning".

Ruts DC contains the three survivors of The Ruts — Segs (bass and lead vocals), Dave Ruffy (drums and vocals) and Paul Fox (guitar and vocals) plus sax and keyboards player Gary Barnacle. Their debut album as Ruts DC, *Animal Now,* was released on Virgin Records in May 1981. Produced by the band and John Brand, it was recorded at the oddly incongruous location of the International Christian Centre in Eastbourne (because it's cheap). The new beginning for Ruts DC was aided immensely by playing a couple of huge concerts as special guests of The Who, followed by their own English and European tour.

band — she met Frank Zincavage, a sculpture student and occasional bassist smitten by art rock and Roxy Music. Deborah persuaded him to compose some music for a video project, which she later ornamented with wordless singing. Impressed with the end effect, they decided to form a band, recruiting Peter Woods (guitar), Benjamin Bossi (sax) and Larry Carter (drums).

In 1981, they released their debut album, *It's A Condition,* which was released on the San Francisco independent label, 415 Records.

Rough Trade

Approaching their 10th year of operation, Toronto's Rough Trade have finally broken out of Canada, the key being the stunning 1983 single *All Touch.*

The core of the band is songwriters Carole Pope and Kevan Staples, who had performed together as The Bullwhip Brothers and O before creating Rough Trade in 1974. By 1976 they had come to critical attention by writing the early New Wave musical *Restless Underwear* and scoring the Alan King film *One Night Stand,* for which they won a Canadian Film Award.

In 1978-'79 they wrote songs for and performed in the CBC TV production *Clowns,* wrote a hit for Tim Curry, and contributed *Shakedown* to the soundtrack of the William Friedkin film *Cruising.* In 1980 they appeared in the film *Deadline,* hosted the CBC *Video Film* television show, and signed with True North Records.

The first True North album, *Avoid Freud,* became a platinum seller and won Carole a prized Juno award for Most Promising Female Vocalist in 1981. This led to a distribution deal with CBS in America, Stiff in England and Big Time in Australia. A national tour of Canada was an absolute sell-out.

A second True North album, *For Those Who Think Young,* featuring background vocals by Dusty Springfield (Carole had sung on a Dusty album which included a couple of Rough Trade songs), also achieved platinum, and won Carole a Chimo award as Best Female Vocalist and a second Juno award. Another huge Canadian tour followed, as well as a jaunt through Denmark.

This third album (the first had been a limited edition direct-to-disc effort in 1976) generated three Canadian hits: *Fashion Victim, High School Confidential* and *All Touch.* All manifest the seamy, often violent sexual imagery of Pope's lyrics, pushing her to the forefront of the small core of female New Music innovators.

Pope and Staples have drawn around them an impressive core of backing musicians. They are Australian bassist Terry Wilkins, drummer Bucky Berger and keyboards player David McMorrow.

Early 1983 saw release of the album *Shaking The Foundations,* featuring some backing vocals by fellow Canadian Bruce Cockburn

RUTS DC

S

audience for what they were doing.

The most talked about aspect of the Cowboys stage act is Gray's frequent forays into the middle of crowds with a loudly whirring (bladeless) chainsaw.

Late in 1982 The Cowboys signed to Australia's White Label Records and released their debut single — *Nothing Grows In Texas* and the band's anthemic *Is Nothing Sacred?*

Sardine v

Sardine originally formed in 1980 to play some songs for guitarist and singer Ian Rilen's publisher. They then decided to continue as they realised the band's potential. After only five weeks rehearsal they played

SARDINE v

In March 1982 Sardine released their debut single, *Sabotage/Sudan*, on Mushroom's White Label. Soon after both Skehill and Hall left the band and they were replaced for a short time by Johanna Piggot, formerly bass player and singer with the defunct XL Capris, and Icehouse drummer John Lloyd. Both have since left Sardine.

In May 1983 the band released, *I Hate You* a 12 inch four-track EP on the independent Phantom. The line-up has changed constantly and the band's future continues to be uncertain.

SACRED COWBOYS

Sacred Cowboys

". . . The Sacred Cowboys are a show of direct hostility towards the flaccid impotence of a borrowed culture. The cause of cringing doubt amongst those who were once certain. Where else can you go and have fun. The Last Big Thing!"

That's how The Sacred Cowboys' lead singer Gary Gray describes the Melbourne-based band he fronts.

The other Cowboys are: Terry Doolan (guitar), Mark Ferrie (bass, guitar), Ian Forrest (keyboards), Janis Freidenfelds (drums), and Andrew Picouleau (bass).

The members each boast previous careers in some of Melbourne's most notorious bands — Freidenfelds and Ferrie were with The Models, Picouleau with X Ray Z, Doolan with Peter Lillie's Leisuremasters, Forrest with True Wheels, and Gray from one of Australia's earlier punk bands, The Negatives.

The Cowboys started off as a joke, performing songs by bands they liked — The Doors, Velvet Underground, Stranglers, Suicide, etc. but soon found there was an

their first gig at Sydney's Rock Garden.

The original line-up of Sardine was Rilen, his wife Stephanie on keyboards, Phil Hall on bass and drummer Greg Skehill. Ian Rilen has a long history in Australian music beginning in the early '70s with Sydney band, Band Of Light, and then with Rose Tattoo. Ian was their original bass player and wrote their hit single from 1977 *Bad Boy For Love*. After he left the Tatts he formed a group named X, who were one of Sydney's first cult punk bands.

Both Stephanie Rilen and Greg Skehill had never played in a band before. Greg had previously concentrated on playing guitar but took up Ian's offer to have a go at drumming. Phil Hall first came to Australia from New Zealand in 1979 where he had played in several bands. His first group in Australia was Socket Set and after their demise Phil spent six months rehearsing with Lobby Loyde, although their intended band never got off the ground.

Helen Schneider

Helen Schneider was born in Brooklyn, and her family later moved to Pomona, New York. In high school, she won scholarships for her classical piano playing. Singing, however, was her real musical love, and she found the perfect outlet for her emotions in the songs of such great blues artists as Otis Spann, Willie Dixon and Bessie Smith. In the late '60s, Helen took to the Massachusetts countryside and put together a band. For six years, they played blues and rock'n'roll in the raucous and rowdy bars of New England.

Finally, Helen returned home to New York City, where appearances at Trude Heller's led to her first recording contract. During the following years, she generated considerable excitement, graduating from small clubs to concert halls throughout the United States and Europe. Helen's first television special, *The Girl From New York*, a European production, was Germany's entry in the Montreux

THE SCREAMING MEEMEES

Film Competition in 1978.

In 1979, she taped her first North American TV special in Los Angeles, *Helen Schneider At The Roxy.*

Prompted by a New York Times review by Robert Palmer, which urged her to " go ahead and rock", Helen formed a New York-based group, The Kick, comprising Thomas Trask (guitar, synthesizer, percussion) Johnny Rao (lead guitar, guitar synthesizer), Ivan Elias (bass) and Jon Revere (drums, timbales).

> **"As long as you can fall in love you can stay young forever."**
> — *Tim Finn, Split Enz*

Signed direct to WEA Germany, Helen Schneider and The Kick had their self-titled debut album issued in Europe in March 1981. Shortly after they embarked on their first continental tour, playing to capacity houses and pushing the album to platinum status.

Schneider racked up an enviable series of international awards during the following year, including the Golden Europa Media Award 1981, the No. 1 Performer of the Year award from Germany's authoritative music trade magazine Musik Markt, the German Phono Academy Award as International Artist of the Year 1982 (the equivalent of the American Grammy Award), and selection as 1981 Singer of the Year by the readers of four German rock magazines — Musik-Express, Bravo, Pop-Rocky, and German Rolling Stone. Clearly setting a precedent for an American artist in Germany, Helen is well on her way to becoming that country's most successful female rock singer.

Helen's second album with The Kick, *Exposed* was released in July 1982, having been produced by

Schneider herself at New York's Power Station studio. The Australian edition included a bonus track in the form of a version of Rose Tattoo's *Rock'n'Roll Gypsy (Outlaw)*, a Europe-only single. In the words of one New York reviewer: "Miss Schneider has a striking ability to create excitement, to provide a dramatic anticipation from the instant she starts a song and to maintain this stimulation."

Screaming Meemees ▬

Premier New Zealand new music unit Screaming Meemees formed in mid-1979 and based itself out of Auckland's XS Cafe, Liberty Stage and The Squeeze. Their first vinyl outing was the track *See Me Go* on the Radio Hauraki *Homegrown '80* album. Then came a top 30 single on the Ripper label, *Can't Take It,* followed by a signing to the Propellor label and the inclusion of *All Dressed Up* on the *Class Of '81* compilation LP.

A re-recorded version of *See Me Go* for Propellor debuted at number one on the singles chart, an absolute

first for a domestic act. A second single, *Sunday Boys,* cemented the band's position and a subsequent major tour resulted in huge attendance figures. Early 1983 saw release of the highly acclaimed album *If This Is Paradise, I'll Take The Bag.* First single from the LP was *F Is For Fear*, which featured a vocal duet with Kim, singer with The Gurlz.

The present line-up is Peter van der Fluit (bass, keyboards), Tony Dumm (vocals), Yoh (drums) and Michael O'Neill (guitars).

Scritti Politti ▬

Green Gartside, guitarist/singer/ songwriter for Scritti Politti, grew up in Cardiff, Wales, and moved to Leeds, England, in the late '70s to go to art school. While there he met Tom Morley, who blew his art college grant on a set of drums to live out the punk ethic with Gartside.

By mid-1978 the group (with various floating members, including 'organiser' Matthew Kay) had moved to London and were playing around the punk clubs, producing

SCRITTI POLITTI

SECRET AFFAIR

Secrets* are laying down a challenge to the wine'n'quaalude formula hard rock stadium bands which enjoy such supremacy across the breadth of the U.S.

Together for almost five years, The Secrets* have recorded one self-titled album, produced by Stan Lynch of Tom Petty's Heartbreakers and Sparks producer Greg Penny. Crisp, sparkling, effervescent pop, it

THE SECRETS*

pamphlets on DIY record making, manufacturing a lone single and two EPs on their own St Pancras label, and over-indulging in drugs. In late 1979, while driving through Wales as support for the Gang Of Four, Gartside had a nervous collapse which led to a heart complaint.

Reading of the state of his health in the music press, Gartside's parents invited him home to Wales to recuperate. While there, he immersed himself in black music and on his return to London in mid-1981 set about restructuring Scritti Politti and their music. Assembling Morley and Kay again, he secured a deal with Rough Trade and in late 1981 they released their debut single, *Sweetest Girl*, which received high praise from the music press.

Their debut album was recorded late in 1981 with producer Adam Kidron, who introduced Jamie Talbot (sax), Joe Cang (bass), Mike MacEvoy (keyboards) and backing vocalists Lorenza, Mae and Jackie to the trio. *Songs To Remember*, a collection of sweet subversive soul, has proved to be one of the most critically acclaimed albums of 1982. Coinciding with its release came Scritti Politti's second single, *Faithless*.

Secret Affair

Secret Affair was formed in September 1978 by singer and keyboardist Ian Page and guitarist Dave Cairns, both formely of The New Hearts, a band that was influenced by '60s pop music and had strong mod connotations. Although The New Hearts released two singles, *Just Another Teenage Anthem* and *Plain Jane* on CBS, they broke up, suffering from the punk credibility backlash.

After playing with several people, Secret Affair completed their line-up by recruiting bass player Dennis Smith (formerly with Advertising) and drummer Seb Shelton, a

member of The Young Bucks. Their first live appearance was in January 1979, supporting The Jam at Reading University. Subsequent London dates built up a large following from the London East End where the second generation mod movement originated.

In mid-1979, Secret Affair signed a licensing deal with Arista Records for their own label, I Spy Records. In August the band released their debut single, *Time For Action*, which garnered them a UK top 20 hit. On completing a nationwide English tour, they added sax player Dave Winthrop, formerly of Supertramp and Juicy Lucy.

The band's debut album, *Glory Boys*, was released in late 1979 and established them at the vanguard of the new mod movement. In early 1980 they successfully toured Europe and released their third single, *My World*, which had a lengthy stay in the British charts. Their second LP, *Behind Closed Doors*, was released late in 1980. Then little was heard of them until *Business As Usual* on Arista in 1982.

The Secrets*

Carrying on the fine tradition of The Shoes, 20/20, (Paul Collins') Beat, The Toms, The Raspberries and other Midwestern American powerpop units, Kansas City's

> **"I just don't feel like a part of the music business. More like a boil on its bum."**
> *Nick Lowe*

was snapped up for British release by the independent Why-Fi Records and soon found Canadian release on the Quality label.

Like most bands of their ilk, this quartet was weaned on Anglo Beat and American garage punk. Their live set is likely to include the odd chestnut from the archives of Mitch Ryder, Dave Clark 5, Bruce Springsteen, The Kingsmen, Them and The Rolling Stones.

The band came to local attention with the irresistible *Uniform*, included on a Kansas City 'homegrown' radio station album. This interest was expanded with a regional hit single, *It's Your Heart Tonight*, which opens the album.

The Secrets* are Brent Hoad (vocals, keyboards, guitars, songwriting), Norman Dahlor (bass, vocals), Steve Davis (guitars, vocals) and Randy Miller (drums). Between them they boast membership of many of Kansas City's seminal rock ensembles, including Mud Creek, Millionaire At Midnight, Catalyst, J.T. Cooke and Bullet.

With vital powerpop ditties of the likes of *Shy Around Girls, Radio Heart* and *Big Girl Now*, The Secrets* make a vital contribution to the cause of Pure Pop for Now People.

THE SELECTER

The Selecter

In 1977, guitarist Noel Davies and drummer John Bradbury sat down and composed an instrumental which they called *The Selecter*. In the 18 months it took to record and release, the pair formed a band, enlisting into their ranks Desmond Brown on keyboards, Kevin

Amanour (guitar), 'Gaps' Hendrickson (vocals), Charley 'H' (drums) and Charley Anderson (bass) were doing the rounds.

Enter Lynval Golding, The Specials' rhythm guitarist, who suggested having *The Selecter* as the B side to their record, thus laying the foundation for the 2 Tone label. He also told Noel Davies about Pauline. Through Lynval, Davies, Brown, Black and Hard Top 22 met and formed The Selecter.

Chrysalis Records signed up the whole 2 Tone label soon after The Specials and Selecter set out on the nationwide 2 Tone tour, to coincide

with The Selecter's debut single, *On My Radio*, which reached number eight in the English charts late in 1979. The group then recorded their debut album, *Too Much Pressure*, produced by Errol Ross and the band, and the single taken from it, *Three Minute Hero*, became a UK top 10 tune in early 1980.

After a successful tour of both Britain and America the group, thoroughly disillusioned with the lack of communication between The Specials and themselves, dramatically left 2 Tone Records. In late 1980 they entered Coventry's Horizon Studios to record a new album — without Desmond Brown, who quit and Charley Anderson, who was sacked. The group recorded their second album, *Celebrate The Bullet,* with producer Roger Lomas and The Blockheads' Norman Watt-Roy doubling on bass. After release in early 1981, the remaining members decided to get the group back to a seven-piece by recruiting keyboard/sax player James Mackie and bassist Adam Williams, formerly with China Street. But the new group was short-lived and in mid-1981, the Selecter disbanded permanently.

Serious Young Insects

Serious Young Insects played their first professional gig in April 1980 after originally being conceived as a

SERIOUS YOUNG INSECTS

Harrison (now with Urge) on guitar and Steve on bass, who once swung with The Swinging Cats.

They called themselves Transposed Men and played a lot of the songs which Selecter were later to play in their first gigs. Just as another Coventry band, The Specials, headed into the studio to record *Gangsters,* Desmond Brown quit and John Bradbury left to replace The Specials' original drummer, Silverton. End of Transposed Men.

Brown joined forces with Silverton and Steve plus a singer called Pauline Black and began rehearsing but played no gigs. Meanwhile, another Coventry band, Hard Top 22, featuring Compton

THE SHAKIN' PYRAMIDS

five-piece band in 1979. Mark White (drums and vocals) and Mick Vallance (bass and vocals) had played together for several years in a variety of suburban Melbourne garage bands, but it wasn't until they met Peter Farnan (guitar and vocals) at a party and then dropped their singer and keyboards player, that this tough power pop trio were on their way.

The band played an average of once a month until the combination of critical acclaim and word of mouth led to a steady increase in the band's audience and the number of gigs. By the end of 1980, Serious Young Insects had supported international tourists such as The Cure, XTC and Magazine. Apart from the fact that all three members are extremely good players in a technical sense, the band attracted a lot of attention with its variety of material. All three write and sing, so instead of having one sound, the band has several distinctive styles.

Serious Young Insects' first single, *Trouble Understanding Words*, was released on Native Tongue in late 1981. In January and February 1982 the group recorded their debut album, *Housebreaking,* at Richmond Recorders in Melbourne with veteran engineer John French. The single from the LP, *Be Patient,* received a lukewarm response and in October 1982 they released their third single, *Faraway Places,* to slightly improved response.

The Shakin' Pyramids ▉

Singer and harp player, Davie Duncan, and guitarists James G. Creighton and 'Railroad' Ken were busking in Glasgow during the summer of 1981 when Ali Mackenzie, who had just launched his own record label called Cuba Libre, wandered by. Ali drummed with his own group, The Cuban Heels, and had set up the label as a direct result of the frustrations he'd endured in his attempts to deal with A&R men from the major companies in London.

Seeing the way The Shakin' Pyramids performed new rockabilly convinced Ali that he should make them the second signing to Cuba Libre. Shortly afterwards, they recorded their first-ever piece of vinyl. Titled *Reeferbilly Boogie*, it was recorded on a four-track and produced by Ali.

The Shakin' Pyramids then came down to London to do what comes naturally (busk), and conveniently chose the foyer of The Venue to do a spot. The Venue is owned by Virgin, and Chairman Richard Branson happened to be there at the time. The Shakin' Pyramids impressed him and when it was discovered they

PETE SHELLEY

had signed to Cuba Libre, the solution was obvious. Virgin Records and Cuba Libre signed a licensing deal, and The Shakin' Pyramids' single, *Take A Trip*, was the first fruit from this new partnership. It was released in March 1982 and made a reasonable but not earth-shattering impact on the charts. Their debut album, *Skin 'Em Up,* was then released and the first chapter of their fairy tale was complete. With the so-called

> **"How can I be a Rude Boy without me hat?"**
> — *Compton Amanour, The Selecter*

"rockabilly revival" at its peak, The Shakin' Pyramids have found an enthusiastic reception everywhere they've gone.

But there is more to them than quiffs and revivalism. The Shakin' Pyramids are very young and their relationship with '50s rock is one of slight influence as opposed to obsession. They also produce their own original material, using the basic structures they have learned, but writing contemporary lyrics that lift their music out of a purely revivalist mode.

Pete Shelley ▉

Pete Shelley picked up his first guitar on January 4, 1970, his prime influence at the time being The

Beatles Songbook. By 1973 he had mastered a few chords and formed his first band, Jets Of Air. For the next couple of years the band played mostly local gigs in Shelley's native Lancashire, mixing his own tunes with a repertoire taken from the likes of David Bowie, Roxy Music and The Velvet Underground.

During the summer of 1976 Shelley, via a want ad for musicians, met up with Howard Devoto. After a few rehearsals they formed a songwriting partnership that eventually led to The Buzzcocks. The band started out playing support to The Sex Pistols at Manchester's Free Trade Hall on July 20, 1976, and in a matter of months, The Buzzcocks had established a firm reputation in the forefront of the New Wave explosion. The next step was to record.

Shelley and Devoto raised the cash themselves and entered the studio at the end of 1976. The result was the *Spiral Scratch* EP on the New Hormones label, released in January 1977. It was, without doubt, a crucial record in the history of the British New Wave.

Howard Devoto however was soon to quit The Buzzcocks to form his own band, Magazine. On March 11, the new, revamped Buzzcocks played support to The Clash at the Harlesdon Colosseum in London. That show alone established the new line-up. The Clash were so impressed with The Buzzcocks' performances, they offered them the support gig on the White Riot tour.

Meanwhile, Shelley planned to follow up *Spiral Scratch* with a single, *Orgasm Addict,* but a severe lack of money meant that it was simply not possible to finance another independent single. Enter Andrew Lauder from United Artists Records, who signed the band on August 16, 1977. By the end of October, *Orgasm Addict* was a UK top 50 hit.

In March the following year the band's debut album, *Another Music In A Different Kitchen*, was released and the single, *I Don't Mind,* saw The Buzzcocks on Top Of The Pops for the first time. Their chart success was further consolidated by their biggest hit single, *Ever Fallen In Love*, and the *Love Bites* album. Throughout this period the band also toured extensively with such groups as The Slits, Penetration and Joy Division as well as playing dates in Europe with Blondie.

By 1980, however, The Buzzcocks were beginning to lose their impetus. Shelley was increasingly frustrated working within the group format and the inevitable limitations thus imposed. Quite aside from The Buzzcocks, Shelley had already

become involved in other projects: his own label, Groovy Records, for instance, and The Tiller Boys (whose *Big Noise From The Jungle* was released in 1981).

Thus when further Buzzcocks sessions failed to work, Shelley handed in his resignation on March 6, 1981. Almost immediately he started work on his debut solo album with producer Martin Rushent. *Homosapien* was released in early 1982 and the dynamic title track was a top 10 hit in England, Australia and parts of Europe.

THE SHOES

Shoes

The Shoes are Jeff Murphy (guitar and vocals), John Murphy (bass and vocals), Gary Klebe (guitar and vocals) and Skip Meyer (drums). The band began in their hometown of Zion, Illinois, in the early '70s, the members not playing live but spending time writing songs and recording in their living rooms.

In 1974 Klebe left for France to study architecture and while he was gone the Murphy brothers made the tapes that became The Shoes' first album, appropriately called *One In Versailles.* They had 300 copies pressed and packed in plain white covers as a surprise for Klebe. When he returned in 1975 they launched their next project, a series of tapes known as *Bazooka* that were

> *"I hate art, I can't stand it. It's treating something that's supposed to be good as precious, and it isn't precious. Anyone can make a record."*
> *Johnny Rotten, Sex Pistols*

circulated to fans but never pressed onto an album.

Then came what The Shoes describe as their first real album, *Black Vinyl Shoes,* recorded on a TEAC four-track tape machine in Jeff Murphy's living room. The album was first sold by mail order in 1978 by the band themselves, before they arranged for wider distribution through Sire. Major companies were impressed by the fact that *Black Vinyl Shoes* contained 15 original songs, a lyric sheet with photos and a T-shirt transfer.

In June 1978 the band also released a single on Greg Shaw's Bomp label, containing two originals, *Okay/Tomorrow Night.* Soon after, The Shoes signed with Elektra and in 1979 they released another LP, *Present Tense,* which included the single, *Too Late,* and a fresh recording of the superb *Tomorrow Night.* In 1980 they released their second Elektra LP, *Tongue Twister,* and another single, *I Don't. Boomerang,* a third album, appeared midway through 1982 and continued The Shoes' unique style of aggressive harmony powerpop. They continue to play occasional live performances and, to date, no photographer has captured them smiling.

Shriekback

It was a music writer for England's staid newspaper, The Guardian, who best articulated the music of Shriekback: "It resembles an algebraic equation, assembled from parts of Ornette Coleman, James Ulmer, Eno & Byrne — funk with emphasis on minimalism but room for eccentricity; rhythms pared to the bone. It is all angles and obtrusions and precious few smooth surfaces, with textures and sounds being slammed together and torn apart. . . While the theory and principles, the design and structure

148

of the moving parts is often absorbing and even admirable, the music itself can leave you surprisingly cold."

Shriekback was founded by disillusioned members of two British upper-echelon new music bands: bassist Dave Allen from Gang Of Four and keyboard player Barry Andrews from XTC. They were joined by guitarist Carl Marsh (from Out On Blue Six), drummer Martyn Baker and percussionist Pedro Oritz. From the outset the unit offered no manifesto, no concrete concept; only the promise of wide experimentation, with the results edited down for record.

Signed to the independent Y label, the group recorded a handful of singles, followed by the obscure album *Tench*. But it was not until the *Care* album early in 1983 that they were able to make a significant impact on British music. Reviewing the LP, NME's Don Watson observed: "I'm beginning to understand the art of their monotony. Suddenly forms are beginning to emerge from the snowstorm of their sound, an overall direction behind their random explorations and a meaning in their tension."

A number of songs on *Care*, such as *Mothloop, Sexthinkone, Cleartails* and (the single) *Lined Up*, found considerable interest in America, where Warner Brothers opted for release of the LP and a maxi-single containing *Hapax Legomena*.

Simple Minds

Simple Minds' beginnings date back to 1977 with Johnny and The Self Abusers who formed in February of that year. One of the more

distinctive of the Scottish New Wave groups, The Abusers built a strong following before differences about the direction of their music caused them to split in November 1977 on the day their only single, *Saints And Sinners*, was released by Chiswick.

By the beginning of 1978, three of The Abusers — singer Jim Kerr, guitarist Charlie Burchill and drummer Brian McGee — had pulled together a new group, adding

> "I decided that the only music which deserves to be taken seriously is that which goes against the Common Mean."
> *Jim Kerr, Simple Minds*

Mick MacNeill on keyboards and Derek Forbes on bass. A second guitarist came in but soon dropped out.

Simple Minds signed to Zoom Records in December 1978, having built a solid live reputation throughout that year in Scotland. Almost immediately, they began working on their debut album, *Life In A Day*, released in the UK in April 1979. It reached number 30 on the charts and the two singles, *Life In A Day* and *Chelsea Girl*, did moderately well.

After touring extensively throughout the UK, the group released their second LP, *Real To Real Cacophony* (again produced by John Leckie), in November 1979, following it with their first European tour. Their third album, *Empires*

And Dance, came out in mid-1980 and gained high critical praise as well as the offer to tour Europe as support for Peter Gabriel.

In 1981 Simple Minds ended their arrangement with Zoom and signed with Virgin Records. With producer Steve Hillage, they recorded two albums, released at first as a double and then separately, titled *Sons And Fascination/Sister Feelings Call*. After a tour of Australia supporting Icehouse in late 1981, the albums and singles, *The American, Sweat In Bullet* and especially *Love Song* (which went top 10), sold highly in that country. By this time, Kenny Hyslop had replaced McGee in the band.

In mid-1982 Simple Minds released a new single, *Promised You A Miracle*, which went again top 10 in Australia, where they were proving to be much more popular than in the UK. With the release of their fifth album, *New Gold Dream*, and the single *Glittering Prize*, the group again toured Australia, this time headlining sell-out concerts. After personality differences, Hyslop departed the ranks during the recording of the album and was replaced by Mel Gaynor.

A&M have earmarked Simple Minds for mainstream American success. Initial advertising sells *New Gold Dream* with the words: "It conjures up a lushness and depth often lacking in today's music. . . Simple Minds make music that is thick, layered, twisting, golden and at the same time danceable and listenable." If the band ever manages to surface from under that dump-load, they may record another fine album.

Siouxsie And The Banshees

Siouxsie And The Banshees have worked hard for the major position they presently hold in British rock. In their early days, back in 1976, many club owners told them never to come back looking for work because they either weren't good enough or were too extreme.

The Banshees' first show was at the 100 Club Punk Festival in London in September 1976. The line-up for that night was Siouxsie Sioux (vocals), Steve Severin (guitar and sax), Sid Vicious (drums) and Marco Pironi (guitar). At this stage, they could barely play their instruments.

One of the few people impressed by the show was Nils Stevenson, who left The Sex Pistols' management to take on The Banshees. There followed a number of line-up changes: Sid Vicious was replaced as drummer by Kenny Morris in February 1977 and John

SHRIEKBACK

SIMPLE MINDS

McKay replaced then-guitarist Peter Fenton.

Record companies simply weren't interested in signing the radical outfit, even though their musical ability had improved and their following increased dramatically, so they appeared on one of John Peel's radio sessions and continued touring throughout England and Europe, gaining a reputation through their live performances.

Suddenly, things were reversed — the record companies began chasing them and in July 1978 they signed with Polydor. A single, *Hong Kong Garden*, was released, becoming a huge British hit. The debut album, *The Scream,* was released early in 1979, and after a second UK hit with *The Staircase,* The Banshees cut their second album, *Join Hands.* On tour to support the album, McKay

and Morris suddenly walked out of the band and various members of support band The Cure helped Siouxsie and Severin complete the schedule.

By the end of 1980, The Banshees' line-up was settled when John McGeoch joined on guitar from Magazine and ex-Slit Budgie became the new drummer. This group recorded the UK hit single, *Happy House*, and the albums, *Kaleidoscope* in late 1980 and *Ju-Ju* in 1981, both with Nigel Gray producing. At Christmas 1981, Polydor released a compilation album, *Once Upon A Time/The Singles.*

In early 1982 Siouxsie was advised to stop singing for an indefinite period to save further damage to her throat. But a year later she returned in full voice with a new album, *A Kiss In The Dreamhouse.*

The Skids

The Skids went through many changes after their formation in 1977. In 1981, with only Richard Jobson remaining from the original line-up, the group produced their fourth and last album, a record which represented a radical departure in musical style for them. The LP, called *Joy,* saw Richard Jobson and co-writer and bass player Russell Webb, both proud Scotsmen, delving further and further into traditional Scottish musical forms.

The record was considerably different from anything The Skids had done previously and a far cry from the sound emitted by the four young men from Dunfermline in 1977. Then, 16-year-old Jobson joined guitarist Stuart Adamson, drummer Tom Kellichan and bassist

Willie Simpson in the embryonic Skids. They recorded a one-off single called *Charles* on manager Sandy Muir's No Bad Records and it was enough to attract the interest of Virgin Records, with whom The Skids signed shortly afterwards.

The Skids were on their way. Their power sound, dominated by Stuart's guitar, put them quickly into the forefront of the New Wave scene. They had their first hit with *Into The Valley* and followed it quickly with their debut album, *Scared To Dance.* The single *Masquerade* reached the top 10 and by the end of 1979, a Mick Glossop production of *Working For The Yankee Dollar* had also scored. Richard Jobson had by now established himself as not only a magnetic stage performer, but an eminently quotable figure. He developed a voracious appetite for information and knowledge which was reflected in his songwriting.

By October 1979 The Skids were, it appeared, well-established. Their second album, *Days In Europa,* was released and acclaimed accordingly.

SIOUXSIE AND THE BANSHEES

This was produced by Bill Nelson and the record displayed a maturity beyond the musicians' years.

At the beginning of 1980 The Skids underwent some notable changes. They replaced their drummer and bass player and

THE SKIDS

recruited Mike Baillie and Russell Webb. In the autumn of 1980, *The Absolute Game* was released. Produced by Mick Glossop, it once again reflected Stuart Adamson's development as a guitarist of distinction and showcased Richard Jobson's thought-provoking lyrics. What nobody realised at the time was that this LP marked the end of this phase of The Skids' career. Drummer Mike Baillie left the band and then, more significantly, Adamson quit. The Skids were now Richard Jobson and Russell Webb and they immediately began planning the next step for the band.

In the meantime, Jobson was for the first time actively pursuing his other interests, acting and writing. He made his West End acting debut in a controversial play titled *Demonstration Of Affection.* Controversial for possibly the wrong reasons, the play proved to Jobson's critics (and he had his fair share) that he could indeed act.

In addition, he completed a book of poetry titled *A Man For All Seasons.* An album of poetry was also forthcoming. Titled *The Ballad Of Etiquette,* it featured Jobson reading a selection of his work accompanied by a complementary musical backing. In 1981 he also took the opportunity to take poetry to the people, conducting a short tour of universities performing selections accompanied by two musicians. After the tour, Jobson concentrated on his latest non-musical project, *Dog Beneath The Skin,* a W.H. Auden/Christopher Isherwood play in which he played 14 characters. The play began in London's New Half Moon Theatre in November 1981, and Jobson was rehearsing for this at the same time as working with The Skids on plans to take *Joy* on the road.

But the conflict of interests became too difficult to reconcile and in the beginning of 1982 Richard Jobson decided to disband The Skids — in part, due to the poor reaction to *Joy,* but mostly to enable him to pursue his acting and poetic aspirations more intently.

The Skids do deserve mention for executing what just may be the most unlikely cover version of all time. Their rendition of the weepy ballad *And The Band Played Waltzing Matilda,* places them alongside other renderers such as Donovan, Rod McKuen and Dame Vera Lynn.

SLOW CHILDREN

THE SLITS

The Slits

The Slits are contemporaries of the original English punk bands, The Sex Pistols, The Clash and Siouxsie And The Banshees. The unit was formed with an original line-up of Arianna Forster, now known as Ari Up (vocals), Palmolive (drums), Kate Korus (rhythm guitar) and Suzi Gutsy (bass). Ari was only 14 when the band was formed and this limited the number of stage appearances The Slits could make in their early days.

All through 1977 The Slits played the English pub circuit and supported The Clash on their legendary White Riot tour. They were obvious targets for the sensationalist English press, who began running headlines like "All Girl Punk Horror".

Palmolive left the band in 1978 and was replaced by male drummer Budgie, previously of Liverpool's The Spitfire Boys. Budgie's position in the band was never permanent and he left soon after to join The Banshees. Kate Korus and Suzi Gutsy also left and they were replaced by Vivien Albertine and Tessa Pollitt. Guitarist Vivien was a former member of Flowers Of Romance, whose lead singer was (later Sex Pistol) Sid Vicious, while bass player Tessa had previously played guitar in a band called The Castrators.

The Slits signed a recording contract with Island early in 1979 and recorded their first album at Ridge Farm Studios with renowned reggae producer Dennis Bovell. The album, *Cut,* was a further contribution to The Slits' reputation as one of the more innovative and original bands playing in England.

In 1981, The Slits signed with CBS and with the addition of their friends — drummer Bruce Smith (from The Pop Group and Rip, Rig And Panic) and keyboardist Steve Beresford — recorded the album, *Return Of The Giant Slits,* which included the single, *Earthbeat.* Soon after the album's release in early 1982, The Slits decided to disband. Rough Trade later issued a *Retrospective* album.

> "The way you go about your music is the way you go about your life."
> — *Ari Up, The Slits*

Slow Children

Slow Children are Pal Shazar and Andrew Chinich. They live in Los Angeles but prior to the formation of the band, Andrew was assistant to the film director Krzysztof Zanussi in Poland.

In 1976, Andrew and Pal began writing together as Slow Children. Their first performance is reported to have been only three minutes long but it was seen by Jules Shear and Stephen Hague, who became friends with Pal and Andrew and eventually produced a series of demo tapes for them.

Slow Children performed through various personnel changes, always returning to their most satisfying configuration — the two of them. A single was released in 1979 but it wasn't until 1980 that they began to record the first Slow Children album. It was produced by Jules Shear (of Jules and the Polar Bears) and Stephen Hague. The recording was completed in London and the self-titled album was released in May, 1981. It was preceeded by a single, *President Am I.*

Patti Smith

Patti Smith grew up in Pitman, a town in South Jersey, near Philadelphia. Her father, a former tap dancer, worked in a factory and her mother, who gave up singing to raise a family, was a waitress. At an early age Patti became infatuated with black music, but it was while she was at high school that she found her real musical standpoint when she discovered Bob Dylan.

While at junior college, Patti became pregnant, had the baby and then gave it up for adoption. She escaped Pitman in 1967 and came to New York, where she hung out at Pratt, the Brooklyn art college. Her interest in poetry, inspired by the 19th Century French Symbolist Arthur Rimbaud, was encouraged by meeting Robert Mapplethorpe, an artist and photographer. Patti next journeyed to Paris with her sister and there teamed up with a street theatre troupe. She began dreaming that Rolling Stone Brian Jones was going to die, and when this did occur, she was so shaken up that she returned to America, moving into New York's Chelsea Hotel with Mapplethorpe.

At the Chelsea, Patti met the hip crowd who used it as a base in the late '60s: the Andy Warhol circle, Jefferson Airplane, Janis Joplin, Dylan cohort Bobby Neuwirth, and the playwright Sam Shepard, among others. After working as a clerk in a bookstore she began scuffling for a living as a rock writer. Patti was still writing poetry (as well as a book of plays with Shepard, *Mad Dog Blues*), and in February 1971, with the encouragement of the Chelsea crowd, and especially rock critic Lenny Kaye who backed her on guitar, performed at a poetry reading at St Mark's in the Bowery.

Patti was still unsure of throwing herself totally into rock and instead delved deeper into poetry, though she still wrote occasional criticism

and a few song lyrics for Blue Oyster Cult. Three volumes of her poetry appeared: *Seventh Heaven* (1971), *Kodak* (1972) and *Witt* (1973). She and Kaye remained in touch, although he spent much of 1973 in Europe, getting together for readings which were slowly evolving into concerts.

With the urging of her new manager, Jane Friedman, Patti and Kaye decided to record a single, *Hey Joe/Piss Factory,* in mid-1974 and then formed a band with ex-Mump drummer Jay Dee Daugherty, keyboardist Richard Sohl and guitar and bass player Ivan Kral, a refugee from the 1968 Czechoslovakian invasion. They played regularly at CBGB's on The Bowery and attracted a lot of interest from the major record companies. In early 1975 Patti signed with Arista, and became the first US new music act to be contracted by a major record company.

In late 1975 her debut album, *Horses* (produced by John Cale), was released to loud acclaim and established her as an immediate star. Her second LP, *Radio Ethiopia* (produced by Jack Douglas),

emerged in 1976, but her career was halted later that year when she fell from a stage in Florida during a performance and broke her neck.

Patti returned in 1978 with a new album, *Easter* (produced by Jimmy Iovine), a new keyboardist, Bruce Brody, and her only hit single, *Because The Night,* written with Bruce Springsteen. In 1979 Patti released her fourth LP, *Wave* (produced by Todd Rundgren), which contained the single, *Frederick.* Since then she has been out of the public eye, living in Detroit with her husband, Fred 'Sonic' Smith of MC5 fame. Poetry has resurfaced in her life via two new books, *Babel* and *Houdini.* She has also written some songs with Tom Verlaine and in 1982, gave birth to a child. Patti and Fred are reported to be working on a joint musical project, though nothing has yet emerged from the collaboration. An interesting bootleg single is in circulation, featuring Patti's rendition of *White Christmas.*

THE SOFT BOYS

The Soft Boys

Unlike most of their contemporaries, The Soft Boys were not influenced by The New York Dolls, David Bowie or Roxy Music but by the golden age of psychedelia.

The band came together in late 1976 in Cambridge (home of Syd Barrett) with Robyn Hitchcock (guitar, vocals), Kimberly Rew (guitar, vocals), Andy Metcalfe (bass) and Morris Windsor (drums). Their first release, the *Give It To The Soft Boys* EP on Raw Records in late 1977, was a combination of punk aggression and the despondent imagery that would characterize most of their songs. Metaphors of crabs, fish and dead flies conveyed extreme bitterness.

In 1978 they were among the first groups signed to Radar Records, releasing one single, *(I Want To Be An) Anglepoise Lamp,* but after several disagreements, they scrapped an entire album to start anew.

PATTI SMITH

153

Their first LP, *A Can Of Bees,* was released independently in 1979 on the group's own Two Crabs label. A very raw and relatively inaccessible record, the influences ranged from early Pink Floyd (Hitchcock's vocal resemblance to Syd Barrett was deliberately played up) to mid-period Led Zeppelin.

The group was criticised for its obvious psychedelic influences and the album otherwise attracted little attention, though by the second album, *Underwater Moonlight,* released in mid-1980 on the Armageddon label, the group had established an identity of its own with a more refined and melodic sound. The albums and two poppy singles, *I Wanna Destroy You* and *Kingdom Of Love* (the latter containing Syd Barrett's *Vegetable Man* as a B side), went by virtually unnoticed. Just before *Underwater Moonlight* was recorded, Andy Metcalfe was replaced by Martin Seligman, who'd previously worked with Alex Chilton & The Local Heroes.

The Soft Boys visited America late in 1980, playing a series of concerts on the East Coast before returning to England to record further material. By this time they had developed a cult following but owing to a lack of any real success or wide

recognition, they decided to break up in January 1981, in favour of various solo projects.

Due to popular demand, Armageddon issued a third album, *Two Halves For The Price Of One* with one side of leftover studio tracks and one live side recorded at London's Hope & Anchor. A single, *Only The Stones Remain* was culled from the LP. Another posthumous

single *Love Poisoning/When I Was A Kid* was given away with a London fanzine A Bucketful Of Brains in March 1982.

Robyn Hitchcock toned down his metaphorical morbidity with two solo albums, *Black Snake Diamond Pole* in 1981 and *Groovy Decay* in 1982. Kimberley Rew, who's already issued one neat pop single, *Stomping All Over The World,* whilst still a Soft

SPANDAU BALLET

SOFT CELL

Boy in 1980, recorded another in 1981, *My Baby Does Her Hairdo Long,* with the assistance of Peter Holsapple, Will Rigby and Gene Holder from The dB's. In 1982 he joined his friends in another Cambridge group The Waves, who released the singles, *Nightmare* and *Brown Eyed Son* during the year.

Soft Cell ▮▮▮▮▮▮

The Soft Cell duo formed in Leeds in 1979. Vocalist Marc Almond had had an obscure prior band, Marc & The Mambas, before he teamed up with synthesizer and percussion player Dave Ball. The group is very much a product of the English Northern Soul club scene and the art school sensibility.

The duo's first single, *Memorabilia,* was released early in 1981 and slipped away without trace, but their second, *Tainted Love,* was a runaway hit in both the UK and Australia later that year. At the end of 1981, Soft Cell issued their third single, *Bedsitter,* and their debut album *Non-Stop Erotic Cabaret,* which rose high in the UK charts.

THE SPITFIRES

In January 1982, they released their fourth single, *Say Hello Wave Goodbye,* and in the middle of the year another single, *Torch,* and *Non-Stop Ecstatic Dancing,* came out. The EP was recorded in New York and featured mostly dub remixes of songs from the first album. The next single, *Numbers,* gave them their fifth consecutive British chart hit.

With fame has come an awesome reputation for petulant behaviour and ludicrous demands. Managed by the volatile Stevo, Marc Almond has become somewhat of an *enfant terrible* of British rock, known for demolishing the foyer of his record company from time to time.

If Soft Cell disintegrated within the next five minutes, their place in the history books of rock would be assured by the extraordinary achievements of *Tainted Love,* a song penned by Ed Cobb, an original member of the Four Freshmen and producer of the Standells. It was originally a minor hit in the late '60s for black American singer Gloria Jones but Soft Cell's version was a number one hit in a score of countries. *Tainted Love* became the longest running hit ever on the American Billboard Hot 100 chart, racking up a staggering 43 weeks. 1983 saw Marc Almond performing more experimental solo work around the London clubs, and the release of the third Soft Cell album, *The Art Of Falling Apart.*

Spandau Ballet ▪▪▪▪▪▪
Spandau Ballet made their first live appearance in London in November 1979 in a private rehearsal room on a Saturday morning in front of an audience of the band's friends — young fashion designers, hairdressers, graphic artists, writers, DJs, and scene-makers. The nucleus of the explosion of pop culture which has come out of the scene originally centred on the West End's fashion conscious clubs — Blitz, Billy's, Hell and St Moritz. Here the customers expressed themselves by

their clothes, which changed exotically week by week, and danced to the largely electronic-based music.

Spandau Ballet were the first band to make music specifically for the scene, which they were part of, and reflected their audience like a mirror, in attitude and appearance. They went on to make appearances at events organised outside of the rock circuit, such as Steve Strange's Christmas party at Blitz, all of which were advertised by word of mouth, and which attracted increasingly larger crowds. Press and media

interest in the band grew, resulting in a distribution label deal for their Reformation label with Chrysalis Records.

The group's first single, *To Cut A Long Story Short,* was released late in 1980 and was an immediate and very large hit. The whole scene surrounding the group exploded, influencing mainstream fashion,

inspiring other groups, giving birth to magazines, and putting pressure on the British music press to cover the new attitudes amongst musicians and fans.

In the UK, Spandau Ballet followed up with further hit singles, *The Freeze, Musclebound/Glow,* and a gold debut album, *Journeys To Glory.* They continually change their appearance to reflect the demanding pace of fashion.

In mid-1981 the group changed their musical style by adding the horn section of black English funk group, Beggar & Co, and recorded *Chant No 1,* which became a club hit all over the world. Their second album, *Diamond,* was released early in 1982, and bolstered their musical credibility. As well as *Chant No 1,* it included the successful singles, *Paint Me Down* and *Instinction.* Chrysalis issued a limited edition boxed set version of the album, featuring four 12 inch singles (with a number of special remixes) and a giant poster. Album three, *True,* recorded at the Compass Point Studio in the Bahamas, appeared in early 1983.

The line-up of Spandau Ballet is Tony Hadley (vocals), Martin Kemp (bass), John Keeble (drums), Steve Norman (percussion) and Gary

SQUEEZE

Kemp (guitar and keyboards). They are the prime target for detractors of the New Romantic movement, for reasons that the accompanying colour photograph can best convey.

Specials ▪▪▪▪▪▪
Founders of the new ska-bluebeat movement, The Specials formed in

THE SPECIALS

mid-1977 as The Coventry Automatics, changing to The Specials a year later. The line-up was Horace Panter (bass), Terry Hall (vocals), Neville Staples (vocals), Jerry Dammers (organ), Roddy Radiation (guitar), Lynval Golding (guitar) and John Bradbury (drums).

Coming from an industrial Midlands city as musically rich as Coventry, The Specials soon had many major record companies checking them out. But the group weren't interested in signing with a big company. What they wanted, and got, was a distribution deal for their own label (2 Tone) that left them with the freedom to record what they wanted and to sign other groups of their choice.

The Specials attracted the interest of Elvis Costello, who produced the band's self-titled debut album late in 1979, the source of a succession of UK hits — *Gangsters, Message To You Rudy* and *Too Much Too Soon* (the last of which was banned by the BBC because of questionable lyrics).

In late 1980 the group's second LP, *More Specials*, was released and it saw a major overhaul and progression of the group's music under the direction of Jerry Dammers. The album was a mix of ska, pop and rock blended into an orchestrated muzak.

In mid-1981, after the release of their number one English hit *Ghost Town,* Hall, Staples and Golding decided to leave the group due to internal dissension. With their departure to form their own Fun Boy Three, The Specials disbanded. However, Jerry Dammers with the remaining three — plus Rico (trombone) and Dick Cluthell (flugelhorn and cornet) — have produced some singles under the name of Special AKA; most notably *The Boiler* (with ex-Bodysnatcher vocalist Rhoda), which was banned by the BBC due to its subject matter — a harrowing monologue from a rape victim.

The Spitfires

Hailing from Adelaide, The Spitfires might well be regarded as Australia's answer to The Cramps. Their own band of "voodoo rock", heavily overlayed with fierce and frantic rockabilly/pub rock, is best manifest in tracks such as *Rumble In The Jungle, Bad Luck Bop* and *I'm In Love With A Vampire* from their debut mini LP *I Was A Teenage Teenager,* issued on the independent Rivet label down under (and dedicated to the Three Stooges).

The Spitfires formed in January 1981, with the aim of playing "real rock'n'roll". The perverse tastes in kitsch, horror movies and cultural trash which prevailed within the ranks soon altered this stance. As support to the Dynamic Hepnotics, Sunny Boys and Rock Doctors, The Spitfires were creating a sensation in Adelaide by the end of 1982, when Rivet thrust them into a studio. In 1983 they stormed the South Australian charts with their debut release.

The group comprises Jeff Stephens (guitar/vocals), Ted 'Stickman' Keeley (lead vocals), Andrew Travers (drums), Greg Ryan (guitar), Rick Gac (bass) and Jeff Karutz (sax/harmonica). In the words of one writer: "Like sex, they are the most fun you can have without laughing."

The Spoons

The Spoons bolster up Canada's fairly dismal contribution to international new music. Managed by former Martha & The Muffins bassist Carl Finkle, the group soared to domestic popularity in 1981 with the hit *Nova Heart* and album *Stick Figure Neighbourhood.* With strong pockets of following in Toronto, Ottawa and Montreal, they landed support stints with Simple Minds, Orchestral Manoeuvres In The Dark and Saga, which led to a recording deal in America with A&M and billings alongside the Police, Flock Of Seagulls and Talking Heads.

Of one performance, Canadian critic Greg Quill observed, "The band was polished and confident, and imbued their youthfully romantic dance music with a passion that's almost atypical of the genre." Similarly, other Canadian critics have highlighted the band's warmth, optimism and Gord Deppe's impressive lyrics.

The Spoons' first international release was the *Arias & Symphonies* album, which was awarded a four star review in The Record. According to Deppe, "We've stepped outside the suburban themes of the first album to explore remote places and uncommon ideas."

THE SPOONS

The Spoons comprise Gord Deppe (vocals, guitar), Sandy Horne (bass, vocals), Rob Preuss (synthesizers) and Derrick Ross (drums). It is worth noting that Preuss is just 17 years old.

Squeeze

The nucleus of Squeeze — Glen Tilbrook (lead guitar and vocals), Chris Difford (rhythm guitar and vocals), 'Jools' Holland (keyboards) and Harry Kakoulli (bass) — formed in Deptford, South London in 1974, with drummer Gilson Lavis joining two years later.

A chance meeting with former Velvet Underground member John Cale, who was touring England, resulted in his producing *Packet Of Three,* an independently released EP This led to securing a contract with A&M Records and Cale remained to produce most of the band's self-titled debut album, which spawned a top 10 English hit in 1978, *Take Me, I'm Yours.*

In 1979 their second LP, *Cool For Cats,* produced by John Wood, was released. It held two English hit singles, *Cool For Cats* (which was also number one in Australia) and *Up The Junction.* Soon after, Kakoulli left and was replaced by former Video Kings bassist John Bently.

Following a lengthy American tour, supporting concerts by Blondie and Patti Smith, Squeeze toured Australia in early 1980, playing pubs and clubs throughout the country. Their third album, *Argybargy,* again produced by John Wood, was released on their return to England and was the last Squeeze product to feature 'Jools' Holland, who left to form his own band, The Millionaires. He was replaced by former Ace keyboardist Paul Carrack, who had been responsible for the contemporary rock classic *How Long?*

1981 saw the release of their most critically acclaimed LP, *East Side Story,* produced by Elvis Costello. The album was a major success in America and consequently, the band decided to concentrate most of their touring in that country. Though Carrack had written their first American hit, *Tempted,* he elected to leave and was replaced by Don Snow, formerly with The Sinceros.

In mid-1982 Squeeze's fifth album, *Sweets From A Stranger,* came out and in October the group dropped a bombshell by announcing that they were breaking up. It was expected that Difford and Tilbrook would continue to work together. A&M bade the group farewell in the manner that record companies know best — by rushing a TV advertised greatest hits album onto the market;

in this case, *Squeeze Singles,* which ranged from *Take Me I'm Yours* to *Annie Get Your Gun.*

Steel Pulse

Steel Pulse began in 1972 in Handsworth, a black working class Birmingham area where all the present line-up except drummer

STIFF LITTLE FINGERS

Steve Nesbitt, grew up.

The original nucleus of the band featured David Hinds (lead vocals and guitar), Basil Gabbidom (lead guitar), and Ronnie McQueen (bass). As they learnt their basic licks, the band gradually drew in other members, mostly their mates at Handsworth Wood Boys Secondary Modern School and later Bournville College. The band's initial gigs were confined to the local pubs and clubs around Birmingham. Eventually they earned enough to finance the first Steel Pulse single, *Kibudu, Mansatta And Abuku,* which was released on Dip, a small reggae label.

The following year, 1977, the band strengthened their line-up with vocalist Michael Riley, percussionist Fonso Martin, drummer Steve Nesbitt and keyboards player Selwyn Brown. At about the same time, Steel Pulse reached a totally unpredicted turning point.

The London punk scene was at its peak when suddenly Steel Pulse received an invitation to play at the Vortex Club, on a bill headed by Generation X. Steel Pulse thus became the first reggae band to play at an all-punk venue.

Later that year, a one-off single, *Nyah Luv,* appeared on the Anchor label and reached the top of the UK reggae charts. That coincided with an invitation to support The Stranglers on part of their British tour. In November '77 the band supported Burning Spear's British tour and for the first time were able to reach a young black mass audience.

In 1978 the band signed a contract with Island Records and their first single for the label was *Ku Klux Klan* which was soon followed by their debut album, *Handsworth Revolution,* which reached the top 10. That year Steel Pulse also played their first headlining tour of Britain, to rapturous response. A stage highlight was the first Island single, for which Riley and Martin donned Klansmen uniforms.

Several internal conflicts resulted in the departure of Michael Riley and the emergance of a much increased Rasta profile. This was emphasised by album two *(Tribute To The Martyrs)* a tour with Bob Marley & The Wailers and a number of appearances on Rock Against

STEEL PULSE

Racism concerts.

Continuing to please both reggae and punk audiences, Steel Pulse recorded a third album, *Caught You,* issued in 1980, followed by an inevitable 'best of' collection. The band has been remarkably quiet in recent times, the only sign of recorded life being the track *Sound System,* included on the *Countryman* film soundtrack album.

Stiff Little Fingers ∎∎∎∎

Stiff Little Fingers come from strife-torn Belfast, Northern Ireland. The nucleus of Jack Burns (guitar and vocals) and original drummer Brian Faloon had been playing in bedrooms, garages and school halls since they were 15 and were later joined by Henry Cluney (guitar and vocals). Stiff Little Fingers were really born in the summer of 1977 with the arrival of Ali McMordie (bass) and the inspiration of the early punk bands — Sex Pistols, Clash and Damned. They took their name from a song by English band The Vibrators.

In the early days Stiff Little Fingers played mostly in self-hired hotel function rooms, selling "invitations" on the sly in the car park. It was at one of these gigs that they met journalists Gordon Ogilvie and Colin McClelland, who realised that the band had enormous potential if they concentrated on writing more songs about their own background. Within a week, Burns wrote *Suspect Device* and *Wasted Week,* and these two songs became the band's first independent single on their own Rigid Digits label.

DAVE STEWART & BARBARA GASKIN
RICHARD STRANGE (BELOW)

London DJ John Peel gave it such extensive exposure that sales boomed, eventually selling more than 30,000 copies.

The group formed a partnership with Rough Trade to distribute their product and a second single, *Alternative Ulster,* and their debut album, *Inflammable Material* (which went top 30 in the UK), were released under this arrangement.

In 1978 Stiff Little Fingers relocated in London, drummer Brian Faloon quit to be replaced by Jimmy

Reilly and the group signed a new distribution deal with Chrysalis. Just prior to Christmas 1978 they released their fourth single, *Straw Dogs,* but it was not until early 1980 that their second LP, *Nobody's Heroes,* was released and quickly scaled the English top 10.

After a triumphant round of sellouts on a UK tour, Stiff Little Fingers ventured to Europe, Scandinavia and America in 1980 and late that year released a live album, *Hanx!* In 1981 their fourth album, *Go For It,* was issued, and in 1982 a fifth, *Now Then,* appeared.

Dave Stewart

Dave Stewart has pulled off an amazing PR campaign for the still-feared synthesizer. By applying it to friendly, familiar '60s pop classics he has removed a great deal of the metal machine's image as a dark, brooding, clunking, burping, emotionless sound box. Stewart has beaten the slick synth duos by operating on his lonesome, aided by select vocalists — which is about as compact as a rock band can become without disappearing up its own anal cavity.

The clever Mr Stewart can be traced back to the early '70s and such ensembles as Egg, Hatfield & The North, and his own National Health. Toward the end of the decade he played in a Bill Bruford (ex-King Crimson, Yes) group.

In the middle of 1980 Stewart enlisted the sensual, breathy voice of former Zombie Colin Blunstone for a classy remake of the 1966 Jimmy Ruffin hit *What Becomes Of The Broken Hearted?* This became a

number one UK hit, so Stewart repeated the formula with Lesley Gore's 1963 smash *It's My Party,* using relative unknown Barbara Gaskin as vocalist. Since that double slam Stewart has been rather quiet, though he has done some work with his group Rapid Eye Movement, which comprises himself (synth), Pip Pyle

THE STRANGLERS

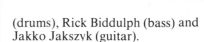

SUNNYBOYS

SW9/THOMAS DOLBY

(drums), Rick Biddulph (bass) and Jakko Jakszyk (guitar).

Richard Strange

Richard Strange first surfaced in 1975 as the singer for English group, Doctors Of Madness, who are now generally acknowledged as a significant influence on many punk and post-punk bands. Joy Division, Simple Minds and Skids have cited them as being the initial inspiration. The group disbanded in 1978 after recording three albums for Polydor.

Strange withdrew for two years and spent his time writing and travelling. In 1980, he released his first solo single, *International*

159

THE STRAY CATS

Language, on Cherry Red Records and in November of that year, Ze Records issued a live album recorded in New York's Hurrah Club entitled *The Live Rise Of Richard Strange.* He also began writing for fellow Ze artist and New York cabaret queen, Cristina.

In December 1980, Strange opened Cabaret Futura in London's Soho. A weekly mixed media club, it proved to be a runaway success and moved to bigger premises. He also produced albums by Sector 27 and Way Out West and, early in 1981, signed to Virgin. The first release was a re-issue of *International Language,* quickly followed by his first solo album, *The Phenomenal Rise Of Richard Strange.* The title track was also released as a single.

To support the album, Strange embarked on a UK tour, backed by the band who appeared on the album — Angus Maclean (guitar), Peter O'Sullivan (bass), Martin Griffin (drums) and Dave Winthrop (sax).

The Stranglers

The Stranglers were originally formed early in 1974 as the Guildford Stranglers, when guitarist and vocalist Hugh Cornwell met a college friend, bass player Jean-Jacques Burnel, and persuaded him to join with Cornwell and drummer Jet Black in forming a band. Prior to this, Cornwell had formed a group in Sweden with two Americans and a Swede but on their return to England they soon broke up. Cornwell set about forming a new group, which was completed when keyboardist Dave Greenfield joined in August 1975.

By 1976 The Stranglers were one of the core bands in the British punk explosion. They were signed to United Artists and released their first single, *Get A Grip On Yourself,* late in 1976, followed by *Peaches,* which was the first New Music hit single to be played on Australian commercial radio.

Around this time, the group backed a female singer called Celia, in the guise of The Mutations, on two singles, *Money Money* and *You*

> **"I really don't know how Freddie Mercury gets away with it. I never see him being slagged off as a poof."**
> **— Marc Almond, Soft Cell**

Better Believe Me. These singles were followed by a succession of Stranglers albums: *Rattus Norvegicus, No More Heroes, Black And White, Live (X Cert)* and in September 1979, *The Raven.*

In early 1979, The Stranglers played a successful though eventful, pub tour of Australia. On their return to England, Hugh Cornwell was jailed for five weeks for possession of drugs. Late 1979 saw both Cornwell and Burnel release solo albums, *Nosferatu* and *Euroman Cometh,* respectively.

While on a tour of France in 1980, all four Stranglers were tossed into jail briefly when fans at a Nice University concert rioted over failed sound equipment and caused a reported $250,000 worth of damage.

After a long hiatus in their career, The Stranglers returned to favour in 1982 with a UK and Australian top 10 single, *Golden Brown,* and the album, *La Folie.* A greatest hits-style album, titled *The Collection: 1977-82,* was issued later in the year.

Stray Cats

The Stray Cats were formed in 1979 in Long Island, New York. Eighteen-year-old guitarist and singer Brian Setzer was still a member of a New York cult band

The Bloodless Pharaohs, which he had joined in 1977, when he began gigging on a part-time basis with old schoolfriends, Lee Rocker (double bass) and Slim Jim Phantom (drums), both aged 17.

When The Bloodless Pharoahs finally split up in 1979 (their only recorded legacy being two tracks on a New York compilation LP, *2x5,* produced by Blondie's Jimmy Destri), The Stray Cats began in earnest, dropping most of their Cochran and Vincent covers in favour of original material.

In July 1980, The Stray Cats became bored with the suburbs of Long Island and decided to try their

Arista Records finally won their signature and in early 1981 their first single, *Runaway Boys,* was released and was a top five hit in most parts of the world. Soon after their debut album, *Stray Cats* (produced half by the band and half by Dave Edmunds), emerged and a second single, *Rock This Town,* did almost as well as the first.

Late in 1981, The Stray Cats completed a successful tour of Australia following a totally sold out UK and European tour. In early 1982 they released their second LP, *Gonna Ball,* produced by the band, but its acceptance was nowhere near as high as the first.

Bilson in Kingscliff on the north coast of New South Wales, Australia. The three boys formed their own band, called Wooden Horse and often played at their high school dances. The Oxley brothers had been musically inclined since they were very young, writing and playing their own songs, and making their own demo tapes at the age of 13.

In January 1979, Peter left his younger brother to finish school and headed with Bill for Sydney. The Shy Impostors were forming at the time and Peter joined them as bass player. Also in the line-up was guitarist Richard Burgman, who had

RACHEL SWEET

luck in London. When they arrived in the UK, they discovered that all the arrangements for gigs and accommodation had fallen through and they finished up staying in a publicist's office, who then hassled club promoters to get them work.

Once they began playing live in London, the sheer vitality of their stage performances did the rest, welding the spirit of the original rockabilly of the '50s with a musical toughness and visual punch that is strictly '80s. Soon they were being courted by half a dozen major labels as well as attracting such luminaries to their shows as Jerry Dammers, The Pretenders, Clash, Banshees and even Jagger, Richards and Ronnie Lane.

They also recorded some tracks with Bill Wyman producing for a projected third LP, *US Breakout,* which has yet to surface. However, their American breakout certainly has. The United States discovered their very own Stray Cats late in 1982 and both *Rock This Town* and *Stray Cat Strut* barrelled into the top 10, followed by a top three album with *Built For Speed,* a Stateside compilation. It was another fine example of the sluggish American market discovering a trend which has already peaked and subsided in the rest of the world.

Sunnyboys ▅▅▅▅▅▅
Peter and Jeremy Oxley (22 and 20 respectively) went to school with Bill

begun playing guitar about 10 years before in school bands and had teamed up with Sydney pub and party band Neon City Sheiks and early punk outfit The Kamikaze Kids, which later included Flaming Hands singer Julie Mostyn.

Meanwhile, Bill Bilson had met up with Steve Mather and they formed a very popular but short-lived group called The Playboy Lords. They did their first gig with The Shy Impostors, then played a number of other gigs, before the desire for a tighter working band led the drummer back to his original friends in music.

When Jeremy finished school, he couldn't wait to get to Sydney and be in his brother's band. With the demise of The Shy Impostors, he was able to step straight into the role of singer/songwriter/guitarist, accompanying Peter Oxley, Bill Bilson and Richard Burgman in their own band, Sunnyboys. On August 15, 1980, they played their first gig.

In late 1980, Sunnyboys released their debut EP on the Phantom label. It proved to be both a cult and commercial success and in early 1981 they signed with larger independent Mushroom Records. Their debut LP, *Sunnyboys,* produced by guitar hero, Lobby Loyde, came out in mid-1981 and enhanced their growing popularity. The group felt it was unfair to fans to include their first hit single, *Happy Man,* on the album, so they simultaneously issued a limited edition which replaced that song with the otherwise unobtainable *Tell Me What You Say.* Fans purchased one version, the general public the other, and everybody's conscience was clear.

The album (both editions) featured a re-recorded version of *Alone With You,* a song from the Phantom EP, and that became a top 10 follow-up hit to the ebullient *Happy Man.* For the second LP, *Individuals,* producer Loyde took the group to Mandrill Studios in Auckland, New Zealand, for the recording and then mixed the tapes at Pasha Studios in Los Angeles. These expensive efforts went somewhat unrewarded, as sales were far from spectacular and no significant hit single was forthcoming. Nonetheless, the album was a fine package of British-style pop-rock in a '60s garage mould.

Surf Punks

Though the music they deliver is nowhere in the realm of punk, Malibu's Surf Punks have carried the style and sound of New Music into the last bastion of resistance — surfing pop. With tongue planted firmly in cheek, Dennis Dragon and Drew Steele have dragged surf culture into the desolate '80s with their signature song *My Beach (Go Home!).*

Dennis Dragon first recorded in 1964 on Capitol as a member of sibling trio, The Dragons. Brother Daryl became The Captain (as in. . . & Tennille), other brother Doug went off and sold insurance and Dennis pursued a varied musical career, which has included numerous surf movie soundtracks, *The Innermost Limits of Pure Fun* and *A Sea For Yourself* among them.

The first, self-titled, Surf Punks album appeared on their own Dayglo label in 1977. In 1979 Shelter Records leased the single *My Beach (Go Home!)* and in 1980 Epic

THE SURF PUNKS

reissued the original album with a few extra tracks and the Shelter single. For the second proper album, *Locals Only* in 1982, the duo reverted to the Dayglo imprint. This LP included the Surf Punks' signature tune — *Spoiled Brats From Malibu.*

Rachel Sweet

Rachel Sweet's 20th birthday in July, 1982, marked 15 years of professional singing. A resident of Akron, Ohio, she started out on the stage at five and began doing commercials at eight, appearing in ads for Dole Bananas (among others), and playing on Broadway in *Up The Up Staircase.*

At the age of 10, Rachel toured 12,000 miles of America as a support act for actor Micky Rooney, travelling with a 24-piece band. Around this time she also opened for Bill Cosby in Reno, Nevada, and in a chance encounter won a $5 bet by duetting with Frankie Valli on *I Believe In Music.*

Aged 12, Rachel first recorded in Cleveland on an independent label. A single, *Faded Rose,* flopped but her producer took the song to Nashville, where she re-recorded it with Roy Baker. In two sessions she recorded seven songs, one *(We Live In Two Different Worlds),* reaching

number, 94 on the US country charts.

In 1977, producer/songwriter Liam Sternberg (her father's best friend) asked her to contribute two tracks to Stiff Records' *Akron Compilation* album — a collection of tracks from bands in the Akron area (home of Devo) that was released with a scratch'n'sniff cover — it smelt of rubber. Rachel's two tracks, *Tourist Boys* and *Truckstop Queen,* led to a recording contract with Stiff and a move to England.

In August 1978, with Sternberg producing, Rachel recorded her first album, *Fool Around,* backed by guitarist Brinsley Schwarz and members of The Blockheads. A revival single, *B-A-B-Y,* was a hit in England and also reached the lower reaches of the top 40 in Australia. Rachel then toured England as part of the Be Stiff tour, culminating at Christmas with eight shows at New York's prestigious Bottom Line.

In early 1979, she recorded a second revival single, *I Go To Pieces,* followed by the old Elvis classic, *Baby Let's Play House.* She then embarked on a US tour, sharing the bill with Graham Parker & The Rumour and finishing off by opening the show for Southside Johnny & The Asbury Jukes in Central Park, New York.

After a second LP, *Protect The*

Innocent, released early in 1980 for Stiff, Rachel signed with CBS and her third LP, titled *And Then He Kissed Me,* produced by Rick Chertoff and Pete Solley, came out in 1981. It featured *Everlasting Love,* a duet with Rex Smith which became a hit in both England and Australia.

Rachel took on the production chore herself for album four, *Blame It On Love,* aided by Marc Blatte and Larry Gottlieb, who also co-wrote eight of the 10 original songs with her.

SW9/Thomas Dolby

SW9 began as a trio in Stockwell, England, with a line-up of Kevin Armstrong (singer, songwriter and guitarist), Mathew Seligman (bass) and Kim Barti (drums). Their debut album, *Drip Dry Zone,* was released in England in October 1980 on the Oval label and won acclaim for the band as one of the figureheads of the new English psychedelic scene. Although perhaps psychedelic in intent then, SW9 call on a broad range of more contemporary influences, from reggae to funk, though the last thing you'd call them is a revival band.

The version of *Drip Dry Zone* which was released in Australia on Gap Records contained three new tracks not included on the original, including the single, *Love Is Essential.* By this time, Seligman had left the group and the new tracks feature the funk influence of Lennie Meade on bass and Thomas Dolby on keyboards. Both of these musicians have performed in Lene Lovich's band and Dolby wrote *New Toy* for her.

Both Dolby and Kevin Armstrong have also been involved in solo projects apart from recording and performing with SW9. Dolby has been most succesful with the album *Golden Age of Wireless,* receiving strong critical support and generating the fine hit *She Blinded Me With Science.*

Sylvia and The Sapphires

Sylvia and The Sapphires are a black English vocal group made up of the three Mason sisters (Sylvia, Ruby and Vicki) from Croydon.

They've recorded two singles for Stiff Records — *Shoppin' Around* and *Baby I'm A Fool For You* — and have been often described as the new

SYLVIA AND THE SAPPHIRES

age Martha & The Vandellas. The trio have sung together since their early childhood and as well as recording for Stiff and making television and radio appearances, they've kept busy singing backing harmonies for Yazoo and The Undertones.

Ruby, born May 23rd, made her debut as a singer in her early school days, performing for her schoolmates. She caused considerable controversy with her parents when, after leaving school, she decided to pursue a singing career. Her first taste of the music business followed when, after winning a sponsored talent competition, she was offered a recording contract which never materialised. However, she got a job handling lead vocals with a soul band and after touring with them, was snapped up by a funk band which desired more vocal harmony.

Her experience has taken her to Australia and twice to New Zealand as a solo artist, and in between her trips, she performed on a seven-week series of *The Cannon And Ball Show*

on English television. She's also worked as a backing vocalist with Junior Campbell, Jimmy Cliff, Cat Stevens, Cilla Black and Rod Stewart.

Sylvia was born December 8th and made her singing debut when Ruby had laryngitis and needed someone to cover for her. She sang in a band at weekends then decided to gain experience in Europe, where she was lucky enough to join a successful band, staying with them for two years.

On her return home, Sylvia sang in a backing group for the television series *Let's Rock,* which had a 15-week run. She also joined Ruby on many backing vocal sessions.

Vicki, born February 26th, was encouraged to sing by her sisters while still at school. As soon as she left she began joining them at recording sessions as a backing vocalist. Vicki soon joined Sylvia on the *Let's Rock* TV series and finally joined her sisters to form Sylvia and The Sapphires, a formidable soul-pop vocal unit.

> **"I never look into the inner meaning of songs. I can't, it makes me nervous."**
> *Rachel Sweet*

T

Tactics

Tactics was formed in Canberra Australia, by vocalist and guitarist Dave Studdert in late 1977. The original line-up was Studdert, Angus Douglas (lead guitar), Ingrid Spielman (piano), Geoff Marsh (bass) and Robert Whittle (drums). In September 1978, the group were persuaded by Sydney group The Thought Criminals to move to Sydney and they quickly attracted an enthusiastic following in the inner-city venues.

In June 1979, Tactics released an EP, *Long Weekend,* on their own Folding Chair label. In June 1980, the group recorded a single, *Outdoors/Hole In My Life,* which they refused to sell and instead gave away at their gigs. The group spent a great deal of time during 1980 recording their debut album *My Houdini,* and it was finally released on Green Records in February 1981. A single, *Second Language,* was taken from it and issued in April.

In November 1981, Tactics released their second LP, *Glebe,* but in the following year, after various line-up changes, the group eventually disbanded, leaving behind a live album, *The Bones of Barry Harrison.*

Talk Talk

"I want to write songs that you'll be able to listen to in 20 years time," is the idealistic, totally original, and unlikely hope of Talk Talk's lead singer and founder member Mark Hollis.

Talk Talk's career began with Mark taking demo tapes into Island Music in 1980, attempting to get a deal. One of the staff members liked his songs and arranged some studio time. At this time Mark was introduced to bassist Paul Webb and drummer Lee Harris. Paul and Lee were in Southend doing a session with producer Ed Hollis who

> "I dislike being called a prodigy. I don't even know what the word means. I'm just a person."
> *Prince*

mentioned to them that his younger brother had some songs. They met, and within a week had not only performed and arranged Mark's songs, but had written some new material together.

The final addition to the Talk Talk line-up was keyboards player Simon Brenner. Next came a series of live dates at the Blitz, Legend and The Embassy, and in November 1981 the band had a contract with EMI. A month later they toured England with Duran Duran, followed not long after by an American jaunt with Elvis Costello.

Following a live session for Kid Jensen on the BBC, Talk Talk cut

TALK TALK

TACTICS

the single *Mirror Mirror* in February 1982, after which came *Today* in June and *Talk Talk* in October. The latter had first appeared, in a snarling punk version, on the 1979 Beggar's Banquet sampler LP *Streets,* performed by the band Reaction.

A year after formation, Talk Talk graced our ears with the album *The Party's Over* and are presently working on a second twelve inch outing. Single four, *My Foolish Friend*, was issued in February 1983.

Talking Heads

Talking Heads, which takes its name from a TV term for a close-up, is one of the most innovative and adventurous new music groups. The band first performed at CBGB's summer festival in June 1975, though all members had been involved with music for many years. The line-up is David Byrne (lead vocals and guitar), Chris Frantz (drums and backing vocals), Tina Weymouth (bass and backing vocals) and Jerry Harrison (keyboards, guitar and backing vocals).

Byrne, Weymouth and Frantz met at the Rhode Island School of Design. Byrne and Frantz had formed their first band, The Artistics, while at school in 1974. Weymouth joined soon after, and the band remained a trio until 1977 when Jerry Harrison, who'd been studying architecture at Harvard, joined. Harrison had spent some time playing keyboards with

> **"People take us far too seriously. We're going to have to start being far more stupid. But there are certain things I feel need to be done in terms of music and performance and what these things amount to is that the world doesn't need another posturing clown yammering away about his 'baby'!"**
> *David Byrne, Talking Heads*

Jonathan Richman's Modern Lovers.

Talking Heads' debut album, *Talking Heads 77,* was produced and recorded by Tony Bongiovi in New York and received unanimous praise, with Rolling Stone calling it "one of the definitive records of the decade". It contained the classic track *Psycho Killer* (parodied by The Fools as *Psycho Chicken*). Next came *More Songs About Buildings And Food,* recorded at Compass Point Studios in the Bahamas with Brian Eno producing, in March/April 1978. It contained the first cover version the band had recorded (Al Green's *Take Me To*

The River, a number 26 US chart hit) and received similar critical reaction to *77,* with John Rockwell from The New York Times naming it number one in his list of top albums for 1978.

During their Australian tour in July 1979, Talking Heads showcased some of the material that would be on their third album, *Fear Of Music,* again produced by Brian Eno with the band. 1980's *Remain In Light,* also Eno-produced, solidified their position as one of the most important and influential new music bands. It saw them experimenting with African rhythms, which then became a vital aspect of their live performances. This fourth album featured guest appearances by Nona Hendryx (formerly of Labelle) and Robert Palmer.

Talking Heads continued to tour extensively throughout America and Europe, performing their unique style of rock'n'roll, best described by David Byrne with the words: "Our music is different. It's driving but very melodious. It's somewhat like the psychedelic stuff of the late '60s but much more refined with much more to say."

Or, as England's Record Mirror rejoiced: "After all these years, someone can still take the five basic components of rock — a singer, a song, a guitar, bass and drums — and come up with something totally fresh."

After the fouth album, the members of Talking Heads became involved in a number of worthwhile individual projects. David Byrne recorded an album with Brian Eno,

TALKING HEADS

THE TEARDROP EXPLODES

the acclaimed *My Life In The Bush Of Ghosts,* as well as a solo album *Songs From The Catherine Wheel* and an EP, *Three Big Songs.* Jerry Harrison went solo with *The Red And The Black* album and Frantz and Weymouth formed the elastic Tom Tom Club, which included Lori Weymouth, Adrian Belew, Lani Weymouth, Tyrone Downie, Monte Brown, James Rizzi and Benjamin Armbrister. This unit cut an album and scored a cult hit with *Wordy Rappinghood.*

In 1982 a double live set was issued, *The Name Of This Band is Talking Heads,* with one disc covering material captured 1977-'79 and the other representing 1980-'81. Sire Records also released an intriguing eight-song cassette aimed at the Walkman market. Titled *Portable Music,* it featured tracks from Byrne and Harrison solo albums, Tom Tom Club cuts (including *Under The Boardwalk*), and two songs from the live album. A new studio album, *Speaking In Tongues,* was released in mid-1983.

The Teardrop Explodes

The origins of The Teardrop Explodes and, in fact, the whole renaissance of Liverpool as a music force, date back to 1977, when the Crucial Three were formed by Julian Cope, Ian McCulloch (now fronting Echo & The Bunnymen) and Pete Wylie (leader of Wah! Heat).

Julian had moved to Merseyside a

year earlier from the Midlands, to study teacher training and drama at college, but these academic aspirations were cut short as a new band — the embryonic Teardrop Explodes — began rehearsing. A series of name and line-up changes ensued, with Mac and Pete Wylie leaving to be replaced by organist Paul Simpson and guitarist Mike Finkler, and with drummer Gary Dwyer coming in for the group's debut gig at Eric's, Liverpool, in November '78. The name The Teardrop Explodes had been adopted by then — taken from a DC comic.

In December of that year, they recorded their debut single, *Sleeping Gas,* for the then recently formed Zoo label. In April '79 a second single, *Bouncing Babies,* was recorded. The summer of '79 saw Paul Simpson depart and David Balfe, (Zoo co-director) join as keyboardist. Previously, he'd played with Big In Japan and Dalek I.

A third single, *Treason,* appeared in February 1980, produced by former Deaf School guitarist and Madness co-producer, Clive Langer. There were more line-up changes — Mike Finkler, for various reasons, was asked to leave. He was immediately replaced by Alan Gill, guitarist with Dalek I. David Balfe and Bill Drummond (the other Zoo director) produced the Teardrops' debut album in Rockfield during the spring and summer of 1980.

When *Kilimanjaro* was released in late 1980, it immediately established the group in the forefront of the new "psychedelic" movement, enhanced by their classic single, *When I Dream,* which was produced by Mike Howlett.

After the album's release, Teardrops underwent more line-up changes, with Gill and Balfe quitting. The remaining members, Cope and Gary Dwyer, decided they would become the core of a flexible

unit, adding guitarists Troy Tate and Hammer.

In July 1982, Tate and bassist Ron Francois quit, leaving the core as Cope, Dwyer and Balfe, who'd rejoined at that time. The trio recorded the second album, *Wilder,* at that time before embarking on more extensive touring, which included dates in Australia.

By late 1982, Cope was frustrated with audience response and decided to split the band. They broke up four years to the day after their London debut. The three remaining members, Cope, Dwyer and Balfe, all plan other projects. Dwyer will assist Cope in future projects and has formed a band with Balfe called Dumbfounding Two.

Besides his work with Teardrops, Cope compiled an anthology album of tracks by his hero, Scott Walker, called *Fire Escape In The Sky — The Godlike Genius Of Scott Walker,* which was released on Zoo Records in 1981.

Tears For Fears

Bath schoolfriends Curt Smidth and Roland Orzabel are the co-founders of Tears For Fears.

When they formed the band, the duo had only two songs written but these attracted the attention of Dave Bates, the man responsible for discocering The Teardrop Explodes, Monsoon, and Trio. He signed them

TEARS FOR FEARS

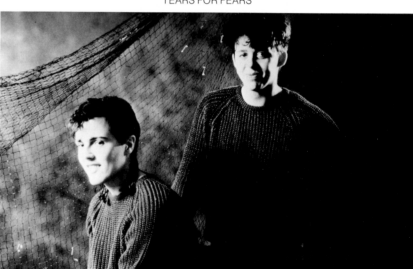

to Polygram.

The first of the two songs, *Suffer The Children,* became their debut single, followed by *Pale Shelter.*

The band's third single, *Mad World,* reached number three on the English charts, staying there for three weeks.

Bassist Curt and guitarist Roland were initially apprehensive about live performances but when the decision to tour was made they were augmented by keyboard players Ian Stanley and Andy Davies, plus drummer Manny Elias. This line-up went on the road supporting the Thompson Twins.

At the conclusion of the tour, Tears For Fears went into the studio with producer Chris Hughes, who'd previously worked with Adam and The Ants and Dalek I Love You. The resulting album, *The Hurting*, included the *Mad World* single plus new versions of the first two singles and the band's fourth single, *Change*.

> **"The modern day music scene is about as vitriolic as a mindless television programme like The Love Boat."**
> — *Julian Cope, Teardrop Explodes*

Tenpole Tudor

Eddie Tenpole first came to attention in the *Who Killed Bambi?* segment of The Sex Pistols' movie, *The Great Rock'n'Roll Swindle*. At one stage, there was a very strong possibility that he would join the Pistols as Johnny Rotten's replacement.

In late 1979, Eddie was motivated to form his own band by the glamour and fame of the movie. Early in 1980, the group — comprising Bob Kingston (guitar), Munch Universe (guitar), Dick Crippen (bass) and Gary Long (drums) — released their first single, *Real Fun,* on Korova Records. They were signed to Stiff and quickly came to attention on the Son Of Stiffs tour which went through Europe, Britain and America.

The group's first single on Stiff came out late in 1980, titled *3 Bells In A Row.* In April 1981, Tenpole Tudor released *Swords Of A Thousand Men,* which soared up the charts in both England and Australia. Two more singles followed in 1981, *Wunderbar* and *Throwing The Baby Out With The Bathwater,* as well as their debut album, *Eddie, Old Bob, Dick & Gary.*

In early 1982 came a second album, *Let The Four Winds Blow,* with the title track released as a single.

The The

The The, a brainchild of notorious Soft Cell manager Stevo, is a utility name for a sole English musician — Matt Johnson. While little can be judged of his musical abilities at this point, a great deal can be determined

TOP / TENPOLE TUDOR. ABOVE / MATT JOHNSON (THE THE)

regarding his business acumen.

In a deal that might be viewed in the same light as The Sex Pistols' famed exploits, Johnson and Stevo managed to persuade CBS Records to part with some £40,000 for what

was essentially a one-sided single.

It all began when Decca Records put up £8,000 for the recording of the track *Uncertain Smile* in New York — without closing contracts. When more money was demanded,

THEATRE OF HATE

Decca demurred and the tape was flogged around other companies. CBS jumped up and down about it and thus began a merry chase. Chairman Maurice Oberstein, unable to arrange a formal office meeting, was instructed to present himself for business at at Tottenham Court Road bus stop at midnight. He complied and before dawn's first light, had coughed up forty big ones which, he hastened to assure, guaranteed him an album and a second single.

At time of writing, The The have yet to call the charts their own — not that they (he?) need a hit anyway. You can live a long time off an advance like that.

Theatre Of Hate

At the time of their disbanding, the nucleus of Theatre Of Hate was Kirk Brandon (vocals), Stan Stammers (bass), and John Lennard (sax).

There were repeated changes of drummers and guitarists.

"Certain people could live up to the Theatre Of Hate idea — others couldn't," is Kirk's explanation of the constant shifts. "You don't stay on the train when it's got to the end of the line."

Theatre Of Hate recorded four albums: *Who Dares Wins (Live At Leeds)* on the SS label, *Do You Believe In The Westworld?*, *Live At The Lyceum,* (cassette only) and *Who Dares Wins (Live In Berlin),* on the Burning Rome label. Plans are afoot for another album of studio material on that label.

Besides the albums, Theatre Of Hate recorded six singles — *Original Sin, Rebel Without A Brain, Nero, The Hop,* plus seven inch and 12 inch versions of *Westworld.*

Third World

The roots of Third World go back to the early '70s and Inner Circle, one of Jamaica's few road bands. Bunny Clarke (vocals), Stephen Core (guitar), Michael Cooper (keyboards), Irvin Jarret (percussion) and Willie Stewart (drums) all came from that group. Only bass player Richie Daley came via another route, a band called Tomorrow's Children.

Third World came to Britain in mid-1975 and were immediately signed by Island Records. The band then toured Britain as support for Bob Marley & The Wailers before releasing their debut album later that year. Third World spent the following year touring almost non-stop through the United States, and with Marley were the first to bring reggae to that country.

In 1977, in addition to releasing the *96 Degrees In The Shade* album, Third World concentrated on live work in the West Indies. This culminated in the band's appearance in a series of shows at Kingston's Little Theatre in Jamaica at the beginning of 1978. Their stage show blended dance, mime and music with a prominent spiritual theme, choreographed by Thomas Pinnock, who has danced with the Jamaican Dance Theatre and the Martha

THIRD WORLD

THE THOMPSON TWINS

basis of many of their current songs. By 1981 the band had expanded to include Joe Leeway on percussion and vocals together with Alannah Currie on percussion and sax.

In mid-1981, The Thompson Twins' debut album, *A Product Of Participation,* was warmly received by the press. But the band were disappointed that it did not capture the seemingly chaotic spirit of their shows. Soon after, producer Steve Lillywhite caught one of their gigs and solved the band's search for a producer.

In early 1982, The Thompson Twins' second LP, *Set,* was released and the single, *In The Name Of Love,* became a minor English hit. Arista in the US picked up the single, it sat at number one on the Billboard dance charts for seven weeks and made a reasonable impression on the R&B/Soul charts. To support the record, the group embarked on their first American visit in June.

Ironically, prior to news of their American success, The Thompson Twins reduced to a trio of just Bailey, Currie and Leeway, in order to accommodate their ever-evolving musical direction. For the future, The Thompson Twins plan to continue mostly in the studio, using guest musicians for live work when

Graham School of Dance in New York.

Third World's *Journey To Addis* album was released in late 1978, following the top 10 success in England and throughout Europe of *Now That We Found Love.* The album reached top 30 in England, coinciding with Third World's first headlining tour of Britain. The followup single, *Cool Meditation,* reached the British charts in early 1979.

In mid-1979 the group released *The Story's Been Told,* an album which further explored their unique blend of black American and Jamaican styles. It was followed in 1980 by the *Prisoner On The Street* album and in 1982 by *You've Got The Power.*

The Thompson Twins ▌▬▬
The Thompson Twins came into being in 1977. Tom Bailey (vocals, keyboards and percussion), Pete Dodd and John Roog, all friends and living in Chesterfield, England, decided to form a band simply because they enjoyed playing music together. The name Thompson Twins was inspired by certain Tin Tin characters.

After spending a couple of years playing around various northern cities in England, the band decided to move to London in 1980, leaving behind their original drummer. Following a brief and unsuccessful

TOTO COELO

liaison with a second drummer, The Thompson Twins auditioned Chris Bell and although he hadn't played drums for some time, he gelled with the other members and was asked to join.

Consequently, the group's musical direction began to evolve from fast, poppy three minute songs to a more experimental, rhythmic sound. Improvisation was then used as the

necessary. Album three, *Quick Step & Side Kick,* was released early in 1983 and yielded the international hit, *Lies.*

Toto Coelo ▌▬▬
"Lots of legs flying everywhere" was one writer's reaction to the sudden appearance of Toto Coelo on Britain's *Top Of The Pops* television show.

The female quintet had landed a spot on the show after exploding out of seemingly nowhere with their bizarre but irresistible hit *I Eat Cannibals.*

Not exactly nowhere. Toto Coelo have a lot more going for them than great legs. Their collective background is quite startling and worthy of documentation. Sheen Doran had appeared on *Ready Steady Go!* as a 12-year-old, singing *You're Ready Now* in the company of Dave Berry and Marianne Faithfull. She also starred in four *St. Trinian's* films as a precocious nymphet (aren't they all?). Lacey Bond starred as a schoolkid in the television series *Grange Hill.* Anita Mahadervan, a former member of Legs & Co., was a familiar face on British television screens through a popular "Milk Has Gotta Lotta Bottle" advertisement. Neither Lindsey Danvers nor Ros Holness have strong screen backgrounds, though both their fathers are recognisable actors.

Toto Coelo was the brainchild of 33-year-old Sheen, who has spent the past 20 or so years on stages, theatre, film and television, all over Britain. She was playing *Sweet Charity* in Manchester when the *Big Spender* production number gave her an ingenious idea. On June 8, 1981, she rang around to her friends and put to them the concept of a theatrically-orientated all-female rock vocal group. The following day, five of them met, drew up plans, and went into six weeks of rehearsals. They made their debut performance at London's Royal Garden Hotel on the Royal Wedding night and then spent a year playing clubs, pubs, assorted dives and supporting a Rose Royce tour.

At one London club, somebody from Radialchoice Records, home of Toni Basil, caught the act and proffered the legendary scrolled recording contract. The girls then commenced sessions with experienced pop producer Bobby Blue and the song *I Eat Cannibals* fairly jumped out and clubbed them on the head. Riddled with sexual innuendo, it took the public's fancy and became a smash hit in England, Australia and a number of European countries.

Recording is a new avenue for the multi-talented members of Toto Coelo, though Sheen did cut a single in Scandinavia in the early '70s — a song given to her by Abba before the world had heard of them. She also scored a European hit with *The Clapping Song,* unfortunately done on a session basis which meant that she got no royalties.

Toto Coelo's second single is *Dracula's Tango.* They are currently working on an album.

TOYAH

Toyah

Toyah Willcox was born in Birmingham on May 18, 1958. After finishing school, she attended the Birmingham Old Rep Drama School. Two months later she was offered the co-starring role in a BBC TV play, *Glitter.* When *Glitter* was telecast in 1977 she was immediately offered a place with the National Theatre, where she stayed for nine months. In the same year she landed the part of Mad in Derek Jarman's punk film, *Jubilee.*

Over Christmas 1977, Toyah began to form her own band, which eventually consisted of Joel Bogen on guitar, Steve Bray on drums, Pete Bush on keyboards and Mark Henry (later to be replaced by Charlie Francis) on bass. During 1978, Toyah continued her acting career with the lead role in the film *Corn Is Green,* starring Katherine Hepburn, the part of Monkey in *Quadrophenia,* as well as the *Quartermass* TV series.

In February 1978, Toyah signed with Safari Records and her debut single, *Victims Of The Riddle,* and an EP, *Sheep Farming In Barnet,* were released later that year. She also appeared in Derek Jarman's movie of Shakespeare's *The Tempest* and the BBC TV series *Dr Jekyll And Mr Hyde.*

In early 1980 her second single, *Bird In Flight,* was released and in May came her debut album, *The Blue Meaning,* which made the UK top 40. To support the album, she embarked on a UK national tour and at its completion broke up the band. Following more theatre and TV acting roles, she released a new single in November, *Danced,* followed two weeks later by a live album, *Toyah! Toyah!*

After winning a number of music polls as Top Female Vocalist, 1982 began with her own BBC TV comedy series, *Dear Heart,* followed in May by a new single, *Brave New World,* and an LP released in June, *The Changeling,* both of which were produced by Steve Lillywhite.

In January 1981, Toyah embarked on a UK tour with a new band: Joel Bogen (guitar), Phil Spalding (bass), Adrian Lee (keyboards) and Nigel Glockler (drums). Recording-wise, 1981 proved to be the breakthrough year. An EP, *Four From Toyah,* reached number four in the UK charts in March, the single *I Want To Be Free,* released in May, became a top five hit, a new LP, *Anthem,* climbed to number two soon after its May release, and in September the single, *Thunder In The Mountains* also went top five.

Trio

Trio came from West Germany. Their address is Regenterstr. 10a, 2907 Grobenkneten 2, phone: 04435/2300. A curious thing about the band is that they put that information on the covers of their records, encouraging people to

TUXEDOMOON

communicate with them.

Trio are, surprisingly, a trio — Stefan, Peter and 'Kralle'. Their story appears to be that they recorded a self-produced mini-album which came to the attention of Klaus Voorman, the famous session bass player and graphic designer, who went into the studio with Trio for some further recording.

Trio's records are marketed by Mercury and the band scored a number one hit in Australia with the extremely silly *Da Da Da, (I Don't*

> "If I want to call someone a cocksucker, I'll call them a cocksucker."
> — *Toyah Wilcox*

TRIO

Love You, You Don't Love Me, Aha Aha Aha).

Their live appearances have essentially been restricted to Europe. Any further information is superfluous.

Tuxedomoon

A peculiar combination of electronic keyboards, violins, saxes, bass, rhythm box and occasional guitar, Tuxedomoon's music covers a wide spectrum of styles and moods, bringing to the contemporary scene a range of textures more associated with classical, jazz or Hollywood film music.

Formed in 1977 when keyboards/sax player Steven Brown and keyboards/violin player Blaine Reininger met whilst studying

electronic music at college, they are now the only survivors, besides The Dead Kennedys, of the early punk flourish of San Francisco, a scene with which they had at best an uneasy alliance.

Expanded to a quartet by the addition of guitar/bass player Peter Principle and Chinese-American actor/vocalist Winston Tong, Tuxedomoon played everywhere in the city except rock clubs — coffee houses, lofts, parties — until financial necessity forced them into places like the Deaf Club (a bona fide club for the deaf, where drinks had to be ordered in sign language). Later they added film-maker Bruce Gedulgig, to pursue their interest in what they call "live movies", a mixed-media combination of music, mime and film.

The most extended example so far of this working method occurred in England a couple of years ago when they worked on an "experimental music and performance" project at Clarendon College, Nottingham. A week's residency entailed a series of lectures at schools in the area and workshop sessions with local dancers, film-makers, performance artists and musicians, culminating in two performances which attempted to tie together the various themes and forms.

Tuxedomoon are signed with San Francisco's Ralph Records, for whom they have recorded two albums, *Half-Mute* and *Desire,* released in 1980 and 1981, respectively. The most recent album, *Divine*, on the Operation Twilight label, features their music from the ballet *Divine* by Maurice Bejart.

171

U

ULTRAVOX

UB40

The name UB40 is taken from the British Government dole registration card and is appropriate to the band's early days. UB40 formed in their hometown of Birmingham, England, Christmas 1978 and without exception no member has ever had any formal musical training. Their common bond therefore was an interest in entertainment, as well as the reflection of their radical humanist approach to politics. Though they were all on the dole, they managed to get instruments and taught themselves to play.

Their first recording contract was with a small independent label, Graduate, which they soon left to form their own label, DEP. As soon as UB40 felt they were good enough to appear in public, they played the English pub circuit. Their pop melodies and dub reggae rhythms proved irresistible to audiences across the nation and they toured incessantly throughout '79 and '80, during which time they were special guests on an extensive UK tour with The Police.

UB40's first single, *Food For Thought/King,* was released early in 1980 and immediately established the band when it went top five. It was followed by the debut album, *Signing Off,* late in the year, and UB40 rapidly became one of the most popular bands in Britain.

The second LP, *Present Arms,* was released in mid-1981 and proved as commercially successful as the first. At the end of the year they also released *Present Arms In Dub*, a re-recorded dub version of their second album. In September 1981, UB40 toured Australia and cemented their high popularity there. They returned in 1982 and later that year recorded album three, titled simply *UB44.* A compilation, *The Singles Album,* became their most successful UK chart album, and was followed by *UB40 Live.*

The line-up of UB40 is Astro (master of ceremonies and trumpet), Ali Campbell (rhythm guitar and vocals), Robin Campbell (lead guitar), Michael Virtue (keyboards), Brian Travers (sax), Norman Hassan (percussion), Earl Falconer (bass) and Jim Brown (drums).

UB40

> **"I admire Fred Astaire more than almost any other person."**
> — *Midge Ure, Ultravox*

Tracey Ullman

Tracey's signing to the Stiff label in England reads like a scene from an old Doris Day movie. The 24-year-old actress/singer fell into conversation in a hairdressing salon with Rosemary Robinson, wife of Stiff founder Dave Robinson. Tracey mentioned she was keen to make a record, Rosemary said she knew just the person to help her and the swift result was the hit single *Breakaway*, a nifty cover of the Jackie DeShannon composition for Irma Thomas.

Tracey won a scholarship at age 12, to the Italia Stage School, commencing her extensive showbiz career. At 16, she appeared in a Berlin ballet production of *Gigi*, then joined the Second Generation Dance Group. At 18, she appeared alongside Shakin' Stevens in the West End stage production of *Elvis* for a year and then moved on to *Grease* at the same theatre. At 20, she played the plum role of Janet in *The Rocky Horror Show* and then starred in three Liverpool stage productions — *Talent, It's A Madhouse* and *Zack*. Back in London, she was seen in the BBC production *McKenzie*, the Central Television production *Four In A Million,* and the BBC series *A Kick Up The Eighties* and *Three Of A Kind.* Moving back to the theatre she took the role of Kate in *She Stoops To Conquer* at the Lyric Theatre.

At the same time as she was signed to Stiff, Paul McCartney engaged her services for his film *Give My Regards To Broad Street.*

Ultravox

Ultravox first came together in April 1974 when singer John Foxx formed the first line-up with drummer Warren Cann, bassist Chris Cross and guitarist Steve Shears (later replaced by Robert Simon). Soon after, they became a five-piece band with the addition of keyboards and violin player Billy Currie.

The band didn't start using synthesizers until they got their first recording contract with Island, but then they quickly established themselves as one of the forerunners of the style with their first album, *Ultravox*, in 1976, which had a few tracks produced by Brian Eno. Unfortunately, being a synthesizer band in England in the punk-ridden late '70s held no credibility whatsoever, and after two further albums, *Ha! Ha! Ha!* and *Systems Of Romance*, which both sold moderately well, Island dumped the band in late '78. Undeterred, in early 1979 the group financed their own tour of America, which was a surprising success, but by then not all the band were on speaking terms and a split was inevitable. In mid-1979, Foxx and Simon departed by mutual consent.

Enter Midge Ure. Guitarist and vocalist Ure had had a very mixed past, beginning in his native Scotland. He was first sighted in a sub-heavy metal band called Salvation, which in the early '70s metamorphosed into a teenybopper group called Slik in emulation of kinsmen The Bay City Rollers. As

U2

that craze died off so did the band. Ure then moved to London, where he teamed up with ex-Sex Pistol Glenn Matlock to form The Rich Kids, which soon fell apart. Soon after, he filled in on guitar for Thin Lizzy on an American tour.

In late 1979, Midge Ure was working in the studio with Magazine members John McGeoch and Dave Formula, Rusty Egan and Billy Currie on Steve Strange's Visage project. Ultravox at this point were

looking for a fourth member to begin again after the split and Ure was willing to play in any group. Thus the second Ultravox was formed.

After a short tour of America, the group returned to England in early 1980 and signed to Chrysalis. Their first album, *Vienna*, was recorded with Kraftwerk producer Conny Plank in Germany with whom they'd worked before, and scored them a worldwide hit single with the title track. In late 1981 the group released their second LP, *Rage In Eden*, again produced by Plank, and it easily emulated the success of the first.

For 1982's *Quartet* they enlisted the aid of veteran producer George Martin and found themselves a lusher sound. Midge Ure also embarked on a sideline solo career during the year, charting moderately with a cover of Tom Rush's *No Regrets* (also a hit for the Walker Bros). His version of Bowie's *The Man Who Sold The World* can be found on the *Party Party* soundtrack album.

The Undertones

The Undertones began in late 1975 in Derry, Northern Ireland, where they all still live. Feargal Sharkey (vocals), John O'Neill (rhythm guitar), Damien O'Neill (lead guitar), Micky Bradley (bass) and Billy Doherty (drums) came together to form a garage band. Two-and-a-half years and numerous practice sessions later, the band were still playing local dates (when such opportunities arose) until a tape they'd made found its way to the independent label, Good Vibrations. They recorded the *Teenage Kids* EP, released on that label in September 1978. It won a crucial early admirer in John Peel, who played it continually on his Radio One show. Within days of this exposure, The Undertones were signed to Sire

THE UNDERTONES

Records.

The next two years saw them carefully grow up and develop. A second single, *Get Over You*, was released in January 1979. Still one of their most popular live numbers, it introduced producer Roger Bechirian, who has worked on all their subsequent recordings. *Jimmy Jimmy* gave them their first top 20 hit (April '79) and prefaced their debut album, *The Undertones*, a month later, which notched up 14 weeks on the album charts.

After another hit from the LP, *Here Comes The Summer*, in July 1979, the group embarked on their first US tour with The Clash and followed it with another top 40 single in October, *You've Got My Number*.

The Undertones recorded their second LP, *Hypnotised*, in Holland in early 1980 and the first single to be released, *My Perfect Cousin*, gave them their first top 10 hit in March. The album followed in April and was also top 10, while the second single, *Wednesday Week*, stuck at number 11. The group set out on their own headlining tour of America and followed it with their biggest foray into Europe.

Despite this success in the UK, the group were unhappy with their progress in the rest of the world and in October 1980, the group left Sire and formed their own label, Ardeck. In June 1981, they issued their third album, *Positive Touch*, featuring the single, *It's Going To Happen*. There followed a gap until *The Sin Of Pride* in early 1983. Despite this world market view, they have remained essentially a garage band.

U2

Late in 1977, drummer Larry pinned a message to the noticeboard at Dublin's Mount Temple school — he was looking for other musicians amongst his fellows to form a band. Of the recruits, only bass guitarist

173

Adam Clayton had any previous experience and that was with a north Dublin garage band.

The two neophytes were singer Bono and guitarist The Edge, who had been so christened by a contingent of neighbourhood friends. Their contribution was to steer U2 towards their own unique style as the band began to rework and remodel the classic four-man line-up, trying to avoid the cliches and excesses of both punk and heavy metal. This resulted in a soaring and intense style of rock that was emotional without being musclebound or bludgeoning.

Working away from the attentions of the London media and record industry, U2 had time to develop without being rushed prematurely into the rock'n'roll circus. With increasing speed they attracted their own audience in Dublin and around Ireland. A three track single, *U-2-3*, was released in late 1979 and their fans responded by seeing it into the Irish charts and by voting the band to the top of five categories in the Readers Poll of the Irish rock magazine The Hot Press.

Meantime, the band were spending increasingly more time playing around England and in 1980 signed to Island. Late that year their debut album, *Boy* and the single, *I Will Follow,* were released and established the group as one of the hottest prospects around.

For most of 1981, U2 toured the length and breadth of America, barely finding time to record their second LP, *October,* again with producer Steve Lillywhite. The single, *Gloria,* was a hit in England and also received favourable exposure in Australia.

TRACEY ULLMAN

telling, evocative lyrics. There really isn't anything quite like it around." (John Rockwell, New York Times)

Verlaine was born 13th December, 1949, in Mount Morris, New Jersey. His formative years, however, were spent in Wilmington, Delaware, where he attended primary and high school. His academic success peaked when he won a place at Erskine College in South Carolina. In the finest rock rebel tradition, he quit after three days.

While in high school, Tom had picked up the rudiments of guitar and gradually gave over his attentions to this instrument. This occurred despite the fact that he had started playing piano at seven and saxophone at 11.

By 1967, Verlaine and drummer friend Billy Ficca had met and decided to make the fateful move to New York City. Tom worked on the Brooklyn waterfront unloading

bananas by day and penning songs and poetry by night. His diligence paid off when Richard Hell, an old high school friend and publisher of a New York poetry magazine, offered to publish some of Verlaine's work.

After a short spell playing solo in local clubs, Verlaine teamed up with Hell, who now played bass and Ficca to form The Neon Boys. With the addition of second guitarist Richard Lloyd, The Neon Boys transmuted into the first Television. Hell then upped and left to form his own band and was replaced by Fred Smith, one-time Blondie bassist.

Looking for a place to play regularly, Verlaine and company were attracted to the burgeoning new wave scene centred on CBGB's, a run-down bar on the Bowery, and played there every Sunday for a six month period. During this time, Television began to be recognised as a radical new force in rock and asserted themselves as a seminal influence on emerging bands.

> "Soft Cell are a couple of fairies, phoney and pretentious. Haircut 100 are cute but a bit wimpy, and the Police are too rock-starrish. They make rock'n'roll look extravagant, pompous and ridiculous."
> — *Johnny Cougar*

TOM VERLAINE

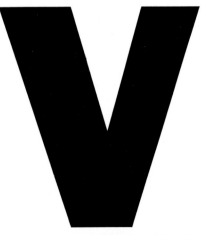

Tom Verlaine ▮▬▬▬▬▬

Tom Verlaine inspires in critics and fans the kind of rabid devotion that is usually reserved for saints and visionaries: "The songs are characterised by Mr Verlaine's raw spat-out singing, by the twanging solidity of the massed guitars and their sweet solo flights and odd, yet

Tom Verlaine first appeared on record backing Patti Smith on *Hey Joe,* a single released on Mer Records in 1974. The first recorded effort by Television was the *Little Johnny Jewell* 12 inch EP, which appeared on Ork Records in August '75 and sold well throughout the United States and Europe.

The cult success off the single led to the band signing to Elektra in 1976. Television released their first album, *Marquee Moon,* in February '77 to mass critical acclaim and by the end of the year had been voted by many as their fave rave of that year. Tom Verlaine, it goes without saying, also featured heavily on that year's guitar polls. *Adventure,* the band's second album, began to break commercial barriers and still retained the critics' approval. *Adventure* entered the British charts at number one in March of '78 and enigmatically, the band decided to go their own ways later that same year.

Tom Verlaine's status as a leading artist was confirmed with the release in July '79 of his first solo album, simply titled *Tom Verlaine.* Once more, both Verlaine and the album showed high in the critics' polls. David Bowie, no less, was of the same critical opinion as the press and chose to record Tom's song *Kingdom Come* on his *Scary Monsters* album.

1981 saw the release of *Dreamtime,* which subsequently proved to be Verlaine's last album for Warner Bros. Despite the fact that Tom felt unhappy with the promotional aspects of the company, the album once again achieved healthy press approval.

Verlaine toured the States in 1981 for the first time as a solo artist; the eight-week jaunt being an unequivocal success. With the basis of this touring band he went into the studio and cut *Words From The Front* for Virgin. Former television cohort Fred Smith, former Patti Smith Band drummer Jay Dee Daugherty and Kid Creole & The Coconuts' guitarist Jimmy Ripp comprised the touring band and this line-up played on the recording of *Clear It Away.* The rest of *Words From The Front* featured Ripp again, with Mink De Ville's rhythm section of Tommy Price and Hoe Vasta.

Tom Verlaine remains largely anonymous to the general public, but the diamond-like quality of Verlaine's performances on vocals and guitar make him and all his albums a rare delight. So much so that a live Television bootleg has been a strong seller for some time.

Visage (Steve Strange)

Steve Strange established the Blitz

VISAGE (STEVE STRANGE)

> **"I'm not interested in fun at all. Sex bores me; it was built up a few decades ago and it's just about to fall to bits."**
> — *Phil Oakey, Human League*

Club in Covent Garden, London, late in 1978 and it could fairly be called the breeding ground of the New Romantic movement. The club's encouragement for bizarre dress attracted a strong following among the young fashion designers, hairdressers and artists in London. As well as inspiring a whole new style of dress, it also cultivated its own mode of music, heavily derivative of disco.

Steve Strange himself became a cult figure and his ever-changing image has been closely watched by fashion magazines the world over. He has often appeared on the cover of England's Ritz magazine and has had a five page spread devoted to him in Vogue.

In 1980, Steve Strange joined with Ultravox guitarist Midge Ure and drummer Rusty Egan to form the non-performing group, Visage. Along with Ultravox's keyboardist and violinist, Billy Currie, and ex-Magazine members Dave Formula (keyboards) and Barry Adamson (bass) they recorded two singles later that year. *Tar* attracted notice, but *Fade To Grey* was a major hit in Europe and the UK, as well as charting in Australia, due in large part to the excellent video clip.

The group released their debut album, *Visage,* in early 1981 and followed it a year later with their second, *The Anvil,* which is currently being transformed into an $800,000 film.

In September 1982, after a series of opening nights at The Rainbow Club, The Barracuda and The Gardens, Steve and Rusty somehow raised close to a million pounds to start a permanent club for New Romantics to pose in. They transformed the old cinema that used to house The Music Machine into something vaguely comparable to Studio 54 and called it The Camden Palace. It became the glittering Mecca for Futurists, New Romantics and record company execs.

Wall Of Voodoo

In 1979, in the suburban wastelands of Los Angeles, five young men and one machine banded together. Mechanisation, alienation and minimalism figured prominently in their musical sensibilities. These traits stemmed from singer/keyboardist Stanard Ridgeway and guitarist Marc Moreland's earliest efforts at collaborative musical composition; efforts which centred around writing unsolicited film scores for sci-fi and horror films. Though few scores were ever accepted, the company they formed through which to sell them played a major role in the band's inception by donating its name — Wall Of Voodoo Inc.

In the ensuing months, Bruce Moreland (bass and keyboards) and Chas T. Gray (bass and synthesizers) joined the enterprise. Having instituted a secret code to ensure security from the rest of the world, the young composers' metamorphosis from soundtrack company to performing group began. They sought further isolation for further study and so established Wall Of Voodoo World Headquarters in a seedy office overlooking Hollywood Boulevard. It was there that a revolutionary "claw method" for keyboards and other "neo-neanderthal" approaches to contemporary music were conceived.

The enterprise reached solid ground when they recruited Ace, a synthetic rhythm machine usually found in cocktail music, which they expanded to provide a swelling, insistent beat. To complement this, the band needed a percussionist who would not feel threatened by Ace's machine precision. A thorough search turned up junk dealer Joe Nanini. In time, Bruce Moreland departed, with Gray taking over his bass duties.

In 1981, the group signed to IRS and released a self-titled five track 12 inch EP, followed by the album *Dark Continent.* The live track *Back In Flesh* was included on the *Urgh! A Music War* soundtrack album. One NME writer described their recorded music as "like early Devo without the wackiness". Early in 1983, Wall Of Voodoo scored their first hit with *Mexican Radio* from the album *Call Of The West,* produced by Richard Mazda.

The Waitresses

Spawned in the musically rich Cleveland/Akron areas, The Waitresses were formed by guitarist Chris Butler (formerly with the bizarre and impressive Tin Huey).

The members include Patty Donahue (vocals), Dan Klayman (keyboards), Bill Ficca (ex-Television drummer), Mars Williams (sax) and Tracy Wormworth (bass).

When the group moved to New York in 1980 they soon attracted attention playing around the clubs with their quirky brand of New Wave. In 1981, The Waitresses signed with Ze Records and early the next year they released their debut album, *Wasn't Tomorrow Wonderful?* The record amply illustrated Butler's ability to write humorous songs for and about women from a woman's standpoint. Patty Donahue's nasal dead-pan delivery perfectly complements the the lyrics.

The Waitresses received no success in their homeland, but the single *I Know What Boys Like* did well in Britain and was a top 10 hit in Australia in mid-1982. The song *Christmas Wrapping* was included on both editions of Ze's *A Christmas Record.* The group also appeared, musically and visually, on the first

> "We're a weird band to pin down. Maybe it's like David Byrne listening to Little Feat at Ornette Coleman's house."
> — *Chris Butler, The Waitresses*

WALL OF VOODOO

THE WAITRESSES

vocal arranger Harry Bowens, Bootsy's Rubber Band percussionist Butch Small, string arranger Johnny Allen (of *Shaft* fame), Irwin Krinsky, a classical pianist of repute, and backup vocalists Carolyn Crawford, Carol Hall, Kathy Kosins, Sheila Horne and Michelle Goulet, who have collectively amassed credits with Motown sessions, Brides of Funkenstein and Bohannon.

Was (Not Was) have never appeared live.

episode of the television series *Square Pegs.* A second album, *Bluesology,* was issued in 1983, after which Patty was replaced by Holly Beth Vincent (sans Italians).

Was (Not Was)

Don and David Was (which are not their real names, neither are they brothers) have been very secretive about their pasts. What little is known is that they both grew up in Detroit and had experience in many minor '70s bands before, in 1980, they decided to set themselves up as Detroit's answer to auteur duos like Steely Dan's Fagen and Becker.

They first attracted notice with a single in 1980 on Ze Records, *Wheel Me Out,* an explosive burst of Zappaesque rock funk. In 1981 they released their debut album, *Was (Not Was)* which garnered heavy critical praise but poor sales. One of the main interests of the record was impressive list of supporting musicians they gathered for the session. Former MC5 guitarist Wayne Kramer, trumpeter Marcus Belgrave (ex-Ray Charles and Charles Mingus), Parliament/ Funkadelic percussionist Larry Fratangelo, David Ruffin's guitarist Bruce Mazarian, former O'Jays

WAS (NOT WAS)

WHAM!

Wham!

Wham!'s press agents claim that the band has "all the vitality of London, but none of its recent pretentions". George Michael and Andrew Ridgeley, who make up Wham!, are two North London teenagers who experimented with various musical styles and line-ups before deciding to work on their own.

As with so many young English bands, things happened very fast for Wham! Four weeks, one demo and one recording contract later, they were ready to record their first single, with George on vocals an and Andrew on guitar.

The song *WHAM! RAP! Enjoy What You Do?* was well received by most people, with the exception of certain authoritarian bodies who sought to have it banned.

Wham! followed this with another single, *Young Guns (Go For It),* which supposedly has something to do with the perils of teenage marriage. In Australia, the hits occurred in reverse order.

Mari Wilson & The Wilsations

Scottish born Mari Wilson, fondly dubbed "The Neasden Queen of Soul", was born Mairrhii Macmillan Ramsay Wilson in 1957. How she came to overcome that fearsome burden and carve her own niche in the world of contemporary music is a tale too tedious to go into here.

For convenience, we jump to 1980 when, as a poorly paid backing vocalist with The Story So Far,

Mari was 'discovered' by manager Tot Taylor and signed to the GTO label. A staunch fan of Dusty Springfield, Peggy Lee, Martha & The Vandellas, Diana Ross (with and without the Supremes), Julie London et al, and sporting a lacquered lid to put Lesley Gore to shame, Mari debuted on vinyl with "an emotionally positive reading of *Loveman"* (so it says right here on the jacket). Backing was rendered by The Imaginations — Teddy Johns, Jimmy Hester, Lester Torvene and Anthony Ante.

After a successful lawsuit by a black female vocal trio, the name The Imaginations gave way to The Wilsations and Mari moved from GTO to her own Compact Organization label. By 1982, Miss Wilson had become one of the best value live drawcards in London, with her rambling, erratic 12-person stage ensemble and a live set that embraced Motown, torch songs, Las Vegas showstoppers, blue eyed soul and sleazy jazz.

Mari has made a greater impression on concert stages than the charts, as evidenced by the less-than-spectacular success of the

> **"Regardless of Women's Lib, women still love to lie by the telephone, waiting for him to call."**
> — *Mari Wilson*

MARI WILSON

singles *Loveman, Beat The Beat, Baby It's True, Dance Card* and *Just What I Always Wanted.*

Enthusiasts might do worse than procure *The Beginner's Guide To Compact,* a boxed set containing assorted 12 inch discs, booklets, posters and other paraphernalia covering the acts Cynthia Scott, Virna Lindt, Tot Taylor and, of course, Mari Wilson & the Wilsations. In February, 1982, Mari released her first album, *Show People,* to mixed reviews. It yielded a single of *Cry Me A River,* the classic Julie London hit.

X

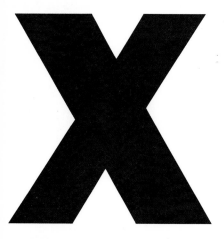

X

X, though little known outside the US, are Los Angeles' premier and original punk band. The group formed in mid 1977 around the nucleus of John Doe (bass) and Billy Zoom (guitar). Doe was born in Decateur, Illinois, and after dropping out of college, played in bands in Washington DC and Baltimore before migrating to Los Angeles. Through a classified ad, he met Billy Zoom, also a native of Illinois, who in the late '60s and early '70s had backed such rock'n'roll legends as Etta James, Bobby Day and Gene Vincent.

John Doe met singer Exene Cervenka when she was working as a waitress in a poetry club in LA, having arrived from her hometown of Chicago with just $60 in her pocket. Soon after, the trio saw drummer Don Bonebrake playing with a group called The Eyes and asked him to join them. Previously, Bonebrake had led a punk combo called Manuel & The Gardeners, which had also contained Charlotte Caffey of the Go-Go's.

X's weird hybrid of heavy metal, rockabilly and rock'n'roll went over a storm with Los Angeles' burgeoning punk scene and in the five years since their debut performance they have become a headline attraction on the West Coast and New York. The group's debut single, *Adult Books,* was released on Dangerhouse Records in April 1978, but they had to wait until 1980 for their next exposure. They contributed three songs to the *Decline Of Western Civilisation* soundtrack LP, and in June of that same year released their debut album, *Los Angeles,* on Slash Records. In May 1981 their second LP, *Wild Gift,* emerged and they had one track, *Beyond & Back,* on the *Urgh! A Music War* soundtrack album. A single, *White Girl,* was released in August 1981.

In 1982, X signed to Elektra and recorded the *Under The Black Sun* album, produced by former Door Ray Manzarek.

XTC

XTC began life in Swindon in 1973 with Andy Partridge (guitar and vocals), Colin Moulding (bass and vocals) and Terry Chambers (drums). They worked under various names including Skyscraper, Star Park and Snakes. In 1975, as The Helium Kids, they recorded for Decca but none of the tracks made it onto vinyl. In 1976 Partridge described their music as "ant music" on handouts and around this time, Barry Andrews joined the group on keyboards. In early 1977 they recorded for CBS but again the results were not released.

Finally, late in 1977 the group signed to Virgin as XTC. Since then they have not looked back and have become one of the most influential and popular New Music groups to emerge from England.

XTC's first release was the *3D-EP* in October 1977, from which one track, *Science Friction,* was released as a single in Australia only. In January 1978, XTC's first album, *White Noise,* was issued along with the single, *Statue Of Liberty.* Two further singles, *This Is Pop* and *Are You Receiving Me?,* followed later that year along with their second album, *Go 2,* in November. After recording that album, Andrews left and was replaced by guitarist Dave Gregory (ex-Alehouse and Dean Gabber & The Gabberdines).

XTC began 1979 with a new single, *Life Begins At The Hop,* in April and in August they released their third album, *Drums And Wires,* and another single, *Making Plans For Nigel.* To coincide with their release, they played a very successful pub and club tour of Australia. 1980 kicked off with a single, *Wait Till Your Boat Goes Down,* in March, and then in August their fourth album, *Black Sea,* was released. This highly acclaimed album spawned four notable singles, *Generals And Majors, Towers Of London, Sgt. Rock* and *Respectable Street* — the last being their only release of 1981.

The group toured Australia again

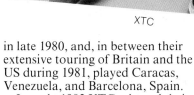

XTC

in late 1980 and, in between their extensive touring of Britain and the US during 1981, played Caracas, Venezuela, and Barcelona, Spain.

In early 1982 XTC released their first double album, *English Settlement,* which produced two singles, *Senses Working Overtime* and *Ball And Chain.* For most of 1982, the group were unable to work, either live or in the studio, due to the illness which beset Andy Partridge. In November of that year, a retrospective double album was released called *Waxworks/Beeswax. Waxworks* contained the A sides of their past singles, while *Beeswax* held the best of their idiosyncratic B sides. In some markets, the set was released as a single album, *Waxworks.* Viewed in such a collected situation, the cream of XTC's output stands up remarkably well as stylised, hard-edged pop-rock, well laden with some devastating hooks and intelligent song structure.

X

Y

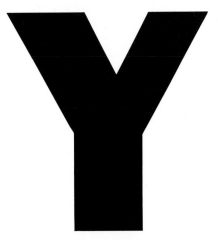

Yazoo

Yazoo are a unique blend of Vince Clarke's bounding synthesizer pop and Genevieve Alison Moyet's warm, bluesy voice. In late 1981, Clarke decided to leave Depeche Mode after having written their first three hits: *Dreaming Of Me, New Life* and *Just Can't Get Enough.* The former truck driver, wages clerk and civil servant opted for a solo career and retired to his Baseldon, Essex flat, (which was filled with electronics), to write songs.

Enter Alison (or Alf, a nickname bestowed by her French father), who had been doing the rounds of the Southend/South Essex rhythm and blues gigs, singing with countless bands like The Vicars and The Screaming Abdabs. Fed up with not getting onto the London circuit, she advertised for "rootsy blues band" and instead met Vince. The partnership was not so unlikely, as Alison had studied musical instrument technology at the London College of Furniture (!).

A debut single, *Only You,* released in March 1982 to test the water for the new duo, became a smash number two hit in England and also rose to number one in Australia. A second single, *Don't Go,* followed quickly and rose to top five in both the UK and Australia. Their debut LP, *Upstairs At Eric's,* produced by Yazoo and Eric Radcliffe, was released in mid-1982.

Yazoo have played live, supported by a micro-computer which controls drum sounds, synthesizer lines and a slide show.

The duo split mid 1983, following the single *Nobody's Diary.*

Young Homebuyers

With the song *She's A Girl,* Australia's Young Homebuyers joined the supreme powerpop echelon of The Records' *Starry Eyes,* Bram Tchaikovsky's *Girl Of My Dreams,* The Rubinoos' *I Wanna Be Your Boyfriend* and The dB's' *Living A Lie.* Their 1982 self-titled album, produced by former Little River Band guitarist David Briggs, just may be the freshest dose of pure pop released anywhere in the world during that year.

Founded by rock journalist Greg Williams in the city of Adelaide, the source of many of Australia's finest bands, Young Homebuyers came

> **"We don't want to shock people for the sake of shocking people. We're not the Plasmatics. We want to shock people into thinking."**
> — *Klaus Flouride, Dead Kennedys*

together in their present formation toward the end of 1980: Williams (lead vocals), guitar), Nigel Lawrence (lead vocals), Paul Ziesing (bass), Mick Teakle (rhythm guitar), Tony Thornton (drums, percussion) and Greg Champion (vocals, guitars). The six came from the ranks of such early New Wave outfits as The Fabulaires, The Bank of France, and Nasty Nigel And The Hellcats.

For the first year, the group toyed with satire and parody, their most popular stage songs including *Penguins Took My Baby, It's All Billy Joel To Me* and *Please Let Me Be On Countdown.* A good-time party band, they were compared to Mental As Anything, The Reels and Sports, because of their casual blend of reggae, rockabilly, British New and Old Wave and bubble pop.

Realising that Australia is simply not large enough a market to support a left-of-centre band in the style to which they wished to become accustomed, Young Homebuyers seriously reorientated their sound toward a more marketable goal and came up with *Take One Step,* an advertising jingle for Hall's Lemon Twist softdrink.

This ditty came to the attention of David Briggs, who signed the band to his Rough Diamond label without them ever having set foot in Melbourne, the label's location. Their long-awaited album appeared late in 1982 and drew both rave reviews and moderate sales. As one critic suggested, perhaps to the band's detriment: "If you hate the atonal wastelands of The Fall, you are sure to love the molodies of Young Homebuyers."

Stop press: the Young Homebuyers disbanded early in 1983. 'Tis a shame.

YOUNG HOMEBUYERS

YAZOO

Z

Moon Unit Zappa

Moon Unit Zappa (that's her real name), daughter of Frank Zappa and sister of Dweezil Zappa, became a 1982 cult sensation in America, and to a lesser extent Australia, with her song *Valley Girls* which was recorded on dad's album *Ship Arriving Too Late To Save A Drowning Witch.*

The song prompted a Californian fashion craze with a whole Valley Girls code of ethics, dress style, and language.

Valley Girls was a clear (as clear as anything Valley-Girl style could be) illustration of what Valley Girls are all about. . . But if you do not talk Val-Speak you would not get the picture.

We'll put it like this. . .Remember the mods and rockers of the '60s? They had their own way of dressing, their own way of talking and their own favourite ways of entertaining themselves. Well that's what the Valley Girls are like. They are, like, *outrageous.*

Uh, like there's this *thing* happening in America right now that a lot of chicks think is *really* mondo bitchen twitchen.

I mean, wo, like, fer shurr, if you don't know how to be a maximum warm babe — like high heels with mini skirts and station wagons are totally skanky — then, like, you're a real geek, you know? Like, what are you, a zod?

But really, no seriously, like it's no biggie if you act like a melvin now because the Val Girls have mondo cool books that explain, like, *everything.*

Simple eh?

FRANK AND MOON ZAPPA

The B-52's
Mesopotamia (Warner)
Design/Illustration: Simon
Levy/Desiree Rohr

Heaven 17
Penthouse & Pavement (Virgin)
Design: BEF/Ray Smith

Urban Verbs
Urban Verbs (Warner)
Design: not credited

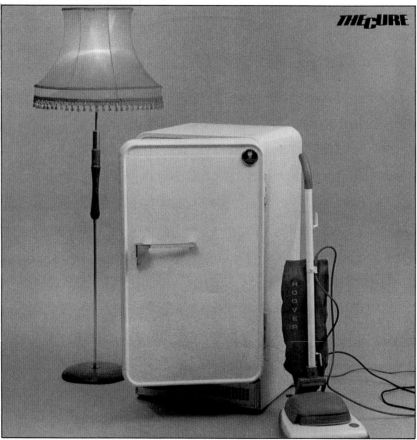

The Cure
Three Imaginary Boys (Fiction)
Design: Martyn Goodard/Bill Smith

The Plasmatics
Coup d'Etat (Capitol)
Design: Butch Star/Leslie Cabarga

James White & The Blacks
Off White (Ze)
Design: Anya Phillips

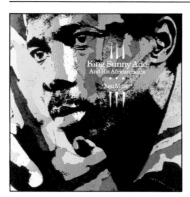

King Sunny Ade
Ju Ju Music (Island)
Design: Bruno Tilley

Machinations
Esteem (White Label)
Design: Pasmal Design

Mari Wilson
Just What I've Always Wanted
(Compact)
Design: Peter Ashworth/Compact

Altered Images
I Could Be Happy (Epic)
Design: David Band

The Incredible Casuals
Let's Go (Eat)
Design: not credited

ART ATTACKS!
COVERING THE NEW ROCK'N'ROLL

The first flush of punk (1975-'77) ushered in a deliberately amateur approach to rock art, eschewing glossy full-colour photographs and painstaking hand lettering in favour of basic primary school materials — scribbles, hand sketches, typewritings, dymo-tapings, rough paste-ups and polaroid photography. If you made your own demo tape and pressed it up for release on your own private record label, there was little sense in employing an art studio to do your sleeves.

Though an inevitable level of sophistication has crept into the visual imagery of New Wave and associated forms, the basic futuristic, progressive and often austere concepts have remained. No more gentle airbrushing and soft focus photography of serene faces — the new art is harsh, impersonal and confrontational. . . well most of the time. It demands attention and evaluation, not mere appreciation.

In many ways, the current 'art school' is the logical extension of the British '70s packaging style which was perfected by the likes of Hipgnosis, Shoot That Tiger and Roger Dean. Less pretentious and obscure, the current art climate deftly combines the original rough'n'ready punk leanings with the cold, concise nature of techno-pop and synth sounds.

There are, of course, many hundreds of stunning sleeves which we could offer as examples of New Rock Art in the '80s. What follows is but a random selection, based primarily on what has taken the authors' fancy and what they could lay their hands on quickly before the photographer arrived.

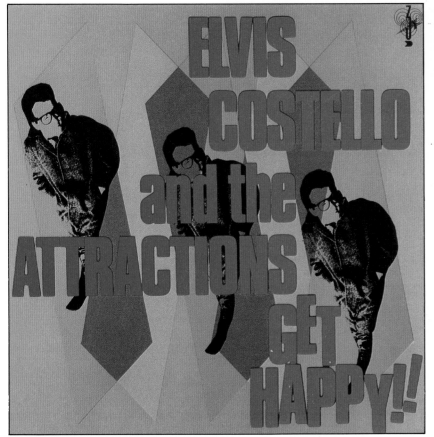

Elvis Costello & The Attractions
Get Happy (F. Beat)
Design: VAT 245 4945 42

The Birthday Party
Junk Yard (Missing Link)
Design: Ed 'Big Daddy' Roth/Neville Brody

Tom Tom Club
Tom Tom Club (Sire)
Illustration: James Rizzi

The Go-Betweens
Send Me A Lullabye (Missing Link)
Design: Jenny Watson

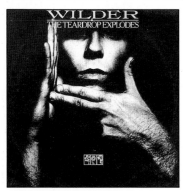

The Teardrop Explodes
Wilder (Mercury)
Design: Martyn Atkins

Japan
Tin Drum (Virgin)
Design: Steve Joule/David Sylvian

The Gun Club
Fire Of Love (New Rose)
Design: L. Thevenon/P. Huart

Various Artists
Permanent Wave (Epic)
Design: not credited

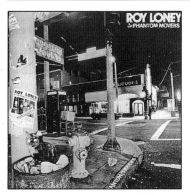

Roy Loney & The Phantom Movers
Roy Loney & The Phantom Movers
(Solid Smoke)
Design: Ellie Byrom/Charly Franklin

U2
War (Island)
Design: RX/Ian Finlay

The Contortions
Buy The Contortions (Ze)
Design: Anya Phillips

Radio Birdman
Eureka Birdman! (bootleg)
Design: Warwick Gilbert (unwittingly)

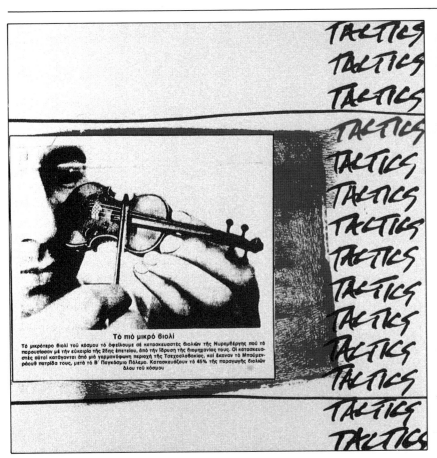

Tactics
My Houdini (Green)
Design: Marjorie McIntosh/Angus
Douglas

The Boys Next Door
Door Door (Mushroom)
Design: not credited

The Milkshakes
After School Session (Upright)
Photography: Eugene Doyen

The Spitfires
I Was A Teenage Teenager (Rivet)
Design: Alan Duffy

XTC
Black Sea (Virgin)
Design: Ken White/Ralph Hall

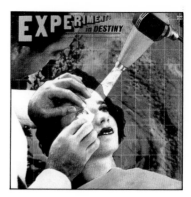

Various Artists
Experiments In Destiny (Bomp)
Design: Diane Zincavage

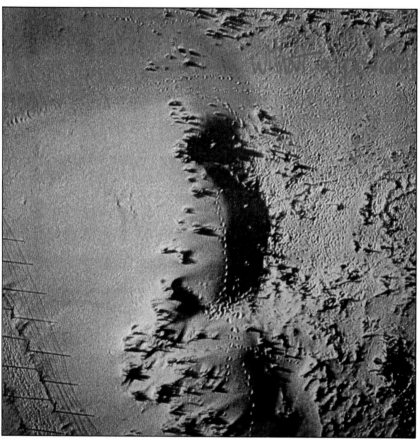

Midnight Oil
Place Without A Postcard (CBS)
Design: Phil Ellott

Dexys Midnight Runners
Too-Rye-Ay (Mercury)
Design: Peter Barrett/Kim Knott/
Andrew Ratcliffe

Orange Juice
You Can't Hide Your Love Forever
(Polydor)
Design: Steve Bush

Au Pairs
Playing With A Different Sex (Human)
Design: Martin-Rocking Russian/Eve
Arnold

**The Makers Of The Dead Travel
Fast**
The Vessels (M Squared)
Painting: Timothy Schultz

Aural Exciters
Spooks In Space (Ze)
Design: J.J. Mahuteau

Soft Cell
The Art Of Falling Apart (Vertigo)
Design: Marc Almond/Peter
Ashworth/Huw Feather

UB 40
Signing Off (Graduate)
Design: Geoffrey & David
Tristram/H.M. Government

a-z affectionately, 1 to 10 alphabetically, from here to eternity without in betweens. still looking for a custom fit in an off the rack world? sales talk from sales assistants when all i want to do is lower your resistance. no rhythm in cymbals no tempo in drums. love's on arrival, she comes when she comes. right on the target but wide of the…

ABC
The Lexicon of Love (Phonogram)
Design: Visible Ink/Neutron Records

Carlene Carter
Musical Shapes (F. Beat)
Photography: Chalkie Davis

New Order
Power Corruption & Lies (Factory)
Painting: Fantin-Latour (1836-1904)

Scars
Author! Author! (Pre)
Design: Rocking Russian

Index

CLOCKWISE FROM TOP LEFT: TONI BASIL/AU PAIRS/CHARGED GBH/CABARET VOLTAIRE

"And you think you're so
clever and classless
and free but you're still
fuckin' peasants
as far as I can see."
— *John Lennon*

Glenn A. Baker

This Glenn's fourth book, his previous titles being *The New Music* (with Stuart Coupe), *Rock Lens* (with Bob King) and *The Beatles Down Under*. He has just completed *Monkeemania — The True Story of The Monkees* for Eel Pie/ Plexus Books.

Glenn, 31, is one of Australia's most active and highly regarded specialist rock writer/researchers and radio/television presenters. Australian editor of Billboard, he has also written for a wide range of international and local publications, including Penthouse, Goldmine, Australian Business, Surfing World, Music Week, Record World, Rolling Stone, Playboy, RAM, Juke, Countdown, History of Rock, People, Daily Mirror, Rock Express and the Australian Encyclopaedia; and was an editorial consultant to the Australian Music Directory.

Glenn is co-compere of the Sydney late night rock TV show *Music Video*, former alternate compere of *After Dark* (ATN7 TV), presenter of the *Rock'n'Roll Trivia Show* on 2WS, owner of Raven and Rivet record labels, compiler of almost one hundred specialist rock anthology albums, special projects consultant to a number of major Australian record companies, custodian of one of the largest private record collections in the Southern Hemisphere, and creative consultant to the television specials *Australian Music Stars Of The '60s, Australia Now!* and *The Wild One*.

Previously, he has been a successful artist manager and songwriter, and was voted 'Best Rock Journalist' in the 1979 Australian Rock Awards.

Glenn lives in Sydney with his wife and four sons and is presently finalising at least two more books on music subjects. On rare occasions he has been known to sleep.

Stuart Coupe

Stuart, 26, has been writing about rock'n'roll and related subjects since he was 15 and has been the Sun-Herald's (Australia's biggest circulation Sunday newspaper) rock critic for the past four years. Prior to that he was editor of Flinders University's Empire Times, a founding editor of Roadrunner, and a staff writer at RAM. Stuart has contributed to a diverse collection of publications, including Dolly, The APRA Journal, Vox, National Times, Rolling Stone, Juke, The Countdown Club Magazine, Form 38, Magazine, The Adelaide Advertiser, Virgin Press, and Stuff.

For the past two years Stuart has also been a freelance publicist working on Australian tours by The Clash, Gary Glitter, Dezo Hoffman, Miles, and The Teardrop Explodes. Before the year ends he expects to work with Frank Sinatra Jnr and The Dead Kennedys.

As co-director of the independent Green label Stuart has been involved with releasing records by Tactics, The New Christs, Allniters, Spy Vs Spy, The Lime Spiders, Do Re Mi, Ducks In Formation, and the soundtrack to *Dingo Girl.*

Stuart presents a weekly radio show on 2SER-FM titled *From Funk To Punk,* and has a deep, meaningful, and financially based relationship with The Hoodoo Gurus.

The first record Stuart bought was The Easybeats' *Friday On My Mind,* and the first concert he attended was by The Seekers. His ambition is to meet Elvis Presley.

Like most famous authors he divides his time between two workplaces, a home/office in Woolloomooloo, and 'the other office' at the nearby East Sydney Hotel. He drinks Victoria Bitter at both. With Glenn A. Baker, Stuart was co-author of *The New Music,* still threatens to finish his book on rock'n'roll and sexuality, and thinks deep hard and long about The Great Novel As Written By Himself.

Stuart is not married, has no kids, and shares a house with his Green Records partner and Tonto the cat.